The Black New Yorkers

THE SCHOMBURG ILLUSTRATED CHRONOLOGY

SCHOMBURG CENTER FOR RESEARCH IN BLACK CULTURE
The New York Public Library

WRITTEN BY

Howard Dodson

Christopher Moore

Roberta Yancy

John Wiley & Sons, Inc.
New York • Chichester • Weinheim • Brisbane • Singapore • Toronto

Copyright © 2000 by The New York Public Library, Astor, Lenox and Tilden Foundations. All rights reserved.

Published by John Wiley & Sons, Inc. Published simultaneously in Canada

Permissions acknowledgments and illustration credits begin on page 453.

Library of Congress Cataloging-in-Publication Data:

Schomburg Center for Research in Black Culture, the New York Public Library.
   The Black New Yorkers : the Schomburg illustrated chronology / written by Howard Dodson, Christopher Moore, and Roberta Yancy.
      p.   cm.
   Includes bibliographical references and index.
   ISBN 0-471-29714-3 (cloth : alk. paper)
   1. Afro-Americans—New York (State)—New York—History—Chronology.
2. Afro-Americans—New York (State)—New York—History—Pictorial works.
3. New York (N.Y.)—History—Chronology.   4. New York (N.Y.)—History—Pictorial works.   5. Afro-Americans—New York (State)—New York—Social life and customs.   6. New York (N.Y.)—Civilization.   7. Afro-Americans—New York (State)—New York—Social life and customs—Pictorial works.   8. New York (N.Y.)—Civilization—Pictorial works.   I. Schomburg Center for Research in Black Culture.   II. Title.
F128.9.N4A54   1999
974.7'00496073—dc21   98-30510

Printed in the United States of America

10 9 8 7 6 5 4 3 2 1

TO REGINA ANDREWS

This book is dedicated to Regina M. Andrews, a pioneer African American librarian. She was also a socially conscious writer, author, civic leader, and activist in the struggle for truth about the African American experience. A native of Chicago, she migrated to New York City in the early 1920s and joined the staff of Harlem's 135th Street Branch of the New York Public Library in 1923. A pivotal figure in the development of the Harlem Renaissance, she assisted and supported many of its young writers. One of the founders of the Harlem Experimental Theatre, she supported the development of black theater in Harlem during and after the Renaissance. Active in local, national, and international civic, cultural, and political affairs, Andrews was also a consummate chronicler of black life, especially in New York City. Thirty years ago, while a consultant to the Metropolitan Museum of Art's exhibition *Harlem on My Mind,* she researched and wrote a draft of the book that gave this work its title and inspired its production and publication. We dedicate this book to her in recognition of her vision, her inspiration, and her commitment to telling the world about the unique and extraordinary role of black New Yorkers in the making of America's greatest city.

CONTENTS

AFTER CENTURIES OF UNMENTIONABLE ABUSE, PHYSICAL AND PSYCHICAL abuse, African American people desperately needed a safe haven, a retreat where they could see themselves, flaunt themselves, sing their hope, dance their promise, test their religion, and air their philosophy. As much as Algerians wanted a Casbah, safe from the prying eyes of the French Colonialist, so did African Americans need a place which would reflect their energy and creativity. They needed a village where the chief resembled them, a series of rites where they were addressed formally, and courteously. Shop windows where their exotic desires were on display. In fact, a city not made with hands, but with need and yearning. Over decades Harlem became that shared promise.

In 1952, the startling dancer Pearl Primus stopped in San Francisco during a North American tour. Her power and the beauty of her dance absolutely stunned me speechless. I had studied dance and even had the temerity to teach at the local Frederick Douglass Community Center. I auditioned for Miss Primus and she said if I would come to New York, she would give me a scholarship. I began immediately to plan the trip with my four-year-old son to New York.

I was an artist—sometimes with an *e* on the word, and I was on my way to New York . . . where it went without saying I deserved to be—being an artiste and all. My future did not intimidate me. I was an artiste after all.

I all but whimpered when I saw the reality of New York, the outlandish skyscrapers, the millions of cars, taxis, trucks, ambulances, bicycles, and then the people—I had to hold on to something inside myself (my memory of my grandmother's dignity) or I would have broken out in a full-fledged run. I mentioned to Miss Primus that I didn't realize there were that many people on earth. "Go to Harlem, you won't believe there are that many black people anywhere outside Africa."

I walked the big wide Harlem avenues and saw more black people just sitting on stoops than I had seen in my entire life. Music poured from each open window and children danced on the pavement. Preachers warned and encouraged from every corner and race men exhorted the audience, "Go home. Go back to Africa."

Barbecue and fried chicken, ladies' perfume and men's cologne made for an intoxicated air—almost too heavy to breathe. In this ambience, I met musicians new to their greatness but familiar to narcotics. As a dancer, it was understood that my body was my instrument, and I could not endanger my instrument. Not one of them ever got so high as to mistreat the instrument, so no one ever offered me drugs.

In Harlem, I met Langston Hughes, who talked to me for hours, but I was so starstruck, I don't remember a single phrase or even a word.

In 1952, I cut my hair and wore it natural. Little children on 125th Street asked me, "Are you a woman or a man?"

Dizzy Gillespie called me the square of the world and Rena Navarro (Fats Navarro's widow) said I was her sister.

When I had the money, I could listen to Lionel Hampton, Dinah Washington, and Moms Mabley at the Apollo Theater. When I was broke, my son and I would join the throng across the street from the theater and wave at the celebrities as they arrived. We had almost as much fun outside as the paying customers inside.

Or if we were flush, we could go to the Baby Grand and listen to Redd Foxx and Slappy White.

Foxx: Hi, I'm Redd.

Slappy: Hi, I'm White.

Foxx: Have you looked lately!

Father Divine's restaurant offered gigantic dinners for twenty-five cents and if I persisted, I could wedge my way into Abyssinian Church and hear the best preaching in the world.

Harlem under my feet and all around me was shakin' and quakin', shakin' till the break of dawn. I dropped the *e* off *artiste*, and finally I dropped the word altogether. And when I described myself, I said I was a dancer from Harlem. I was not really, but boy, I wanted to be. Let me off uptown.

My story was repeated millions of times in New York. I would not be myself without Harlem. I would not be myself without New York. I would not be myself without black New Yorkers. That is why *The Black New Yorkers: The Schomburg Illustrated Chronology* is a book for all New Yorkers and for all Americans. It chronicles our story—the lives and times of people who for nearly four centuries have been creating a presence and a voice for themselves in the city, the nation, and the world.

Maya Angelou

INTRODUCTION

T HE BLACK NEW YORKERS: THE SCHOMBURG ILLUSTRATED CHRONOLOGY traces nearly four hundred years in the lives of people of African descent in New York City, documenting the evolution of the entire black New York experience.

Here is an unparalleled reference source designed to answer your questions about the history of black New York. Here, too, is a fascinating story of great achievement and struggle in a dynamic global context.

Highlights from a Storied Past

From the arrival of Jan Rodriguez in 1613 to the present day, black New Yorkers have drawn on the richness of their heritage as well as the genius and daring that resided in themselves. In every era, they have been active agents in the making of their history. If you follow the narrative thread from the beginning of their story, you will discover the major forces behind their efforts.

The strongest of these forces spanned the centuries. European and Euro-American colonialism and militarism, for example, not only helped shape the modern world, but also had crucial consequences for black New York history. So, too, did the ongoing relationship between African peoples on the African continent, in the United States, and throughout the diaspora. Of profound necessity,

African peoples virtually everywhere have been connected through their efforts to define themselves and their worlds and to exercise their rights as human beings in every period of history covered in this book.

Every effort by black New Yorkers to challenge and rebuff assaults on their rights and dignity has, by its nature, been political. So, too, has been their individual and collective initiative in all spheres of human endeavor.

In *The Black New Yorkers: The Schomburg Illustrated Chronology,* these driving forces, key dates, and seminal events are explored in a general introduction to each period, followed by a chronology that details the specific personalities, movements, and activities through which black New Yorkers expressed their engagement with their times. *Italics* indicate events that occurred outside the geographical boundaries of the five boroughs of New York City (Manhattan, Brooklyn, The Bronx, Staten Island, and Queens) that also had a significant impact on the lives of black New Yorkers. These entries serve as markers, helping to locate specific black New York events along the broader timelines of history. Contemporary geographical locations are included in brackets to help you identify early New York sites. The names of people who are included in the Selected Biographies are set in **bold** type the first time they appear in the chronology.

Who Are the Black New Yorkers Today?

The fruit of this rich history is the largest black urban population in the nation today. If the 2.3 million contemporary black New Yorkers were organized as a discrete political entity, they would rank as the fourth largest city in the United States, after New York, Los Angeles, and Chicago. This means that the black New York population is larger than the total populations of Philadelphia (1.5 million), Houston (1.7 million), San Diego (1.2 million), Dallas (1.1 million), and Detroit (1 million). Indeed, it is about four times the population of Washington, D.C., and more than twice as large as San Francisco. New York City's black and black Hispanic populations contribute in significant ways to giving New York State the largest black population in the nation—an estimated 4.1 million people or almost twelve percent of the black population in the United States.

Geographically, the largest concentration of black New Yorkers is neither in Harlem nor in the borough of Manhattan. That honor goes to Brooklyn, whose black and black Hispanic population totaled 924,862. That's larger than the total populations of Washington, D.C., and San Francisco, and almost as large as the total population of Detroit. The borough with the second largest black New York population is the Bronx, with 507,144 (350,565 black and 156,579 black Hispanic). Queens is third, with 439,474 (399,079 black and 60,395 black Hispanic). Manhattan, of which Harlem is a part, ranks fourth with 413,153 (275,407 black and 137,746 black Hispanic). Staten Island, the smallest borough in terms of size and population, has the smallest black New Yorker population: 36,318 (32,148 black and 4,370 black Hispanic).

Demographically, then, neither Harlem nor Manhattan is the center of black life in New York City. Politically, culturally, and to some extent economically, however, Manhattan in general and Harlem in particular have dominated public consciousness. *The Black New Yorkers: The Schomburg Illustrated Chronology* reflects this public perceptual bias, relying as it does on available scholarship, which has tended to emphasize Harlem and black Manhattan at the expense of black New Yorkers living in the "outer boroughs."

A Global Heritage

Census designations of "black" and "black Hispanic" mask one of the most salient characteristics of black New Yorkers—their diversity. *The Black New Yorkers: The Schomburg Illustrated Chronology* reveals the nature of that diversity and complexity as it has unfolded over time.

The majority of black New Yorkers are native-born African Americans who have come to the city from other parts of the country. During the period of the great migration, most came from the American South, and their states of origin frequently served as a basis for social, economic, and political organization. Migrants from Virginia, North Carolina, Georgia, and South Carolina founded clubs and organizations named for their states of origin. The vast majority fashioned their newfound sense of collective identity as black New Yorkers within the cauldron of the social, economic, and political struggles they encountered.

It was through their involvement in this dynamic African American social and group-making process that most black New Yorkers from the Caribbean, the African continent, and Central and South America negotiated their relationships with the city and forged their greater black New York identity. This shared sense of a pan-African black New York group identity has been most prevalent during periods of social crisis and political mobilization.

The persistence of racism in American society in general and New York City in particular has been critical in fostering a belief among black New Yorkers of diverse backgrounds that they share a common plight and a common destiny, as well as a storied past.

The primary sources of black immigrants have been the islands of the Caribbean and continental Africa. But black immigrants have also come from Brazil, Colombia, Costa Rica, Ecuador, Honduras, and other parts of Central and South America, Canada, France, and England, as well as other parts of Europe and Asia.

Caribbean immigrants have dominated this global African migration to New York City. Indeed, the pioneer black New York settlers were primarily from the Caribbean. More than eighty percent of the enslaved and free black residents of colonial New York traced their African roots through the Caribbean. The majority of enslaved colonial African New Yorkers were not transported directly from Africa, but rather came after some period of residence in the islands of the Caribbean.

During the 1980s, an estimated 80,000 continental-born Africans also took up residence in New York City. Interestingly enough, this total from one decade significantly surpassed the number of Africans transported to New York City during the entire slave trade. Nigerians, Liberians, Egyptians, Ethiopians, and Ghanaians dominated this immigration flow, but Malians, Somalis, South Africans, and Ivorians also participated. This pattern continued into the 1990s, with some fifty African nations contributing to the immigrant pool.

Diverse Voices

The diversity of the black New York population is also reflected in the languages they speak. Among native-born African Americans, standard English has been enriched by unique African American vocabulary as well as African-influenced syntax, intonation, and rhythms. English speakers from the Caribbean and the African continent have put their unique cultural stamps on the language as well. The Jamaican accent is markedly distinct from the Barbadian and the Trinidadian. The same is true of the Ghanaian, the Nigerian, and the South African. Though all these forms of English are mutually intelligible, their practitioners often take pride in this sign of their unique ethnic identity.

Prior to the 1980s, Puerto Ricans of African descent constituted the largest Spanish-speaking group among the Afro-Hispanic population. Like their English-speaking Caribbean counterparts, they too, have added a black flavor to the Spanish they speak. Their presence has, in turn, distinguished Puerto Rican Spanish from that spoken in Spain and in other parts of the Spanish-speaking world in South and Central America. Since the 1980s, immigrants from the Dominican Republic, a significant percentage of whom have African ancestry, have added their island's unique brand of Spanish to the Afro-Hispanic mix in New York City. Colombians, Ecuadorians, Guatemalans, Cubans, Hondurans, Venezuelans, and other Spanish-speaking people of African descent have added their voices to the black Hispanic linguistic mix of black New Yorkers.

The languages spoken by Haitian immigrants and their descendants dominate the linguistic presence of French-speaking populations of black New York. Theirs is a uniquely Haitian French, however. Indeed, it is so distinct that it is called Creole and is treated as the national language of Haiti; it is the language of choice of most Haitian American immigrants. Most Haitian American immigrants also speak a brand of standard French with a Haitian accent that is intelligible to other Francophones, but Haitian Creole is generally spoken and understood only by Haitians and their descendants. Immigrants from Martinique and Guadeloupe, as well as African immigrants from the former French colonies on the African continent are also counted among the black New York French-speaking residents. They include the Senegalese, Malian, Ivorian, Guinian, and Zairian (Congo) natives who have taken up residence in New York City. Continentally born African immigrants also speak their indigenous languages, which number in the hundreds, as do Afro-Brazilians, who speak New-World African Portuguese, and New-World African immigrants from Suriname and Aruba, who speak the Dutch-based Creole, papiamento.

Diverse Religions

Black New Yorkers today practice most of the forms of religious expression known in the Atlantic world. They worship in the Kamitic, Christian, Judaic, and Islamic traditions. As Christians, they are active in both the Catholic and the Protestant traditions. Most U.S.-born African Americans are Baptists or Methodists. Most Hispanic and Francophone black New Yorkers are Catholics. Black New Yorkers from the British Caribbean tend to worship in the Episcopal Church. But black New Yorkers practice in a wide variety of other religious and faith traditions. Ethiopians continue to practice in the Ethiopian Orthodox Church, the founding Christian Church on the African continent. Some Haitians, Puerto Ricans, and Cubans practice New World African religions—vaudou in the case of the Haitians, and Santeria in that of the Cubans and Puerto Ricans. Jamaican immigrants have nurtured Rastafarianism in New York City since the 1970s. Black Jewish congregations in New York City date back to the 1920s and maintain a vibrant, active presence in New York's black religious life. Islamic communities emerged in New York City during the late nineteenth century, and in addition to those practitioners of the Nation of Islam's black Muslim traditions, there are black New Yorkers from the continent and from the United States who are congregants in the diverse Islamic traditions of the world.

Beginning in the 1920s with such figures as Daddy Grace and later Father Divine and Reverend Ike, black New Yorkers created numerous sects and cults, which have expanded the religious landscape and given rise to some of the most unique religious movements in the country. In sum, the vast majority of black New Yorkers are religious people, but their religion of choice is shaped by their ethnic and cultural identities.

Diverse Cultures

The cultural diversity of black New Yorkers is best exemplified by their wide-ranging and profound contributions to the field of music. Since New York has been one of the centers of musical production in the United States, black New Yorkers have left their imprint on many of the established African American idiomatic forms, especially gospel, jazz, rhythm and blues, and rock and roll. Rap, and the hip-hop industry that has grown up around it, had its origins among black New Yorkers in the Bronx during the late 1970s.

While the blues had its origins elsewhere, black New Yorkers were instrumental in giving the blues worldwide currency through record companies like Pace Records and the sheet music company of W. C. Handy, the "Father of the Blues." Rock and roll and rhythm and blues artists did not achieve true national recognition until they had played Harlem's Apollo Theater. And many of the leading jazz artists of the twentieth century, including Duke Ellington, Count Basie, Ella Fitzgerald, Charlie Parker, Louis Armstrong, Dizzy Gillespie, Sarah Vaughn, and Miles Davis established their national reputations while living and working in New York City.

As rich as the African American musical heritage is, black New Yorkers from the Caribbean and the continent have brought their African-based rhythms and indigenous cultural styles and forms with them to New York City. The Afro-Cuban rhythms of Mario Bauza, "Machito," and Chano Pozo became infused with African American jazz and sparked the development of a Latin jazz idiom. Jamaican reggae and rocksteady are found here, as are Trinidadian *soka,* Puerto Rican *bomba y plena,* Dominican *merengue,* Colombian *cumbia,* Congolese *soukous,* Haitian *rara,* Malian *wassoulou,* South African *mbaganga,* Senegalese *mbalax,* and Nigerian *juju* and highlife.

Black New Yorkers are also counted among the world's leading performers of European classical music. Marian Anderson, Leontyne Price, Kathleen Battle, and Jessye Norman head the list of black New York divas.

The cultural diversity found in music is also to be noted in dance, food, dress, family and community rituals, and art.

A New Perspective on History

Like the black New York experience itself, *The Black New Yorkers: The Schomburg Illustrated Chronology* offers an abundance of eye-opening information on a wide range of topics, including:

- Business and economics
- Performing and visual arts
- Film
- Immigration
- Law and social justice
- Literature
- Media
- Music
- Organizations and institutions
- Discrimination and civil rights
- Politics
- Religion
- Science and exploration
- Slavery and freedom
- Sports
- Theater

The book's orderly format makes it easy and stimulating to use. Several elements enhance its intrinsic value. These include a section of concise biographical sketches, a bibliography, a selection of historical documents, a subject index, and more than two hundred illustrations. Beyond the information you are looking for, we hope these pages give you a mind-expanding perspective on the human experience.

BLACKS IN
COLONIAL NEW YORK

1613–1783

THE BLACK EXPERIENCE IN NEW YORK HAD ITS ORIGINS IN THE EURO-
pean colonization of the Americas and the expansion of the
transatlantic slave trade. Two colonial powers—first the Dutch and
later the English—presided over the unfolding of this first chapter
in black New York historical and cultural development. In 1613
when Dutch merchants first arrived in the New World to establish
a trading post, Jan Rodriguez, a free African from the West Indies,
was with them and helped them build it. In 1625, the year before
the Dutch settlement was officially named New Amsterdam, the
first enslaved Africans arrived to become its labor force.

From Exploration to Colonization

By the time Rodriguez arrived in New Amsterdam, people of
African descent had been involved in the complex process of colo-
nizing and settling the New World for more than a century. European colonial powers had already transported more than 500,000
enslaved Africans to Central and South America and to the
Caribbean. Between 1450 and 1870, 50 percent of the Africans who
crossed the Atlantic would live in South and Central America and
43 percent in the Caribbean. Only 7 percent would live in North
America, where the earliest had settled in South Carolina in 1526.

In Brazil, Mexico, Peru, Argentina, and the Caribbean Islands, Africans had been mining gold and silver, tending cattle, and constructing forts, churches, and public buildings for a century. Throughout the New World, the Africans raised sugar cane, tobacco, and other cash crops for the world market, and at times served in the military forces.

Christopher Columbus's voyage on behalf of Spain to the Western Hemisphere in 1492 had unleashed the economic forces that led to the African migration. Within two years after Columbus's "discoveries," Pope Alexander VI sought to settle any disputes about who would profit. The Pope awarded to Spain all of the Americas except Portuguese settlements in Brazil, and to Portugal all of Africa and Asia. In the view of the other European powers, however, title to the newly opened territories rested less on papal decrees than on exploration, conquest, occupation, and settlement. Spain's and Portugal's claims would be challenged by the Dutch, the English, and the French, among others, all of whom had imperial designs on the Western Hemisphere.

Africans Build a Dutch Trading Colony

The United Provinces of the Netherlands, the seven northern provinces of the Netherlands led by Holland and Zeeland, aligned themselves against both Spain and Portugal. The Dutch had declared their independence from Spain in 1581. Then, in 1602 the United Provinces subsidized and authorized the East India Company to challenge Portuguese claims to Africa and Asia by establishing a Dutch monopoly on trading from the Cape of Good Hope through the Pacific. Henry Hudson, the English seaman sailing for the Dutch East India Company, was seeking a new route to Asia when he wandered into New York Bay in 1609 and sailed up the North River (later renamed the Hudson River in his honor).

To the Dutch West India Company, founded in 1621, the United Provinces gave a trade monopoly in the Americas and West Africa, and the added mission to support the ongoing Dutch war against Spain in the Americas and on the Atlantic Ocean. By 1625 the company had established the village of New Amsterdam on Manhattan Island, and had begun importing enslaved African labor to assist them in salvaging their North American imperial venture. The first enslaved black workers cleared land; built houses, roads, fortifications, and bridges; and planted and harvested crops. But because village merchants were more interested in trading than in farming, a plantation economy did not emerge.

The legal status of Africans varied during the early period of Dutch colonial rule, and Africans—free, half-free, and slave—frequently enjoyed some of the same rights as white residents. Some owned property, bore arms and practiced Christianity, created families, and engaged in the same commerce, both legal and extralegal, as whites. Beginning in 1655, however, colonial authorities transformed New Amsterdam into a slave trading port and increased restrictions on the African residents.

The Slave Trade Supports a British Colony

The English won control of New Amsterdam in 1664, and renamed it New York. Within a few years, it was positioned as a major outpost in the British colonial empire.

Under British rule, the emerging city became an even more aggressive actor in the transatlantic slave trade. The Duke of York—for whom the city and the colony were renamed, and who later became James II—was a major shareholder of the Royal African Company, the British firm that held the monopoly in the British slave trade. Among his first actions were granting port privileges to ships engaged in the slave trade, and encouraging New York residents to become more actively involved in it. At the same time the British colony of New York developed elaborate slave codes designed to control and restrict the behavior of enslaved Africans, and strip free and half-free blacks of the rights and property they had held, however tenuously, under Dutch rule. The English began enforcing the slave codes in 1702 and a slave market was established on Wall Street in 1711. The slave revolt of 1712 and the infamous "Negro plot" of 1741 put New Yorkers on notice that the seeds of rebellion, if not revolution, were in their midst.

The Quest for Freedom

By the turn of the eighteenth century enslaved and free black New Yorkers had become sufficiently familiar with the law to both openly break it and try using it to advance their own interests and causes. They developed alliances with whites—both rich and poor—and waged consistent struggles, individually and collectively, against the constraints of their colonized and enslaved existence.

The ideals of freedom, justice, and liberty—the central themes of black struggle throughout the colonial period—were given new force and meaning by the Declaration of Independence and the Revolution. Black New Yorkers, like blacks in the other new American states, took these professed national ideals to heart. Some ran away and joined forces with the British. Others volunteered for military service in the hope that they would be granted freedom. In September 1776 the British occupied New York City and established it as their military headquarters, which it would remain throughout the balance of the war. Traveling with the British were thousands of "black refugees," enslaved Africans from southern colonies who had run away and joined the British forces during military campaigns in Virginia, South Carolina, and Georgia. Some became members of the Black Brigade and fought on the side of the British during the occupation period. When the war ended in 1783, more than three thousand black refugees—men, women, and children—shipped out of New York harbor with the British, headed for Nova Scotia. Some eventually returned to Africa to help found Sierra Leone. Some of the three thousand were native-born black New Yorkers.

1492

Christopher Columbus makes his maiden voyage to the Western Hemisphere.

1493

Pope Alexander VI divides the Americas, Africa, and Asia between Portugal and Spain.

1502

The first enslaved Africans in the New World arrive in Hispaniola [Haiti and the Dominican Republic].

1522

December 26. The first documented slave revolt in the Americas takes place in Hispaniola on a sugar plantation owned by Christopher Columbus's son, Admiral Diego Colon.

1525

Black Portuguese navigator Esteban Gomez sails into the bay [between Long Island and Staten Island] "discovered" by Italian explorer Giovanni da Verrazzano the previous year. He reports exploring a wide and long river with "fine fur-bearing animals." Gomez names the waterway *Deer River* (renamed for English explorer Henry Hudson after his 1609 voyage).

1526

The first enslaved Africans in continental North America arrive in South Carolina to provide labor for Spanish colonizers; they rebel and flee into the wilderness frontier a few months later.

1546

Enslaved Africans in Mexico mount a significant revolt. (Others follow in 1570, 1608, and 1650.)

1552

The first documented ship carrying enslaved Africans from Africa arrives in Brazil.

1602

The Dutch East India Company is established to trade in Africa and Asia.

1605 ca.

Fugitives from Brazilian mines and plantations form dos Palmares, a quilombos—a wilderness colony of escaped blacks. (The largest of Brazil's many quilombos, Palmares lasts until 1695, with its population reaching more than ten thousand.)

Manhattan Island in 1600. Native Americans row toward their settlement.

Jan Rodriguez establishes a trading post with Native Americans.

1609

English explorer Henry Hudson sails a Dutch ship, the *Half Moon,* past the island Native Americans call Manahatta.

1613

Spring. Jan Rodriguez, a free black sailor working for a Dutch fur trading company, is left alone on Manhattan Island to live and trade with the Native Americans.

1619

August. The first twenty enslaved Africans in Virginia arrive at Jamestown; all are sold as laborers for the British colony.

1621

The Dutch West India Company is established to trade in West Africa and the Americas.

1625

Eleven enslaved African men arrive in New Amsterdam [Manhattan] with the Dutch West India Company and become the first municipal labor force. The workers build Fort Amsterdam, clear fields, and construct roads and homes. They also clear land for farms beyond New Amsterdam [Staten Island, Brooklyn, Queens, and the Bronx]. Some of their surnames—Angola, Congo, Santomee (São Tomé)—may indicate their origins.

1626

New Netherland Director-General Peter Minuit "purchases" Manhattan Island from the native Algonquian people with glass jewelry and trinkets worth twenty-four dollars.

1638

A school is established "to train the youth of the Dutch and the Blacks in the knowledge of Jesus Christ" [the Collegiate School, one of the nation's oldest private schools].

1639

African laborers work daily in Manhattan Island's northern forest region [upper East Side and Harlem] clearing timber and cutting lumber at the colony's saw mill [74th Street and Second Avenue].

May 7. Anthony Jansen van Salee, a free black from Morocco, sells his Manhattan farm to Dutch baker Barent Dircksen. The sale includes the land, house, and barn but excludes all fruit trees (twelve apple, forty peach, seventy-three cherry trees, twenty-six sage plants, and fifteen vines), which van Salee removes.

August 1. Anthony Jansen van Salee receives a land grant from the governor, Willem Kieft. The two-hundred-acre farm is located "upon Long Island, opposite Coney Island" [in Brooklyn].

October 2. Barent Jan Pieters, the son of enslaved workers Pieter and Susanna San Tomé, is baptized at New Amsterdam's Protestant Dutch Reformed Church—the church's first recorded baptism of a black child. (By the baptisms of Louis and Lara Angola's triplets—Lucretia, Elisabeth, and Anthony—on July 12, 1665, sixty-three black children are baptized at the church.)

1641

January. Jan Primero, an African worker, is found murdered. Without explaining why he was killed, eight of Primero's cowork-

M A N A T V S

Gelegen op de Noort Rivier

Staten Eyland

Achter t' Col

Noort Rivier

Red Hoeck

Conijne Eyland

Wick Quawanck

t' Eyland Manatus

Zeedendal

Techkonis

Mareckwick

(This style of houses occupied by savages)

Keskachaue

Hell Gaet

INDICATION OF THE CHIEF PLACES ON THE
MANATVS

1 - Company's Farm with an imposing House.	21 - Farm of Senikant (Predekant).	36 - Two plantations and two farms of Wolfert Geritsz and two of his partner, (Van Couwenhoven and Andries Hudde).
2 } 3 } 4 } Five abandoned farms of the Company which are vacant, where of 5 } from now on, 1639, three are again 6 } to be occupied.	22 - Farm of Anthony The Turck (Anthony Jansen Van Salee).	37 - Plantation of Gegoergesyn.
	23 - Farm of Jan Claesen.	38 - Three plantations of Gegoergesyn.
	24 - Plantation of Davit the Provoost.	39 - Plantation of Claes Norman.
7 - Plantation of Tomes Sanders (the blacksmith).	25 - Plantation of Hendric the Tailor.	40 - Farm of Dieryck the Norman.
8 - Plantation of Old Jan (John Seals).	26 - Plantation of Tymen Jansz.	41 - Farm of Cosyn (Cosyn Gerritsen Van Putten).
9 - Plantation of Jan Pietersz.	27 - Farm of Van Vorst. (Cornelis, at Ahasimus).	
10 - Plantation of Twiller.	28 - v (Farm of Hendrick Cornelissen Van Vorst at Hoboken).	42 - Commenced farm of Poelen Pietersz. in its entirety as the same has been laid out from the river to the Sandhill.
11 - Plantation of Boere Beecker.	29 - Farm of Jan Everts (Bout at Communipaw).	
12 - Plantation of Mr. Lesle de Neve Sinx.	30 - Plantation on the Laeter Hoeck (Jan de Lacher's).	43 - Commenced farm of Jonas Bronck.
13 - Plantation of Tomas Bets. (Bescher).	31 - Three Plantations at Poueles Hoeck.	44 - Plantation of Pieter Schorstinveger (Chimney sweeper).
14 - Plantation of Jan Van Rotterdam.	32 - Plantation of Maerynes (Maryn Adriaensen, Wehawken).	45 - Plantation of the Tailor.
15 - Plantation of Hendrick Pietersz.	33 - Plantation of Davidt Pieters (De Vries).	A - Fort Amsterdam.
16 - Brewery of Boere Backer.	34 - Nooten (Governor's) Island with a plantation of Twiller.	B - Grain Mill.
17 - Plantation of Jacob Collaar (Jacob Van Corlaer).	35 - Two beginnings and 3 Plantations of Pannebackery (Pannebacker's).	C - Saw Mill.
18 - Farm of Cornelis Van Thienhoven.		D - Saw Mill.
19 - Farm of Loen Ontangele.		F - Quarters of the Blacks, the Company' Slaves.
20 - Farm of Twiller in the Hell Gate.		

ers confess to the murder. Dutch authorities decide that because they are valuable slaves, only one should be put to death for the crime. Manuel de Gerrit de Reus draws the short straw, but at his hanging the rope breaks and he falls to the ground. Bystanders call Manuel's good fortune "an act of God," and he is pardoned of the crime.

Manhattan Island (Eyland Manatus) in 1639. Joan Vingboom's map includes a legend citing Dutch properties as well as the farm of free black Anthony Jansen van Salee (22) [before his move to Brooklyn] and the Dutch West India Company's slave quarters (F).

May 5. Anthony van Angola and Lucie D'Angola are married at the New Amsterdam church. The wedding, the earliest recorded marriage of Africans in the colony, is the second for both Anthony (widower of Catalina van Angola) and Lucie (widow of Laurens van Angola). (During the next decade, black marriages and baptisms are more than one quarter of those recorded for the village.)

1643

February 25. Dutch soldiers led by British Captain John Underhill, known for leading the 1639 massacre of three hundred Pequots in their Connecticut settlement, attack Native American settlements north of New Amsterdam [the vicinity of the Manhattan Bridge] and in New Jersey. More than a hundred residents are killed; the soldiers suffer no fatalities. Following the attack, Native Americans burn farms on Manhattan Island and in the surrounding areas [Brooklyn, Staten Island, and the Bronx]. As farms are abandoned and destroyed, the colony suffers a food shortage.

July 13. Land grants are given to free blacks Catalina Anthony and Domingo Anthony and to three other black settlers the same year. Authorities hope that these properties, located in the unsettled frontier territory [Chinatown] north of New Amsterdam, will serve as a buffer zone between the village and Native American settlements. (Surviving Dutch records indicate that Governor Kieft was implementing a new policy for use of frontier land abandoned by colonists after raids by Native Americans.)

1644

February. Captain Underhill leads Dutch soldiers in a nighttime attack on an Algonquian settlement [the northern Bronx], killing seven hundred residents. The buffer zone inhabited by free blacks becomes increasingly important to colonists who fear retaliation by surviving Native Americans.

February 25. Eleven enslaved black workers successfully petition the local Dutch government, winning their freedom in the first group manumission in colonial North America. Each is given

Black Landowners in Manhattan's "Land of the Blacks"
1643–1664

Landowner	Acreage	Farm Grant Received
Catalina Anthony (widow of Jochem)	8	July 13, 1643
Domingo Anthony	12	July 13, 1643
Cleyn (Little) Manuel	10	ca. December 1643
Manuel Gerrit de Reus	12	ca. December 1643
Manuel Trumpeter	18	December 12, 1643
Marycke (widow of Lawrence)	6	December 12, 1643
Gracia D'Angola	10	December 15, 1644
Simon Congo	8	December 15, 1644
Jan Francisco	8	December 15, 1644
Pieter San Tomé	6	December 15, 1644
Manuel Groot (Big Manuel)	8	December 21, 1644
Cleyn (Little) Anthony	6	December 30, 1644
Paulo D'Angola	6	December 30, 1644
Anthony Portuguese	12	September 5, 1645
Anna D'Angola (widow of Andries)	6	February 8, 1647
Francisco D'Angola	6	March 25, 1647
Anthony Congo	6	March 26, 1647
Bastiaen Negro	6	March 26, 1647
Jan Negro	6	March 26, 1647
Manuel the Spaniard	4	January 18, 1651
Mathias Anthony	2	December 1, 1655
Domingo Angola	4	December 2, 1658
Claes Negro	2	December 2, 1658
Assento Angola	2	December 2, 1658
Francisco Cartagena	2	December 2, 1658
Anthony of the Bowery	2	ca. 1658
Anthony the blind negro	2	ca. 1658
Manuel Sanders	4	ca. 1662

Manhattan Island frontier farmland and freedom on the condition that he grow food for the Dutch West India Company. Named are Paulo Angola, Big Manuel, Little Manuel, Manuel de Gerrit de Reus (who survived an attempted hanging in 1641), Simon Congo, Anthony Portuguese, Garcia D'Angola, Pieter San Tomé, Jan Francisco, Little Anthony, and Jan Fort Orange. Their wives are also freed, but the manumission document stipulates "that their children at present born or yet to be born, shall be bound and obligated to serve the Honorable West India Company as Slaves." The black farm region known as "the land of the blacks" now spans more than a hundred square city blocks [Chinatown, Little Italy, SoHo, and Greenwich Village].

1646

May. The slave ship *Tamandare* arrives in New Amsterdam from Brazil.

1647

August. Peter Stuyvesant arrives from Holland to replace Kieft as governor. An anti-Catholic and anti-Semite, Stuyvesant oversees

Dutch West India Company slave-trading interests in New Amsterdam and Curaçao. (He eventually becomes the colony's largest slaveholder, owning forty men, women, and children.)

1648

A Dutch territorial council passes a resolution authorizing the importation of slaves into New Netherland, and encouraging trade with Brazil and Angola.

The New Amsterdam Town Council passes the first ordinance to curb the number of runaway slaves. Fines are levied against any citizen who harbors a fugitive.

1651

Citizens of Gravesend [a part of Brooklyn] request an increase in the number of slaves imported into the colony.

1653

March 15. Construction of a city wall is approved by the New Amsterdam Town Council. The West India Company's slaves are ordered to build a barricade with logs "twelve feet long, eighteen inches in circumference, sharpened at the upper end" from river to river across Manhattan Island [contemporary Wall Street].

The world population is estimated at 500 million. More than 500,000 enslaved Africans have been imported to South America and the Caribbean, with less than one percent of that total transported to North America.

Manhattan Island in 1656.

1654

The Portuguese drive the Dutch from Brazil. Some refugees migrate to New Amsterdam.

1655

September 15. A Dutch slave ship, the *Wittespaert* (*White Horse*), arrives carrying three hundred Africans from Guinea, the first shipped directly to New Amsterdam from Africa.

1658

Approximately 2,000 people are scattered on Manhattan Island and beyond [within the boundaries of the five boroughs]; an estimated ten percent of them are enslaved. About 100 free blacks live in New Amsterdam and western Long Island [Brooklyn].

New Haarlem [Harlem] is established as the colony's second permanent settlement. To inspire settlers to migrate to the wilderness region in northern Manhattan, the village is named after a town in Holland that fought valiantly before falling to the Spanish in the sixteenth century. Stuyvesant orders enslaved workers to construct a road from New Amsterdam to the new settlement [the vicinity of 110th Street and the East River].

1660

England's Royal African Company is founded, principally to engage in the African slave trade.

1661

Free black "Francisco the negro" is one of the twenty-three founders of Boswijk [Bushwick in Brooklyn].

Emannuel Pieterson and Dorothy Angola, adoptive parents of enslaved eighteen-year-old Anthony, petition the Town Council for their son's freedom. The council grants the request.

Barbados passes a comprehensive slave code, the Act for the Better Ordering and Governing of Negroes, which will serve as a model for codes in other British colonies.

1663

The Maryland legislature, concluding that it is necessary to fix the status of blacks in the colony, enacts legislation to reduce all blacks to slavery even though some are already free, and seeks to impose slave status on all blacks born in the colony regardless of the status of their mothers. (In 1681 the law is brought in line with established practices by declaring that black children of white women and children born of free black women will be free.)

1664

August. A Dutch slave ship, the *Gideon,* arrives in New Amsterdam carrying nearly three hundred enslaved men, women, and children; village residents complain that there is not enough food to adequately feed them.

August. The English sail warships into New Amsterdam harbor and demand a Dutch surrender. Stuyvesant wants to fight but is opposed by even his staunchest allies. Food provisions are too low to sustain a war.

September 8. The Dutch surrender New Amsterdam to the English. Dutch soldiers are sent back to Holland aboard the empty slave ship *Gideon.* (In his first address following the Dutch defeat, English governor Richard Nicolls issues a proclamation for the capture of a runaway slave. It states, "The Negroe is a lusty young fellow about 20 years of age, he was cloathed in a red waistecoat, a pair of linen breeches, somewhat worne, a grey felt hat, but no shoes or stockings.")

October. The colony is renamed New York, after the Duke of York (later James II), brother of King Charles II.

1665

The English dictate lenient terms of surrender. The terms recognize the legality of all Dutch-claimed property, including slaves. They also demand to know how blacks can be free and own property in "the land of the blacks" area. Stuyvesant gives a formal explanation, responding affirmatively on behalf of free blacks and detailing their status as property owners.

Governor Nicolls establishes the Duke's Laws, which become the foundation of colonial New York's legal system. Their slave code restricts the use of white indentured servants (those willing to sell themselves into bondage), and grants port privileges and warehouse priority to ships engaged in the slave trade. The duke is a major shareholder in the Royal African Company, a slave-trading enterprise.

Francisco, an early Boswijk [Bushwick] farm owner.

1667

Cartmen form a guild and contract with the city to perform public works. The cartmen, whose one-horse wagons are the city's primary carriers of commodities, transport rubbish, maintain roads and fortifications, and perform other public works. (By 1691, the colonial legislature passes several ordinances that make race a qualification for a city carting license. Blacks, free and enslaved, and Native Americans are prohibited from working as licensed cartmen.)

1669

A slave revolt takes place in Jamaica. (Others follow in 1672, 1673, 1678, 1682, 1685, 1690, 1733, and 1734.)

1673

August 8. The Dutch recapture the New York colony. (They relinquish control to the English a year later. The negotiated settlement requires the Dutch to give up the colony in exchange for English-controlled Suriname.)

1674

September 24. Free black Francisco Bastien purchases four acres of land from Judith Stuyvesant, widow of the late Dutch governor. Bastien's land is in a region the Native Americans call "Crommessie" [Gramercy Park]. (The transaction is approved by Dutch authorities, having been made during the brief period when the Dutch regained control and called the city "New Orange." Bastien buys an additional fifteen-acre plot [at 34th Street and Sixth avenue] in 1684.)

1679

October 2. The New York Common Council responds to slave-owners' complaints about slave runaways by passing a law that establishes a large fine (25 pounds) for harboring fugitives or failing to send them home or to local magistrates.

New York Governor Edmund Andros prohibits the enslavement of Native Americans in eastern Long Island. The region becomes a refuge for enslaved Africans seeking freedom.

Jaspar Danckaerts, a European traveler, observes in his diary: "We went from the city following the Broadway. . . . upon both sides of this way were habitations of negros, mulattos and whites. . . . they are on this road, where they have ground enough to live on with their families."

1680

The British Parliament grants the New York colony a monopoly on the bolting (sifting) and production of wheat, substantially increasing the need for slave labor in the Hudson Valley region.

December. Solomon Pieters, the eldest son of Pieter San Tomé, one of the eleven slaves freed in 1644, purchases a thirty-acre estate "into the woods, northeast of the swamp" [the vicinity of 23rd street and Broadway]. The sale is the first to a free black approved by the English colonial government since the Dutch surrender. (In 1667, Pieters and his younger brother, Lucas, the colony's first known black physician, had inherited and split equally their father's six-acre farm.)

1682

A revised slave code requires slaves to carry passes. Additional slave laws are enacted or updated almost annually during the 1680s and 1690s. The new laws prohibit slaves from possessing guns; levy fines against anyone caught trading with an enslaved black or Native American; prohibit more than four enslaved blacks or Native Americans from meeting together; and forbid any black male to be out at night without carrying a lantern to light his face. The laws also regulate black funerals; nighttime burials are not allowed, and no more than twelve blacks are permitted to attend a funeral.

1688

A small group of Mennonites and Quakers pass the first recorded resolution by whites officially protesting slavery at a meeting in Germantown, Pennsylvania.

1690

Farmers in Harlem complain about a nearby "band of Negroes, who have run away from their masters at New York and commit depredations on the inhabitants of the said village." The accused are said to be part of a maroon (runaway slave) colony.

1702

A comprehensive statute, An Act for Regulating Slaves, is passed by the colonial legislature. Increasing fines and strengthening existing laws, the measure permits slaves to be whipped up to forty lashes, and makes legal virtually any punishment of a slave except death or dismemberment. A public office, Common Whipper of Slaves, is established, with the whipper paid three shillings for each slave punished. The number of slaves permitted to assemble, unless for their owner's profit, is dropped from four to three. In criminal trials, slaves are allowed to testify only against other slaves, not against a white or free black person.

1704

A school of religious instruction for black adults and children is opened in his home by Elias Neau, a French Protestant, whose efforts are sponsored by the Society for the Propagation of the Gospel in Foreign Parts, a missionary organization seeking to gain converts among enslaved Africans and Native Americans. (Within a year the enrollment grows to thirty persons and the school is moved to Trinity Church.)

1706

A law is enacted ensuring the slave status of any child born to an enslaved woman. The law protects white males from the normal application of paternity claims.

July. Lord Cornbury, the governor of New York and New Jersey, issues a proclamation against runaways and rebellious slave activity in Brooklyn: "Whereas I am informed that several negroes in Kings County have assembled themselves in a riotous manner, which if not prevented may prove of ill consequence . . . and if any of them refuse to submit themselves, then to fire on them, kill, or destroy them, if they cannot otherwise be taken."

1711

The Wall Street slave market opens on an East River pier in Manhattan. Slaves are also sold at other markets in Manhattan and Brooklyn.

1712

Rev. John Sharpe, an English clergyman living in New York, makes a diary entry about observing Africans burying their dead north of the town's commons. (This is the first known mention of the cemetery, north of today's City Hall, now known as the African Burial Ground.)

April 7. A group of enslaved Africans sets fire to a building on Maiden Lane, on the outskirts of the city. The Africans ambush whites who come to put out the blaze, killing eight white men. In response, a complete search of Manhattan Island is immediately conducted. Several blacks commit suicide rather than be captured. Thirteen slaves are hanged, one is chained and starved to death, one is burned at the stake, and another is "broken on the wheel" (his bones are broken by the movement of a wheel-like apparatus until he dies).

Following the Maiden Lane incident, more severe legislation is enacted—An Act for Preventing Suppressing and Punishing the Conspiracy and Insurrection of Negroes and other Slaves. Among other restrictions, blacks, Native Americans, and "mulattos" are denied the right to inherit or transfer land to their heirs.

1716

July 17. Land owned by Francisco Bastien, the last black landowner in colonial lower Manhattan, is sold by his heirs. (The land is perhaps sold because of the severe inheritance law enacted in 1712.)

1726

The Trinity Church rector and vestry observe "upwards of a hundred English and Negro servants" attending catechism on Sundays. After classes they sing psalms.

1730

May 25. New York's first newspaper, *The New-York Gazette* (founded in 1725), publishes an advertisement about Clause, a twenty-seven year old runaway slave who "has got with him a Homespun Coat of Linen and Wool, with Brass buttons, an Ozenbrig Vest with black Buttons and Buttonholes, and an old striped

For they that carried us away captive
  required of us a song;
And they that wasted us required us
  mirth, saying,
Sing us one of the songs of Zion.
How shall we sing the Lord's song in a
  strange land?

—Psalm 137: 3, 4

RUN AWAY

THE 18th Inftant at Night from the Subfcriber, in the City of New-York, four Negro Men, Viz. LESTER, about 40 Years of Age, had on a white Flannel Jacket and Drawers, Duck Trowfers and Home-fpun Shirt. CÆSAR, about 18 Years of Age, clothed in the fame Manner. ISAAC, aged 17 Years cloathed in the fame Manner, except that his Breeches were Leather; and MINGO, 15 Years of Age, with the the fame Clothing as the 2 firft, all of them of a middling Size, Whoever delivers either of the faid Negroes to the Subfcriber, fhall receive TWENTY SHILLINGS Reward for each befide all reafonable Charges. If any perfon can give Intelligence of their being harbour'd, a reward of TEN POUNDS will be paid upon conviction of the Offender. All Mafters of Veffels and others are forewarn'd not to Tranfport them from the City, as I am refolved to profecute as far as the Law will allow.   WILLIAM BULL.
N. B. If the Negroes return, they fhall be pardon'd.   · 88

vest, Leather Breeches, new homespun Worsted Stockings, black shoes with buckles, he has a Hat and Cap and he can play upon the fiddle and speaks English and Dutch. Whoever can take up the said Negroe and bring him to his said Master, or secure him and give Notice, so that his Master can have him again, shall have reasonable satisfaction besides all reasonable charges." Weekly, the newspaper publishes advertisements selling slaves and seeking runaways.

1737

White coopers (barrel makers) petition the New York colonial legislature to prohibit blacks from working as coopers, claiming the need for protection against "the pernicious custom of breeding slaves to trades whereby the honest and industrious tradesmen are reduced to poverty for want of employ." Race becomes a qualification for other occupations, such as dock worker and coachman. Colonial laws also limit economic opportunities for enslaved blacks by levying fines against anyone found trading with them and requiring the return of goods received.

A

JOURNAL

OF THE

PROCEEDINGS

In the Detection of the

CONSPIRACY

Formed by some White People, in conjunction with Negro and other Slaves, for burning the City of NEW-YORK in AMERICA and murdering the Inhabitants.

Which conspiracy was partly put in execution, by burning his Majesty's house in fort George, within the said city, on Wednesday the 18th of *March*, 1741, and setting fire to several dwelling and other houses there, within a few days succeeding. And by another attempt made in prosecution of the same infernal scheme, by putting fire between two other dwelling-houses within the said city, on the 15th day of *February*, 1742; which was accidentally and timely discovered and extinguished.

CONTAINING,

I. A narrative of the trials, condemnations, executions, and behaviour of the several criminals, at the gallows and stake, with their speeches and confessions; with notes, observations and reflections occasionally interspersed throughout the whole.
II. An appendix, wherein is set forth some additional evidence concerning the said conspiracy and conspirators, which has come to light since their trials and executions.
III. Lists of the several persons (whites and blacks) committed on account of the conspiracy; and of the several criminals executed; and of those transported, with the places whereto.

By the Recorder of the City of NEW-YORK.

Quid faciant Domini, audent cum talia Fures? Virg. Ecl.

Printed at NEW-YORK:
LONDON, Reprinted and Sold by JOHN CLARKE under the Royal Exchange, Cornhill. MDCCXLVII.

(Above) *Burning at the stake. This punishment, along with hanging and deportation, was inflicted upon enslaved Africans convicted of participation in the 1712 and 1741 uprisings.*

(Left) *Account of 1741 conspiracy trials. An excerpt from the journal of Daniel Horsmanden, one of the trial judges.*

1739

September 9. A slave revolt occurs in Stono, South Carolina; twenty-one whites and an estimated forty-four blacks are killed.

1741

March 18. A slave accused of setting a fire that causes damage to the governor's mansion and destroys a church is also accused of taking part in the "Negro plot," an alleged conspiracy by blacks to

Enslaved Africans attend a funeral at the African Burial Ground, ca. 1746. Colonial laws forbid more than twelve blacks to assemble at funerals.

take control of the city. More than 150 blacks are arrested during the investigation.

May 11–August 29. Thirty-one blacks and four whites are executed for their role in the alleged conspiracy to take over the city. Eighteen black men, two white men, and two white women are hanged; thirteen black men are burned at the stake. Seventy enslaved black men are transported out of the colony.

1746

August. A wall is constructed across Manhattan Island from the Hudson River to the East River [across Chambers Street] to protect the city during the French and Indian War, but the African Burial Ground and the Jewish Burying Ground [Chatham Square] are left outside of it.

1761

Dear Jesus by thy precious Blood,
The World Redemption have:
Salvation now comes from the Lord,
He being thy captive slave.

—Jupiter Hammon, "An Evening Thought. Salvation by Christ, with Penitential Cries"

Jupiter Hammon's poem "An Evening Thought. Salvation by Christ, with Penitential Cries," composed on December 25, 1760, is published. A slave living on a Long Island estate [Queens], Hammon is the first published black poet in North America. His poems are distributed as broadsides and small pamphlets.

1762

January 15. Samuel "Black Sam" Fraunces, a West Indian of mixed French and African descent, opens the Queens Head Tavern at the intersection of Pearl Street and Broad Street.

1763

The Treaty of Paris ends the French and Indian War. England, France, and Spain agree to divide regions of North America among themselves.

1770

March 5. Crispus Attucks, a former slave, is the first person killed by the British in the Boston Massacre. He is called the first martyr of the American Revolution.

Census of slaves in Brooklyn in 1755.

CENSUS OF SLAVES.

BROOKLYN.

A List taken from the Negro's belonging to the Inhabitance, under the Command of Saml Hopson Captn of the West Company of Brookland in Kings County

Negroes Names	To Whom Belonging	Negroes Names	To Whom Belonging
One Negro Man cald Francis		One Negro Man cald Will........	
Do Sambo......	Isaac Sebring	Do Cezer.................	Derk Bargay
One Do Wench Judy..........		One Negro Man cald prince......	Simon Booram
One Negro Man Cald Roger......		One Negro Man cald Ceser.......	Cornel Sebring
Do Harry.......		One Negro Man cald Dick........	
Do Peter......		Do Prince......	Saml Hopson
Do Josey.......	John Bargay	One Do Wench Dine............	
Do Esquire.....		One Negro Man cald Robin	Peter Van Pelt
One Negro Wench cald Mary....		One Negro Man cald Tight.......	Micael Bargan
Do pegg........		One Do Wench Dine............	
One Negro Man cald Thom......		One Negro Man cald Coffe.......	Abrm Brewer
Do Jack.........	Chrispr Seehar	Do Wench Judy.............	
Do Wench Bett...........		One Negro Man cald Tight	Israel Hosfield
One Negro Man cald Toney		One Negro Man cald Willing	Jacob DeBevoice
Do Wench cald Mary	John Carpenter	One Negro Man cald France......	Jacob Bennet
Do Tracey.....		Do Wench Elizabeth	
One Negro Man cald Tobey.......		One Negro Man cald Sam	
Do Wench cald Flora	Whitead Cornwell	Do Wench Dine........	Jery Bruer
One Negro Man cald Ceaser	John Middagh	Do Deyon.......	
Do Wench Jane............		One Negro Man cald prime	George DeBevoice
One Negro Man cald James	John Vandike	One Negro Man cald Ceaser	Jury Bloue
Do Wench Bett		Do Wench Lil..........	
One Negro Man cald Sam		One Negro Man cald Isaac.......	Winant Bennet
Do Thom	Clos Vanvaughty	One Negro Man cald Jo	Mrs Vandike
Do Wench Jane.............		Do Wench Jane.............	
One Negro man cald Clos........	John Griggs	One Negro Wench Cald Jane.....	Earsh Middagh
One Negro Man cald Chalsey.....	Israel Hosfield Junr	One Negro Man Cald Harry......	
One Negro Man cald Thom	Peter Stots	Do Nease.......	
Do Wench Jane............		Do Dick......	Jacob Bruington
One Negro Man cald Harry	Sam: De Bevoice	Do Charles	
Do Wench Libe......		Do Wench Peg...........	
One Negro Man cald Frank.......	Mr Van Doune		43 Negro Men
Do Thom			24 Do Women
Do Wench Anne			
One Negro Man cald Harry.......	Jacob Sebring	Total	67
Do Wench Phillis..........			

The above is a just account of Negrees to the Best of my knowledge belonging to the Inhabitants of the West Company of Brookland
SAML HOPSON.

A view of Harlem from Morrisania in 1765.

1773

June. Massachusetts slaves petition the colonial legislature for freedom. (Continued to the January 1774 session, the petition inspires "a Bill to prevent the Importation of Negroes and others as slaves into this Province," but the governor refuses to sign it.)

A Baptist church, the first independent black church, is founded in Silver Bluff, South Carolina.

1775

March 6. In Boston, Prince Hall and a group of black men join a Masonic lodge sponsored by British Army officers, starting the black Masonic movement in North America.

In Virginia, Britain's Lord Dunmore issues a proclamation granting freedom to male slaves who join the British army. General George Washington opposes the recruitment of free or enslaved blacks to fight for the Patriot cause.

May. Following the British and American clashes in Massachusetts at Lexington and Concord, preparations are made for the expected British invasion of New York. Enslaved black laborers are used to build military barricades and fortifications throughout the city, and

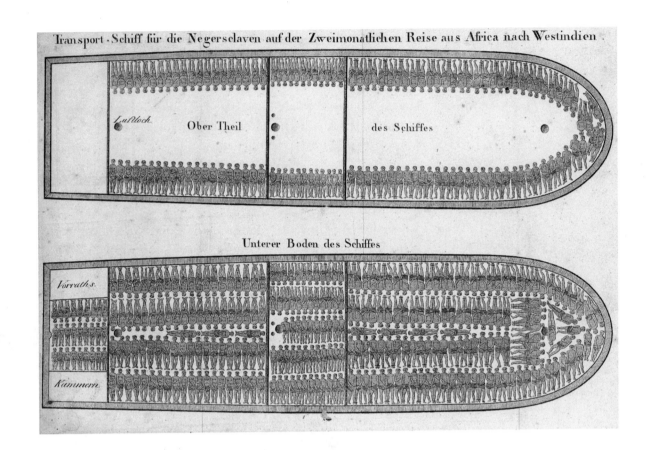

Transport-Schiff für die Negersclaven auf der Zweimonatlichen Reise aus Africa nach Westindien.

Luftloch. Ober Theil des Schiffes

Unterer Boden des Schiffes

Vorraths.

Kammern.

are required to work every day on building the city's defenses. Free black men must work every other day.

August 23. British ships in New York harbor open fire on the city; cannonballs damage the roof of Samuel Fraunces's tavern.

An interior view of a slave ship, depicting the inhumane conditions under which enslaved Africans endured the Middle Passage.

1776

The American Declaration of Independence proclaims that "all men are created equal," the first statement of the universal principle of human equality.

July 21. General Nathanael Greene alerts General George Washington that the British navy is anchored outside New York harbor. He adds: "A negro belonging to one Strickler, at Gravesend, was taken prisoner (as he says) last Sunday at Coney Island. Yesterday

Of the first 6.5 million people who have crossed the Atlantic and settled in the Americas, 5.5 million are Africans, the vast majority of whom are still enslaved.

he made his escape, and was taken prisoner by the rifle guard. He reports eight hundred negroes collected on Staten Island, this day to be formed into a regiment."

August 26. The Battle of Long Island begins as a large British force attacks Americans. General Washington and his smaller band of Patriot troops retreat to Manhattan Island.

September 22. The British employ a black hangman for their execution of Nathan Hale, the American patriot convicted of spying.

November 16. The Patriot forces are defeated at Fort Washington as the British take complete control of New York City.

December. British General Lord William Howe employs enslaved blacks as soldiers and laborers. Many serve as blacksmiths, carpenters, wagon drivers, river pilots, and teamsters, building military installations for the English forces. Some join with Delaney's

Hangman adjusting a noose.

Rangers, a Tory guerrilla force, and others with Colonel Tye, a black pro-British rebel commander in New Jersey.

ca. December. Fort Negro is constructed on a ridge overlooking the Hudson River [in the Bronx]. Black soldiers fighting for the British are stationed at the fort.

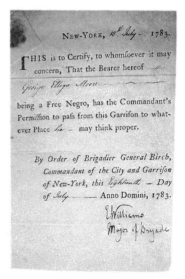

Free Paper issued to George Moore, 1783.

1780

February 10. Seven free blacks, including ship captain and merchant Paul Cuffee and his brother John, protest in a petition to the Massachusetts legislature that they are being subjected to taxation without the right to vote. (Two years later, suffrage is granted to black males subject to taxation.)

Pennsylvania abolitionists lead their legislature to pass the first state statute abolishing slavery, An Act for the Gradual Abolition of Slavery.

1781

The New York General Assembly authorizes the enlistment of slaves, promising freedom in exchange for service.

1783

The American Revolution ends. An estimated five thousand blacks have served in the Patriot army and navy; about twenty thousand have served in the British army.

November. The British depart from New York City, taking with them more than three thousand former slaves who fought on England's side during the war. General Washington tries to stop the departure, claiming it is a theft of property. British General Sir Guy Carleton insists on making good on the British promise, and Washington relents. Most of the newly freed blacks go to Canada; some return to Africa to Sierra Leone.

December 4. General Washington bids farewell to his former officers at a gathering at Samuel Fraunces's tavern.

FROM THE AGE OF REVOLUTION
TO THE CIVIL WAR

1784–1864

Overleaf:

The presentation of colors to the U.S. Colored Troops 20th Regiment at the Union League Club House, 1864.

Portraits: top left, *James Varick, founder and first bishop of the African Methodist Episcopal Zion Church;* top right, *Sojourner Truth, abolitionist and women's rights crusader;* bottom, *Samuel Cornish (left) and John Russwurm (right), founders of* Freedom's Journal, *America's first black newspaper.*

THE AMERICAN REVOLUTION USHERED IN AN AGE OF REVOLUTION THAT shook the foundations of European colonialism in the Americas. The French Revolution of 1789 triggered the Haitian Revolution of 1791. By 1804 the Haitian people, under the leadership of Toussaint L'Ouverture, Jean Jacques Dessalines, and Henri Christophe, had defeated the armies of Britain, Spain, and Napoleonic France and established the first black republic in the Americas. Between 1810 and 1825 all of Spain's American colonies except Cuba and Puerto Rico revolted and declared their independence. Brazil declared its independence from Portugal in 1822. By 1865 the European colonial empires in the Americas, which had fueled Europe's development for over three hundred years, had dwindled to a handful of French, British, Dutch, and Spanish islands in the Caribbean and the British stronghold in Canada.

The Decline of Slavery in the Americas

The systems of slavery that had served as the foundation of most of the European colonial economies of the Americas, were also shaken and eventually destroyed by the ideological and political currents of the Age of Revolution. The Haitian Revolution announced to all slave-holding societies of the Americas not only that enslaved Africans were capable of resisting through flight and rebellion, but that societies based on slave labor were inherently unstable. The Haitian Revolution also demonstrated that enslaved Africans were capable of both destroying slavery and taking control of and governing former slave societies. The successes of the Haitian Revolution inspired slave revolts and conspiracies throughout the Caribbean, the United States, and the South American mainland. Slave regimes began to fall throughout the hemisphere. In 1794 France abolished slavery in Santo Domingo, Haiti, Cayenne, Guadeloupe, and Martinique. Most of the Spanish-American colonies abolished slavery shortly after they declared their independence. England, which had led the struggle to end the slave trade, abolished slavery in her dominions in 1838.

While the new American government refused to abolish slavery, several northern colonies either included its abolition in their state constitutions or enacted laws abolishing slavery during and shortly after the American Revolution. Vermont led the way one year after the Declaration of Independence.

"King Cotton" Revitalizes American Slavery

The New York State Legislature did not address the issue of abolition until 1799, when it passed an act for the gradual emancipation of enslaved Africans. This act was amended in 1817 to provide for the abolition of slavery in the state on July 4, 1827, freeing ten thousand enslaved African New Yorkers.

Among the former southern colonies, where slavery remained the backbone of the economy, only Virginia made any serious effort to abolish it prior to 1860. For throughout the American South, where new plantation economies based on slave labor were established toward the end of the eighteenth century, the growth and eventual triumph of "King Cotton" expanded slavery exponentially.

Prior to the Revolutionary War, southern plantations raised tobacco, indigo, sugar, and rice. By the 1790s cotton had emerged as the main crop. The invention of the cotton gin in 1793 made it possible to increase the production of cotton 250-fold. Cotton plantations in Georgia and South Carolina soon expanded to new lands in Alabama, Mississippi, Louisiana, and Texas. Maryland, Virginia, Kentucky, North Carolina, and Tennessee, meanwhile, turned to producing and selling enslaved Africans to the cotton-producing deep South. By the 1830s, 80,000 African Americans were being sold in the cotton-growing states each year. This internal slave trade met the labor needs that the transatlantic slave trade—abolished since 1807—could no longer provide. The struggle between the expanding slave states of the South and the free states of the North and West eventually led to the Civil War.

During the period from 1783 to 1865, the new American nation experienced enormous growth and development. From a base of 5 million inhabitants in 1790, the population had grown to more than 31 million people in 1860. The African American population—both slave and free—also increased dramatically. Thanks primarily to abolition initiatives in the North, the free black population increased from 59,000 in 1790 to 488,000 in 1860. The enslaved African population increased at an even more dramatic rate. According to the 1790 federal census, there were only 697,624 enslaved Africans in the country. By 1860 there were almost 4 million (3,953,760).

New York Dominates the Cotton Trade

By 1860 the country had extended its boundaries to the Pacific Coast, including fifteen slave states and nineteen free states, and claimed all the unsettled territories between the two oceans. New roads, canals, and railroads had been built linking the Atlantic Coast with the interior. Steamships, the telegraph, and the cotton gin had been invented. Factory-based industrial economies had been established in the Northeast. When combined with the development of the cotton plantation South and the agricultural Midwest, the three regions had knit together an interdependent national economy, with the cotton plantation at its base.

New York City occupied a unique position in the evolving national economy. As late as 1780, New York handled only about ten percent of the American colonies' foreign trade. This percentage grew during the period of the British occupation, and by 1812 New

York had established itself as the dominant port in the country. In 1800 New York City's population surpassed that of Philadelphia, and it became the largest city in the country. Throughout the period leading up to the Civil War, New York was able to maintain its numerical supremacy and commercial dominance because of its ready access to domestic exports and foreign imports, its concentration of mercantile and financial institutions, and its unique ability among all American cities to handle both imports and exports. New York's unique relationship to the South's cotton plantation economy accounted in no small measure for its preeminence.

After the War of 1812 New York emerged as the paramount port in the development of the "cotton triangle trade"—the shipment of raw cotton from southern plantations to British mills, and the importation of finished British cotton and woolen goods for American markets. During the period leading up to the Civil War, New York established its preeminence in the textile field by gaining control of this import/export traffic. The cotton bale became the most important article in American commerce prior to the Civil War. By 1860 cotton exports paid for three fifths of all American imports. Raw cotton was also the most valuable item in British imports, and eighty percent of it came from the southern states, transhipped through New York. It should not be surprising to learn, therefore, that when the South seceded from the union to protect and extend its cotton plantation economy, the Mayor of New York, Fernando Wood, introduced a resolution in the Common Council proposing that New York also secede. The resolution was voted down.

Building the Antebellum Black Community

Throughout the period, black New Yorkers founded some of the earliest African American churches, schools, and publications. They established and ran successful businesses, and created viable communities and institutions in sometimes hostile environments. They established the first African American theater and the first black newspaper and journal and invented new genres of music and dance. They created Underground Railroad stations, assisted and defended fugitive slaves, and helped organize and run anti-slavery and abolitionist societies. Black New Yorkers waged persistent struggles for civil rights for the city's free black population. They worked as laborers, coopers, stevedores, cooks, waiters, carpenters, and teachers, and when racial discrimination forced them out of certain industries, they led the struggle to break down those barriers.

1784

The New York African Society, a spiritual and benevolent association, is formed in Manhattan, and presents poet Jupiter Hammon as one of its first lecturers.

1785

A bill introduced by Aaron Burr proposing an immediate end to slavery is rejected by the New York State legislature in favor of legislation granting freedom but severely limiting political and social rights: blacks cannot vote, hold public office, or testify against whites in any court in the state, and interracial marriages are banned.

The New York Society for Promoting the Manumission of Slaves (New York Manumission Society) is established to push for an emancipation statute. Led by John Jay as president and Alexander Hamilton as vice president, the society also fights against bounty hunters who openly seize blacks on city streets, and offers enslaved blacks free attorneys and legal aid.

1787

Delegates to the Constitutional Convention draft the United States Constitution, including a fugitive slave clause.

The African Free School is founded by the New York Manumission Society, and provides instruction in reading, writing, and arithmetic for forty boys and girls in a single room at 245 William Street, Manhattan. Cornelius Davis, a white teacher, trains boys in navigational skills for seafaring careers. A woman is hired later to instruct girls in needlework and other domestic crafts.

Jupiter Hammon's sermon *An Address to the Negroes in the State of New York* is published.

1788

The New York State Legislature passes a comprehensive slave code making it illegal to sell slaves imported into the state after 1785, and declaring all illegally imported slaves free. The legislation also grants slaves the right to trial by jury when accused of a capital offense.

Doctors and medical students caught digging up bodies from city graveyards for experimentation are attacked by angry mobs, setting

African Free School No. 2, Mulberry Street, Manhattan. This engraving is based on a drawing (ca. 1829) by Patrick Reason, a thirteen-year-old student at the school.

off the Doctors Riots. The African Burial Ground is one of the cemeteries desecrated.

1789

John Jay, a proponent of gradual manumission, becomes the first chief justice of the United States Supreme Court.

March 4. The first session of Congress is convened in New York City, first capital of the United States.

April 30. George Washington is inaugurated as president of the United States, and Samuel Fraunces, of Fraunces Tavern, becomes the presidential steward, managing culinary affairs at the presidential mansion at 3 Cherry Street, Manhattan.

1790

August 12. The United States Congress meets for the last time in New York City, as the capital moves to Philadelphia.

1791

The first ten amendments to the Constitution—the Bill of Rights—are ratified.

Enslaved blacks revolt in Haiti.

1792

Denmark is the first nation to abolish the slave trade.

Benjamin Banneker's Almanac, *published in Philadelphia, is the first scientific book by an African American.*

1793

Congress passes its first Fugitive Slave Law. It requires that persons removing a fugitive slave from a state first get a certificate of removal from a local, state, or federal judge.

African American Catherine Ferguson, a cake maker, gathers together black and white children in her Manhattan neighborhood to form the city's first Sunday school.

New York City's black population is 3,470, or 10.5% of the total of 33,131. About a third of the city's blacks are free. The city's free and enslaved black population ranks second in size behind Charleston, South Carolina, with 8,270 blacks, who comprise more than half of the city's total of 16,359.

1794

Eli Whitney is granted a patent on the cotton gin. Its use increases the demand for slave labor in the southern states. (Cotton production rises from 138,000 pounds exported in 1792 to 17,790,000 pounds in 1800.)

Slavery is abolished throughout the French colonies.

1795

The African Burial Ground in lower Manhattan is closed, and a new cemetery is established on Christie Street.

1796

Peter Williams Sr. purchases his freedom from the John Street Methodist Church. (Born a slave, Williams was purchased by the church in 1783, and served as its sexton and undertaker.) As a member of the free black community, he operates a tobacco shop and funeral establishment.

August. A group of African Americans, primarily from Class Number 31 of the John Street Methodist Church, requests permission to become a separate society of Methodists after holding a series of secret meetings in the home of **James Varick** at 4 Orange Street [Baxter Street], Manhattan. They are dissatisfied with their second-class treatment at John Street, where they are forced to sit in the gallery, required to wait until whites receive the sacramental elements, and are baptized after white candidates. The group organizes Zion Church, a leading force in the abolition movement. Among the original members are James Varick, Abraham Thompson, June Scott, William Miller, Francis Jacobs, William Brown, Peter Williams, William Hamilton, Thomas Miller, and Samuel Pontier. (Zion moves from a rented house on Cross Street to a newly erected edifice on the corner of Church and Leonard Streets in 1800.)

1799

New York State passes a second gradual emancipation act stipulating that all male children born to slave mothers after July 4, 1799, are to be freed at the age of twenty-eight, and all female children are to be freed at the age of twenty-five.

Wall Street and City Hall in Manhattan, 1797.

1800

United States federal offices are moved from Philadelphia to Washington, D.C. The new capital city has a population of 2,464 free black inhabitants and 623 enslaved.

August 30. Gabriel Prosser and more than one thousand enslaved supporters prepare to attack whites in Richmond. Virginia Governor James Monroe sends troops to stop the planned slave revolt. (Monroe is elected president of the United States in 1816, with Daniel D. Tompkins of New York as his running mate.)

1801

Thomas Jefferson is inaugurated as the third president of the United States. Jefferson found blacks to be "inferior to whites in the endowment of both body and minds."

1803

The African Burial Ground is covered over with landfill, up to twenty-five feet deep in some places, to make way for the construction of buildings and a section of Broadway. The nearby Collect Pond, a thirty-acre lake, is drained and also covered with fill.

A Pinkster Ode for the Year 1803 *is published in Albany, detailing the African-Dutch religious and cultural celebration conducted annually in that city. (An African ceremony that coincides with the Christian observance of Pentecost, Pinkster is believed by historians to have originated during the era of Dutch local rule. In 1890, James Fenimore Cooper's novel* Satanstoe *describes a Pinkster celebration in New York City as it may have occurred in the seventeenth and eighteenth centuries. Similar African carnival traditions are evident in New Orleans, the Caribbean, and Brazil.)*

1805

October 8. William Richmond, born free in Staten Island, is defeated by British heavyweight boxer Tom Cribb in a bout lasting an hour and a half. (After migrating to Yorkshire, England, in 1778, Richmond became a semi professional boxer; by 1800 he had opened a tavern in London.)

1807

England prohibits the slave trade.

August 10. Seeking burial space, Zion Church successfully petitions for a portion of the Potter's Field at West 4th Street [currently Washington Square Park]. The search for a cemetery comes after city inspectors discover Zion "has no burying ground, but inter all their dead in a vault under the church." (According to the inspectors report, seven hundred and fifty bodies were buried beneath the church between 1802 and 1807.)

1808

A federal law bans the importation of slaves.

January 1. James Varick delivers his "Sermon of Thanksgiving on the Occasion of the Abolition of the African Slave Trade" at a celebration at Zion Church as the new federal statute takes effect. Parade marchers carry antislavery signs stating "Am I not a man and a brother?"

June 6. The New York African Society for Mutual Relief, a benevolent association, is established in Manhattan. William Hamilton, a free black carpenter reputed to be the son of Alexander Hamilton, is president, and John Teasman, a teacher at the African Free School, is vice president. (The society is incorporated on March 23, 1810.)

A paternity trial, *The Commissioners of the Almshouse v. Alexander Whistelo* (a black man), includes "experts" on race called to help the court come to a decision. The judges are confused because the girl child is of lighter complexion than her mother, Lucy Williams, and the alleged father, Alexander Whistelo. The testimony of the medical doctors is split, some arguing that the girl must have a white father, while others assure the court that an accident—including ink being spilled in the mother's shoes during her pregnancy—could explain the difference in hue. Whistelo is exonerated.

The New York State legislature passes An Act to Prevent the Kidnapping of Free People of Colour, the second act of its kind passed in the nation, and the first passed in a state where slavery is still legal. However, blacks continue to be kidnapped illegally by slave-hunting posses known as "blackbirders" and sent to Cuba and South America.

The Abyssinian Baptist Church is founded on Anthony Street [Worth Street] in Manhattan by black members of the First Baptist Church who are unwilling to accept segregated seating, and a group of Ethiopian merchants. The congregation is assisted by Rev. Thomas Paul, organizer of Boston's African Baptist Church in 1805.

1809

The New York State legislature passes laws that recognize slave marriages, prohibit the separation of enslaved spouses, and legitimize the children of slaves.

1810

Black enrollment at the African Free School is growing due to a statute requiring masters to teach their slaves' children to read the Bible.

The Brooklyn African Woolman Benevolent Society is founded by Peter and Benjamin Croger, Joseph Smith, and Henry Thompson. Its constitution is adopted directly from that of the New York African Society for Mutual Relief.

Zion Church (known as Mother A.M.E. Zion Church as the denomination evolves) establishes the African Marine Fund, a benevolent society with a constitution stipulating that "All monies paid in by the members, and made by collection, is to be appropriated to the use of schooling the poor African children, whose parents are unable to educate them." The constitution stipulates that both male and female members "on their joining this society, paying the sum of one dollar, shall be entitled to vote for the officers."

1812

The United States declares war on Britain. Blacks fight in land and water battles during the war.

During the War of 1812, free and enslaved black men help to erect fortifications, including Castle Clinton [in Battery Park], Fort Williams [on Governor's Island] and Fort Gansevoort [in Manhattan, near 14th Street and the Hudson River]. Slaves who enlist in the war effort receive their freedom upon discharge. Fourteen-year-old Thomas Jennings serves as a volunteer digging trenches.

February 16. Boyer No. 1, a lodge for black Freemasons, is established in New York City and sanctioned by the Prince Hall Grand Lodge of Massachusetts. Often referred to as the African Lodge of New York, it is officially named after Jean-Pierre Boyer, a military hero and later president of Haiti.

The Wilberforce Philanthropic Association is founded and incorporated in New York City. The organization becomes famous for its pageantry at African celebrations.

1815

Peter Croger, a whitewasher, advertises that he is holding an evening "African School" at his home in Brooklyn.

1816

The Village of Brooklyn is incorporated within the Town of Brooklyn. The Village of Brooklyn begins accepting blacks in its first public school (opened in 1815), but places them in a separate room.

1817

New York passes a new emancipation act declaring that all slaves in the state will be free after July 4, 1827, with two exceptions: those born between 1799 and 1827 are to remain indentured servants until they reach the ages specified

(Above) *A manumission document, 1817. George, an enslaved man, is certified as satisfactory for manumission.*

(Left) *A certificate of freedom for John E. Moore, 1813.*

in the 1799 statute, and visiting slaveholders are allowed to bring slaves into the state for up to nine months.

Advocating a plan to colonize American blacks in Africa on the grounds that they are incapable of serving useful lives in the United States, the American Colonization Society is formed in the hall of the House of Representatives. Supporters include Henry Clay, Andrew Jackson, James Madison, and Thomas Jefferson.

African Americans opposed to the American Colonization Society stage a national meeting in Philadelphia. Three thousand delegates declare it their "right and intention to remain in the United States." A small minority of blacks feel, however, that colonization may be the only solution to end the misery of blacks in the United States.

While most blacks are opposed to the views of the American Colonization Society, the idea of colonization in Africa appeals to some blacks as a practical alternative to being subjected to continual humiliations. Within New York City's black leadership, Rev. Peter Williams Jr., **Rev. Samuel Cornish,** and Thomas Jennings, members of the Haytian Emigration Society of Coloured People, favor black emigration to Haiti instead of to Africa.

1818

The African Wesleyan Methodist Episcopal Church [Bridge Street Church], the first black church in Kings County [Brooklyn], is founded by blacks who withdrew from Sands Street Church because of the proslavery rhetoric of Rev. Alexander McCaine and the demand that they pay ten dollars quarterly for the "privilege" of worshipping in restricted pews.

1820

New York City's black population is 10,086, or just over eight percent of the total, 123,706. The city's black population is the nation's fourth largest, behind Baltimore, Charleston, and the District of Columbia.

Congress enacts the Missouri Compromise. Missouri is admitted as a slave state, and Maine as a free state. With a dividing line drawn at 36° 30' north latitude across the territory of the Louisiana Purchase, slavery is banned in states north of the line, except for Missouri; slavery is allowed in states south of the line.

The Washington Colonization Society founds Liberia as a site for the repatriation of former American slaves.

Free African American Thomas Downing opens a restaurant and catering business, the Oyster House, at Broad and Wall Streets, Manhattan.

February. The *Mayflower of Liberia* sails from Manhattan with eighty-six black emigrants aboard, arriving in Sierra Leone on March 9.

August. A fever epidemic claims the lives of 296 city residents, 138 of them black.

August 18. The New York African Society for Mutual Relief buys a tenement house on Orange [Baxter] Street for $1800.

1821

New York State legislation restricts the voting rights of free black men, requiring that they own at least $250 in property and be residents for three years, *compared to the $100 in property and one-year residency requirements for white males.*

The African Grove Theatre in Manhattan's Greenwich Village is founded by a Mr. Brown, the West Indian owner of a Bleecker Street ice cream parlor and outdoor garden frequented by free ladies and gentlemen "of color." The home of the first professional black theater company in America, it features performances by James Hewlet from Long Island [Queens] and **Ira Aldridge,** who was educated at the African Free School.

Samuel Cornish organizes the Demeter Street Presbyterian Church at the corner of Marion and Prince Streets, Manhattan. (Born of free parents in Delaware, Cornish was trained for the ministry by Rev. John Gloucester, pastor of Philadelphia's First African Church, and worked as a missionary to slaves on the Eastern Shore of Maryland before moving to New York.)

Shakespearean actor Ira Aldridge.

1822

January. The African Grove Theatre is shut down by police after white rowdies disrupt a Saturday night performance. Despite an order by police to keep the theater closed, the Grove's actors try to stage *Richard III* the following Monday night, but are arrested on stage minutes after the play begins. (The Grove reopens, but closes forever in 1823.)

May. Denmark Vesey, a free African American, organizes a slave revolt in Charleston, South Carolina. Betrayed by a follower, Vesey and more than forty rebels are executed.

1823

November. A smallpox epidemic kills 394 Manhattan residents, 113 of them blacks.

1824

Student James McCune Smith welcomes French Revolution hero the Marquis de Lafayette to Manhattan's African Free School Number 2 on Mulberry Street, as "a friend of African Emancipation."

1825

Andrew Williams, a shoe shiner, purchases three lots of land [near West 80th Street and Central Park West] for $125. This is the origin of the neighborhood known as Seneca Village.

1826

Property requirements reduce black voting strength to nil. Of a total black population of 12,499 in New York County, only 16 meet the $250 property qualification to vote.

Tuberculosis kills 820 New Yorkers, 117 of them black.

1827

Black leaders meeting at the home of M. Boston Crummell at 139 Leonard Street, Manhattan, decide to launch a newspaper to answer scurrilous attacks on free blacks by the white press and to advocate the abolition of slavery.

March 16. The first issue of *Freedom's Journal*, the first black newspaper in the United States, is published. Edited by Samuel Cornish and **John Russwurm,** the paper operates from Zion Church at 152 Church Street. (Born a slave in Port Antonio, Jamaica, Russwurm was a graduate of Bowdoin College in Maine, one of the earliest black graduates of an American college.)

July 4. Zion Church and other black churches conduct day-long indoor celebrations commemorating New York State's Emancipation Day, despite warnings by city officials that white backlash might cause rioting. Though the act frees more than ten thousand black New Yorkers, no outdoor parades are held, to dispel white fears of violence.

July 5. More than two thousand blacks gather in the vicinity of St. John's Park and march to Zion Church at Church and Leonard Streets, Manhattan, after being urged by members of the New York State legislature to celebrate emancipation on the fifth, since July 4 is revered by white citizens as the day of national independence.

Brooklyn's first African Free School is formed. [Later named Colored School #1, it moves to 51 Saint Edwards Street, and is now P.S. 67.]

We wish to plead our own cause. Too long have others spoken for us. Too long has the publik been deceived by misrepresentations, in things which concern us dearly. . . . Our vices and our degradation are ever arrayed against us, but our virtues are passed by unnoticed.

—First editorial in *Freedom's Journal*, March 16, 1827

I hope you are not to be classified with those, who think that our mathematical knowledge should be limited to 'fathoming the dish-kettle,' and that we have acquired enough of history if we know that our grandfather's father lived and died. . . . Ignorant ourselves, how can we be expected to form the minds of our youth, and conduct them in the paths of knowledge?

—First article by a woman ("Matilda") in *Freedom's Journal*, August 10, 1827

1828

Black New York women found the Dorcas Society to aid needy African Americans.

1829

Slavery is abolished in Mexico.

David Walker's Appeal, in Four Articles: Together with a Preamble, to the Coloured Citizens of the World, but in particular and very expressly, to those of The United States of America, *published in Boston, appeals to blacks to revolt against their oppressors.*

Robert Alexander Young publishes the militant pamphlet *The Ethiopian Manifesto, Issued in Defence of the Blackman's Rights* in New York City.

The New York African Clarkson Association, a benevolent society, is chartered. Officers of the New York African Society for Mutual Relief assist in its organization.

Converted to the cause of colonization in Africa, John Russwurm resigns as editor of *Freedom's Journal* and moves to Liberia. Samuel Cornish resumes editorship, publishing the paper under the new name, *The Rights of All.*

1830

July 4. Speaking against the American Colonization Society, Rev. Peter Williams Jr. charges that its effort to transport blacks back to Africa is a program to rid the country of its black population. Williams accuses the society's supporters of wanting to make conditions so miserable for blacks in the United States that they will want to leave. (The son of one of the founders of the Zion Church, Peter Williams Jr., after attending the African Free School, was confirmed as an Episcopal priest and organized the St. Phillip's African Church in 1818.)

The New York Union African Society, a benevolent association, is organized and incorporated.

This day we stand redeemed from a bitter thralldom. . . . THE AFRICANS ARE RESTORED! No more shall the accursed name of slave be attached to us—no more shall negro and slave be synonimous [sic]. . . . This day has the state of New-York regenerated herself—this day has she been cleansed of a most foul, poisonous and damnable stain.

—William Hamilton, Zion Church, July 4, 1827

The black population is about seven percent in New York County [Manhattan], almost ten percent in Kings County [Brooklyn], and thirteen percent in Queens County.

While wealthy patrons dine upstairs in Thomas Downing's Oyster House, his young son George provides shelter and assistance to runaway slaves en route to Canada in the cellar, which serves as an Underground Railroad station. Downing also helps support the African Free Schools.

Rev. James W. C. Pennington is among the founders of the Brooklyn Temperance Association.

1831

Nat Turner leads a slave revolt in Virginia. Fifty-seven whites are killed by Turner and his raiders. Turner and at least forty more blacks are killed in response.

The time must come when the Declaration of Independence will be felt in the heart as well as uttered from the mouth, and when the rights of all shall be properly acknowledged and appreciated. God hasten that time. This is our home, and this is our country. Beneath its sod lie the bones of our fathers; for it, some of them fought, bled, and died. Here we were born, and here we will die.

—Address to the Citizens of New York, statement adopted at the Mass Meeting on January 25, 1831, African Hall, Manhattan

January 25. Philip A. Bell and Samuel Ennals lead a black anticolonization mass meeting at the African Hall on Nassau Street, Manhattan, to protest the organization of a New York branch of the American Colonization Society.

William Hamilton and Thomas Downing are New York delegates to the First National Negro Convention in Philadelphia. The convention passes a resolution calling for the establishment of "a College for the instruction of young men of colour, on the manual labour system, by which the children of the poor may receive a regular classical education, as well as those of their more opulent brethren." It also calls upon the American Colonization Society to "desist; or, if we must be sacrificed to their philanthropy, we would rather die at home."

1832

White abolitionist William Lloyd Garrison founds the New England Anti-Slavery Society in Boston. The Society vigorously opposes the American Colonization Society's colonization efforts.

At the insistence of black parents, the New York Manumission Society begins to employ black instead of white teachers at its black schools.

Finding that its black schools have become a heavy financial burden, the New York Manumission Society proposes transferring the

African Free School's nearly 1,400 pupils to the Public School Society, which operates schools for poor white children.

The character Jim Crow is "born" in New York City, as white comic entertainer Thomas Dartmouth "Daddy" Rice performs the dancing black-face character at the Bowery Theater.

1833

June. The Phoenix Society, a benevolent organization devoted to the overall improvement of black New Yorkers, is formed under the leadership of Rev. Christopher Rush, Rev. Theodore Wright, Thomas Jennings, and Benjamin Hughes. Arthur Tappan, a wealthy white philanthropist and abolitionist, gives financial support to the new group. The organization mandates itself: "To visit every family in the ward, and make a register of every colored person in it—their name, sex, age, occupation, if they read, write and cypher—to induce them, old and young, and of both sexes, to become members of this Society."

October 2. Mobs attack members of the New York City Anti-Slavery Society.

William Peter Powell, an African American from Brooklyn, joins William Lloyd Garrison, the radical white publisher of the *Liberator*, and others at the founding meeting of the American Anti-Slavery Society in Philadelphia. The Society establishes its headquarters in New York. Powell, born a slave in New York, works as a shipsmith (marine ironworker) on the New York City docks.

1834

March. Black youth leaders **Henry Highland Garnet,** William H. Day, and **David Ruggles** form the Garrison Literary and Benevolent Association of New York, gathering 150 black youths under the age of twenty-one in a public school for their first meeting. They vow in the preamble of their constitution that "forming ourselves into an associated body will be the means of spreading information and diffusing knowledge, and we hope to do good to soul and body." The group is told by a city official that they will have to change its name if they want to continue using public facilities. They opt to retain their name and rent space.

June. Rev. Samuel Cox, a white antislavery minister, is criticized by members of his Laight Street Presbyterian Church for inviting Samuel Cornish to attend Sunday service. Cox answers with a sermon questioning the whiteness of Jesus. The *Courier and Enquirer* newspaper blasts Cox for suggesting Jesus was black. An enraged white merchant bellows, "He called my Savior a nigger! God damn him!"

June 2–13. The fourth annual National Negro Convention is chaired by William Hamilton and held in Manhattan. In attendance are fifty delegates from Pennsylvania, New York, New Jersey, Connecticut, Massachusetts, Rhode Island, Maryland, and Ohio as well as a visitor from Canada and one from Haiti. Hamilton strongly denounces what he calls the "divide and conquer" views of the American Colonization Society.

July 4. An interracial celebration at Chatham Street Chapel, a white Presbyterian church, marks the seventh anniversary of the end of slavery in New York State. Angry white spectators break up the commemoration.

July 7. At Chatham Street Chapel, members of the all-white New York Sacred Music Society clash with a black choir over use of rehearsal space in the building. Police arrest six blacks.

July 9. Black and white abolitionist homes, businesses, and churches are attacked by whites who are angered by the formation of the American Anti-Slavery Society. St. Philip's African Episcopal Church and the African Baptist Church are badly damaged by rioting white crowds. Over two thousand demonstrators stage an antiblack protest at Chatham Chapel. Mocking blacks, some in the angry mob "struck up a Jim Crow chorus"—imitating Thomas Rice's popular theatrical act.

The town of Brooklyn is chartered as the City of Brooklyn.

The African Free Schools merge with the Public School Society, and are continued as separate schools. The Society also establishes part-

Under present circumstances it is highly necessary the free people of colour should combine, and closely attend to their own particular interest. All kinds of jealousy should be swept away from among them, and their whole eye fixed, intently fixed, on their own peculiar welfare. . . . [They need] to take into consideration what are the best means to promote their elevation, and after having decided, to pursue those means with unabating zeal until their end is obtained.

—William Hamilton, address to the fourth annual National Negro Convention, June 2, 1834

time "normal" schools, one for blacks and one for whites, the purpose of which is to train teachers.

1835

November 20. The New York Committee of Vigilance is organized to assist fugitive slaves and to prevent the kidnapping and enslavement of free blacks. Among its founding members are David Ruggles, Robert Brown, and Thomas van Rensellaer, who notes that black New Yorkers are giving donations to the cause that exceed anything he has ever seen before.

The American Anti-Slavery Society distributes more than one million antislavery handbills, pamphlets, and other literature throughout the North and South. Southern postmasters demand that antislavery materials be extracted from southbound mail.

Maria W. Stewart publishes the pamphlet *Productions of Mrs. Maria W. Stewart*, which includes devotional thoughts and essays on the condition of black people. Stewart encourages black women to strive for education and political rights. (Stewart, called America's first black woman political writer, was forced by public opposition to her work to move to New York City from Boston. She worked as a school teacher in Brooklyn and Long Island.)

O, ye daughters of Africa, awake! awake! arise! no longer sleep nor slumber, but distinguish yourselves. Show forth to the world that ye are endowed with noble and exalted faculties.

—Maria Stewart, *Productions of Mrs. Maria W. Stewart*, 1835

1836

April. A city policy against granting carting licenses to blacks is challenged by William S. Hewlett, a porter living on Pearl Street, Manhattan. Attempting to become the first licensed black cartman, Hewlett petitions to start a business selling books from a cart, but is refused a license on the basis of "public opinion" (denied because of his race).

July 23. David Ruggles is unable to free fugitive slave George Jones, who is arrested at 21 Broadway in Manhattan. Ruggles writes, "In less than three hours after his arrest, he [Jones] was bound in chains, dragged through the streets, like a beast to the shambles. My depressed countrymen, we are all liable; your wives and children are at the mercy of merciless kidnappers." (Ruggles, who uses his bookstore and boarding house on Lispenard Street as an Underground Railroad station, is credited with aiding hundreds of former enslaved blacks to freedom.)

The Association for the Benefit of Colored Orphans, known as the Colored Orphan Asylum, is founded by two Quaker women, Anna H. Shotwell and her niece, Mary Murray. Located at 12th Street and Sixth Avenue, the institution houses thirty-seven children in a two-story wood-frame house.

1837

January. Philip A. Bell begins publishing the *Weekly Advocate* newspaper in Manhattan with Samuel Cornish as editor and Charles Bennet Ray as general agent. (The paper becomes the *Colored American* in March 1837. Ray becomes part owner with Bell in 1838, and later sole owner, and sole editor from 1839 until it ceases publication in 1842. A member of the American Anti-Slavery Society, Ray works as a "conductor" for the Underground Railroad, providing information and shelter to black runaways.)

February. Black men petition for equal suffrage at a meeting at Phoenix Hall in Manhattan. They also petition for jury trials for alleged fugitives and an end to the policy permitting out-of-state slave owners to bring enslaved blacks into the state for a period of nine months. Nearly two thousand names are on the petitions, which the state assembly rejects by a vote of seventy-one to twenty-four.

The American Anti-Slavery Society claims 1,350 branch offices and more than a million members nationwide.

March 2. *The Emancipator,* a weekly newspaper published by the American Anti-Slavery Society, warns New York's black citizens about kidnappers or "blackbirders": "Look out for Kidnappers. . . . Colored people should be on their guard. Let no white man into your house unless you know who he is, and what his business is. If he says he is an officer and has a warrant to arrest a fugitive slave, don't let him in unless he shows a search warrant."

September 16. In a *Colored American* editorial, Samuel Cornish demands that Mayor Cornelius Lawrence end the prohibition

A kidnapping by "blackbirders." Free blacks kidnapped and sold into slavery in the South are a valuable source of revenue for their captors.

against granting carting licenses to blacks, calling the policy an "inhuman measure of taking from the colored man the means of getting his bread."

The New York Committee of Vigilance reports that it has helped more than six hundred fugitive slaves pass through New York City to Canada in its first two years.

James McCune Smith, the city's first degree-holding black doctor, establishes a medical practice and pharmacy.

1838

August 1. William Lloyd Garrison delivers an address at the Broadway Tabernacle "at the request of the people of color of New York City." The speech commemorates the emancipation of 600,000 enslaved blacks in the Caribbean on that day in 1834.

August. The *Mirror of Liberty,* possibly America's first black magazine, is published by David Ruggles. It is an advocate for the rights of blacks.

September 4. Frederick Washington Bailey, a fugitive from Maryland, arrives in lower Manhattan disguised as a sailor. Finding shelter at Ruggles's boarding house, he awaits the arrival of his fiancée, Anna Murray, a free black woman from Maryland. Married in a service performed by Rev. James Pennington, the two resume Bailey's freedom journey to Massachusetts, where he changes his name to **Frederick Douglass.**

Free African American James Weeks purchases part of the Lefferts estate in Brooklyn [Weeksville].

1839

June. Captives aboard the Amistad *revolt, taking command of the slave ship.*

Abolitionists petition the New York State Legislature to mandate jury trials for all alleged slaves. They also petition for the repeal of the nine-month law, so that all slaves brought into the state would be immediately set free.

Anthony Provost, attempting to start a small business, challenges city policy against issuing carting licenses to black vendors. Denied a license, Provost defiantly loads his goods on "as good a horse and cart as was to be seen on any dock" and attempts his business without a license. Provost is fined following a complaint by a white cartman. (Effectively kept off the streets, he sells his horse and cart months later.)

The Abyssinian Benevolent Daughters of Esther Association is established by black women in Manhattan with a detailed constitution. Benefits include unemployment insurance, sick aid, burial payments, and interment in the society's cemetery.

William Peter Powell establishes the Colored Sailors' Home at 2 Dover Street, Manhattan. The home encourages reading, conversation, prayer, and self-discipline for the visiting sailors, and prohibits alcohol and gambling. (It eventually registers over five hundred sailors per year for both short- and long-term stays.)

1840

April 27. The Jamaica Convention, held in Queens County, adopts a resolution vowing to "exert ourselves by the use of all legitimate means to obtain redress" from the denial of voting rights, and access to libraries and public transportation. Officers appointed are

Thomas van Rensellaer of New York, president; Aaron Wood of Flushing, vice president; Rev. James W. C. Pennington of Newtown and William P. Johnson, secretaries.

The fifth annual report of the New York Vigilance Committee notes that the committee has helped 1,373 fugitive slaves since its formation.

New York passes An Act to Prevent the Free Citizens of this State from Being Kidnapped or Reduced to Slavery, and also An Act to Extend the Right of Trial by Jury.

African American abolitionists Charles Ray, Samuel Cornish, Rev. Theodore Wright, and Rev. James Pennington join with white abolitionists Lewis and Arthur Tappan to form the American and Foreign Anti-Slavery Society.

Following a split in the American Anti-slavery Society, African American abolitionists Rev. Henry H. Garnet, Rev. Samuel Ward, and Charles Ray join with white abolitionists to form the national Liberty Party. James Birney, a white abolitionist from Alabama who helped found the University of Alabama and was the publisher of the Cincinnati *Philanthropis*, runs as the party's presidential candidate, receiving seven thousand votes.

James Covey, a Mende sailor working aboard a British ship docked in New York, agrees to help the Africans arrested for their revolt on the slave ship *Amistad*. Covey travels to Connecticut, where he serves as a translator for the defendants.

William Powell's Colored Sailors Home moves to 61 Cherry Street. The boardinghouse provides banking, postal, and employment services for black sailors. (Frederick Douglass's newspaper, the *North Star*, later describes it as "an Oasis in the desert, when compared with the many houses where seamen usually congregate. . . . The best seamen are here always to be found, and the mutual interests of themselves and employers are thus promoted.") About twenty-five percent of the sailors working aboard vessels that sail in and out of New York are African Americans.

1841

The USS Creole, *carrying slaves from Virginia to Louisiana, is seized by slaves and sails into Nassau, in the Bahamas, where they become free.*

January. The *Colored American* reports that most blacks are not using public transportation because of official segregation, and that Thomas Downing was recently beaten by agents of the Harlem Railroad when he attempted to board a train car. Some cars are set aside for blacks, but black riders complain about the infrequency of these cars.

The Colored Orphan Asylum moves to Fifth Avenue between 43rd and 44th Streets, on the outskirts of the city. Its new three-story brick building shelters more than two hundred children, and includes a school, a nursery, a playground, and an infirmary. At the age of twelve, the children become indentured laborers (girls until age eighteen, and boys until twenty-one) bound to farm families in New Jersey, Connecticut, Long Island, and upstate New York.

New York State amends the gradual emancipation act of 1799 by removing the nine-month grace period for slaves in transit. Thereafter any slave brought into the state by a slaveholder is immediately free.

The Colored Orphan Asylum on Fifth Avenue, Manhattan.

Sixteen African American teachers from Manhattan, Brooklyn, and Queens issue a *Journal of Education*. Calling for improved education and equal voting rights, the teachers write: "Hundreds of children that are now shut out from the blessings of education, call loudly up to you to come. If there ever was a time that called for united action, it is now. If there ever was a time for colored freemen to show their love of liberty, their hatred of ignorance, and determination to be free and enlightened, it is now."

Free black oyster-gatherers arrive in New York from Baltimore, following discrimination against black oyster-gatherers in the Chesapeake Bay region. Many of them buy homes in Sandy Ground, a Staten Island community.

Rev. James W. C. Pennington publishes *A Textbook on the Origin and History of the Colored People.*

Pierre Toussaint gives the first donation, $100, for the construction of a Roman Catholic Church [now St. Vincent de Paul's on West 23rd Street] in Manhattan for French-speaking people.

Dr. James McCune Smith delivers a lecture, "Toussaint L'Ouverture and the Haytian Revolution," to benefit the Colored Orphan Asylum.

1842

The Philomathean Literary Society, an association of black men and boys interested in literature, oratory, and music, becomes a lodge within the Grand United Order of Odd Fellows. Peter Ogden, a black Jamaican sailor who became an Odd Fellow while in England, takes their petition to his Victoria Lodge in Liverpool after white Odd Fellows in the United States refuse to initiate black men.

1843

June 1. Isabella Baumfree reveals that she is "called in spirit" and changes her name to **Sojourner Truth** on the Christian day of Pentecost. She leaves her home on Canal Street to carry her abolitionist and equal rights message outside the city, saying, "the Lord gave me the truth because I was to declare the truth to my people."

Philanthropist Pierre Toussaint.

August 16. Henry Highland Garnet delivers an "Address to the Slaves of the United States" at the National Convention of Colored Citizens in Buffalo, New York. Calling for massive slave rebellions, his speech marks a turning point in the antislavery movement.

1845

The Brooklyn African Tompkins Association is organized to raise funds to encourage education and support the families of deceased members.

William Henry Lane, "Master Juba," is a featured dancer at Irish social clubs in Manhattan's Five Points district. One of America's most influential dancers of the nineteenth century, Lane improvises on the Irish clog dance, creating American tap dancing.

1846

A statewide referendum on equal suffrage for blacks and whites is defeated by a vote of 224,336 to 85,406. Horace Greeley's *New York Tribune* endorses equal voting rights for blacks, but eligible New York City voters overwhelmingly oppose the measure 29,948 to 5,137.

"Coloured Seamen—Their Character and Condition" by William Peter Powell, the first comprehensive report on black sailors, is published by the American Anti-Slavery Society.

The first issue of the *Ram's Horn* newspaper is published, with Thomas van Rensellaer and Willis Hodges as editors.

The A.T. Stewart Store, the city's first department store, opens at 280 Broadway, site of the former African Burial Ground. Remains unearthed during excavation for the building are dug up and carted off for use as landfill.

1847

Frederick Douglass begins publishing his newspaper the North Star *in Rochester, New York.*

Louis Napoleon, a black dock worker, appeals to the New York Mayor's Court on behalf of George Kirk, a slave brought into the state as a stowaway on a ship arriving from Savannah. Kirk is

Abolitionist Henry Highland Garnet.

Brethren, arise, arise! Strike for your lives and liberties. Now is the day and the hour. Let every slave throughout the land do this and the days of slavery are numbered. You cannot be more oppressed than you have been—you cannot suffer greater cruelties than you have already. Rather die freemen than live to be slaves.

—Henry Highland Garnet, Address to the Slaves of the United States, August 16, 1843 defended by John Jay, grandson of former Chief Justice John Jay, and is ordered released by Judge John W. Edmonds on the grounds that Georgia law does not apply in New York.

Members of the Abyssinian Baptist Church in Manhattan organize Concord Baptist Church in Brooklyn.

Antislavery minister Henry Ward Beecher, brother of Harriet Beecher Stowe, is called to pastor at Brooklyn's newly organized Plymouth Congregational Church.

1848

Bethel Tabernacle A.M.E. Church is founded in Weeksville, Brooklyn.

Rev. James Gloucester establishes Siloam Presbyterian Church in Brooklyn.

Ruling in *the Matter of Joseph Belt, an Alleged Fugitive,* Judge John Edmonds orders Belt released from custody. (Belt had been captured on a New York City street and held for two days while his captors waited for passage to Maryland.)

1849

Charles Reason is named professor of belles lettres and French at New York Central College, McGrawville, New York.

1850

Congress enacts the Compromise of 1850, allowing California into the Union as a free state. Settlers in other former Mexican lands will be allowed to vote whether or not to permit slavery. To gain southern support, the act contains a Fugitive Slave Law that is harsher than the 1793 legislation. Federal marshals are required to help enforce the law, which denies jury trials to runaway slaves and levies heavy fines on anyone aiding runaways.

September 18. Following the passage of the Fugitive Slave Act, the Manhattan Anti-Slavery Society petitions Mayor Caleb Woodhull to protect free blacks from being seized and taken into slavery. But Wall Street businesses celebrate the Compromise of 1850 as "Glorious News from Washington," according to the New York *Journal*

Master Juba, creator of tap dancing.

A view of Brooklyn in 1846.

of Commerce. A one-hundred-gun salute is fired from the Battery, and the *Journal of Commerce* reports, "the market is steadier [and] the prospect of an entire settlement of the vexed questions which have agitated the country, has a favorable influence upon all classes, and none feel it more than capitalists whose means are always at a greater risk in troublesome times."

September. James Hamlet, an escaped slave living as a free man in the City of Williamsburgh [Brooklyn], is the first person seized under the new federal Fugitive Slave Law and is returned to Maryland. Fifteen hundred supporters rally at Zion Church on Leonard Street in Manhattan, and raise $800 to buy Hamlet's freedom.

October 5. Several thousand supporters of James Hamlet hold a demonstration at City Hall Park to welcome him back to New York, and more than two hundred blacks escort him to his home in Williamsburgh.

The Seneca Village [Central Park] area now includes twenty percent of the city's seventy-one black landowners and ten percent of its eligible voters.

Sojourner Truth dictates her *Narrative of Sojourner Truth* to a white friend, and raises funds by selling copies at her lectures.

The New York Vigilance Committee privately reports that within recent months more than four hundred fugitives have arrived at Underground Railroad locations in New York. Committee member Rev. Charles B. Ray notes that his home has become a "daily receptacle" for escaped slaves. Fugitives passing through New York ports—perhaps the Underground Railroad's busiest junction—are sent on to New Bedford and Boston, Massachusetts; and Albany and Troy, New York. Underground Railroad stations include black churches and Quaker organizations.

1851

Sojourner Truth delivers her "Ain't I a Woman" speech at the National Convention for Women's Rights in Akron, Ohio.

Harriet Tubman begins her travels to the South as an Underground Railroad conductor rescuing enslaved blacks. (Having escaped from slavery in Maryland in 1849, she makes nineteen trips south to lead more than three hundred others out of bondage. Rewards for her capture mount to $40,000. She settles in Auburn, New York.)

Berean Baptist Church is founded in Brooklyn.

A convention of black New Yorkers meets to discuss plans for forming a bank, encouraged by the fact that blacks have savings in New York City banks totaling $40,000 to $50,000 that could be transferred to the black bank.

1852

Harriet Beecher Stowe's antislavery novel, Uncle Tom's Cabin, *is published.*

Louis Napoleon learns that eight enslaved blacks have been brought into Manhattan from Virginia by the Lemmon family, and successfully files for a writ of habeas corpus, obtaining their release.

1853

March. Elizabeth Taylor Greenfield, known as the "Black Swan," performs before an all-white audience at Manhattan's four-thousand-seat Metropolitan Hall. Frederick Douglass and many other blacks criticize Greenfield and urge her to repeat the concert from which blacks were excluded. Greenfield, who was born into slavery in Natchez, Mississippi, before becoming the first African American singer to tour the United States and England, gives a benefit performance for the Colored Orphan Asylum and the Home of Aged Colored Persons.

March 31. *The New York Times* reports that a waiters' union is formed by black and Irish workers seeking higher wages and reduction of hours.

August. Blacks are attacked by whites at a performance based on Harriet Beecher Stowe's *Uncle Tom's Cabin* at Purdy's National Theatre, where a special parquet has been installed for black seating.

Business and real estate holdings in New York City and its environs have increased over a hundred percent during the past two decades. Black investments in business enterprises total $839,100: $755,000 in Manhattan, $79,200 in Brooklyn, and $4,900 in Williamsburgh. Real estate holdings exclusive of indebtedness total $1,160,000: $733,000 in Manhattan, $276,000 in Brooklyn, and $151,000 in Williamsburgh.

A confederation of black waiters successfully demands an increase in wages to $16 a month. A black waiter attending a white waiters' meeting urges his white counterparts to "agitate" for wages higher than their current $12 a month.

The Public School Society turns over its segregated charity schools to the New York City Board of Education, including nine colored schools in Manhattan and three in Brooklyn.

1854

Congress passes The Kansas-Nebraska Act, repealing the 1820 Missouri Compromise, which barred slavery in the region. Allowing settlers in the Kansas and Nebraska Territories to vote on the slavery issue, the law leads to bloody confrontations between pro- and antislavery forces.

July 16. Elizabeth Jennings, a public school teacher and organist at the First Colored American Congregational Church, defies the seg-

I had seen their tears and sighs, and I had heard their groans, and I would give every drop of blood in my veins to free them.

—Harriet Tubman

That little man in black there say a woman can't have as much rights as a man cause Christ wasn't a woman. Where did your Christ come from? From God and a woman! Man had nothing to do with him! If the first woman God ever made was strong enough to turn the world upside down, all alone, together women ought to be able to turn it rightside up again.

—Sojourner Truth, Woman's Suffrage Convention, Akron, Ohio, 1851

Sojourner Truth, abolitionist and women's rights crusader.

Underground Railroad conductor Harriet Tubman.

regated policies of the Third Avenue streetcar and boards the car. Jennings, the daughter of Thomas Jennings, is injured when a conductor and a police officer physically toss her off the car. The Black Legal Rights Association hires Chester A. Arthur as her attorney. (Arthur succeeds to the presidency of the United States in 1881 following the assassination of James A. Garfield.)

The publication of *Twelve Years a Slave* by Solomon Northup leads to the identity and capture of Northup's kidnappers, Alexander Merrill and Joseph Russell, but they are unsuccessfully prosecuted in New York. (Born free in Minerva, New York, Northup was kidnapped in 1829 and transported to Washington, D.C., where he was sold as a slave and shipped to Louisiana. Northup's narrative sells more than thirty thousand copies during his lifetime.)

The Singing Luca Family performs at the Old Tabernacle on Broadway to an audience of more than five thousand.

1855

February. Elizabeth Jennings is awarded $225 and court costs by a white jury in a decision that upholds the right of "colored persons, if sober, well behaved, and free from disease" to ride on the city's streetcars.

The City of Williamsburgh and the Town of Bushwick merge with the City of Brooklyn. [The final "h" in Williamsburg drops out of use by the late nineteenth century.]

A second convention meets in New York City to urge black entrepreneurs to create a fund to encourage beginning businesses. Deposits by blacks in downtown Manhattan banks have grown to $60,000. Nothing comes of this or of the 1851 bank proposal.

Samuel Ringgold Ward's *The Autobiography of a Fugitive Slave: His Anti-Slavery Labours in the United States, Canada and England* is published.

As blacks are excluded from most skilled professions in favor of immigrant Europeans, the majority of them are employed in service professions. Of New York City's 4,788 employed blacks, 1,291 are

A Partial Listing of Black Manhattan Businesses in 1855

Owner	Type of Business	Location
T. S. Boston and M. J. Lyons	Photographers	4 Beach Street
W. F. Brown and W. I. Scott	Ice cream parlor	70 Bleecker Street
B. A. Burgalew	Watchmaker	352 Canal Street
Lawrence Chloe	Restaurant	5 Front Street
Edward V. Clarke	Jewelry dealer	352 Canal Street
Thomas Downing	Restaurant	3–5 Broad Street
Alexander Duncan	Undertaker	15 Laurens Street
Edward Felix	Tinsmith	148 Church Street
Henry Johnson	Restaurant	13 Fulton Market
Stephen Lawrence	Engineer and agent for steam pressure gauges	35 William Street
James R. W. Leonard	Printer	219 Centre Street
Patrick H. Reason	Engraver	56 Bond Street
Thomas van Rensellaer	Restaurant	Corner Wall and Water Streets
Henry Scott	Pickle maker	217 Water Street
Stephen Simmons	Restaurant	Corner of Broad and Pearl Streets
James McCune Smith	Pharmacist	55 West Broadway
William Wally	Soap and candlemaker	161 Broadway
Philip A. White	Pharmacist	Gold and Frankfort Streets
John J. Zuille	Printer	396 Canal Street

Solomon Northup is reunited with his family.

domestic servants, 574 are waiters, and 437 are laundresses. The remainder are seamen, laborers, porters, cooks, stewards, housekeepers, sweepers, and bootblacks.

1856

March 18. The *Falmouth*, an illicit slave-trading schooner, leaves a Manhattan pier, but is spotted by officials from the Brooklyn Navy Yard. The vessel is intercepted in the Narrows—the narrow waterway separating New York's Upper and Lower Bays—and returned to port. Twelve men are arrested. Ten crew members are acquitted, and the ship's captain and owner are each fined $2,000 but avoid jail.

1857

The Dred Scott *decision by the United States Supreme Court opens all federal territory to slavery and denies citizenship to black Americans.*

May. Frederick Douglass comments on the *Dred Scott* decision in an address in New York City commemorating the anniversary of the American Abolition Society: "You may close your Supreme Court against the black man's cry for justice, but you cannot, thank God, close against him the ear of a sympathising world, nor shut up the Court of Heaven. All that is merciful and just on earth and in Heaven, will execrate and despise this edict of Taney." (Taney is chief justice of the Supreme Court.)

The close of business on Wall Street.

August 5. The *New York Tribune* reports on the social aristocracy of Manhattan's "Africano-American" community, emphasizing "its castes, its first society hotels, and Young America bowling alleys."

New York City ports dominate the illegal international slave trade to plantations in Cuba, Brazil, and the American South. The *New York Journal of Commerce* asserts, "Few of our readers are aware of the extent to which this infernal traffic is carried on, by vessels clearing from New York, and in close alliance with our legitimate trade; and that down-town merchants of wealth and respectability are extensively engaged in buying and selling African Negroes." A typical slave expedition starts with the purchase and outfitting of a vessel, including the acquisition of iron handcuffs and manacles, along the South Street seaport.

The New York State Supreme Court affirms the decision, in the 1852 Lemmon Case, that any slaves brought into New York by their owners are immediately free.

1858

Seneca Village is destroyed to make way for Central Park. A campaign to gain support for the neighborhood's destruction describes the predominantly black community of black-owned homes, shops, churches, and a cemetery as "rundown and seedy."

The African Civilization Society is organized and advocates emigration to "the Yoruba country" [Nigeria]. The society argues that growing cotton in Africa would cut the demand for slaves in the American South. Supported by Martin Delaney and Rev. James W. C. Pennington, Henry Highland Garnet serves as president. Frederick Douglass and George Downing strongly criticize the effort.

1859

May. An African Civilization Society exploration party leaves New York City on the ship *Mendi* to investigate the Niger Valley in Africa as a possible colonization site.

June. A ship sails from New York carrying forty-five emigrants to Liberia. (The total number of emigrants to Africa under the auspices of the American Colonization Society eventually reaches 15,386.)

October 16. John Copeland of Williamsburgh and Shields Green join abolitionist John Brown in an attack on the federal arsenal at Harper's Ferry, Virginia, aiming to arm enslaved blacks and start a war against slavery. (Within two days the assault is put down by troops under Colonel Robert E. Lee. Brown and his black supporters are captured and executed.)

December 15. A John Brown Memorial is held at Manhattan's Cooper Union as antislavery activists mourn Brown's death. A group of blacks seek to have the bodies of Green and Copeland, who were executed for their involvement in the raid, returned to New York for burial but are unsuccessful.

1860

February 22. The *New York Times* publishes the Atlanta *Daily Confederacy's* "black and white" list, exposing New York businesses hostile to Southern slave-holding interests. Forty New York firms are listed as abolitionist and forty-seven as "constitutional." The *Daily Confederacy* concludes, "We have true southern born men in New York who will keep us posted as to the status of each firm or concern who are attempting to do business with the South."

April 23. More than one thousand people fill Zion Church for a debate on the African Civilization Society. George Downing and

Frederick Douglass, orator, journalist, reformer, and public servant, 1856.

Already slaveholders go to bed with bowie knives, and apprehend death at their dinners. Those who enslave, rob, and torment their cooks, may well expect to find death in their dinner-pots. . . . The world is full of violence and fraud, and it would be strange if the slave, the constant victim of both fraud and violence, should escape the contagion. He too, may learn to fight the devil with fire, and for one, I am in no frame of mind to pray that this may be long deterred.

—Frederick Douglass, American Abolition Society Address, May 1857

others speak against the society, calling it "an auxiliary to the Negro-Hating" African Colonization Society, but a disturbance breaks out when Henry Highland Garnet attempts to speak in its favor. The meeting ends when the pastor puts out the lights. (The *Anglo-African* calls the gathering "one of the most unsatisfactory and unhappy demonstrations ever made in this city.")

December 20. "What would New York be without slavery?" ponders commerce analyst James Dunmore De Bow in a New York *Daily News* article. De Bow concludes, "the ships would rot at her docks; grass would grow in Wall Street and Broadway, and the glory of New York, like that of Babylon and Rome, would be numbered with the things of the past."

Abraham Lincoln launches his campaign for the presidency with a lecture at Cooper Union in Manhattan organized by Rev. Henry Ward Beecher and Henry Bowen of the *Independent*.

The *New York Herald* warns that a Republican presidential victory will mean "the north will be flooded with free Negroes, and the labor of the white man will be depreciated." Despite Republican Abraham Lincoln's victory, he loses the New York City vote.

A statewide referendum on equal voting rights for black and white males is defeated 337,984 to 197,503. New York County voters reject equal suffrage 65,082 to 10,483.

1861

April 12. The Civil War begins with the Confederate attack on Union forces at Fort Sumter, South Carolina.

July 26. Black New Yorkers offer three regiments of troops with "their arms, equipment, clothing and pay provided by black residents in the state," but the governor refuses their assistance, saying he is not authorized to enroll blacks. Earlier in the year blacks staged military drills at a private hall, but they were warned to stop by the chief of police who told them he "could not protect them from popular indignation and assault."

New York City's black population is 12,472, or 1.55% of the total of 805,608. The city's black population is the nation's seventh largest, behind Baltimore, New Orleans, Philadelphia, Charleston, the District of Columbia, and Richmond. The United States Census indicates that there are only eighty-five black owners of real estate in the city's black community.

Mayor Fernando Wood proposes that New York City join the Confederacy. He points to the strong commercial ties between Manhattan and the South while blasting the Republican Party for bringing on a secession crisis and a Civil War that threaten local business interests.

1862

February 21. Convicted of slave trafficking off the coast of West Africa, Captain Nathaniel Gordon is hanged at the Tombs Prison in lower Manhattan, the only person ever executed in the United States for trading in slaves. (His ship, the *Erie*, was apprehended off the coast of West Africa carrying eight hundred men, women, and children, ages six months to forty years, destined for the slave market in Cuba.)

July. Congress passes a bill introduced by Senator Preston King of New York to accept blacks into war service. (Nearly 179,000 African Americans were inducted into the Union Army.)

A study of black sailors by William Powell indicates that 3,271 black seamen sail to and from the Port of New York each year, with about 250 in port at any one time. He reports that nationally 35,271 of the country's 300,000 sailors are African American.

1863

January 1. President Abraham Lincoln issues the Emancipation Proclamation, freeing all slaves except those in states or parts of states that are not at war with the Union.

January 1. The Emancipation Proclamation is celebrated by thousands at Cooper Union's Great Hall. Rev. Henry Highland Garnet reads the proclamation to an enthusiastic audience, but, quoting Wendell Phillips, he adds, "The Emancipation Proclamation freed the slave but ignored the Negro."

July 1–3. Union forces defeat Confederate troops at the Battle of Gettysburg, the Civil War's bloodiest battle.

July 11–16. Draft rioters kill more than one hundred blacks and whites in Manhattan and Brooklyn. A federal law giving wealthy young men the privilege of avoiding military service by paying

PRESENTED by AUGUST AU, Esq.

LIBERTY.

Liberty. This mid-nineteenth-century drawing is considered by some to be an early model for the Statue of Liberty.

others to take their places outrages poor European immigrants. Blaming blacks for the Civil War, angry mobs stage a four-day rampage of murders, lynchings, and burnings. A mob gathers in front of the Colored Orphan Asylum. Two hundred children are led out a back door as the building is fire-bombed and set ablaze. A little girl hiding under a bed dies in the attack.

Many blacks seek to arm themselves in self-defense. At Manhattan's Fifth Police Precinct, more than four hundred African Americans request and are issued firearms. Others find protection in black communities in Flatbush and Weeksville [in Brooklyn]. The *Christian Recorder* newspaper reports that in both neighborhoods, black men "armed themselves . . . determined to die defending their homes." William Powell's Colored Sailors' Home is attacked and "completely rifled of all its furniture, books, and clothing." The building is badly damaged and Powell, his family, and boarders are "compelled to escape over the roof for their lives."

Rev. James Pennington writes that the rioting has had a tragic impact on the city's black population: "The breaking up of families; and business relations just beginning to prosper; the blasting of hopes just dawning; the loss of precious harvest time which will never again return; the feeling of insecurity engendered; the confidence destroyed."

Sarah Smith Tompkins Garnet is named the first black woman principal of a public school (Grammar School No. 80) in Manhattan. Daughter of Sylvanus Smith, a Weeksville butcher and meat merchant, she had served since 1854 as a teacher at the African Free School in Williamsburgh, Brooklyn. A founder of the Equal Suffrage League, one of Brooklyn's earliest equal rights organizations, she is the sister of Dr. Susan Smith McKinney Steward. (After the death of her first husband, James Tompkins, an Episcopal minister, she marries Henry Highland Garnet in 1879.)

1864

February 9. At Rikers Island, the U.S. Colored Troops 20th Regiment trains for military service. (Other black New York soldiers are members of the U.S. Colored Troops Regiments 26 and 31, which train on Rikers and Hart Islands.)

Draft Riots, 1863: A black man is hanged by the mob while a nearby house burns, 32nd Street, between Sixth and Seventh Avenues.

March. The U.S. Colored Troops 20th Regiment, led by a military band, parades down Broadway. Thousands cheer as the soldiers march from Union Square to the Hudson River Pier at 26th Street, where they board a steamship headed to the war zone. (More than four thousand black New Yorkers fight in the Civil War.)

June. A white streetcar conductor and a policeman remove a black woman from an Eighth Avenue streetcar. In an editorial the *New York Tribune* upholds the woman's right to ride a streetcar, especially since her husband, an army sergeant, has died in the Civil War.

The Coachmen's Union League Society is established. Its constitution is influenced by that of the New York African Society for Mutual Relief, but it is organized as a trade association. (By 1925 the Coachmen have more than a thousand members and own a three-story Harlem building.)

THE FIFTEENTH AMENDMENT.

THE MAKING OF
THE NEW NEGRO

1865–1916

Overleaf:

The Fifteenth Amendment. This 1870 lithograph depicts African Americans and their antislavery allies celebrating the ratification of the Fifteenth Amendment.

Founding members of the Niagara Movement, 1905. Top row: H. A. Thompson, New York; Alonzo F. Herndon, Georgia; two unidentified members. Second row: Fred McGhee, Minnesota; unidentified boy; J. Max Barber, Illinois; W. E. B. DuBois, Georgia; Robert Bonner, Massachusetts. Bottom row: Henry L. Baily, Washington, D.C.; Clement G. Morgan, Massachusetts; W. H. H. Hart, Washington, D.C.; and B. S. Smith, Kansas.

QUIETLY, WITHOUT MUCH FANFARE, NORTHERN BUSINESS INTERESTS— financiers, bankers, company promoters, railroad builders, and manufacturers—accelerated the growth and consolidation of the American national economy during the Civil War. Responding to the need for munitions and military provisions, as well as for the capital to wage a successful war, northern businessmen, in partnership with an expansive federal government, forged the first American military-industrial complex.

Industries boomed, major business corporations evolved, and cities grew rapidly. In short, while the world's attention was focused on the war and the dying, the Civil War was fostering the economic and political consolidation of a rapacious nation-state— one that was enthusiastically committed to liberal, democratic political principles, a free enterprise economic system, and a belief in its ultimate "manifest destiny" to rule the world. Against this backdrop, black New Yorkers celebrated the defeat of the Confederacy, mourned the assassination of Abraham Lincoln, and continued their struggles for human dignity.

The First Fruits of Freedom

For a period of time the South, which had been the major battleground of the war, became the major arena in which northern and southern blacks began to practice their new-found freedom. The passage of the Thirteenth Amendment to the Constitution, once and for all, had abolished slavery throughout the land. Then came the other Reconstruction acts—the Fourteenth and Fifteenth Amendments and the Civil Rights acts of 1866 and 1875—all measures designed to recognize blacks as full-fledged citizens of the United States and to secure the rights of citizenship for them and their progeny. The majority of the black voting population in the South used their votes to elect blacks to local, state, and national office. Some black New Yorkers went south to participate in this new experiment in democracy. Henry Highland Garnet was in the vanguard of those who left, as was Thomas Cardoza. Garnet went to work in Washington, D.C., while Cardoza opened schools for black children in North Carolina. Even as New York was sending emissaries to the South, increasing numbers of southern blacks were moving to New York. But the pace of black migration was completely overshadowed by the rate of European migration to the United States in general and to New York in particular.

The migration had started three decades before the war, but accelerated its pace from the 1870s through the end of the century. Between 1815 and 1915, an estimated 33 million people moved to the United States. Three quarters of them passed through New York. Seventeen million of the more than 23 million people who migrated to the United States between 1880 and 1919 entered through New York City. Most of them settled in cities, with a significant percentage remaining in New York, where employment opportunities were plentiful. They worked on the waterfront, in manufacturing and the garment industries, and in trade. The expansion of the city's infrastructure also created a demand for construction workers.

Between 1870 and 1900, the population of the five boroughs of New York City increased from 1,478,103 to 3,437,000. By 1910 the population totaled 4,767,000. This dramatic influx of European immigrants during the second half of the nineteenth century displaced black New Yorkers in many fields of economic endeavor. The demographic imbalance produced by this massive wave of European migration reduced black voting power and further marginalized blacks in other spheres of human endeavor. By the turn of the century, however, black New Yorkers had begun to regroup and assert themselves in several economic, political, and cultural arenas.

Between 1890 and 1900 New York's black population increased by some 25,000. Nevertheless, at the beginning of the new century, there were only 60,000 black New Yorkers scattered throughout Greater New York (the five boroughs). The vast majority of them lived on the west side of Manhattan in today's midtown, between 20th and 64th Streets. The heaviest concentrations were in "San Juan Hill" and the "Tenderloin." San Juan Hill, one of the most congested areas in the city, was located between 60th and 64th Streets and Tenth and Eleventh Avenues. It was named, sardonically, for the Spanish American War battle, because of the interracial battles that regularly took place there. The boundaries of the Tenderloin district were less clearly defined, but its main street was West 53rd Street between Sixth and Seventh Avenues.

By 1900, West 53rd Street could boast of having two black-owned hotels, a variety of small businesses, the Colored Men's YMCA, Mount Olivet Baptist Church, St. Marks Methodist Episcopal Church, St. Benedict the Moor Roman Catholic Church, and the offices of major fraternal societies and political clubs. The "Y," the first all-black YMCA established in a northern city, became the center of black New York intellectual and social life during the first decade of the century.

The Backlash

The race riot of 1900 shook black New York at its foundations and sparked a series of developments that laid the social and political foundations for the famous Harlem Renaissance of the 1920s. The riot was symptomatic of the declining status of blacks throughout the nation in the last quarter of the nineteenth century. Racial segregation, stereotyping, and discrimination had become national norms, and lynching a national pastime. The decade of the 1890s recorded some 1,665 lynchings of blacks throughout the country. Blacks denied access to New York City's longshoremen, street cleaners, baggage handlers, hod (cement) carriers, and garment workers unions fought back by taking jobs when unions in these crafts and industries went on strike. Black New Yorkers also brought numerous lawsuits against white hotels, restaurants, and theaters that denied them service.

On the evening of August 15, 1900, a mob of several thousand whites raced up and down Eighth Avenue and the side streets between 27th and 42nd Streets, assaulting and brutally beating every black man, woman, and child in sight. The riot shocked black New Yorkers into action; by the end of the decade, they had been instrumental in organizing both the local Citizen's Protective League, the National Association for the Advancement of Colored People (NAACP) and National Urban League.

Hints of a Cultural Renaissance

James Reese Europe in 1910 organized the Clef Club, an association of black professional instrumental musicians that served as a club and booking offices for black entertainers throughout the city. Two years later W. C. Handy moved to New York City and established the Handy Publishing Company, an African American-owned sheet music publishing firm. Precursors of the Harlem Renaissance of the 1920s, entertainers Bert Williams, George Walker, and Ernest Hogan, and musicians Will Marion Cook, James Reese Europe, Ford Dabney, W. C. Handy, Bob Cole, and J. Rosamond Johnson, among others, pioneered in the development of innovative African American theater and musical forms, including jazz and the blues. In 1912 James Reese Europe organized a concert at Carnegie Hall featuring an orchestra of 125 of black New York's most distinguished musicians. It presented works by African American composers and celebrated the fact that African American music and musicians were emerging as the defining voices of twentieth-century American music.

It was the 1913 Emancipation Exposition, however, that sought to present a comprehensive survey of black achievement in all fields of endeavor. Organized around a series of conferences, congresses, and exhibitions of the religious, political, and cultural aspects of African peoples' historical development, the exposition commemorated the fiftieth anniversary of the Emancipation Proclamation. It attracted more than 30,000 visitors during the last ten days of October 1913. Many of the issues and themes that dominated public discourse during the Harlem Renaissance surfaced and were developed during the exposition. By the second decade of the twentieth century, black New Yorkers had also started to make Harlem the center of black life in New York.

1865

March. The Freedmen's Bureau is created by the federal government to protect the legal rights of former enslaved blacks and to provide them with education and medical care, oversee labor contracts between them and their employers, and lease land to black families.

April 14. Abraham Lincoln is assassinated, and is succeeded by Andrew Johnson.

April 24. City planning commissioners authorize the widening of Sixth Avenue north of Central Park to the Harlem River. It is widened twenty-five feet on each side.

Only forty-four black males throughout New York State meet the $250 free-hold (total property value) qualification entitling them to vote.

December. The Ku Klux Klan is founded in Pulaski, Tennessee, to restore white supremacy in government, race relations, and land ownership.

December 18. The Thirteenth Amendment, abolishing slavery in the United States, is ratified.

1866

January 1. Fisk University opens in Nashville, Tennessee.

In the 1860s nearly eighty-five percent of Brooklyn's black population resides in two black communities: just over fifty-three percent in the Borough Hall–Fort Greene section, which extends southward and eastward from the Brooklyn Navy Yard to and along Atlantic Avenue until it reaches the western border of the Bedford-Stuyvesant area and Brooklyn Heights; and nearly thirty-one percent in the southern portion of Williamsburg to the northern extension of Stuyvesant Heights.

The Move Northward in Manhattan

Date	Area	Location
1790–1840	Free African Community	Region northwest and east of the African Burial Ground: residents, businesses, churches, and boarding houses located on Duane, Reade, Baxter, Mulberry, Worth, and Lispenard Streets, and West Broadway
1820–1863	Stagg Town	Mulberry and Baxter Streets, Five Points
1863–1890	Little Africa/Little Liberia	Thompson, Sullivan, and Bleecker Streets, and Minetta Lane
1880–1910	Tenderloin	23rd Street to 42nd Street along Eighth and Ninth Avenues
1890–1910	San Juan Hill	58th Street to 65th Street between Eighth and Eleventh Avenues.

February 7. A black delegation, led by Frederick Douglass and George Downing, calls on President Andrew Johnson to urge that voting rights be granted to former enslaved blacks. The meeting ends in disagreement as Johnson reiterates his opposition to black suffrage.

April 4. City planning commissioners approve the construction and widening of two major roadways—Harlem Lane [St. Nicholas Avenue] and Manhattan Avenue—north of Central Park through Harlem.

Brooklyn's Howard Colored Orphan Asylum is founded by a black woman, S. A. Tillman, at Pacific Street and Ralph Avenue to shelter homeless children. The orphanage is directed by Rev. William F. Johnson.

The New York Colored Mission is founded by the Society of Friends (Quakers). Among its aims is "to conduct in the city of New York a Sabbath School for Religious Instruction."

April 9. Congress passes a Civil Rights Act over President Johnson's veto, granting citizenship to all persons born in the United States except Native Americans, and providing for the punishment of anyone preventing the free exercise of these rights.

June. Congress approves the Fourteenth Amendment, prohibiting voting discrimination, and it is sent to the states for ratification.

September 25. Black jockey Abe Hawkins wins the first race at the newly opened Jerome Park in the Bronx. More than twenty thousand fans, including Gen. Ulysses S. Grant, witness the inaugural event.

1867

The Colored Orphan Asylum moves uptown to the northwest corner of Amsterdam Avenue and 143rd Street, in the West Harlem neighborhood known as Carmensville.

"Sketches of New York City Life—'Hot Corn,'" 1868. Street vending provides the opportunity for individuals with almost no initial capital to become economically independent. This is built upon the struggle in earlier years for the right to sell from carts.

Thanksgiving dinner at the Colored Orphan Asylum, 1874.

January. Congress grants suffrage to black males, over President Johnson's veto.

March. Congress passes the first Reconstruction Act, over President Johnson's veto. The act divides the South into five military districts, temporarily bars many Confederates from voting or holding office, calls for the creation of new governments in the South with black men given the right to vote, and prohibits the readmission of southern states to the Union until ratification of the Fourteenth Amendment.

Howard University in Washington, D.C., is chartered by an act of Congress, and named for General Oliver Howard, head of the Freedmen's Bureau (and later the university's president).

1868

July 21. The Fourteenth Amendment is ratified.

November 3. Ulysses S. Grant is elected president of the United States. Black voters in the South provide the decisive margin, as the majority of white southerners vote for Grant's opponent, Democrat Horatio Seymour.

1869

January 13. The first national convention of Negro Labor in the United States meets at Union League Hall in Washington, D.C., with 161 accredited delegations. Delegates split on the question of relations between white and black labor.

November 11. Black workers hold a convention to select New York representatives for the National Negro Labor Congress meeting to be held the following month. Delegates from various fields include: fifty engineers, four hundred waiters, seven basketmakers, thirty-two tobacco twisters, fifty barbers, twenty-two cabinetmakers and carpenters, fourteen masons and bricklayers, fifteen smelters and refiners, two rollers, six moulders, five hundred longshoremen, and twenty-four printers.

The Corporation of Caterers, a consortium of twelve black-owned catering establishments, is formed in Manhattan to "encourage and promote" the business interests of its members. Individual caterers manage banquets, weddings, and other social functions and own imported silverware and china. The Corporation initiates the United Public Waiters Mutual Beneficial Association, a waiters' and cooks' benevolent organization, "to insure both medical and brotherly aid when sick and to assist respectably interring its deceased members." To strengthen their position in this occupation in which blacks have a chance to attain economic success, the group also seeks to control the quality of service workers and to prevent "irresponsible men attempting to cater at weddings, balls, parties, and some hotels on special occasions."

The Hamilton Lodge of the Grand United Order of Odd Fellows begins its annual Civic and Masquerade Ball.

Manhattan's black population has decreased from 18,595 in 1840 to 15,755. During the same period Brooklyn's black population has increased from 2,846 to 5,653. The movement is attributed largely to racial animosity toward blacks in Manhattan on the part of the new wave of European immigrants. During the same period, the city's overall population has increased from 391,114 to 1,478,103.

1870

January 20. Hiram Revels, a Mississippi State Senator, becomes the first African American member of Congress when he is elected to the United States Senate by the state legislature. (Seated after acrimonious debate, he serves only until the end of the term, March 1871.)

March 30. The Fifteenth Amendment passed by the Congress in 1869 is ratified. (New York State approves, then rescinds its adoption of the amendment, joining California, Tennessee, Oregon, Delaware, Kentucky, and Maryland in opposing the measure.) Passage, however, is not enough to guarantee the franchise to blacks. Poll taxes, literary tests, and "grandfather clauses," all in differing degrees, will preclude equality at the polls for nearly another century.

Negro Labor of New York organizes three professional groups: the Saloon Men's Protective and Benevolent Union, the Colored Waiters' Association, and the first Combined Labor Institute.

Susan Maria Smith from Weeksville, Brooklyn, is valedictorian of her graduating class at the New York Medical College for Women. She is the first black woman to practice medicine in New York State and the third in the nation. Also musically talented, she serves as organist and choirmaster at Brooklyn's Bridge Street African Methodist Episcopal Church.

The Fisk Jubilee Singers perform a concert of spirituals in New York City to raise funds for Fisk University in Nashville, Tennessee.

1871
Jockey Harry Bassett wins the Belmont Stakes.

1872
December 9. Lieutenant Governor P. B. S. Pinchback becomes acting governor of Louisiana while the white carpetbag governor, Henry Clay Warmoth, is suspended because of impeachment proceedings.

1873
Black males are granted suffrage by the New York State Assembly, which rescinds the $250 property-ownership requirement.

The Town of Harlem is annexed by New York City, joining Manhattan and the Bronx.

The Nazarene Congregational Church is organized in Brooklyn.

Susan Maria Smith, physician and social activist.

1874

November 8. James Theodore Holly, who emigrated to Haiti in 1861, is consecrated missionary bishop of the republic at Manhattan's Grace Church; he is the first black bishop in the Episcopal Church.

1875

March 1. Congress passes a Civil Rights Act guaranteeing equal rights in public places, and prohibiting the exclusion of blacks from jury duty.

November 2. Mississippi Democrats use fraud and violence to keep blacks from voting. The so-called "Mississippi Plan" (political assassinations and economic intimidation) is used later to toss out Reconstruction governments in other southern states.

The St. Augustine Protestant Episcopal Church is founded in Brooklyn.

Amanda Berry Smith becomes a charter member of the Brooklyn branch of the Women's Christian Temperance Union (WCTU).

1876

Manhattan's Ninth Avenue elevated train ("el") is extended northward from its terminal at 59th Street to 155th Street and Eighth Avenue.

Black inventor **Lewis Howard Latimer,** son of a fugitive slave, renders the drawings of Alexander Graham Bell's telephone for the patent application.

1877

The "Exoduster" movement begins, with thousands of blacks migrating to Kansas.

April. President Rutherford B. Hayes, making good on a campaign promise to southern states, withdraws federal troops from the South. Antiblack Democrats take control of local governments.

June 15. Henry O. Flipper becomes the first black graduate from West Point.

Evangelist and missionary Amanda Berry Smith.

September 27. John Mercer Langston is named minister to Haiti. (He is one of the thirteen African American diplomats, among them Frederick Douglass and George W. Williams, to serve in foreign capitals by the end of the century.)

1878

Antonio Maceo, a black Cuban patriot, visits New York to raise funds for Cuba's war effort against Spain.

The Ninth Avenue elevated train line extends to 61st Street [to 155th Street by 1881]; a Third Avenue line runs from South Ferry to 129th Street; and a Second Avenue line from Chatham Square to 129th Street.

1879

Edwin P. McCabe leaves his job on Wall Street to organize the migration of thousands of African American families from the Southern states to Kansas in the Exodus of 1879. In Kansas, McCabe is elected state auditor, becoming the first black elected to a state office in the United States during the post-Reconstruction period.

1880

Riverside Drive is completed in Manhattan, extending from 72nd Street three miles northward to 125th Street.

Lewis Latimer supervises the installation of the first electric street lighting system in New York City, and follows with installations in Philadelphia and England.

The Society of the Sons of New York and the Society of the Daughters of New York are organized by black native-born New Yorkers. Black residents born in other states follow suit, organizing the Sons of Virginia, the Sons of North Carolina, and the Sons and Daughters of South Carolina. Churches conduct special services (such as South Carolina Days and Virginia Days) to honor members from individual southern states.

April 13. St. Philip's Episcopal Church passes a resolution to take up a collection to assist refugees from Arkansas awaiting transportation to Africa.

Inventor Lewis Howard Latimer.

Arkansas refugees rest at Mt. Olivet Baptist Chapel, 1880. A group of 150 blacks from Arkansas arrive in New York City in tattered clothing and find respite at this church at 218 West 37th Street in Manhattan. Discouraged by the lack of opportunities in the West, they are seeking a ship bound for Liberia, Africa.

1881

Dr. Susan Maria Smith McKinney is among the founders and serves on the staff of the Brooklyn Women's Homeopathic Hospital and Dispensary at Myrtle and Grand Avenues [later the Memorial Hospital for Women and Children, which closes in 1918]. She is also on the staff of the New York Medical College and Hospital for Women at 213 West 54th Street, Manhattan.

March 4. Frederick Douglass, first black marshal of the District of Columbia, leads the traditional march escorting the outgoing president, Rutherford B. Hayes, and the incoming president, James A. Garfield, from the Senate chamber to the Capitol rotunda for the presidential inauguration. Garfield appoints him as the first black recorder of deeds for the District of Columbia.

December. Tennessee initiates segregation policies by introducing a Jim Crow railroad car. (It is followed by Florida, 1887; Mississippi, 1888; Texas, 1889; Louisiana, 1890; Arkansas, Georgia, Alabama, and Kentucky, 1891; South Carolina, 1898; North Carolina, 1899; Virginia, 1900; Maryland, 1904; and Oklahoma, 1907.)

1882

Dr. Philip S. White becomes the first black person to sit on Brooklyn's Board of Education. (He is followed by attorney Thomas McCants Stewart, and inventor Samuel Scottron. Consolidation in 1898 brings Brooklyn's public schools under the control of the New York City Board of Education.)

Forty-nine blacks are reported lynched during 1882.

1883

July. The city's first black Catholic church opens in Greenwich Village at the northeast corner of Bleecker and Downing Streets, and is named after St. Benedict the Moor, a black saint who lived in Sicily in the late 1500s.

Brooklyn School Board member Thomas McCants Stewart.

Students at a colored school learn about objects. After 1871, trustees appointed to the New York City Board of Education for each ward have the responsibility to appoint teachers and contract for school repairs, and help bridge the gap between city leadership and neighborhood interests.

T. Thomas Fortune, publisher and journalist.

Lewis Latimer begins working with Thomas A. Edison, serving as an engineer, chief draftsman, and expert witness on the Board of Patent Control, after receiving a patent in 1881 for carbon filaments for the first Maxim electric incandescent lamp.

1884

T. Thomas Fortune founds the *New York Freeman* newspaper. Fortune, born a slave in Florida, advocates the use of the term "Afro-American" to describe Americans of African descent.

Historian and journalist John Edward Bruce adopts "Bruce Grit" as his column head in the *New York Age* and the Cleveland *Gazette*. (Born a slave in Piscataway, Maryland, Bruce becomes the leading black syndicated columnist of the late nineteenth and early twentieth centuries.)

November–February 1885. The Berlin Conference of fourteen European nations divides the African Continent among themselves.

1885

July. The Astor Place Colored Tragedy Players, a black theatrical troupe, stages a benefit performance to raise money for the Grant Memorial under the leadership of Richard T. Greener, secretary of the Grant Monument Association, a position earned by service to the Republican party. Greener, who had served on the Howard University Law faculty and practiced law in South Carolina—before Reconstruction—and Washington, D.C., is also chief examiner of the municipal civil service board for New York City.

The Fleet Street A.M.E. Zion Church is organized in Brooklyn.

1887

July. The *New York Freeman* reports that Jim Crow conditions are on the decline at many of the city's finer hotels, noting that "now in many of the best restaurants, hotels and churches decent colored people receive courteous treatment." Visiting black politicians like P. B. S. Pinchback, John R. Lynch, and John Mercer Langston are observed staying at the Hoffman House, the Metropolitan Hotel, and the Fifth Avenue Hotel.

John Edward Bruce, historian and journalist.

The *New York Freeman* becomes the *New York Age*, with T. Thomas Fortune and Jerome B. Peterson as joint owners.

Harlem Hospital opens at 126th Street and the East River with twenty-six beds to serve the local population.

A fancy dress ball on Seventh Avenue, 1872. W. E. B. DuBois writes in 1901 that black New Yorkers live in their own protected world "closed in from the outer world and almost unknown to it, with churches, clubs, hotels, saloons and charities; with its own social distinctions, amusements and ambitions."

1888

Mezzo-soprano Flora Batson Bergen is presented with a diamond-cut bead necklace by the citizens of New York, after being declared "The Double-Voiced Queen of Song" at a concert in Philadelphia a month earlier. (She gained prominence in 1885 at a great temperance revival in New York where she sang "Six Feet of Earth Make Us All One Size" on ninety consecutive evenings in the great hall of the Masonic Temple. Moved to tears, thousands signed the pledge.)

Mezzo-soprano Flora Batson Bergen.

Census figures record 41,183 "colored" people living in Manhattan, the Bronx, Queens, Staten Island, and Brooklyn. Included in that number are more than 4,000 Chinese, Japanese, and Native Americans. Over 36,000 people of African descent live in the city: approximately 23,000 in Manhattan and the Bronx, 10,000 in Brooklyn, 3,000 in Queens, and 900 on Staten Island.

Republican party leader Richard T. Greener.

1890

March. Former students of the African Free School form the John Peterson Association to preserve the memory of a favorite teacher who taught at the school for over fifty years. Among the school's alumni are clergymen and activists Henry Highland Garnet and Alexander Crummell, restaurateur and caterer Thomas Downing, teacher Charles L. Reason, engraver Patrick Reason, abolitionist Samuel Ringgold Ward, physician James McCune Smith, and actor Ira Aldridge.

June 25. Jockey Isaac Murphy rides in the nation's most celebrated horse race of the year, a special match race between thoroughbreds Salvator and Tenny at Brooklyn's Sheepshead Bay track. Salvator, with Murphy riding, wins the race by a head. A color lithograph, commissioned by a champagne company, is used as an advertisement and adorns bars throughout New York. (Earlier in the year, Murphy won the second of his record-setting three Kentucky Derby victories.)

June 27. Boxer George "Little Chocolate" Dixon defeats featherweight champion Fred Johnson with a fourteenth-round knockout in Coney Island, becoming the first black world titleholder and $4,500 richer.

August 12. The Mississippi Constitutional Convention begins systematic exclusion of blacks from political life. The Mississippi Plan (literacy tests) is later adopted by other southern states along with other devices to exclude black voters.

Charles Anderson is elected president of the Young Men's Colored Republican Club of New York County. Anderson, employed as a gauger at the Internal Revenue Service's district office, is emerging as a leading figure among local black politicians.

Newspapers advertise "Desirable Properties for Colored People" in Harlem, which has more than two hundred tenements and apartment houses occupied by black residents. The Colored Knights of Pythias forms a lodge in Harlem and a few black churches begin to use the Harlem and East Rivers for baptisms.

Black minstrel show performer Ernest Hogan writes *All Coons Look Alike To Me,* introducing "coon songs" to Broadway, vaudeville, and the minstrel circuit. Many black critics find the songs degrading but the genre sweeps the city and the nation.

Inventor Granville T. Woods moves to New York City and continues his work on inventions that advance the development of electrical and mechanical equipment. (Born in Columbus, Ohio, Woods began working in a machine shop at the age of ten, and by 1907 would patent thirty-five inventions, including a telegraph system for communication between moving trains, and inventions used by American Engineering, General Electric, and Westinghouse Electric, among other companies.)

Jockey Isaac Murphy.

1891

Dr. Verina Morton Jones becomes the city's second black woman physician, practicing in Brooklyn.

1892

April 3. **Arturo Alfonso Schomburg** assists Rosendo Rodriguez and Rafael Serra with organizing Las Dos Antillas (The Two Islands), an organization formed to "actively assist in the independence of Cuba and Puerto Rico." Rodriguez is named the club's president and Arturo Schomburg its secretary. The organization receives support and financial assistance from groups sympathetic to their Caribbean cause. Schomburg lists contributions of rifles, machetes, and medical supplies sent to compatriots in the Caribbean.

Ellis Island opens as the city's depot for immigrants.

Two black police officers are hired in Brooklyn.

Victoria (Smith) Earle Matthews, inspired by an antilynching lecture given by Ida B. Wells, helps found the Woman's Loyal Union Club of New York and Brooklyn, and is elected club president. Advocating women's suffrage, the group is sometimes ridiculed by black men who say the women should be home in the kitchen; but

Victoria Earle Matthews, journalist, lecturer, social activist, and pioneer in travelers' aid work.

Bibliophile Arturo Alfonso Schomburg, ca. 1896.

the women respond to male fears by telling them they want to vote in order to put black men in elective office.

Black literary societies are active in Manhattan and Brooklyn. The *Brooklyn Eagle* reports that there is no class of city residents "fonder of literary pursuits than the Afro-American." Black churches, the

Guadeloupean women at Ellis Island, 1911.

Ethiopian immigrants arrive at Ellis Island, ca. 1910.

Soprano Sissieretta Jones, known as "Black Patti."

primary sponsors of the societies, often have small lending libraries and reading rooms, and also offer concerts, lectures, and discussion groups.

M. Sissieretta Jones performs at Madison Square Garden's "Jubilee Spectacular and Cakewalk." Her specialty is soprano arias from grand and comic operas, and her stage name, "Black Patti," is derived from the name of Spanish soprano Adelina Patti.

Bill "Bojangles" Robinson makes his New York debut, tap dancing with a touring minstrel show.

1893

Lincoln Hospital and Home is founded by a group of wealthy white women concerned about poor health within New York City's black population and about the lack of non-segregated hospitals.

June 23. Jockey Willie Simms wins five out of six races at Sheepshead Bay. (The first black jockey to win international fame, Simms became the first American jockey to win a race in England aboard an American horse. He is among the group of black jockeys and performers who congregate regularly at the Marshall Hotel on West 53rd Street in the heart of the neighborhood known as "Black Bohemia.")

Victoria Earle Matthews, using the pen name Victoria Earle, publishes *Aunt Lindy*, a novel about a former slave living in Georgia after the Civil War. Matthews also writes for several newspapers, including the *New York Times*, the *Boston Advocate*, and the *New York Age*.

Bethany Baptist Church is founded in Brooklyn.

1894

August 24. At Jerome Park in the Bronx, black jockey Willie Simms duplicates the feat he performed the previous year at the Sheepshead Bay racetrack, winning five of six races.

P. B. S. Pinchback, former Reconstruction governor of Louisiana, takes a job as a U.S. marshal at the U.S. Customs House in Manhattan. Active in Republican politics, he uses the influence of Charles W. Anderson and Booker T. Washington to get the position, but stays for only a short time before moving to Washington, D.C.

Singer and composer Harry T. Burleigh wins a competition for baritone soloist at St. George's Episcopal Church. Burleigh also becomes a soloist and a member of the choir of Temple Emanu-El.

1895

James D. Carr, an 1895 graduate of Columbia University, is appointed Assistant District Attorney of Manhattan.

July. Victoria Earle Matthews participates in a conference of black women in Boston to help form the National Federation of Afro-

Harry T. Burleigh, baritone soloist and composer.

American Women. Among the founders are Margaret Murray Washington and Boston native Josephine St. Pierre Ruffin. Matthews serves as chairwoman of the federation, a consortium of more than sixty black women's groups.

The Sons of North Carolina is founded when a group of black men who migrated from that state come together to respond to the plight of a fellow migrant. (By 1925 the organization has over four hundred members and a multistory meeting house in Brooklyn.)

September 18. Booker T. Washington delivers a major address (later known as the "Atlanta Compromise" speech) at the opening of the Cotton States International Exposition in Atlanta. In asking African Americans to "cast down your buckets," Washington calls upon them to pursue their livelihoods in the South; he also, however, asks white Americans to make room for black workers over European immigrants.

1896

The National Association of Colored Women is organized at 9 Murray Street, Manhattan, under the leadership of activists Victoria Earle Matthews and Mary Church Terrell from Washington, D.C. This coalition of black women's groups, which includes the Woman's Loyal Union Club, the National Federation of Afro-American Women chaired by Matthews, and Terrell's National League of Colored Women (formerly the Colored Woman's League of Washington), adopts the motto "Lifting as we climb," and receives the blessing of Booker T. Washington. Terrell serves as president of the new association, and Matthews as its national organizer.

May 18. In Plessy vs. Ferguson, *the United States Supreme Court upholds the doctrine of "separate but equal." It rules that asking Homer Plessy, a black man, to leave a white railroad car was an act of segregation that did not violate the United States Constitution.*

October 12. The nation's three best-known black divas, Sissieretta "Black Patti" Jones, Flora Batson, and Marie Smith Selika, perform to a standing-room-only crowd at Carnegie Hall. Selika, who sings in Europe and the United States, is regarded as America's first black concert coloratura.

1897

The American Negro Academy is organized, with **W. E. B. DuBois** *as a founder and vice president.*

The Bermuda Benevolent Association is founded by businessmen Clarence Robinson and George Joell in the San Juan Hill area of Manhattan. The Association later purchases a building in Harlem and extends mortgages to longtime members.

February 11. The White Rose Mission is founded by Brooklyn civic leaders Victoria Earle Matthews and Maritcha Lyons to create a "Christian, nonsectarian Home for Colored Girls and Women, where they may be trained in the principles of practical self-help and right living." Operating from headquarters in Manhattan's San Juan Hill district, organization members meet boats at piers, and provide meals and lodging for migrants from the South and the West Indies.

The Household of Ruth, a sister affiliate of the Grand United Order of Odd Fellows, is founded to address black women's needs. It advocates that black women are "largely wage earners in industry and their labor needs the protection of the ballot."

1898

New York City consolidates all five boroughs, joining Brooklyn, Queens, and Staten Island with Manhattan and the Bronx.

February 15. The United States battleship Maine *is blown up in Havana Harbor, and America declares war against Spain, befriending Cuba in its revolt against the colonial power.*

April 4. Black producer and writer Bob Cole creates a black production company for his first musical comedy, *A Trip to Coontown.* Playing at the Third Avenue Theater, the play is the first full-length musical comedy produced, performed, written, and directed by blacks. (Later in the year the show plays at the Grand Opera House at Eighth Avenue and 23rd Street, billed as *The Kings of Koon-dom.*)

June 6. George "Little Chocolate" Dixon defeats Eddie Santry in New York City for the world featherweight title in a twentieth-round knockout.

June 28. *Clorindy: The Origin of the Cakewalk* opens at Broadway's Casino Roof Garden, starring fourteen-year-old Abbie Mitchell, Ernest Hogan, and Belle Davis, with ragtime-style music by Will Marion Cook and lyrics by Paul Laurence Dunbar. Mitchell marries Cook the following year.

During the Spanish-American War, black soldiers in the 24th and 25th Infantry Regiments of the 9th and 10th Cavalry accompany Theodore Roosevelt's Rough Riders in the campaign to take San Juan Hill.

August 2. Arturo Schomburg attends a meeting of the Cuban Revolutionary Party at Chimney Corner Hall on Sixth Avenue and 25th Street after the Spanish-American War ends in July. As the war strikes the death knell for the independence movement, with Spain ceding the Philippines, Cuba, and Puerto Rico to the United States, Schomburg begins to direct his interest less toward the Puerto Rican liberation movement and more toward the cause of American blacks.

September 15. Rev. Alexander Walters and T. Thomas Fortune organize a meeting of black leaders in Rochester, N.Y. Out of the meeting, the National Afro-American Council is created with Walters as its president. Walters speaks out strongly against the U.S. Supreme Court's Plessy v. Ferguson "separate but equal" decision. The Council is the country's largest organization of black leaders.

Cyclist Marshall "Major" Taylor.

Richard T. Greener declines an appointment as consul to Bombay, India, but accepts a post in Vladivostok, Russia.

Tammany Hall creates the United Colored Democracy for its black politicos, headquartered on West 53rd Street. Edward E. Lee, head bellman at a downtown hotel, serves as UCD chairman. During elections Lee directs the spending of Tammany money for campaign purposes in black neighborhoods.

Lincoln Hospital and Home opens a nursing school for black women.

Cyclist Marshall "Major" Taylor wins a match race against Jimmy Michael at Manhattan Beach. With a 121-point total nationwide (including twenty-one first-place victories, thirteen second-place

Lincoln Hospital Nursing School graduating class.

berths, and eleven third-place showings) he is declared the national champion at the end of the season, making him the nation's first black national champion in any sport.

Willie Simms wins the Brighton Handicap riding Ornament, the Toboggan Handicap at Belmont Park riding Octagon, and his second Kentucky Derby aboard Plaudit. He rides most of the time contracted to Richard Croker and Michael F. Dwyer. (Black jockeys won twelve of the first twenty-two Kentucky Derbies, but were prohibited from the Derby after 1911.)

1899

Mount Olivet Baptist Church in Manhattan opens the city's first black YMCA.

St. Phillip's Protestant Episcopal Church and the First Baptist Church are established in Brooklyn.

William L. Buckley is appointed principal of P.S. 80 on West 40th Street in the heart of a neighborhood known as the Tenderloin.

Welterweight Joe Walcott, the "Barbados Demon," defeats Billy Edwards, Dan Creedon, Dick O'Brien, and Bobby Dobbs in New York bouts.

1900

The First Pan-African Congress is convened in London. W. E. B. DuBois assesses American race relations, stating that the number-one problem of the twentieth century is the "color line."

New York City's black population is 60,666, or 1.76% of the total, 3,437,202. The city's black population ranks fifth behind the District of Columbia, Baltimore, New Orleans, and Philadelphia. Of Manhattan's 36,246 black residents, the largest concentrations are in the San Juan Hill area with 4,982, and Harlem with 4,652. Brooklyn has 18,367 black residents; Queens, 2,611; the Bronx, 2,370; and Staten Island, 1,072. There are more than 50,000 foreign-born blacks from the West Indies, Cuba, the Philippines, and West Africa. There are 809 black men to every 1,000 black women in New York City. Howard University Professor Kelly Miller writes that the "excess" of black females is "a most striking feature" of black populations in most northern cities.

Black migrants arrive from states bordering the Atlantic. The Old Dominion Steamship Company runs biweekly trips between Virginia and New York City. Steerage fare is $5.50, with a meal included. Steamers also run regularly from Charleston, South Carolina, and Florida to Hudson River ports. Jim Crow accommodations (blacks in separate berths and at separate dining tables) are the rule on all the shipping lines.

Segregated schools are discontinued in New York. William L. Buckley, the last African American principal of a colored school, retires to France.

The Colored Men's YMCA opens in Manhattan on West 53rd Street. Founded by the Reverend Dr. Charles T. Walker to expand the "Y" services started the previous year at Mount Olivet Baptist Church, the facility offers lectures, musical performances, plays, and classes in industrial skills training.

August 12. African American Arthur Harris fatally stabs Robert Thorpe, a white plainclothes police officer who has allegedly made unwelcome advances to Harris's black common-law wife, May Enoch, at the corner of 41st Street and Eighth Avenue in the Tenderloin district. Harris takes a train to his mother's home in Washington, D.C. (Robert Thorpe dies at Roosevelt Hospital the following day.)

August 15. Turbulent race rioting erupts in the Tenderloin. Angry white mobs attending the wake for slain police officer Robert Thorpe chase electric streetcars on Eighth Avenue, pulling blacks off at random and beating them. Hundreds of whites pour into the streets, attacking black men, women, and children with virtually no restraint from white police officers. Houses are sacked and burned, and places that employ blacks are raided. Comedian Ernest Hogan locks himself in a theater overnight to escape harm, and Paul Laurence Dunbar is among the injured. Scores of white policemen are reported taking part in the attacks. (A grand jury later refuses to indict any of the policemen.)

August 16. The *New York Times* reports, "For four hours last night Eighth Avenue, from Thirtieth to Forty-second Street, was a scene of the wildest disorder that this city has witnessed in years."

September 12. A mass meeting is held at Carnegie Hall in support of the newly formed Citizen's Protective League. Organized at St. Mark's Church on West 53rd Street, the League demands the removal of all officers who attacked blacks during the summer riot. (The police department conducts its own investigation. Blacks who testify that they had been beaten complain that police investigators are treating them as criminals. A grand jury investigation produces no indictments of any police officers.)

October 29. Arthur Harris, arrested in Washington, D.C., and brought back to New York to stand trial, is found guilty of second-degree murder for the August death of police officer Robert Thorpe. Harris is sentenced to the state prison at Sing Sing "at hard labor for the term of his natural life." An Arthur J. Harris Liberation Fund is formed. (Harris dies in prison on December 20, 1908, at the age of thirty. The cause of his death is unknown.)

December 22. A *Harper's Weekly* editorial notes, "The Negro is not a newcomer in New York. He has been here for two centuries and a half . . . but even during the time of bondage his condition was not much worse than now. . . . It is quite true that the Irish seem to have a natural antipathy to the Negroes, but the other north-of-Europe races seem to have no natural feeling of repugnance and the Italians are quite devoid of it. The strangest thing about this strange problem is that so many native Americans should feel hostile—not actively hostile, but in sympathy with the lawless Negro-baiters. I heard many native Americans, even New Englanders, say after the riot that they would have been glad if many of the Negroes had been killed."

A Brooklyn trolley line drawing-room car, 1896.

A New Negro for a New Century is published, ushering in the "new Negro" generation. The book features essays by Booker T. Washington, lecturer and social welfare reformer Fannie Williams, and other prominent blacks. Washington stresses education as key to the advancement of the "new Negro," and Williams stresses the involvement of black women in clubs.

Booker T. Washington founds the National Negro Business League, and T. Thomas Fortune, editor and publisher of the *New York Age,* is appointed chairman of the executive committee. (The organization grows to more than forty thousand members.)

James Weldon Johnson *writes the words, and his brother, J. Rosamond Johnson, writes the music, to* Lift Ev'ry Voice and Sing. *(It becomes known as the Negro National Anthem.)*

Bert Williams and George Walker, the first internationally famous team of black performers, produce *Sons of Ham* on Broadway. (The multitalented team—they are singers, dancers, and comedians—follows with a string of stage hits including *In Dahomey* (1902) and *Bandana Land* and *In Abyssinia* (1908), and forms their own company with their wives, Ada Overton Walker and Lottie Thompson Williams, and Jesse Shipp, Will Marion Cook, and Alex Rogers.)

Vaudevillians Ada and George Walker, 1905.

Two hotels—the Marshall and the Maceo—on West 53rd Street in the heart of "Black Bohemia," are creating a "revolutionary" new center of black artistic life. (According to a later report by James Weldon Johnson, "There gathered the actors, the musicians, the composers, the writers and the better-paid vaudevillians; and there one went to get a close-up of Cole and Johnson, Williams and Walker, Ernest Hogan, Will Marion Cook, Jim Europe, Ada Overton, Abbie Mitchell, Al Johns, Theodore Drury, Will Dixon and Ford Dabney. Paul Laurence Dunbar was often there. A good many white actors and musicians also frequented the Marshall, and it was no unusual thing for some of the biggest Broadway stars to run up there for the evening."

Major Taylor wins the American cycling title for a third straight year. His victories include defeating Frank Kramer in a one-mile match race at Manhattan Beach, and Tom Cooper at Madison Square Garden. Cooper leads an effort to bar Taylor from the nation's tracks. Taylor then begins to race in Europe as well as America, eventually establishing a sports reputation second only to jockey Isaac Murphy's in the previous century.

1901

"Pig Foot" Mary (Lillian Harris) sets up shop at Amsterdam Avenue and 61st Street, where she sells pig feet cooked in her own special style from a wash boiler atop a baby carriage. (Arriving from the Mississippi Delta penniless, she becomes one of the city's shrewdest businesspeople, later moving her thriving business to 135th Street and Lenox Avenue. At one point her bank account rose to $375,000.)

William Mack Felton opens an auto school and garage, becoming one of the nation's first driving instructors. (Felton came to New York in 1898 with "a dollar tucked away" in his shoe, and worked first as a clock and bicycle repairman. He later invents a device to wash cars automatically.)

October 16. Dr. Booker T. Washington, head of Tuskegee Institute, is invited to dine at the White House by President Theodore Roosevelt. The invitation causes great controversy among whites opposed to the visit.

1902

Jockey Jimmy Winkfield wins the Champion Stakes at Sheepshead Bay, riding Von Rouse.

1903

W. E. B. DuBois's The Souls of Black Folk *is published, and includes a response to Booker T. Washington's 1895 Atlanta Exposition speech.*

November 13. Andrew Hassell Green, the eighty-three-year-old multimillionaire leader of the Greater New York campaign that led to the city's 1898 consolidation, is shot and killed by Cornelius Williams, a black furnace-tender. The trial casts the public's attention on Hannah Elias, a wealthy black woman with whom Williams was reportedly infatuated. According to the press, Elias is courted by several wealthy white men. Reportedly the owner of two apartment buildings and a mansion at 236 Central Park West, Hannah is also said to have numerous bank accounts. (The district attorney concludes that Green had no relationship with Elias and convicts Williams as a deranged killer.)

In all things that are purely social we can be as separate as the fingers, yet one as the hand in all things essential to mutual progress.

—Booker T. Washington,
Atlanta Exposition Speech, 1895

[I]n the history of nearly all other races and peoples the doctrine preached . . . has been that manly self-respect is worth more than lands and houses, and that a people who voluntarily surrender such respect, or cease striving for it, are not worth civilizing. . . . Negroes must insist continually, in season and out of season, that voting is necessary to proper manhood, that color discrimination is barbarism, and that black boys need education as well as white boys.

—W. E. B. DuBois,
The Souls of Black Folk, 1903

W. E. B. DuBois.

1904

January 6. Booker T. Washington convenes a group of black leaders at Carnegie Hall to review the problems facing blacks in the United States. W. E. B. Du Bois, Washington's prime antagonist, appears on the same platform in an attempt to resolve differences and find common ground. The group agrees that the collection and dissemination of information about black history and culture is critical to promoting understanding and harmony between the races, and self-improvement and advancement within the black community. Arthur Schomburg tells both men of his personal efforts to gather materials on black history and offers his services toward the group's aim.

May 15. Sigma Pi Phi is organized in Philadelphia. Open to black male college graduates and men engaged in professional activities within their communities, the organization is the nation's first black Greek-letter fraternity.

June 15. Philip A. Payton Jr. founds the Afro-American Realty Company and launches a drive to bring blacks to Harlem. He uses outdoor billboards to advertise, and is among the first to put ads in elevated and subway trains. (Payton attributes his first opportunity to a dispute between two white landlords on West 134th Street. "To get even, one of them turned his house over to me to fill with colored tenants. I was successful in renting and managing this house, and after a time I was able to induce other landlords." This enables him to build a thriving business among black immigrants to Harlem.)

October 27. The Interborough Rapid Transit (IRT) subway system is completed to 148th Street and Lenox Avenue in Harlem, with trains running at forty miles per hour and carrying 600,000 passengers daily. The ride from City Hall to 14th Street takes twenty-six minutes for a fare of five cents. (The subway triggers the rapid urbanization of upper Manhattan and the surrounding boroughs.)

Charles Anderson organizes the Colored Republican Club of New York City and leads the campaign to get black male voters to the polls to re-elect Theodore Roosevelt.

Real estate pioneer Philip A. Payton.

1905

The Niagara Movement, led by W. E. B. DuBois, creates a more militant voice to counter the conservative policies of Booker T. Washington.

December 25. "Negroes Move Into Harlem" is the *New York Herald* headline for an article pointing out that "During the last three years the flats in 134th Street between Lenox and Seventh Avenues, that were occupied entirely by white folks, have been captured for occupancy by a Negro population. . . . The cause of the colored influx is inexplicable."

President Theodore Roosevelt appoints Charles Anderson collector of internal revenue for the Second New York District, which includes Wall Street. Anderson, the city's most powerful black politician, arranges the appointments of attorneys and district attorneys, deputy U.S. marshals, election examiners, deputy collectors, and customhouse inspectors. He is also a vigorous supporter of Booker T. Washington, defending him from attacks by W. E. B. DuBois and political activist Hubert H. Harrison.

Charles W. Anderson, the leading black political figure in the North.

The White Rose Travelers' Aid Society is formed by the White Rose Mission. (The Society greets more than fifty thousand black women migrating from the South over the next ten years.)

Eva del Vakia Bowles is hired as secretary of the Colored Young People's Christian Association in New York City (later the 135th Street YWCA in Harlem). She is the first black woman on the staff of the Young Women's Christian Association.

1906

December 4. At Cornell University, Alpha Phi Alpha is founded as a Greek-letter fraternity for undergraduates. (From 1826—when the first black student attained a degree from an American university—to 1905, an estimated 7,488 black students have graduated from colleges and professional schools.)

The biracial Committee for the Industrial Improvement of the Condition of the Negro in New York is formed. Though its goal is to expand employment opportunity for the city's minority community, it sends letters to southern newspapers urging blacks to stay in the South.

Lawyer and songwriter James Weldon Johnson is appointed U.S. consul to Venezuela. The post comes from Johnson's contacts with the New York Republican party. (Leaving Venezuela in 1908, Johnson next serves as consul to Nicaragua until 1912.)

1907

December 10. John E. Nail and Henry C. Parker, both salesmen with the Afro-American Realty Company, open their own Harlem-based real estate firm as Philip Payton's closes. (With Nail as its driving force, the new business thrives and becomes the agent for the move of the black YMCA to Harlem, and handles the sale and rental of Equitable Life Assurance Company properties, including the elegant townhouses on 138th and 139th Streets between Seventh and Eighth Avenues that become known as Strivers' Row.)

Scott Joplin moves into an office at 128 West 29th Street to compose and arrange ragtime music.

Henry Parker and John Nail. The realtors become known as the "Little Fathers of Negro Harlem."

St. Philip's Church Housing Complex, ca. 1915. The New York Age *said of this Nail and Parker real estate deal, "It puts on the books of St. Philip's Church the wealthiest colored church corporation in the country, the best property owned by colored people in Manhattan or in any other borough, and it opens up to colored tenantry the best houses that they have ever had to live in."*

Harlem's Colored Orphan Asylum moves to Riverdale for a "cottage plan" style of living in the Bronx.

1908

The Union of South Africa is established.

January 15. Alpha Kappa Alpha is founded at Howard University as the first sorority for black women.

May. The Lincoln Settlement House is founded at 129 Willoughby Street in Brooklyn. Directed by Verina Morton-Jones, the house offers day care, a medical clinic, free kindergarten, and classes in carpentry, cooking, and sewing. The institution is an extension of white social reformer Lilly Wald's Henry Street Settlement House on the lower East Side. [The Lincoln Settlement house later moves to 105 Fleet Place.]

August. Fifty-two nurses gather at St. Mark's Episcopal Church to found the National Association of Colored Graduate Nurses. The whites-only policy of the American Nurses' Association prompts the black nurses to form their own organization. The Lincoln Hospital School of Nursing Alumnae association,

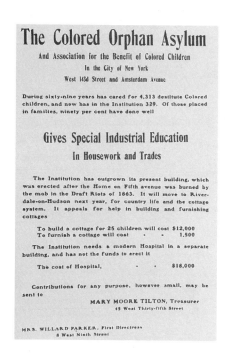

(Above) *Colored Orphan Asylum administration building and housing for younger children in Riverdale.*

(Left) *Fund-raising handbill for the Colored Orphan Asylum.*

headed by Adah Belle Samuels Thoms, sponsors the first meeting. (Martha Franklin, a black Connecticut nurse who chairs the three-day conference, is elected president of the new organization. In 1906 Franklin sends fifteen hundred letters to black nurses nationally, questioning them about racial discrimination in their profession.)

August. In Springfield, Illinois—Abraham Lincoln's birthplace—the false claim that a black man raped a white woman leads to a race riot that leaves eight blacks dead and no rioters arrested.

In intercity basketball competition between black teams, the Smart Set Club from Brooklyn defeats the Washington, D.C., Crescent Athletic Club at home and away.

Jockey Jimmy Lee wins the Grand Trial Stakes at Brooklyn's Sheepshead Bay track, and the Great American Stakes at Aqueduct Race Track, riding Sir Martin.

1909

January. Spurred on by the Springfield, Illinois, race riot of 1908, concerned whites Mary White Ovington, Henry Moscowitz, and journalist William English Walling issue a call for a conference on the "Negro question" to be held on the centennial of Lincoln's birth. The call, drafted by Oswald Garrison Villard, publisher of the *New York Evening Post* and a grandson of William Lloyd Garrison, is signed by an interracial group. Black signers include Niagara Movement participants W. E. B. DuBois, Bishop Alexander Walters, Ida Wells Barnett, and Rev. Francis Grimke.

February 12. The National Negro Conference, meeting at the Charity Organizational Hall in Manhattan, creates the National Negro Committee (initially known as the National Committee for the Advancement of the Negro) to further develop an organization that will improve the status of blacks in America.

April. Explorers Matthew Henson and Admiral Robert Peary become co-discoverers of the North Pole on their seventh joint expedition.

The Lincoln Theatre opens at 56–58 West 125th Street. A place for silent movies and live stage entertainment, the theater is named after the former U.S. president.

May 3. *The Red Moon* opens on Broadway. With book, lyrics, and music by Bob Cole and J. Rosamond Johnson, the show stars Cole, Johnson, Ada Overton Walker, and Abbie Mitchell. Black critics note the absence of racially derogatory characters.

June 5. Alpha Phi Alpha forms a chapter for black male students at Columbia University.

1910

July 4. As Jack Johnson fights Jim Jeffries for the heavyweight championship of the world in Reno, Nevada, many spectators are heard shouting "Kill the nigger!" After Johnson's victory over the "white hope," whites throughout the country retaliate by assaulting African Americans, resulting in at least eight deaths and the banning of screenings of the fight film. Six African Americans are killed in New York City violence.

Heavyweight champion Jack Johnson.

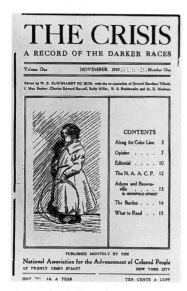

The first issue of the NAACP journal
The Crisis: A Record of the Darker
Races, *1910.*

New York City's total black population is
91,709: Manhattan, 60,534; Brooklyn,
22,708; Bronx, 4,117; Queens, 3,198;
and Staten Island, 1,152.

Many predominantly black blocks in the Tenderloin area are
demolished, and thousands of people are displaced, to make way
for the construction of the Pennsylvania Railroad Station. Most of
the dislocated black families move to Harlem.

The National Negro Committee, meeting in Manhattan, adopts a
new name—National Association for the Advancement of Colored
People (NAACP)—and targets racial hatred and discrimination as
the root causes holding African Americans back socially and economically. The organization establishes its office at 20 Vesey Street.
The phrase "colored people" is used to emphasize the broadest concerns of its founders, and not to limit the range of the organization
to the United States. W. E. B. DuBois, a member of the board of
directors, is invited to serve as the association's director of publicity
and research, and as editor of its monthly journal, *The Crisis: A
Record of the Darker Races.* The first issue is published in November
1910. (The NAACP's structure and purpose inspire the creation of
other civil rights groups, including South Africa's African National
Congress in 1912.)

At the invitation of Alva Belmont, a southern-born New York
socialite married to wealthy banker Oliver Belmont, more than two
hundred black women meet with white women suffragists. Later in
the year, more than one hundred black New York women join the
"colored" branch of the Political Equality Association. Mrs. Belmont pays for a small permanent headquarters in Harlem for the
black suffragists, promising to provide a larger space when the
group increases in size. (The black women are not aware when Alva
Belmont later secretly donates $10,000 to the Southern Woman
Suffrage Conference, an organization that opposes enfranchise-
ment for southern black women.)

James Reese Europe organizes the Clef Club, a union comprising
many of the best African American musicians in the city. The Club's
building serves as a booking office that can supply groups of three
to thirty musicians virtually day and night. Through Europe's leadership with the Clef Club, and later the Tempo Club, which offers
dance orchestras for hire, he is the first to bring prestige and some

James Reese Europe and the Clef Club Orchestra, 1915.

We colored people have our own music, that is the product of our souls. It's been created by the sufferings and miseries of our race. Some of the melodies we play were made up by slaves, and others were handed down from the days before we left Africa. We have developed a kind of symphony music that lends itself to the playing of the peculiar compositions of our race.

—James Reese Europe

degree of professional order to the lives of black musicians in New York City.

Bert Williams is hired by Florenz Ziegfeld to star in the *Ziegfeld Follies.*

1911

April 9. Arturo Schomburg and others interested in black history and culture meet at the home of black journalist John E. Bruce. The group forms the Negro Society for Historical Research, an organization designed to collect information and conduct research into the history and culture of black people worldwide. Bruce serves as its president and Schomburg as secretary-treasurer.

August 12. Samuel J. Battle is appointed New York City's first black policeman.

October. The National League on Urban Conditions Among Negroes (National Urban League) is founded in New York City, consolidating three organizations: the Committee on Urban Conditions Among Negroes, the Committee for Improving the Industrial Condition of Negroes in New York, and the National League for the Protection of Colored Women. George Edmund Haynes, a co-founder of the League with Mrs. William H. Baldwin Jr., becomes its first executive director. (Haynes, in 1912 the first African American awarded a Ph.D. by Columbia University, studied economics there during a period of marked concern about problems of rapidly increasing urbanization, emigration, and migration. While working on his doctoral dissertation, "The Negro at Work in New York City," Haynes met with Baldwin and her associate Frances Kellor to discuss the urgent need for social work among blacks in New York. After becoming executive secretary of the League, Haynes created a program with Fisk University to combine the objectives of serving the masses of disadvantaged blacks and training black social workers to meet their needs.)

Mary Eliza Mahoney is named supervisor of the Howard Orphan Asylum for black children in Brooklyn. Mahoney, who graduated

Bert Williams.

Lots a folks puts on religion on Sundays same as if it was a clean shirt.

Some folks carries dare troubles wid 'em everwhare day goes. I reckin dey'd take 'em tuh heabin wid 'em if dey thought dey could git in.
—Bert Williams, "Philosophacs and Philosophibs,"
from *Bert Williams's Joke Book*

THE GREAT COOPERS

Are offered as real artists—they amuse, entertain and mystify. For pleasing, refined and astonishing novelties they cannot be equaled. Mr. Cooper tells stories in dialect, tears beautiful designs from paper and does free-hand drawing. Not to hear Mr. Cooper and his mischievious boy "Sam" is to miss one of the greatest treats in the amusement world.   He is an artist of natural talent and gained his high standing after years of success before the public.

Mrs. Cooper, while blindfolded, will tell the numbers placed on the blackboard, the kind of watch you carry, also the exact time of the same and many other wonderful feats.

from the New England Hospital for Women and Children in 1879 as the nation's first college-trained nurse, was also a founding member of the National Association of Colored Graduate Nurses, which was started in 1908.

Saint Philip's Episcopal Church and Rectory is constructed at 214 West 134th Street, built to the designs of two black New York architects, Vertner W. Tandy and George W. Foster Jr. (Active supporters of the migration of New York's black community to Harlem, St. Philip's pastor Rev. Hutchens C. Bishop and parishoner John Nail engineered a deal worth over a million dollars including land for the new church and for apartment buildings to be rented to black

The Great Coopers broadside, ca. 1910.

households. Vertner Tandy, a graduate of Tuskegee Institute, is the leading black architect in Harlem and provides training opportunities for other black architects.)

March 19. Booker T. Washington is beaten by a white attacker in the hallway of 11½ West 63rd Street. President William Taft is among the hundreds of well-wishers who send letters and telegrams.

Hubert Henry Harrison writes letters critical of Booker T. Washington. The letters are published and Harrison, who emigrated to the United States from St. Croix at the age of seventeen, is fired from his job at the United States Post Office. He is hired by the Socialist Party, and becomes a leading party speaker and campaigner.

Composer and pianist Scott Joplin completes *Treemonisha,* a folk opera. However, he is unable to get a full production of his favorite work.

The New York Lincoln Giants baseball team plays in Harlem at 135th Street and Fifth Avenue on Olympic Field.

Baseball legend John Henry "Pops" Lloyd.

The Brooklyn Royal Giants are purchased by John Connor, a black businessman. (Giants star John Henry "Pops" Lloyd, called by some the best player ever, played on the Havana Stars in a series of six games in Cuba in 1910 against the major league Detroit Tigers. Lloyd batted .500 against major-league pitching in twenty-two at bats. The Havana Stars tied the Tigers, with three wins each. American League President Byron Bancroft Johnson was so embarrassed that he demanded a clause in the contracts of major-league teams playing in Cuba that said that no American blacks could play on any Cuban team when playing against American League clubs.)

1912

January 6. Sigma Pi Phi's Zeta chapter is established at the office of *The Crisis* at 20 Vesey Street. W. E. B. DuBois is a charter member and chief organizer of the chapter.

November 11. Howard Porter Drew, the first African American known as "the world's fastest human," breaks the world indoor record in the 100 meters at the 23rd Regiment Armory in Brooklyn.

Hubert H. Harrison publishes *Socialism and the Negro,* in which he concludes that color prejudice is based on economic foundations. (Harrison forms the Colored Socialist Party but, deciding that white socialists offer little to help the advancement of blacks within American society, begins to support the more action-oriented Industrial Workers of the World.)

The Autobiography of an Ex-Coloured Man, by James Weldon Johnson, is published.

The Brooklyn Royal Giants, 1917.

Explorer Matthew Henson.

Matthew Henson, unheralded co-discoverer of the North Pole with Lt. Robert Peary, publishes his autobiography, *A Negro Explorer at the North Pole.*

Julian Abele designs the most prominent building in New York by a black architect, the James B. Duke Mansion [now the Institute of Fine Arts] at Fifth Avenue and 78th Street, Manhattan. First black graduate of the Ecole des Beaux-Arts, Abele is the chief designer for the firm of Horace Trumbauer and Associates in Washington, D.C.

James Reese Europe takes an orchestra of more than 125 African American musicians to Carnegie Hall, introducing black music to much of the city's white cultural elite for the first time.

1913

William Monroe Trotter, in a White House confrontation, accuses President Woodrow Wilson of lying when Wilson denies responsibility for segregation in government cafeterias in Washington, D.C.

February 12. A "Concert of Negro Music" is held at Carnegie Hall in commemoration of the 50th Anniversary of the Emancipation Proclamation (and in recognition of Abraham Lincoln's birthday). It features the Clef Club Orchestra conducted by James Reese Europe. The concert benefits the Music School Settlement for Colored People of New York.

October. The Emancipation Proclamation Commission of the State of New York presents a ten-day national exposition at the 12th Regiment Armory in Manhattan to celebrate the fiftieth anniversary of emancipation. The Commission, composed entirely of black men (unlike those in other states, which are white-dominated), presents a program including a major exhibition and pageants surveying the history of African Americans from their African origins through their emancipation from American slavery, an honor roll of two hundred men selected by their fellows as being representative leaders, and two public concerts. W. E. B. DuBois chairs the committee on exhibits. At the urging of DuBois, sculptor Meta Warrick Fuller creates *Spirit of Emancipation,* a three-figure piece standing eight feet high, noted for its depiction of strong and dignified African Americans.

1914

March. Roland Hayes performs at a Carnegie Hall benefit concert for the Music School Settlement for Colored People. The Georgia-born tenor is the son of former slaves.

June 8. Manhattan's Bijou Theatre, closed because of racial troubles, re-opens as a segregated theater, exclusively for blacks.

Madame C. J. Walker builds a townhouse in Harlem at 108–110 West 136th Street, including a fully equipped beauty parlor at 110.

St. James Presbyterian Church moves from West 55th Street to West 137th Street in Harlem [the church later moves to its present home on 141st Street].

The Libya Hotel opens at 149 West 139th Street, as Harlem becomes the center of black life.

William Roach, Joseph Sweeney, and Hodge Kirnon are among the founders of the Montserrat Progressive Society, a Caribbean benevolent association. (By 1925 the Society has 750 initiates and owns a Harlem building.)

Madame C. J. Walker.

1915

March 3. The NAACP leads protests against D. W. Griffith's film *The Birth of a Nation,* which has its world premiere at the Liberty Theater in New York City. The film features vicious racial stereotypes and glorifies the activities of the Ku Klux Klan.

Arturo Schomburg, now using the first name Arthur, completes his *Bibliographical Checklist of American Negro Poetry,* assisted by

Madame C. J. Walker's Harlem residence, 1914. Located at 108–110 West 136th Street, the town house includes at number 110 "the most completely equipped and beautiful hair parlor that members of our Race have ever had access to," as described by the Chicago Defender.

The Libya Hotel, 1914, at 149 West 139th Street.

James Weldon Johnson. The fifty-seven-page booklet is considered a landmark effort to record the works of black poets.

Father Divine (George Baker) establishes a church on Myrtle Avenue in Brooklyn. He proclaims himself the only living God and demands complete loyalty and sexual abstinence from his followers. (Migrating from Valdosta, Georgia, to Harlem in 1914, Father Divine served an apprenticeship under St. John the Divine Hickerson before moving out on his own.)

A group of Danish West Indian women in Harlem establish a benevolent society (reorganized in 1917 as the American West Indian Ladies Aid Society).

September 9. Carter G. Woodson, George Cleveland Hall, W. B. Hargrove, Alexander L. Jackson, and J. E. Stamps found the Association for the Study of Negro Life and History at a Chicago meeting, with Woodson as director. (Woodson becomes editor of the Journal of Negro History *established the following year. The name of the organization is changed in the 1960s to the Association for the Study of Afro-American Life and History.)*

November 14. Booker T. Washington's death ends the reign of the "Tuskegee Machine" as the dominant political force in black America.

November. Anita Bush forms the Anita Bush Players in Harlem at the Lincoln Theater to perform serious theater for black audiences. Bush, a former member of the Williams and Walker theatrical troupe, says she wants to prove that black actors can be just as good at legitimate theater as their white counterparts. Members of the new acting troupe include Bush, Charles Gilpin, Dooley Wilson, and Carlotta Freeman. (The Bush players soon move to the Lafayette Theater, where they became known as The Lafayette Players.)

Ferdinand Q. Morton is elected chairman of the United Colored Democracy. UCD's members are largely southern and West Indian immigrants. (In 1912 the UCD moved uptown to 136th Street to be in the midst of the growing black population in Harlem.)

1916

November 2. The *New York Age* reports that construction companies will not honor their agreement to protect strikebreakers. More than three hundred unemployed black men hired to replace Italian hod carriers on strike from construction jobs in Manhattan, the Bronx, and Brooklyn are immediately discharged when the companies reach agreement with the union.

Edward A. Johnson from the 23rd Assembly District in Queens is the first black elected to the New York State Assembly.

Adah Thoms is elected president of the National Association of Colored Graduate Nurses. Thoms meets with the NAACP and the National Urban League on a campaign to improve conditions at black hospitals and training schools.

City zoning laws protect apartment building owners but do not protect racial and ethnic minorities. Housing covenants continue to bar blacks from apartment buildings throughout the city.

WAR, RENAISSANCE, AND DEPRESSION

1917–1934

Overleaf:

The Harlem Hellfighters march up Fifth Avenue. Members of the 369th Regiment march home to Harlem after serving 191 days in combat, longer than any unit in the armed forces.

Party for Langston Hughes, Harlem, 1924. Left to right: Ethel Ray (Nance), Langston Hughes, Helen Lanning, Pearl Fisher, Regina Anderson (Andrews), Rudolph Fisher, Luella Tucker, Clarissa Scott, Hubert Delany, Marie Johnson, E. Franklin Frazier. Bending over: *Esther Popel and Jessie Fauset.*

BY 1917 THE EUROPEAN POWERS HAD DIVIDED THEMSELVES INTO TWO death-dealing camps: the Allied Powers led by Britain and France, and the Central Powers led by Austria-Hungary and Germany. Strapped for labor and troops capable of bearing arms, the Allied forces had already resorted to drafting and/or recruiting African peoples from their African and Caribbean colonies to join their peasant and working-class European counterparts on the dying fields.

Black Americans in general—and black New Yorkers in particular—were divided over whether or not they should again respond positively to the nation's patriotic call. Some decided to go to Europe and defend democracy there, assuming America would permit them to enter the fray. Others decided to stay at home and fight—for democracy, for a new African nationalism, or for a socialist or communist alternative to America's racist antidemocratic practices.

Origins of the Great War

In many respects, Europe had been in a perpetual state of war since the late fifteenth century. Hardly a year passed when two or more of the European nation states were not engaged in some form of military conflict. There were wars to defend the honor and dignity of princes and kings; wars to defend national borders or expand national boundaries; wars to capture and hold colonial territories; wars to disrupt trade and capture precious metals or equally precious cargoes of colonial products; and, of course, wars to advance and defend Christendom. Europe's battles reshaped the globe.

At the Berlin Conference in 1885, the major European powers divided up the African continent and scrambled to take possession of the newly "acquired" territories. By 1900 the continent had been virtually occupied, leaving people of African descent throughout the world (except the Liberians, the Ethiopians, and the Haitians) living under some form of white domination.

The United States had limited its nineteenth-century imperial activities to taming the West and enforcing control over the Native American and Hispanic peoples. (Further European expansion in the Americas had been declared off limits through the Monroe Doctrine of 1823.) The United States launched its own colonial empire in 1898 when it annexed Puerto Rico, Hawaii, Guam, and the Philippines during the Spanish-American War and made Cuba an American protectorate. A year after the onset of World War I, the United States, continuing the pursuit of its imperial agenda, would invade Haiti, further reducing the number of self-governing people of African descent around the world.

By the second decade of the twentieth century, war had become an established tradition in European politics, and military conflicts were prevalent in other parts of the world as well. But nothing in the European or global past compared in any way with the havoc and devastation wrought by the Great War of 1914. Indeed, the cumulative impact of four centuries of European warfare did not begin to match the destructive force of the first three years of what would become known as World War I. It is probable that more people were killed between 1914 and 1917 than had died in the previous four hundred years of European fratricidal warfare.

European pleas for military assistance from the United States fell on deaf ears, as President Woodrow Wilson and Congress tried desperately to keep Americans from getting entangled in this deadly European conflict. America, however, was never completely neutral. While the Europeans were busy destroying one another, the United States was busy getting rich by exporting supplies and capital. Once again, war was fueling the American national economy. New York City, the center of the nation's international banking and export trade, was a principal beneficiary. But by 1917 the United States could no longer remain even nominally neutral.

German submarine attacks on commercial shipping in the spring of 1917 precipitated a change in United States policy. The so-called Zimmermann telegram—a secret message from Germany's foreign minister ordering its Mexican ambassador to offer Mexico Germany's assistance in retaking Texas, New Mexico, and Arizona from the United States—was the last straw. In April President Wilson asked Congress to declare war "to make the world safe for democracy," seemingly oblivious to the wanton undemocratic practices victimizing the country's disenfranchised African-American citizens. The contradictions in this slogan were not lost on black people living in the United States.

Nevertheless, black New Yorkers signed up for duty in the 369th Regiment, an all-black unit dubbed the Harlem Hellfighters. They went to Europe and established a distinguished record of service—so distinguished that the French government awarded the entire regiment its highest military honor, the Croix de Guerre, for its heroic efforts on the front. Meanwhile, James Reese Europe had organized the 369th Regimental Marching Band, a unit comprised of many members of his former Clef Club band. Together, they introduced jazz to Europe in general, and to Paris in particular. Chastised by the United States Government for breaking the American racial code between blacks and whites while they were in Paris, the men of the 369th were, nevertheless, welcomed back to New York City with a triumphal victory parade up Fifth Avenue to Harlem.

The Rise of Pan-African Nationalism

Within months of their return, racial riots involving African American veterans broke out in twenty-six cities across the country. Labeled the Red Summer of 1919, the riots differed from those of the previous two decades. This time armed veterans returned the fire, defended their communities, and gave attacking white citizens and policemen all they could handle. Service on the battlefields of

Europe had demonstrated to black New Yorkers, and to African peoples in general, that whites were mere mortals and that they bled and died like ordinary human beings. This realization fractured the myth of white invincibility and challenged the myth of white supremacy. It opened the door for blacks to begin to extricate themselves from the mental shackles of European and American colonialism and racial domination.

The seeds of postwar strife had taken root as America's unique position in the wartime economy unleashed an economic boom that had a profound impact on urban economies, especially in its northeastern and midwestern cities. News of the expanding job markets and rumors of improved race relations enticed millions of southern African Americans to leave farms and moribund southern cities and head north to urban industrial centers such as New York City, Philadelphia, and Chicago, among others. Caribbean migrants also set their sights on New York, and by the time America entered the war, black New Yorkers who had staked out Harlem as the next center of black New York life were being inundated by southern and Caribbean migrants. Harlem not only became the largest black urban community in the United States and future black capital of the world, it also became a dynamic, ethnically diverse black urban population.

Caribbean migrants had always been a part of the ethnic mix of New York's black population. Indeed, upwards of eighty percent of the black population of colonial New York had come from the Caribbean. But the Caribbean immigrants of the 1910s and 1920s frequently brought with them a sense of racial identity and political nationalism that fundamentally transformed the nature of African American political and social discourse. Their impact was also felt in literature, the arts, and various fields of economic enterprise. No single individual—immigrant or otherwise—had a more dramatic impact on black New York's political and social landscape than the Jamaican-born African nationalist, Marcus Mosiah Garvey.

Garvey arrived in New York in 1916, a year before America entered World War I. By 1917 he had established his Universal Negro Improvement Association (UNIA), a multiethnic, multinational, worldwide movement of African peoples. At its height in the mid-1920s, the UNIA had millions of members and had organized hundreds of chapters in Africa, in the Americas, and throughout the Caribbean. His newspaper, the *Negro World,* became one of the leading American black weeklies and a highly successful vehicle for promoting his philosophies. The first international convention of the UNIA, in 1920, drew over 25,000 delegates to New York City's Madison Square Garden, and announced to the world that the "New Negro" that had surfaced at the turn of the century had burst full force onto the historical stage, and "knew no fear."

The magnetic appeal of Garvey and Garveyism heightened the struggle for political hegemony in Harlem and black America triggered by the death of Booker T. Washington in 1915. Other new and old political forces were also trying to fill the vacuum created by the demise of Washington's "Tuskegee Machine," the political apparatus he had used to define and control black politics nationally since the turn of the century. Although W. E. B. DuBois had been presumed to be Washington's heir apparent, several new aspirants, in addition to Garvey, had surfaced in Harlem by the early 1920s. There were socialists A. Philip Randolph and Chandler Owen, with their journal the *Messenger;* and Cyril Briggs, the Marxist African nationalist editor and publisher of the *Crusader,* official organ of the African Blood Brotherhood. Charles Johnson and the National Urban League used their journal, *Opportunity,* to compete for the allegiance of the new urban migrants. But for a time, none of them—individually or collectively—could compete with Garvey.

Garvey's competitors and opponents eventually ended up siding with novice Assistant Attorney General J. Edgar Hoover to bring about Garvey's imprisonment and the demise of the UNIA. By then, however, Garvey's message of Pan-African nationalism, economic self-sufficiency, anticolonialism, racial pride, and assertiveness had both tapped and fueled a spirit of resistance in its urban adherents.

The New Negro Renaissance

During the first half of the 1920s, Garvey and Garveyism, more than any other single force, created the political and ideological context from which the New Negro Renaissance (Harlem Renaissance) emerged. The Renaissance became the dominant intellectual and literary expression of the New Negro Movement. W. E. B. DuBois, James Weldon Johnson, and Alain Locke had planted the seeds and nurtured it. Arthur Schomburg was its bibliographer, and the 135th Street Branch of The New York Public Library one of its principal repositories and forums. Langston Hughes, Zora Neale Hurston, Claude McKay, Countee Cullen, Jean Toomer, and Wallace Thurman were among its most gifted writers.

But there was more to the Renaissance than literature. There were exhibits of artworks by African American artists and of traditional African art, organized and presented by Arthur Schomburg and the Harmon Foundation. There were the music of Duke Ellington and Fletcher Henderson; the theatrical productions of Eubie Blake and Noble Sissle; the nightlife at the Savoy, the Cotton Club, and Connie's Inn; the Lafayette and Alhambra theaters; and A'lelia Walker's *Dark Tower*. Occuring as it did during the Roaring Twenties, the New Negro, or Harlem, Renaissance was also part of the Jazz Age and the age of Prohibition. Its reach extended beyond Harlem to Washington, D.C., and to Chicago, Kansas City, the Caribbean, and Brazil. Wherever black folk were during the 1920s, there was a renewed sense of the possibilities of affirming their African identities and transforming their social condition.

Economic Depression and Rekindled Racism

Black New Yorkers returned from the Great War to find the city about to embark on the most extensive housing construction boom in its history. Railroad and subway lines constructed since the city's consolidation had opened new areas of growth throughout the five boroughs. In addition, a series of building projects completed on the eve of and during the early stages of the Great Depression transformed New York's cultural infrastructure and skyscape. Foremost among these were the Riverside Church (1929), the Museum of Modern Art (1929), the Empire State Building (started in 1929 and opened in 1931), the Chrysler Building (1930), the Daily News Building (1930), Brooklyn College (1930), the Waldorf Astoria (1931), and the Whitney Museum (1931). The Holland Tunnel had opened in 1927, and the Lincoln Tunnel and George Washington Bridge were both completed during this period.

Late nineteenth- and early twentieth-century European immigration created extraordinary demands for new housing. By 1920 the boom was on. Between 1921 and 1930, over 70,000 new dwelling units were completed each year, reaching a peak of 107,185 units in 1927. (The next highest average for a decade was 30,500 between 1956 and 1965. Fewer than 10,000 units have been constructed annually since 1980.) Blacks inherited many of the properties newly vacated by white out-migration and overdevelopment. But restrictive covenants limited their choice of locations in many parts of the city.

New York, the banking and commercial capital of the world, was the epicenter of the Crash of 1929. It brought on the Great Depression and reverberations from it were felt around the world. Under President Herbert Hoover's leadership, the nation and the bankrupt national economy limped along for three years.

Meanwhile, the war had left an indelible mark on the international scene. It changed the map of Europe's political geography. The 636-year-old Austro-Hungarian Empire collapsed. New borders were drawn for Germany, Austria, Hungary, and Romania. The new nations of Poland and Czechoslovakia, and the kingdoms of Serbia, Croatia, and Slovenia [later Yugoslavia] were established. Equally significant, the Lenin-led Marxist Revolution against the tsarist regime in Russia changed the political landscape of Europe and the modern world.

The war also ushered in a new era of racism and totalitarianism in Europe. Benito Mussolini seized absolute power in Italy in 1926 and by the early 1930s his Fascist revolution was in full swing. Laws abolishing freedom of expression were passed, the Italian parliament was abolished, a special police force was established to suppress political opposition, and the death penalty was instituted. By 1934 Adolf Hitler had come to power in Germany, bringing with him a new and heightened public assertion of Aryan (white) superiority. In the United States, the racist Ku Klux Klan, whose membership had peaked at four million in 1925, was fighting a rear-guard action to remain a vital force in American politics. Although its membership had dwindled to 100,000 by 1930, the economic crisis of the Great Depression and the rising tide of racism, Fascism, and Nazism in Europe rekindled the spirit of racism and xenophobia in America and New York for the rest of the decade.

In 1932 New York Governor Franklin D. Roosevelt was elected president of the United States. His "New Deal" economic and social policies put New York and the nation on the road to recovery.

1917

April. As the United States joins the Allied forces in the Great War, New York black political and religious leaders advocate support of the war while demanding democracy for the black masses.

April 5. *Three Plays for a Negro Theatre*, by Ridgely Torrence, opens at the Garden Theatre. Written by a white playwright, the plays—*Granny Maumee*, *Simon the Cyrenian*, and *The Rider of Dreams*—are the first serious dramas about African Americans to reach the Broadway stage. (James Weldon Johnson calls the production "the most important single event in the entire history of the Negro in the American Theatre.")

April 6. America enters the Great War (World War I). President Woodrow Wilson, who has just instituted a policy of segregation in government agencies, tells Congress that "the world must be made safe for democracy."

May. **Marcus Mosiah Garvey** organizes the first American branch of the Universal Negro Improvement Association (UNIA) in Harlem to advocate economic improvement and independence for African Americans.

June 12. Hubert H. Harrison introduces Marcus Garvey at a meeting to launch the Liberty League of Afro-Americans at Bethel

This is the time to say to the American white government from every pulpit and platform and through every newspaper, "Yes, we are loyal and patriotic" . . . [but] we do not believe in fighting for the protection of commerce on the high seas until the powers that be give us at least some verbal assurance that the property and lives of the members of our race are going to be protected from Maine to Mississippi. . . . It is infinitely more disgraceful and outrageous to hang and burn colored men and boys and women without a trial in times of peace than it is for Germans in times of war to blow up ships loaded with mules and molasses.

—Adam Clayton Powell Sr., sermon, April 1917

Political activist Hubert H. Harrison.

A.M.E. Church in Harlem. The assembly of more than two thousand people adopts a resolution written by Harrison stating that "a. We therefore ask, first that the similar rights of the 250,000,000 Negroes of Africa be conceded. . . . b. We invite the government's attention . . . to the continued violation of the Thirteenth, Fourteenth, and Fifteenth Amendments, which is a denial of justice and the existence of mob-law for Negroes from Florida to New York."

July 1–3. Whites in East St. Louis, Illinois, riot violently against blacks, killing two hundred and leaving thousands homeless. Over three hundred buildings and forty-four railroad cars are destroyed by fire. Thousands of blacks flee to St. Louis, Missouri, seeking safety.

July 4. Hubert H. Harrison begins publishing the *Voice*, "A Newspaper for The New Negro," as the organ of the Liberty League of Afro-Americans.

W. E. B. DuBois and Martha Gruening, a white associate, investigate the East St. Louis riot for the NAACP, reporting that whites drove six thousand blacks from their homes, two hundred of whom were murdered by shooting, burning, or hanging.

July 28. During a silent protest parade against lynching in New York City, fifteen thousand blacks march silently down Fifth Avenue to the roll of muffled drums. Black Boy Scouts pass out leaflets saying in part, "We march because we want our children to live in a better land and enjoy fairer conditions than have been our lot." Leading the march are the Rev. Dr. H. C. Bishop, president of the parade; Rev. Dr. Charles D. Martin, secretary; Rev. F. A. Cullen, vice president; and J. Rosamond Johnson, first deputy marshal. Rev. G. M. Plaskett and Dr. W. E. B. DuBois are also in the line of officers. Other leaders include A. B. Cosey, C. H. Payne, Rev. E. W. Daniels, Allen Wood, James Weldon Johnson, and John Nail.

August 1. A delegation of prominent African Americans goes to the White House to present a petition to President Woodrow Wilson, urging him to support legislation making lynching a federal crime. However, they are denied an audience by presidential secretary Joseph Tumulty, who tells them that Wilson's schedule is too

The Silent Protest Parade at 42nd Street and Fifth Avenue, July 28, 1917.

busy. The delegation includes Fred Moore of the *New York Age*, W. E. B. DuBois of *Crisis* magazine, James Weldon Johnson of the NAACP, realtor John Nail, cosmetics mogul Madame C. J. Walker, Rev. Adam Clayton Powell Sr., and Rev. George Frazier Miller.

September. Annie K. Lewis, president of the Colored Woman Suffrage Club of New York City, is elected vice president of the statewide New York Woman Suffrage Party. (The election is among the few occasions when black women gain leadership positions in interracial women's organizations. Throughout the city and state, black women urge male voters to support the proposed amendment to strike the word "male" from the New York state constitution, thus allowing women the right to vote.)

November. In a *Crisis* editorial, W. E. B. DuBois urges black men to support a statewide referendum to give women of all races the right to vote.

November 6. New York State voters pass the full suffrage bill, enfranchising more than seventy-five-thousand women. New York is the first state east of the Mississippi River to do so.

November. James C. Thomas is the first black representative elected to the New York City Board of Aldermen.

Eighteen-year-old dressmaker Ann Lowe opens a shop on Madison Avenue. Born in Alabama and the daughter and granddaughter of seamstresses, Lowe develops a reputation for delicate needlework that attracts clients like the Rockefellers and Astors.

December 11. Thirteen black soldiers are hanged for their alleged participation in an August riot in Houston, Texas, between members of the 24th Infantry Regiment and white residents, in which two blacks and eleven whites were killed.

James Weldon Johnson and George Miller meet with Woodrow Wilson to present a petition of twelve thousand signatures requesting executive clemency for members of the all-black 24th Infantry convicted for their alleged participation in the August riot in Houston, Texas. (Nineteen soldiers are hanged and ninety-one are imprisoned, fifty-one of them for life.)

The *Messenger,* a monthly journal subtitled "The Only Radical Magazine Published by Negroes," is founded by **A. Philip Randolph** and Chandler Owen. The magazine opposes United States participation in the Great War and counsels African Americans to resist the military draft. Randolph and Owen are jailed and their offices ransacked as the publication, targeted as subversive, comes under close surveillance by the federal government.

December. The U.S. Army Nurses Corps alters its segregation policy, stating that it will accept limited enrollment of black nurses. (The Corps, however, does not accept its first black applicants until July 1918. The first eighteen black nurses are not appointed until December, after the war has ended.)

Federal agents search the offices of the NAACP and *Crisis* magazine during the "Red Scare."

Joe Oliver leaves New Orleans and settles in Chicago, where he is joined by other musicians, triggering a jazz migration.

Harry T. Burleigh's musical arrangements of "Deep River," the first known arrangements of a Negro spiritual for solo voice with independent piano accompaniment, bring him acclaim as a pioneer and authority. Burleigh becomes one of the founders of ASCAP (American Society of Composers, Authors, and Publishers).

Edward A. Johnson becomes the first black elected to the New York State legislature, winning in Manhattan's Nineteenth Assembly District, one of two districts (the other is the Twenty-first) with registered black voter constituencies large enough to prompt both the Republican and Democratic parties to run black candidates.

The UNIA moves from its office at 235 West 131st Street in Harlem across the street to 238 West 131st Street. (The organization soon expands to larger offices at 2305 Seventh Avenue.)

1918

February 23. The Tuskegee Institute Singers perform a concert of Negro spirituals at Columbia University's Horace Mann auditorium.

July. Race riots flare in Pennsylvania in Chester and Philadelphia.

July 2. Marcus Garvey's UNIA is incorporated in the State of New York, with Garvey, Isaac B. Allen, Irene M. Blackstone, Walter J. Conway, Carrie B. Mero, and Harriet Rogers listed as directors on the certificate of incorporation.

August. The UNIA begins publishing the *Negro World* in English, Spanish, and French editions. The newspaper has a circulation of two hundred thousand copies weekly. Published with a policy against "demeaning" advertisements, it declines ads for skin lighteners and hair straighteners.

August. West Indian immigrant Cyril Briggs founds a monthly magazine titled *The Crusader*. (The magazine serves as the publicity

Until the workers of all races, creeds, nationalities and color are joined hand in hand against their common foe—the capitalist exploiters, for the achievement of a common aim—their emancipation, their fight will be futile, useless.

As long as the black and white working dogs keep fighting over the bone of race prejudice, the yellow capitalist dog will run up and grab the meat in the form of big profits.

Race wars like wars between Nations are fought for the benefit of the Owning Class.

"Black and White Workers Unite," the Messenger.

organ of The Hamitic League of the World from January 1919 to December 1920, and it serves as the organ of The African Blood Brotherhood from July 1921 to its final issue in January 1922.)

September 3. Five more soldiers are hanged for their alleged participation in the 1917 Houston riot.

November 11. An armistice is signed, ending the Great War. Official records document service by 370,000 black soldiers and 1,400 black commissioned officers. Three black regiments, the 369th, 371st, and 372nd, are awarded the French Croix de Guerre for valor.

Soldiers receiving the Croix de Guerre.

Henry Johnson and Needham Roberts of the 369th Infantry Regiment, who suffered disabling wounds while destroying a German raiding party, are the first Americans to receive the French Croix de Guerre. The unit receives the award as well.

December. Ida B. Wells-Barnett and A. Philip Randolph are chosen to represent the UNIA at the upcoming Versailles Peace Conference. However, the United States Department of State denies travel clearance for both.

The *Messenger* urges black Americans to align themselves with trade union and socialist movements. Editor A. Philip Randolph helps to organize the Socialist Party's first black political club in New York. Postmaster General Albert Burleson revokes the journal's second-class mailing privileges because of their party activities.

Walter White becomes assistant executive secretary of the National NAACP.

The Women's Political Association of Harlem advocates birth control. The association is one of the first African American organizations to take a positive stand on the issue.

Madame C. J. Walker moves from Harlem to Villa Lewaro, her luxurious Westchester County mansion designed by Vertner W. Tandy. She intends to maintain the mansion both as her personal home and as a showplace and inspiration to other blacks that they, too, can achieve the "American Dream."

We return.
We return from fighting.
We return fighting.
Make way for Democracy! We saved it in France,
and by the Great Jehovah, we will save it in the
United States of America, or know the reason why.

–W. E. B. DuBois,
The Crisis, May 1919

Black New Yorkers celebrate Armistice Day in Harlem, November 1918.

Dressmaker and fashion designer Fanny Criss moves to New York from Richmond, Virginia, following her forty-year career as one of Richmond's finest seamstresses and designer for a large wealthy white clientele. (Many of Criss's creations are in the collection of Richmond's Valentine Museum.)

The White Rose Home and Industrial Association founded by Victoria Earle Matthews establishes permanent headquarters in Harlem on West 136th Street.

The five-hundred-member National Association of Colored Graduate Nurses locates its headquarters in Harlem at the YWCA's 137th Street branch. The association establishes a national registry to assist black nurses in finding employment.

Will Marion Cook organizes the New York Syncopated Orchestra. (Later called the American Syncopated Orchestra, it tours the United States and Europe, and plays a command performance at Buckingham Palace.)

1919

February. The Pan-African Congress organized by W. E. B. DuBois meets in Paris. Blaise Diagne of Senegal is elected president and DuBois, secretary.

February 17. James Reese Europe's all-black military band leads the victorious 369th Infantry Regiment up Fifth Avenue. Known as the Hellfighters, they march in precision formation past the reviewing stand salute of Governor Al Smith, then parade north to Harlem. Turning up Lenox Avenue at 130th Street, the band breaks into "Here Comes My Daddy" to the cheers of several thousand spectators. Joyous family members and sweethearts join the marchers as they are exuberantly welcomed uptown.

April 18. The Epsilon chapter of Omega Psi Phi fraternity is established in New York City for students at Columbia University, New York University, and City College.

Twenty-six race riots occur between April and October, a period dubbed the "Red Summer." Locations include Charleston, South Carolina; Knoxville, Tennessee; Chicago; Washington, D.C.; Longview and Gregg counties in

Texas; and Phillips County, Arkansas. Seventy-six blacks are lynched during the year.

Responding to racial hatred sweeping the country, Jamaica-born writer Claude McKay writes a sonnet, "If We Must Die," which is published in Max Eastman's *Liberator* magazine.

October 14. George Tyler, an angry UNIA follower, rushes into the UNIA office and fires a shot at Marcus Garvey, grazing his forehead. Blood streaming down his face, Garvey runs into the street. Many bystanders believe that his survival of the potentially fatal attack is a sign of his invincibility. (Tyler commits suicide the following day while in jail.)

James Reese Europe and his band returning from the war. Europe's band entertained French, British, and American troops in Europe and introduced jazz to French civilians.

November 23. Marcus Garvey successfully launches the Black Star Line from its berth at 135th Street and the Hudson River. Its flagship, the SS *Yarmouth,* rechristened the SS *Frederick Douglass,* makes its maiden voyage from New York to the West Indies and Central America. The shipping line is a triumph in Garvey's plan for a black-owned and operated enterprise that sails between America, the Caribbean, and Africa.

December. The UNIA purchases Liberty Hall at 120 West 138th Street from the Metropolitan Baptist Church. Marcus Garvey regularly draws more than five thousand people to hear him invoke his message "Up, you mighty race!" Arnold Ford, a black Jew, becomes the hall's musical director and writes the UNIA anthem.

Audley Moore joins the UNIA, embracing Pan-Africanism.

The NAACP publishes its annual report on racial violence in America, "Thirty Years of Lynching in the United States, 1889–1918."

W. E. B. DuBois hires Jessie Redmon Fauset as literary editor of *The Crisis,* which publishes and nurtures the young black writers of the New Negro Renaissance (later known as the Harlem Renaissance).

The Commandment Keepers: Church of the Living God, a denomination of black Jews, is founded in Harlem by Wentworth Arthur Matthew and eight other men. Rabbi Matthew serves as bishop and becomes closely aligned with fellow black Jewish leader Rabbi Arnold J. Ford. The Commandment Keepers believe they are the descendants of the ancient Hebrews, whom they believe were black people.

George Baker Jr. (Father Divine) moves his growing congregation from Myrtle Avenue in Brooklyn to Sayville, Long Island.

Mamie Smith's Garden of Joy at the corner of 138th Street and Seventh Avenue becomes a popular Harlem nightspot. Designed by architect Vertner Tandy, the Garden is constructed upon a large rock that proved too expensive for laborers to remove, and includes an open-air movie theater.

Claude McKay.

If we must die—let it not be like hogs,
Hunted and penned in an inglorious
   spot . . .
Like men we'll face the murderous,
   cowardly pack,
Pressed to the wall, dying, but fighting
   back!

—Claude McKay, 1919

A Black Star Line stock certificate. With stock sold only to blacks, at five dollars per share, the Black Star Line raises $610,860 in its first year of operation and purchases three ships.

Marcus Garvey in a 1924 UNIA parade. Garvey is proclaimed "the Black Man of Sorrows" at the August 1924 UNIA convention, where delegates from nearly a thousand divisions around the world profess faith in the motto "One God, One Aim, One Destiny."

Oscar Micheaux produces his first film, *The Homesteader*, based on his 1917 novel.

Versatile cellist Marion Cumbo plays at vaudeville houses and concert halls. Cumbo, a member of the Negro String Quartet, studied music at the Institute of Musical Art [today's Juilliard School of Music].

Ethel Waters, billed as Sweet Mama Stringbean, performs nightly at Edmund's Cellar, a basement cabaret at 132nd Street and Fifth Avenue in Harlem.

Rabbi Wentworth Arthur Matthew (far right, behind altar) and temple members, 1939.

A scene from Oscar Micheaux's film,
Harlem After Midnight, *1934.*

OSCAR MICHEAUX'S
PRODUCTION OF

WITH AN ALL STAR
COLORED CAST

'HARLEM AFTER MIDNIGHT'

1920

January 16. Prohibition goes into effect in the United States.

January 23. Marcus Garvey's Negro Factories Corporation files a certificate of incorporation to provide loans and technical assistance to blacks who need help developing their own small businesses. (With stock sold at five dollars per share, the venture is less successful than the Black Star Line, but it helps to develop a chain of cooperative grocery stores, a restaurant, a laundry, a tailor and dressmaking shop, a millinery store, and a publishing house.)

January. Marcus Garvey's Black Star Line returns to New York City from the Caribbean carrying four hundred tons of log wood and more than two hundred passengers.

January. The first issue of *The Brownies' Book,* a magazine aimed at building pride among black children, is published by the NAACP, edited by W. E. B. DuBois and Jessie Redmon Fauset.

The black population, at 10,463,131, is 9.9 percent of the United States population. New York City's black population is 152,467, or 2.71% of the city's total, 5,620,048. The black population ranks first in the nation, ahead of Philadelphia, the District of Columbia, Chicago, and Baltimore.

The first issue of the NAACP's The Brownies' Book, *1920.*

February 13. Andrew "Rube" Walker organizes the National Association of Professional Baseball Clubs, usually called the Negro National League.

May. The Universal African Black Cross Nurses is organized as a women's auxiliary of the UNIA. Black Cross nurses are trained to provide medical service for their local communities.

July 17. The New York Lincoln Giants play the Atlantic City Bacharach Giants at Brooklyn's Ebbets Field before a crowd of sixteen thousand fans. The game marks the first time two Negro League teams have played at a major league stadium.

July 26. Heavyweight boxer Harry Wills, known as the Brown Panther, knocks out Fred Fulton at Manhattan's First Regiment Armory. The victory makes Wills the first black number-one contender for the heavyweight title since Jack Johnson's 1915 loss. Champion Jack Dempsey, however, refuses to fight Wills.

August. The Nineteenth Amendment is ratified, giving women the right to vote in national elections.

August 2. Marcus Garvey's UNIA holds its first International Convention of Negro Peoples of the World for the entire month. Claiming an international following of blacks and whites, Garvey rouses the crowd of twenty-five thousand at the opening session at Madison Square Garden with a call for a free Ireland, as well as for the end of imperialism in Africa. He vows to rally blacks worldwide "to retake every square inch of the 12,000,000 square miles of African territory belonging to us by Divine right." The convention elects Garvey as Provisional President of Africa, and he creates the "Court of Ethiopia," patterned after the British monarchy.

Twenty-five black longshoremen being used as strikebreakers by the Morgan Line are attacked by fifty white longshoremen on 14th Street and Ninth Avenue, Manhattan. Four of the black men suffer skull fractures, and two white men are shot.

The Friends of Negro Freedom is founded by A. Philip Randolph to combat Marcus Garvey's strong influence among the immigrant

UNIA Black Cross Nurses.

Clad in their white costumes, with their flowing white caps and black crosses, these beautiful women of a sorrowed and bleeding but determined race, thrilled us men with pride and devotion to the cause that eventually will send us the call to make the supreme sacrifice on the battle plains of our beloved Africa.

—*Negro World Convention Bulletin,*
August 3, 1920

work force. The group meets on Sunday mornings at Harlem's Lafayette Theatre on Seventh Avenue to discuss political and racial issues. Among its members are George Schuyler, Robert Bagnall, William Pickens, and Chandler Owen.

A. Philip Randolph runs for election as the Socialist Party candidate for state comptroller, the first African American nominated for a statewide post this high. He loses the election but attracts 202,361

UNIA Convention Parade, 1920.

A. Philip Randolph, the Socialist Party candidate for state comptroller.

votes—a substantial number, considering that Eugene Debs, Socialist candidate for president, polls only about a thousand more votes.

Black Republican Mary Church Terrell leads the party's efforts to attract black women voters in New York City, encouraging black women to vote for Warren G. Harding in the November presidential election. Rumors circulate across the country that Harding is of African American descent. Meanwhile, party leaders emphasize his willingness to support women and black causes. The National Association of Colored Women (NACW), however, takes a less than enthusiastic stance. Charging that the Republican Party convention issued "not a plank, but a splinter on lynching," NACW president Mary B. Talbert sends a telegram to Harding urging fairness to women and attention to black issues, but including no endorsement of his candidacy.

Probation officer Grace Campbell tries unsuccessfully for a state assembly seat in the Nineteenth District, running as a Socialist Party candidate.

November. Charles Gilpin stars in Eugene O'Neill's play *The Emperor Jones* at the Provincetown Playhouse in Greenwich Village. Gilpin is praised by *The New Republic* as one of the finest artists on the American stage. (He is awarded the 1921 Spingarn Medal for his outstanding performance.)

November. James Weldon Johnson becomes the first black executive secretary of the NAACP.

The African Blood Brotherhood, a paramilitary organization, advocates armed defense of American black communities and proposes a worldwide confederation of all African groups. (Under the leadership of Cyril Briggs, the Brotherhood affiliates with the Communist Party and eventually claims 150 affiliate branches and 50,000 members.)

Socialist Party candidate Grace Campbell.

The Abyssinian Baptist Church, located on West 40th Street, purchases lots in Harlem near Seventh Avenue. To get the congregation accustomed to moving to Harlem, Rev. Adam Clayton Powell Sr. conducts summer services at the 138th Street site, where the new church will be constructed, beneath tents dubbed the Abyssinian Baptist Tents.

Bishop Charles Emanuel Grace ("Sweet Daddy Grace") establishes his United House of Prayer in New York. Grace, of African American and Portuguese ancestry, invites anyone, without regard to race, to join. An early black owner of Harlem real estate, he purchases the building at 555 Edgecombe Avenue. (The bishop sponsors a line of commercial products including Daddy Grace Soap [which promises to heal, cleanse, and reduce body fat], tea, coffee, and cookies. He also organizes a home-buying association, an insurance company, and a burial society.)

Dr. Louis T. Wright is hired by Harlem Hospital, becoming the facility's first black doctor. Demanding still more doctors, the black

James Weldon Johnson.

"Sweet Daddy Grace," Bishop Charles Emanuel Grace of the United House of Prayer.

community says there are more available than only the Harvard-trained Wright, referring to graduates of two black medical schools—Howard University and Meharry Medical College.

The City of New York opens the Katy Ferguson Home for black unwed mothers. Described as the only one of its kind for black women, the home is named for the nineteenth-century Sunday School founder.

The St. Vincent Benevolent Association is established in Brooklyn.

Catherine Allen Latimer is the first black woman hired by the New York Public Library.

The Theatrical Owners and Bookers Association (TOBA) is founded. The black performing circuit becomes known as "Tough-On-Black-

Actors" because of the difficulties of life on the road experienced by many black performers.

Harlem singer Mamie Smith records "Crazy Blues," composed by Perry Bradford, for the Okeh label. Backed by a band that included Willy "the Lion" Smith, the record is often considered the first blues recording, and it was the first to sell more than one million copies.

Louis T. Wright, the first black physician to serve in a New York City hospital.

1921

March. Harry H. Pace founds the Pace Phonograph Corporation with capital stock of thirty thousand dollars. Operating from offices in Pace's basement at 257 West 138th Street in Harlem, the company lists as its directors W. E. B. DuBois, John E. Nail, Matthew V. Boutte, and Viola Bibb. (Formerly **W. C. Handy**'s partner at the Pace and Handy Music Company, Pace produces best-selling "race records" on his Black Swan label. Ethel Waters records the label's first hit record, "Down Home Blues," which sells five hundred thousand copies within six months. Former Pace-Handy employee Fletcher Henderson joins Pace as a recording manager. Also on board are William Grant Still as an arranger, Fredi Washington as stenographer, and her sister Isabel Washington [later the wife of

Harlem Hospital, 1920s.

Charles Gilpin as Emperor Jones, 1920.

Blues recording star Mamie Smith.

Adam Clayton Powell Jr.] as a messenger between the office and the factory.)

May 23. The black musical comedy *Shuffle Along* opens on Broadway at the Belasco Theater. With a story by comedians Flournoy Miller and Aubrey Lyles and music by Noble Sissle and **Eubie Blake,** the show is hailed by critics as a departure from conventional revues, and is lauded for its choreography and fast-paced dancing. Cast members include Florence Mills and Lottie Gee, and classically trained musicians Hall Johnson and William Grant Still are in the orchestra. Hit songs include "Love Will Find a Way" and "I'm Just Wild About Harry." (Josephine Baker and **Paul Robeson** become replacement cast members.)

May 24. Hubert Julian, known as "the Black Eagle of Harlem" for his skill as an airplane pilot, receives a Canadian patent for his invention of an air-safety device. (Born in Port of Spain, Trinidad, Julian is one of America's most popular aviators. Among his air-stunt specialties, reported widely by both black and white newspapers, are his parachute jumps over Harlem rooftops, playing the saxophone as he descends.)

June. *The Crisis* publishes the poem "The Negro Speaks of Rivers" by **Langston Hughes.** (Literary editor Jessie Fauset later recalls that after reading the piece—submitted by Hughes when he was a Cleveland, Ohio, high school senior—she took the "beautiful dignified creation" to W. E. B. DuBois, saying, "what colored person is there, do you suppose, in the United States who writes like that and is yet unknown to us?")

July. The New York headquarters of the African Blood Brotherhood receives a report from the commander of its Tulsa, Oklahoma, post regarding a riot during which (according to the *Boston Herald*) more than ten thousand whites invaded the black section of the city, setting fires and brutally murdering black men and women. The incident was sparked by the false press report that Dick Rowland, a nineteen-year-old black man, had attacked a white female elevator operator, whose arm he had grabbed merely to save himself after stumbling as he got on the elevator.

August. The Second Pan-African Congress meets in London, Brussels, and Paris.

Noble Sissle and Eubie Blake with the Shuffle Along chorus, 1921.

August 1. The 135th Street Branch Library opens an exhibition of works by African American artists, including Meta Fuller, Henry Tanner, and Laura Wheeler Waring.

September 28. Marcus Garvey organizes the African Orthodox Church. The church represents Mary, Jesus, and God as black. Rev. George Alexander McGuire, an Episcopalian minister, serves as pastor.

October 1. Former child prodigy pianist Helen Hagen makes her New York debut at Aeolian Hall. Black critic Theophilus Lewis

O' silent church, O' lying press,
Speak up against this lawlessness—
Alas! 'tis you, alone, to blame
For this, our country's greatest shame—
Speak out or Truth shall write your name
Down with the mobs!

—Andrea Razafkeriefo [Andy Razaf],
"Black Tulsa's Answer,"
The Crusader, August 1921

Aviator Hubert Julian, "the Black Eagle."

I've known rivers:
I've known rivers ancient as the world
   and older than the flow of human
   blood in human veins.
My soul has grown deep like the rivers.
                    —Langston Hughes,
          "The Negro Speaks of Rivers"

urges white theatergoers who enjoy "trash" like *Shuffle Along* to go see Hagen and "take a night at the feet of a real Negro artist." (Hagen studied piano and musical composition at Yale University at age thirteen.)

Young political activist J. Raymond Jones campaigns for Democratic mayoral candidate John F. Hylan. A member of the Five Cent Fare Club, Jones helps to convince black voters that Hylan will save the five-cent subway fare. (Though credited with delivering several thousand black votes for Hylan's successful run, Jones receives neither the customary cash payment nor the city

Langston Hughes, 1930.

Political strategist J. Raymond Jones, "the Harlem Fox."

job that white campaign workers commonly received. An immigrant from the Virgin Islands, Jones was introduced to political organization and the potential of the black vote as a member of the UNIA.)

Henrietta Vinton Davis is chairperson of major UNIA meetings at Liberty Hall, Carnegie Hall, and Madison Square Garden. (Long the only woman among the UNIA leadership, Davis was a teacher and an actress before joining the organization. Serving as international organizer, she travels on organizational tours throughout the Caribbean aboard UNIA ships. One of the UNIA's most popular spokespersons, Davis is called by Garvey "the greatest woman of the Negro race today.")

Claude McKay is hired as associate editor of the radical literary magazine *The Liberator.* McKay, who also writes for the magazine, is the first black in an editorial position. Rising New Negro Renaissance talent Jean Toomer is among the writers submitting manuscripts.

Bellevue Hospital announces it is opening its doors to black nurses, and admits six black nurses for postgraduate work. The change from its discriminatory policy comes after two years of negotiations with Dr. George O'Hanlon, the hospital's general medical superintendent.

Augusta Savage struggles to remain a student at Cooper Union, a noted New York art school. Hearing of her financial plight, black patrons arrange for the young artist to do commissioned portraits and busts of W. E. B. DuBois and Marcus Garvey.

The Awakening of Ethiopia, a sculpture by Meta Warrick Fuller depicting the history and great expectations of African Americans, is exhibited at New York City's "Making of America" festival. Fuller's work is viewed as a compelling symbol of the New Negro Renaissance.

1922

An antilynching bill passes in the House of Representatives but is killed in the Senate by a filibuster.

March 10. Florence Mills performs at a late-night benefit for *The Liberator.* Editor Claude McKay's memorandum approves a $100 payment to Mills to sing three songs "between midnight and 2 A.M." at the New Star Casino at 107th Street and Lexington Avenue.

April. Paul Robeson makes his first appearance on the professional stage, in the play *Taboo.*

June. Marcus Garvey travels to Georgia, where he meets secretly with Edward Young Clark, an imperial wizard of the Ku Klux Klan. Disclosure of the meeting causes a major rift within the UNIA.

June. Following his freshman—and only—year at Columbia University, Langston Hughes begins a series of odd jobs before traveling abroad to Europe and Africa. Hughes works during the summer months at a farm on rural Staten Island, where he manages to continue writing, but also weeds, waters, and picks onions, carrots, lettuce, and beets on a vegetable farm at 2289 Richmond Avenue.

Claude McKay's collection of poetry, *Harlem Shadows,* is published. Praised by many literary critics, it is regarded as the first major book of the New Negro Renaissance.

September. Claude McKay leaves New York for the Soviet Union. James Weldon Johnson hosts a going-away party that he describes as the first time "black and white literati" have gotten together on a purely social plane. (McKay works his way abroad as a freighter crewman, sailing to Russia to attend an international Communist conference. He delays his return to the United States for twelve years, living in various places throughout Europe during the period.)

The Awakening of Ethiopia *by Meta Warrick Fuller, 1921.*

November 27. *Liza,* a musical comedy by Irvin C. Miller and Maceo Pinkard opens on Broadway. The show brings the dance, the Charleston, which is already popular in Harlem nightclubs, to the Broadway stage. Aurora Greely, a student at Harlem's Wadleigh High School, dances nightly in the chorus. (Pinkard, a composer and song publisher, is perhaps best known for writing "Sweet Georgia Brown" and "Gimme a Little Kiss, Will Ya, Huh?")

The NAACP issues its annual report on racial violence in America, "The Shame of America: 3,436 People Lynched, 1889–1921."

J. Raymond Jones and a group of Caribbean-born friends, almost all from the UNIA, form a Democratic Party club. Inside the party, the club allows Jones and his companions to broker their ability to garner Caribbean votes. The group directly usurps power from the United Colored Democracy (U.C.D.), a club of predominantly indigenous African Americans. Some observers see Jones's overtures to white political groups as a sign he is a new breed of black politician, one who turns away from socialist and separatist alternatives to work within the framework of capitalism and integration. Most Harlem political clubs are "whites only," even though blacks comprise a majority of the population. Martin J. Healy's Democratic club in Harlem's Nineteenth Assembly District regularly directs interested blacks away from his club to the U.C.D.

The UNIA sponsors concert performances by Roland Hayes and **Marian Anderson** at Carnegie Hall.

Librarian and writer Nella Larsen is named children's librarian at the 135th Street Branch Library. (During her library tenure Larsen writes two novels, *Quicksand* and *Passing*.)

The Harmon Foundation is founded by white real estate tycoon William Elmer Harmon. The foundation launches a series of black artist exhibitions—the first at the 135th Street Branch Library. (At the urging of Alain Locke and George Edmund Haynes, Harmon decides to finance the Harmon Awards, cash prizes for noteworthy black achievements.)

C. B. Powell, the first African American admitted to Bellevue Hospital to study radiology, opens an office in Harlem providing X-ray treatments. He is the city's first black radiologist.

The Alpha Kappa Alpha sorority's Lambda chapter is organized for students in the New York City region.

Duke Ellington and his six-piece band, the Washingtonians, arrive in Manhattan after a successful season at the Howard Theatre in Washington, D.C.

1923

Resolutions adopted at the Pan African Congress convened in London and Lisbon demand that Africans have a voice in their government, and that development in Africa should be "for the benefit of Africans, and not merely for the profit of Europeans."

January 4. Claude McKay speaks out in Russia about racism in the United States, criticizing American socialists as being unwilling or unable to transcend racism.

January 15. NAACP Branch Director Robert Bagnall cosponsors an open letter to Attorney General Henry Daughterty, urging prosecution of Marcus Garvey for mail fraud. (In March, 1923, Bagnall ridicules Garvey in a *Messenger* editorial, characterizing Garvey as "a Jamaican Negro of unmixed stock, squat, stocky, fat, and sleek with protruding jaws, and heavy jowls, small bright piglike eyes and rather bulldoglike face.")

January 23. Claude McKay delivers a speech before the Communist International in Moscow. In reaction, the Commintern launches an investigation into the race question in the United States.

January. The first issue of *Opportunity: A Journal of Negro Life* is published by the National Urban League, with Charles S. Johnson as its editor.

April. Crowds thrill to pilot Hubert Julian, "the Black Eagle," as he jumps from an airplane over Harlem. His target is a vacant lot on 138th Street between Seventh and Eighth Avenues. Julian lands about two blocks away on the roof of a U.S. Post Office.

May 15. Willis Richardson's one-act play, *The Chip Woman's Fortune,* opens at the Frazee Theatre on Broadway for a one-week run.

The first issue of Opportunity: A Journal of Negro Life, *journal of the National Urban League.*

The play, which originated at Harlem's Lafayette Theatre, is the first serious play by a black writer to appear on Broadway.

May 18. Marcus Garvey's trial on mail fraud begins in New York with Garvey defending himself. He is charged with misrepresenting the fact that the Black Star Line owned several steamships in order to "induce large numbers of poor persons to part with their money and invest in the stock." (Found guilty by the jury, Garvey is sentenced to five years in jail on June 21. He is unaware that he is the first black leader targeted by J. Edgar Hoover, an assistant to the United States Attorney General, who uses secret operatives in his attempt to uncover evidence of criminal acts by Garvey and the UNIA.)

Marcus Garvey's *Philosophy and Opinions of Marcus Garvey* is published by Universal Publishing.

June. Bessie Smith records the popular "Jailhouse Blues" at Columbia studios in Manhattan, accompanied by Fletcher Henderson on piano. (Songs by Smith recorded in other sessions during the year include "Downhearted Blues," "Baby Won't You Please Come Home," and "'Tain't Nobody's Business If I Do.")

September. Jean Toomer's *Cane* is published. Avant-garde critics hail the work as a literary landmark. Charles S. Johnson notes that Toomer has had "the most astonishingly brilliant beginning of any Negro writer of this generation."

October. The United States Department of Labor reports that over 500,000 blacks left the South during the year.

October. Former *New York Age* publisher T. Thomas Fortune becomes assistant managing editor of the UNIA newspaper, the *Negro World.*

October 29. The musical *Runnin' Wild* opens on Broadway. Written by *Shuffle Along* authors Flournoy Miller and Aubrey Lyles, with music by J. P. Johnson and Cecil Mack, the show popularizes the

Jean Toomer, the author of Cane.

An everlasting song, a singing tree,
Caroling softly souls of slavery,
What they were, and what they are to me,
Caroling softly souls of slavery.

—Jean Toomer,
Cane

Bessie Smith, "Empress of the Blues."

Charleston, which was introduced on Broadway in *Liza* the previous year.

The Renaissance Ballroom and Casino is constructed at the corner of 138th Street and Seventh Avenue. Mamie Smith's Garden of Joy is leveled to make way for the new entertainment complex.

November 3. Brooklyn's best-known basketball team, the Spartan Five (formerly the Spartan Braves) is relocated to Harlem by the team's owner, **Robert J. "Bob" Douglas,** and renamed the New York Renaissance Big Five (the Rens), the first full-salaried black professional basketball team. They win their debut game against the Collegiate Big Five by a score of 28 to 22. Named for Harlem's Renaissance Ballroom, the team's starting five are captain Hilton Slocum, Frank Forbes, Hy Monte, Zack Anderson, and Harold Mayers. (The Rens are quickly regarded as one of America's best professional teams. Their style of play contrasts sharply with the nation's better-known black basketball team, the Harlem Globetrotters. Unknown to most white fans, the Globetrotters are actually Chicago-based, but owner Abe Saperstein selects the name "Harlem" for its instant black identification.)

November 25. Florence Mills performs at the Lafayette Theatre in a benefit performance for the Dressing Room Club, a newly formed benevolence guild founded by black theater performers. Actor Leigh Whipper serves as chairman of the special event.

December 16. The Mutual Association of Eastern Colored Baseball Clubs (also known as the Eastern Colored League) joins the Negro National League. The New York Lincoln Giants and the Brooklyn Royal Giants are now included in the expanded league.

Charles Anderson is appointed collector of the newly created Third District of the Internal Revenue Service.

The Colored Women's Democratic League is formed as an auxiliary of the United Colored Democracy.

United Colored Democracy leader Ferdinand Q. Morton is appointed Civil Service Commissioner.

Caribbean-born Sheik Daoud Faisal establishes the Islamic Mission to America on State Street in Brooklyn.

At James VanDerZee's photographic studio at 109 West 135th Street, young and old Harlemites pose in front of romantic backdrops and pristine settings to mark marriages, births, and other life milestones.

A National Guard Armory is constructed for the 369th Regiment, the Harlem Hellfighters, at 2366 Fifth Avenue (between West

142nd and 143rd Streets). Artist Elmer Stoner is commissioned to execute oil portraits of the regiment's four black colonels: Woodruff Chissum, Chauncey M. Hooper, Elmer Sawyer, and Miles Paige of Brooklyn's 3rd Separate Battalion.

December. Tenor Roland Hayes returns to America a celebrity following a triumphant European tour. Securing the professional management of the Boston Symphony Orchestra Company, he embarks on a major tour including a critically acclaimed concert at Carnegie Hall.

The Pace Phonograph Corporation is forced to close, with Harry Pace noting that "radio broadcasting broke and this spelled doom for us."

Fletcher Henderson forms his own orchestra. Appearing at Harlem nightspots, Henderson employs guest instrumentalists **Louis Armstrong**, Coleman Hawkins, and Don Redmon.

The chairman of the New York State Athletic Commission orders Jack Dempsey to fight black challenger Harry Wills for the heavyweight title.

Orchestra leader Fletcher Henderson.

1924

March 21. At a dinner at the New York Civic Club to celebrate "The Debut of the Younger School of Negro Writers," black writers are introduced to white publishers. Among the New Negro Renaissance writers at the event, which is sponsored by Charles S. Johnson and *Opportunity*, are Gwendolyn Bennett, Countee Cullen, Jessie Fauset, Helene Johnson, Alain Locke, and Eric Walrond. Bennett, a 1921 graduate of Brooklyn's Girls' High is singled out, as her poem "To Usward" is chosen as the dinner's keynote reading. Johnson hails Alain Leroy Locke, who is based at Howard University, as the "dean" of the New Negro movement. (Langston Hughes later describes Locke as one of three "midwives" of the movement, along with Charles Johnson and Jessie Fauset.)

April. Frederick W. Wells, a student at Columbia Law School, attracts protests when he moves into the Furnald Hall dormitory. It is alleged that the New York City Ku Klux Klan is responsible for the burning of a seven-foot cross outside the dorm. Klansmen send Wells threatening letters and make bomb threats in the days that follow.

May 1. A fight between heavyweight champion Jack Dempsey and Harry Wills, the so-called "colored heavyweight champion" is announced for September 6. However, the fight is canceled, as Dempsey takes another bout with Gene Tunney. (Sports historians regard Dempsey's "ducking" of Wills as one of sport's greatest evasive maneuvers. Promoters fear "another Jack Johnson," and Dempsey is reluctant to test Wills in the ring.)

May 15. Paul Robeson stars in Eugene O'Neill's play *All God's Chillun Got Wings*, which opens at the Provincetown Playhouse. The play is about an upper-class black man married to a poor white woman.

July 8. William DeHart Hubbard becomes the first black in Olympic history to win an individual gold medal, winning the long jump.

August 10. Five thousand UNIA members accompany the Harlem funeral march for *Negro World* contributing editor John Edward Bruce.

September 1. The home of Samuel Brown in West New Brighton, Staten Island, is attacked by a group of white residents. (Brown moved into the area in July and refused offers from local white groups to purchase his house at a $1,500 profit. He begins receiving threats, including letters signed with crosses, after the refusal.)

September 1. The musical *Chocolate Dandies* opens on Broadway at the Colonial Theatre, with music and lyrics by Noble Sissle and Eubie Blake, and dialogue by Sissle and Lew Payton. The cast includes Josephine Baker. Musician, singer, and dancer Valaida Snow makes her Broadway debut as the character Mandy. Known as "Queen of the Trumpet," the multitalented Snow can play every instrument in the pit orchestra.

October 19. *Dixie to Broadway*, a musical imported from England, opens on Broadway starring Florence Mills.

December 27. The Delta Sigma Theta sorority holds its sixth national convention at the Harlem YWCA on West 137th Street. More than two hundred delegates and additional sorors from

James VanDerZee's portrait of a Garveyite family.

twenty-two states are described as an assembly of "the largest group of Negro college women at any given time." (On New Year's Day, Kappa Alpha Psi fraternity hosts an open house party at A'Lelia Walker's studio on 136th Street for the Greek-letter groups visiting the city during the Christmas holidays.)

December. Ernestine Rose, librarian of the 135th Street Branch Library, hosts a community meeting at which an organization is formed to develop a reference library of books and documents relating to black life. Arthur A. Schomburg, James Weldon Johnson, Hubert Harrison, and John Nail are elected officers.

Marcus Garvey forms the Universal Negro Political Union to encourage African American voters to be interested in national politics.

Fletcher Henderson's orchestra, the first to make a name with big-band jazz, opens at Roseland on Broadway. Trumpet player Louis Armstrong leaves King Oliver's Creole Jazz Band in Chicago to join Fletcher Henderson's band at the Roseland Ballroom.

Black ownership of the successful Black Swan recording label ends as Harry Pace sells it to the Paramount Company.

The Cotton Club opens at 644 Lenox Avenue on the northeast corner of 142nd Street in Harlem, with Andrew Preer conducting the first Cotton Club Band. Owned by white mobster Owney Madden, the club's policy excludes black customers, although all of the performers are black. Light-complexioned blacks sometimes gain entrance. Connie's Inn, at Seventh Avenue and 131st Street, also maintains a whites-only policy. LeRoy's at 2250 Seventh Avenue, however, bars white patrons.

The apartment shared by Ethel Ray (James Weldon Johnson's secretary) and Regina Anderson (a librarian at the 135th Street Branch Library) at 580 St. Nicholas Avenue is a popular Harlem gathering spot for newcomer writers. Among those welcomed are Wallace Thurman, Dorothy Peterson, Edwin Coates, Llewellyn Ransom, Richard Bruce Nugent, Jean Toomer, Elmer Stoner, Rudolph Fisher, Nella Larsen Imes, Countee Cullen, Bertha McNeil, Esther Popel,

Clarissa Scott, Angelina Grimke, Miguel Covarrubias, Gladys and Walter F. White, and Dorothy and Jimmie Harris.

1925

February. Marcus Garvey's appeal of his mail fraud conviction is denied by the U.S. Circuit Court of Appeals, Second Circuit. Arrested in New York, he is incarcerated in the Atlanta Federal Penitentiary.

March. The *Survey Graphic,* a white publication, devotes an entire issue to "contemporary Negro life." Hiring Alain Locke to edit the

New Negro literary figures gather at a party in honor of Langston Hughes hosted by Regina Anderson (Andrews) and Ethel Ray (Nance): (left to right) Langston Hughes, Charles S. Johnson, E. Franklin Frazier, Rudolph Fisher, and Hubert Delany.

special edition, the publication sells out two printings (more than forty-two thousand copies) and becomes the magazine's most widely read issue ever. Notably, the issue does not present blacks as a "problem," focusing instead on Harlem's vibrant culture.

May 1. *Opportunity* magazine holds its first literary awards dinner in Manhattan at the Fifth Avenue Restaurant on 24th Street. Zora Neale Hurston, Countee Cullen, and Langston Hughes win prizes funded by Casper Holstein, the West Indian boss of the Harlem numbers racket.

May 8. The Division of Negro Literature, History and Prints opens in the 135th Street Branch Library. Gifts and loans for the collection come from black collectors Arthur Schomburg, Hubert Harrison, Charles Martin, George Young, Louise Latimer, and Mrs. John Bruce.

The staff of the 135th Street Branch mount an exhibit in the New York Public Library's Central Building on 42nd Street using many items from Arthur Schomburg's collection. The first of its kind, the exhibit runs for four months.

July 17. The Staten Island home of Samuel Brown is attacked a second time by a group of white men, who smash windows, uproot trees and shrubs, and break up the outdoor furnishings. This time detectives are assigned to protect Brown's property and a grand jury is convened to investigate the violence.

The Staten Island Branch of the NAACP is organized following the racially motivated harassment of the Samuel Brown family.

August 25. A. Philip Randolph leads the first successful movement to organize black labor nationally with the founding of the Brotherhood of Sleeping Car Porters. Despite the Pullman Company's success in crushing many earlier efforts at union organization, the Brotherhood represents the largest single African American working group. The minimum wage paid by the Pullman Company to porters is $12.50 per month, but the Brotherhood demands $150 per month. The organization's headquarters is established at 2311 Seventh Avenue in Harlem.

The Literary Event of the Year!

The Records of a Race in Literature
History, Art and Science

GRAND OPENING
OF THE
**Department of Negro History
Literature and Art**
IN THE
135th Street Branch of the N. Y. Public Library
103 West 135th Street

Friday, May 7th, 8:30 P. M. At

Speakers :

Dr. Hubert Harrison, staff lecturer, New York Board of Education.
Dr. Alain Locke, of Howard University.
Dr. E. H. Anderson, director of the New York Public Library and others.

SINGING OF NEGRO SPIRITUALS

Large loan collection of Negro literature by:
Mr. Arthur Schomburg　　Dr. Charles Martin
Dr. Hubert Harrison and others

ALL ARE WELCOME

Auspices of Negro Literary and Historical Society and the New York Public Library

Opening of the Division of Negro Literature, History and Prints, 1925.

SURVEY GRAPHIC

HARLEM
MECCA
OF THE NEW
NEGRO
MARCH 1925

The New Negro issue of Survey Graphic, *March 1925.*

The American Negro must remake his past in order to make his future. . . . History must restore what slavery took away. . . . The Negro has been a man without a history because he has been considered a man without a worthy culture.

–Arthur A. Schomburg,
"The Negro Digs Up His Past,"
Survey Graphic, March 1925

October. NAACP lawyers confer with attorney Clarence Darrow in New York City in preparation for the upcoming (October 30) Detroit trial of Dr. Ossian Sweet. (Sweet, who had purchased a house in a white neighborhood, was charged with murdering a white man during an attack on his new home by a white mob. Darrow and the NAACP lawyers take the position that Sweet acted in self-defense.)

October 13. Garland Anderson's full-length play *Appearances* opens at the Frolic Theatre on Broadway. (Leaving his job as a bellhop in San Francisco, he made a cross-country auto tour to publicize the play.)

The Hesperus Club of Harlem becomes the first ladies' auxiliary of the Brotherhood of Sleeping Car Porters.

A member of the Brotherhood of Sleeping Car Porters.

The American Negro Labor Congress replaces the African Blood Brotherhood as an auxiliary of the Communist Party. A. Philip Randolph, troubled by the Soviet Union's seeming manipulation of American blacks, opposes the group.

The Krigwa Players is founded by W. E. B. DuBois and a group of writers, some from *Crisis* magazine. The group (originally called Crigwa, or Crisis Guild of Writers and Artists) is assembled from those who sent in manuscripts for the Amy Spingarn Prizes in Literature and Art. Performances are held in the basement of the 135th Street Branch Library.

Mother A.M.E. Zion Church is completed at 140 West 137th Street in Harlem. The neo-Gothic stone church is designed by George W.

Foster Jr., one of the first black architects in New York State and one of the first two African American architects registered in New Jersey.

The Edgecombe Sanitarium, the first black-owned hospital, opens in Harlem at 328 West 137th Street. Surgeons practicing at the hospital include Louis T. Wright, Allen Graves, Hudson Oliver, and Ralph Young.

Zora Neale Hurston moves to New York City after winning an award for her story "Spunk," which was published in *Opportunity* magazine. Obtaining a scholarship to Barnard College, she studies anthropology with Franz Boas. Hurston creates the term "Negrotarians" for whites who support the New Negro movement.

The "First American Jazz Concert" is staged at Aeolian Hall.

Ada "Bricktop" Smith, a singer at Connie's Inn, leaves New York City and travels to France, where she opens a nightclub and names it after herself. Bricktop's fast becomes one of Paris' most popular nightspots.

Edgecombe Sanitarium Women's Auxiliary.

Marian Anderson wins a recital competition sponsored by the New York Philharmonic Symphony at Lewisohn Stadium in Harlem. Anderson, raised in Philadelphia, performs concerts at local churches.

The *Inter-State Tattler*, a newspaper focusing on black socialites and their activities, begins publishing. Popular society columnist Gerald (Gerry) Dismond is a featured contributor.

1926

January 17. The Negro String Quartet, featuring Felix Weir, first violin; Arthur Boyd, second violin; Hall Johnson, viola; and Marion Cumbo, cello, performs a concert of chamber music at Grace Congregational Church on 139th Street in Harlem.

Carter G. Woodson organizes Negro History Week. The week encompasses Abraham Lincoln's birthday, February 12, and the generally accepted date of Frederick Douglass's birthday, February 14. (In the 1970s the event becomes Black History Month.)

February 26. Theodore "Tiger" Flowers wins the world middleweight title over Harry Greb at Madison Square Garden. Flowers, known as the "Georgia Deacon" because he reads Bible verses before and after every fight, becomes the first black middleweight champion. (A year later Flowers is knocked out during a fight and dies four days later from brain injuries.)

March. The *Booker T. Washington* (SS *General Goethals*), a ship in the UNIA's Black Cross Trading Company fleet, is sold at auction for one-quarter of its purchase price.

May 19. NAACP lawyers and Clarence Darrow return to New York victorious after a Detroit jury reaches a "not guilty" verdict in the trial of Ossian Sweet.

May 19. Arthur Schomburg's collection of more than ten thousand books, manuscripts, newspapers, and assorted items of African and African American history and culture are delivered to the New York

Zora Neale Hurston.

I feel most colored when I am thrown against a sharp white background. For instance at Barnard. "Beside the waters of the Hudson" I feel my race. Among the thousand white persons, I am a dark rock surged upon, and overswept, but through it all, I remain myself. When covered by the waters, I am; and the ebb but reveals me again.

—Zora Neale Hurston,
"How It Feels to Be Colored Me," 1928

Public Library main building at 42nd Street. More than one hundred boxes of materials are processed for later transfer to the 135th Street Branch. (Through the efforts of National Urban League officials Charles S. Johnson, L. Hollingsworth Wood, and Eugene Kinckle Jones, the Carnegie Corporation provided a grant of ten thousand dollars for The New York Public Library to acquire Schomburg's collection. The payment amounts to a fraction of the collection's actual value. Schomburg's personal treasure is the base from which the Schomburg Center for Research in Black Culture evolves.)

May 25. The musical comedy *Lucky Sambo* opens on Broadway at the Columbia Theatre. (A *New York Times* critic, heartened by the

Selected items from Arthur Schomburg's collection on view in the reading room of the 135th Street Branch Library, 1928.

show's continued use of minstrel blackface, champions "blackening up" in all comic shows. He adds, "The paler hues are all very well for heroes and chorus, but comedians must be definitely black.")

June 16. *The Negro-Art Hokum,* a controversial essay by journalist George Schuyler is published in the *Nation.* The article, urging black artists to embrace Western culture as their own, is rebutted by Langston Hughes, who argues for black artists to create art within their own racial heritage and experience.

September 24. The musical revue *Blackbirds of 1926* opens at the Alhambra Theatre. Florence Mills stars, singing "I'm a Little Blackbird Looking for a Bluebird." (The hit show travels to Paris and London.)

November. *Fire!,* a magazine created by younger Renaissance writers, is published as an experimental alternative to the older *Opportunity* and *Crisis.* Wallace Thurman edits the avant-garde publication, which includes contributions from Zora Neale Hurston, Gwendolyn Bennett, Langston Hughes, John P. Davis, Richard Bruce Nugent, and Aaron Douglas. (It is the only issue published.)

December. Countee Cullen wins the first Harmon Foundation literary prize—a gold medal and four hundred dollars—for *Color,* his first volume of poetry. Artist Palmer Hayden, a Cooper Union student who works as a custodian to pay for art supplies and room and board, wins the art prize.

December 30. *In Abraham's Bosom,* a play by Paul Green, opens at the Provincetown Playhouse. (The play, starring Rose McClendon, Abbie Mitchell, and Jules Bledsoe, is awarded the Pulitzer Prize in 1927.)

Catherine Allen Latimer is appointed reference librarian at the 135th Street Branch Library. Latimer supervises the Division of Negro Literature and History.

May Edward Chinn is the first black woman to obtain a medical degree from Bellevue Hospital Medical College. (A former pianist and singer who accompanied such notables as Paul Robeson, Chinn also becomes the first black woman to have an internship at Harlem Hospital, and the first woman to ride with Harlem Hospital ambulance crews on emergency calls.)

The Savoy Ballroom opens on Lenox Avenue between 140th and 141st Streets. Boasting a dance floor that can accommodate more than three thousand people, the Savoy is open to blacks and whites. Fletcher Henderson's band leads the opening night celebration. (The popular dance hall is home to many other big bands and performers, including Big George and the Diamonds, Leon Abbey and the Savoy Bearcats, and Fess Williams and the Royal Flush Orchestra. Dances introduced at the Savoy include the Camelwalk, the Shimmy, and the Black Bottom.)

The Alhambra Theatre opens on Seventh Avenue at 126th Street. The theater offers movies and live entertainment. For dance events, blacks and whites are separated by an alternate-night policy.

Choral singer Eva Jessye forms the Original Dixie Jubilee Singers with singers she meets in Harlem and Brooklyn. Kansas-born Jessye directs and composes for the choir, which tours locally and nationally.

Voodoo: A Grand Opera in Three Acts by composer H. Lawrence Freeman is performed at the 52nd Street Theatre. (Freeman, once a child prodigy in Cleveland, composes music for concerts, musical comedies, operas, and ballets.)

Hazel Scott, a five-year-old Trinidad-born pianist, performs at Town Hall.

Carl Van Vechten's novel *Nigger Heaven* is published. The white author's work becomes popular among white social voyeurs but gets a cold and angry reception in black Harlem.

1927

January 20. The Arthur A. Schomburg Collection is officially opened in the 135th Street Branch Library's Negro Division. The collection is the largest and most comprehensive library of black-related materials in the nation.

March 9. *Earth,* a play about voodoo rituals written by white playwright Em Jo Basshe, opens at Broadway's 52nd Street Theatre. *Messenger* critic Theophilus Lewis blasts the play as the "latest Broadway forgery of Negro drama."

April 20. Paul Robeson and Lawrence Brown give a concert at Town Hall to promote a Museum of African Art. Proceeds of the event complete a fund for the purchase of a portion of the Blondiau–Theatre Arts Collection of African art, which is deposited in the Negro Division at the 135th Street Branch Library.

July 11. *Africana,* a musical revue starring Ethel Waters, opens at the Daly 63rd Street Theatre.

August 21. The Fourth Pan-African Congress is convened in New York City, with more than two hundred delegates from the United States, the West Indies, South America, Africa, Germany, and India. The resolutions repeat those adopted at the 1923 conference, with the addition of calling for the withdrawal of the American Marines from Haiti.

October 10. *Porgy,* a play written by white playwrights DuBose and Dorothy Heyward, opens on Broadway featuring an all-black cast. The play stars Frank Wilson and Rose McClendon as the characters Porgy and Bess.

November 6. Several thousand fans and mourners attend the Sunday funeral of Florence Mills, Broadway's most popular female entertainer, who died from appendicitis on November 1. (Newspapers report that more than 125,000 mourners filled 137th Street in front of Mother A.M.E. Zion Church, where funeral services were held. Though reviews of her performances were rhapsodic, there are no known recordings or films of her work.)

November 18. President Calvin Coolidge commutes Marcus Garvey's prison sentence. He is released after serving thirty-three months in the Atlanta Federal Penitentiary and taken to New Orleans in federal custody.

December 2. Marcus Garvey is ordered to be deported to Jamaica and to never return to the United States.

Singer and dancer Florence Mills.

December 3. A Saturday midnight "Monster Testimonial Benefit" is held simultaneously at three Harlem theaters (Alhambra, Lafayette, and Lincoln) to raise funds for the Florence Mills Memorial Fund. Actor Jesse A. Shipp chairs the effort with Mills's widower, U.S. "Kid" Thompson, as treasurer. The fund acknowledges "our 'Flo' . . . a conspicuous example of the artistic talent of her Race, and a beloved, admired and respected member of the theatrical profession."

December 4. The Cotton Club hires Duke Ellington and his orchestra as its permanent band.

December 9. Marcus Garvey, speaking from the SS Saramacca just before his departure from New Orleans, tells supporters, "I sincerely believe that it is only by nationalizing the Negro and awakening him to the possibilities of himself that this universal problem can be solved." One of the leaders of a delegation of UNIA officers from New York, Chicago, Cincinnati, Cleveland, and Pittsburgh announces that association members have given Garvey a gift of ten thousand dollars to defray expenses of his trip and help with his resettlement in Jamaica. (Though Garvey continues to be active from his base in Jamaica, his influence on the New York parent body lessens substantially. In 1935 he moves his base of operation to London, where he remains until his death in 1940. Declared Jamaica's first National Hero in 1964, he is reinterred in a permanent memorial at National Heroes Park in Kingston.)

Following Marcus Garvey's deportation, Carlos Cooks takes over the leadership of the UNIA in New York City. Garvey names Henrietta Vinton Davis his senior administrator in Jamaica. (During Garvey's imprisonment (1925–1927), Davis oversaw UNIA affairs in British Honduras.)

December 27. *Showboat,* a musical by the team of Jerome Kern and Oscar Hammerstein, opens at the Ziegfield Theatre. Jules Bledsoe plays the role of Joe, singing "Ole Man River."

The Brotherhood of Sleeping Car Porters secures shorter working hours for Pullman porters. From its headquarters at 239 West 126th Street, A. Philip Randolph wages a national campaign to gain full union recognition for the porters. Black columnist Edgar

Fourth Pan-African Congress

OPENING SESSION

St. Mark's M. E. Church—Rev. John W. Robinson, D. D., *Pastor*

Sunday, August 21, 4 p. m.

Organ Prelude

Invocation:—Bishop J. S. Caldwell, A. M. E. Zion Church

Music

Introduction of General Presiding Officer—By Mrs. A. W. Hunton, President Circle for Peace and Foreign Relations

History of Pan-African Congresses—Dr. W. E. B. Du Bois

Greetings

AFRICA	Chief Amooh III	CANADA . . .	Hon. J. F. Jenkins
BAHAMAS .	Hon. T. Augustus Toote	EAST INDIES . .	Mr. H. K. Rakhit
BARBADOES . .	Bishop R. G. Barrow	HAITI . . .	M. Dantes Bellegarde
	VIRGIN ISLANDS . .	Hon. Adolph Sixto	

And from representative Negroes in other parts of the World

Report of Brussels Conference of Oppressed Races—Dr. William Pickens

Benediction

MONDAY AUGUST 22

MORNING SESSION 10 O'CLOCK

Exposition of Conditions in Africa—Discussion opened by Mrs. Coralie Franklin Cook

AFTERNOON SESSION 2 O'CLOCK

Subject:—African Missions

Address:—Mrs. Helen Curtis

Discussion:—Led by Rev. Florence Randolph—Mrs. A. B. Camphor

Address:—The Colored American Woman and Missions—Mrs. Addie W. Dickerson

4 O'CLOCK

Reception to Delegates and Friends

Y. W. C. A. 137th Street

EVENING SESSION 8 O'CLOCK

St. James Presbyterian Church—Rev. William Lloyd Imes, D. D., *Pastor*

Organ Prelude

Invocation

Music

Subject:—History of Africa

Addresses:—Dr. Charles H. Wesley, Howard University, Prof. Melville Herskovits, Columbia University

Subject:—The Dispersed Children of Africa

Address:—M. Dantes Bellegarde, Port au Prince, Haiti, Commander of the Legion of Honor, Former Minister to France

Program for the fourth Pan-African Congress, New York City, 1927.

TUESDAY AUGUST 23

MORNING SESSION 10 O'CLOCK

Exposition of Conditions in the Caribbean Islands

Discussion opened by Dr. Georges Normail Sylvain

AFTERNOON SESSION 2 O'CLOCK

Beth Ephillah Fourth Moravian Church—Rev. Charles D. Martin D. D., *Pastor*

Subject:—The Future of Africa

Address:—Mr. W. Tete Ansa

Discussion:

Subject:—The History of Africa (Continued)

Address:—Prof. Leo William Hansbury

Discussion

4 O'CLOCK

Visit the 135th Street Branch Public Library to see the African Exhibit and Schomburg Collection

EVENING SESSION 8 O'CLOCK

Salem Methodist Episcopal Church—Rev. F. A. Cullen, D. D., *Pastor*

Organ Prelude

Invocation:—Bishop P. A. Wallace—A. M. E. Zion Church

Music

Subject:—The Economic Development of Africa

Addresses:—Chief Amooh III., Dr. Leslie Pinckney Hill

WEDNESDAY AUGUST 24

MORNING SESSION 10 O'CLOCK

Exposition of Conditions in Europe and the United States and Possessions

Discussion:—Opened by Hon. J. F. Jenkins—Rev. George Frazier Miller, D. D.

AFTERNOON SESSION 2 O'CLOCK

Subject:—Political Partition of Africa

Addresses:—Dr. Y. Hikada, Prof. H. H. Phillips, Prof. Rayford W. Logan

EVENING SESSION 8 O'CLOCK

The Abyssinian Baptist Church, 138th Street, East of 7th Avenue

Organ Prelude

Invocation:—Rev. A. Clayton Powell, D. D., *Pastor*

Music

Subject:—Education in Africa

Address:—Dr. Wilhelm Mensching

Subject:—Art and Literature

Addresses:—Mr. John Vandercook. Mr. Arthur Schomburg

Closing Address:—Dr. W. E. B. Du Bois

The Duke Ellington Orchestra. Hired in 1927, the orchestra serves as the Cotton Club's band for six years.

Grey issues an appeal for "all Negroes to stand behind A. Philip Randolph."

Hubert T. Delany is appointed an assistant United States Attorney for the Southern District of New York.

Virginia Proctor Powell becomes the first African American to take and pass the New York State high school librarian's examination. Born in Pennsylvania and a graduate of Oberlin College, Powell is appointed librarian at Brooklyn's Seward High School.

Four Negro Poets is published, featuring works by Countee Cullen, Langston Hughes, Claude McKay, and Jean Toomer.

The Harlem Experimental Theatre is formed. Co-founders include Rose McClendon, Dorothy Peterson, Regina M. Andrews, Benjamin Locke, and Jessie Fauset. Performances are held at St. Philip's Episcopal Church and in the basement of the 135th Street Branch Library.

The Girl Friends, Inc. is founded in New York City. (The club becomes a national social and cultural organization.)

1928

Oscar DePriest from Chicago is the first black elected to Congress from the North.

January. The Harmon Foundation sponsors the nation's first major all-black art exhibition at the International House in Manhattan. (The exhibition then travels to several American cities. Artists Aaron Douglas and Romare Bearden criticize the foundation for primarily exhibiting black art work that imitates the work of white artists.)

February 27. *Keep Shufflin'* opens on Broadway at Daly's 63rd Street Theatre. (Flournoy Miller and Aubrey Lyles wrote the book for this short-lived *Shuffle Along* sequel, which includes music by several composers including Andy Razaf, Henry Creamer, James P. Johnson, and Fats Waller. The show is the last Miller and Lyles collaboration on Broadway. Miller will become a contributing writer for the *Amos 'n Andy* radio show and later for the television series.)

March. Claude McKay's novel *Home to Harlem* is published. The critically acclaimed book becomes the first best-selling novel by a black writer.

April 9. Nina Yolanda DuBois, the daughter of W. E. B. DuBois, marries Countee Cullen at Salem Methodist Church. The wedding is black New York's social event of the year, with more than five thousand people trying to attend. (Cullen leaves for Paris with his best man. His wife follows later, but on her arrival, the marriage ends.)

May 9. The musical *Blackbirds of 1928* opens at the Liberty Theatre. The show, inspired by the popularity of the 1926 version, stars Bill "Bojangles" Robinson, Elisabeth Welch, Adelaide Hall, and Tim Moore. Music from the show includes "I Can't Give You Anything But Love."

June 29. A black man, John Brown Jr., is threatened with lynching by a white mob in Jamaica, Queens, when a white woman working in the hotel in which Brown lives accuses him of harassment. Two policemen pull revolvers and nightsticks to hold off the mob.

Harlem's Dunbar Apartments are constructed at 2588 Seventh Avenue. Named for poet Paul Laurence Dunbar, the six apartment buildings are financed by John D. Rockefeller, who sees the project as a model for solving Harlem's housing problem. The Dunbar becomes home to such notables as W. E. B. DuBois, Countee Cullen, A. Philip Randolph, Bill "Bojangles" Robinson, and Matthew Henson.

The Dunbar National Bank is founded in Harlem, under the leadership of John D. Rockefeller. African Americans sit on the bank's board of directors. The staff of the bank, which is located at 135th Street and Seventh Avenue, is predominantly black.

Zora Neale Hurston dubs Iolanthe Sydney's house at 267 West 136th Street "Niggerati Manor." Among the many Renaissance artists who live at the boardinghouse rent-free is Wallace Thurman, a gay writer who helps to give the renovated tenement a reputation as Harlem's "bohemian" center—the black Greenwich Village. Other "Manor" associates include Richard Bruce Nugent, Langston Hughes, and Aaron Douglas.

Wallace Thurman's *Negro Life in New York's Harlem* is published by Haldemann-Julius.

Charles Johnson resigns from the National Urban League, leaving Opportunity *magazine to become the chairman of the social science department at Fisk University. (Johnson becomes Fisk's first black president in 1946.)*

New York City–born saxophonist Benny Carter forms his own orchestra. (Carter will write the scores for several Hollywood films, including *The Snows of Kilimanjaro*.)

Employees of the Dunbar National Bank.

The Hobby Horse bookstore opens at 205 West 136th Street. The shop features books by black writers and exhibits black artwork and photography. (It closes in 1930.)

1929

A "Don't Buy Where You Can't Work" campaign begins in Chicago and spreads to other cities.

March. *Hearts in Dixie,* the first all-black talking film produced by a white studio—20th Century Fox—opens at New York theaters. The film stars Clarence Muse, Gertrude Howard, and Stepin Fetchit.

Sixteen-year-old Broadway chorus girl Nina Mae McKinney, performing in *Blackbirds of 1929,* is spotted by film director King Vidor and cast as Chick in the movie *Hallelujah.* Her performance is that of the first "black temptress" in talking pictures. Born in South Carolina and raised in New York, the young actress is signed to a five-year contract with MGM.

May 4. *Pansy,* an "All-Colored Musical Novelty," opens on Broadway. With book by Alex Belledna and music by Maceo Pinkard, the show features Bessie Smith. The short-lived musical closes after three performances. *New York Times* critic Brooks Atkinson calls *Pansy* "the worst show of all time." The same year Smith appears in her only film, *St. Louis Blues*.

June. MGM's *Hallelujah!*, a film with a southern black story line directed by King Vidor, opens in New York movie theaters. MGM holds premiers uptown in Harlem, and downtown, where blacks are barred from the opening night show. Eva Jessye's Original Dixie Jubilee Chorus provides songs for scenes depicting black church services.

June 20. *Hot Chocolates* opens at Broadway's Hudson Theatre. Begun as a floor show at Harlem's Connie's Inn, the musical review features music by Fats Waller and Andy Razaf. Dancer Paul Meers and orchestra leader Cab Calloway are among the cast members. The show introduces the Waller/Razaf hit "Ain't Misbehavin'."

July. *The Crisis* publishes Mahatma Gandhi's "Message to the American Negro."

September. Former champion cyclist Major Taylor makes an appearance in Harlem to sign copies of his book, *The Fastest Bicycle Rider in the World.* (Taylor self-published the autobiography following its rejection by several publishers.)

September 23. Caspar Holstein is kidnapped by rival gang members and held for $50,000 ransom. (Within a few days he is released and left on a street corner roughed up and bleeding.)

October 24. The New York stock market crashes, triggering a global depression.

Colonel Charles W. Fillmore becomes the first black district leader in the Republican Party.

Republican Oscar De Priest, the recently elected black congressman from Chicago, is defended by white Republican Congressman Fiorello H. LaGuardia from New York City when several House members object to De Priest being given an office near theirs. Within a few months southern politicians are again

Caspar Holstein, policy banker and literary patron.

Let not the 12 million Negroes be ashamed of the fact that they are the grand children of ~~the~~ slaves. There is no dishonour in being slaves. There is dishonour in being slave-owners. But let us not think of honour or dishonour in connection with the past. Let us realise that the future is with those who would be truthful, pure and loving. For, as the old wise men have said, truth ever is, untruth never was. Love alone binds and truth and love accrue only to the truly humble.

Sabarmati,
1st May, 1929.

M. K. Gandhi

Mahatma Gandhi's "Message to the American Negro."

up in arms when De Priest's wife is entertained at the White House by the first lady. The critics cast the reception as unprecedented. From his home in Brooklyn, Arthur Schomburg sends a letter to the New York Times *reminding all that Thomas Jefferson was the first president to officially entertain a person of color.*

Louis Armstrong and his band, the Stompers, take up residency at Connie's Inn.

The National Colored Players is organized at the West End Theatre on St. Nicholas Avenue at 125th Street in Harlem.

The Phi Beta Sigma fraternity holds its national convention, or "conclave," at City College. Carter G. Woodson is the keynote speaker. A welcoming dance hosted by Phi Delta Kappa is held at A'Lelia Walker's studio.

Wallace Thurman's play *Harlem* opens on Broadway, starring Isabel Washington. His novel, *The Blacker the Berry,* is also published during the year. Both develop the theme of prejudice against West Indians.

Popular band leader Duke Ellington resigns from the Cotton Club to pursue other musical opportunities. The Cotton Club hires Cab Calloway and his orchestra as the permanent club band.

1930

Ras Tafari becomes Emperor Haile Selassie of Ethiopia.

The Gold Star Mothers, a label of respect given to the mothers of men who died in World War I, are honored with a government-sponsored tour of United States military cemeteries in Europe. At the last minute, officials decide that the white mothers should travel separately, and first. The black Gold Star Mothers wait for a second, and inferior, ship.

April. **Adam Clayton Powell Jr.,** a senior at Colgate University, preaches his first sermon at Abyssinian Baptist Church on Good Friday evening. (After graduating from Colgate in June, Powell Jr. travels to Europe, Egypt, and Jerusalem—a three-month graduation present from the church.)

October 22. *Blackbirds of 1930* opens on Broadway starring Ethel Waters and the dance team Buck and Bubbles. (The show runs for only twenty-six performances.)

December. The Young Negroes Cooperative League (YNCL) is founded in Harlem by journalist George Schuyler to harness the economic power of African Americans through buying clubs, cooperative grocery stores, and food distribution networks. **Ella Baker** serves as the organization's first national director. Baker and her colleagues view the league as uplifting the principles of communalism, an alternative to the cutthroat capitalist competition that many felt led to the 1929 stock market crash and the resultant social disaster. Headquartered in New York City, the league represents nearly two dozen affiliate groups nationwide.

The Harlem Citizens' Committee for More and Better Jobs is formed, with Rev. Adam Clayton Powell Sr. among its founders. The organization attempts to persuade Harlem merchants to hire

Over 350,000 people live in Harlem.

A Cotton Club handbill.

A view of 125th Street and Eighth Avenue during the 1930s.

black sales clerks, but its polite tactics and gentle persuasion do not yield a sympathetic response from white merchants. No efforts are made to picket white stores.

Despite Harlem's large African American population, few white businesses employ blacks. The community's twenty-four A&P grocery stores employ only nine blacks—all in menial positions. There are no black employees in the thirteen United Cigar stores. Community protests force Harlem's largest department store, Blumstein's, to hire black elevator operators, including one who is a graduate of City College. Koch's department store closes rather than hire a single black salesperson.

Black pilot Hubert Julian trains the Ethiopian Air Force for Emperor Haile Selassie's coronation.

Riverside Church is constructed at 122nd Street and Riverside Drive. Its dedication as an "interracial, interdenominational and international" church body makes it among the nation's first avowedly interracial churches.

The word *negro* is abolished by the Universal Holy Temple of Tranquility. The Temple's founder, Bishop Amiru Al-Minin Sufi Abdul Hamid, is denounced by critics as anti-Semitic, as he repeatedly calls for boycotts of Jewish-owned businesses in Harlem.

Zora Neale Hurston and Langston Hughes meet regularly to write a folk comedy play, which they call *The Bone of Contention* (later *Mule Bone*). At Louise Thompson's apartment at 435 Convent Avenue, Hurston acts out the play's male and female characters to the delight of her co-author, as Thompson, serving as secretary to the two writers, types the manuscript.

Charlotte Mason (called "Godmother" by the Harlem Renaissance recipients of her stipends), the wealthy white Park Avenue patron, breaks with Langston Hughes. (She had provided full financial support to Hughes since their first meeting in 1928, and to others, including Zora Neale Hurston, Claude McKay, Richmond Barthé, Aaron Douglas, Hall Johnson, and folklorist Arthur Huff Fauset.)

The National Pan-Hellenic Council is established at Howard University as a national coordinating body for the nation's African American fraternities and sororities.

1931

January 1. After successful political campaigns, Democrats James S. Watson and Charles Toney are inducted as municipal court judges. Harlem political leaders consider the two a "mixed ticket"—representing and combining the emerging political power of native-born and non-native-born blacks. Both are lawyers, but Watson is a West Indian immigrant and Toney is "an indigenous Negro."

March. Walter White succeeds James Weldon Johnson as executive secretary of the NAACP.

April 6. The first Scottsboro trial begins in Scottsboro, Alabama, with nine black youths accused of raping two white women on a freight train.

May 4. Ethel Waters stars in *Rhapsody in Black,* Broadway revue with music by several black composers, including W. C. Handy, J. Rosamond Johnson, and Cecil Mack. Waters performs Handy's "St. James Infirmary."

September 15. *Fast and Furious: A Colored Revue in 37 Scenes* appears on Broadway. Zora Neale Hurston and Jackie "Moms" Mabley write for and perform in the musical. (Mabley, who started her career in southern minstrel shows, is a popular comedienne at Harlem nightclubs. She eventually appears at Harlem's Apollo Theatre more times than any performer in its history.)

Bertram L. Baker, born in Nevis, establishes the United Action Democratic Association of Kings County. Baker pushes for representation on the Kings County Democratic Committee.

Father Divine's mystic powers seem to be validated following the arrest of more than eighty of his followers in Sayville, Long Island, on a disorderly conduct charge stemming from a noisy demonstration that turns the white community against them. Four days after condemning Father Divine to prison, the judge drops dead of a heart attack. Father Divine is reported to have said from his prison cell, "I hated to do it." Many of his converts have been recruited in Harlem.

Duke Ellington hires Ivie Anderson as his band's first featured singer. (Anderson's recording of "It Don't Mean a Thing (If It Ain't

A bread line in Harlem, 1931.

Got That Swing)" is her first hit with Ellington's band. Other Anderson band hits include "Stormy Weather," "Solitude," "Mood Indigo," and "I Got It Bad and That Ain't Good.")

1932

The median income of skilled black workers in New York City drops from $1,995 in 1929 to $1,003 in 1932. Fifty percent of Harlem families receive city relief payments, and twenty-five percent are families headed by women. The city's Home Relief Bureau pays eight cents per meal per family. The annual salaries of semiskilled and unskilled workers drop by forty-three percent. Mortality rates at Harlem Hospital are nearly twice as high as at Bellevue Hospital. Sixty percent of black women work, compared to less than twenty percent of white women.

June 25. Father Divine is released from prison and welcomed by seven thousand of his church members at Harlem's Rockland Palace (Manhattan Casino), 155th Street and Eighth Avenue, at a "Monster Rally to Our Lord" celebration.

June 30. Communist Angelo Herndon is convicted by an all-white Atlanta jury of possessing literature calling for an independent black state. The charge against Herndon is based on an 1861 statute meant to guard against slave revolts by punishing insurrectionists.

The Communist Party chooses New Yorker James Ford as its vice presidential candidate, the first time in the century that a black person is selected to run for the nation's second highest office.

Countee Cullen and Langston Hughes endorse the Communist Party ticket for the presidency.

June. Langston Hughes and nineteen other black Americans make a pilgrimage to the Soviet Union. Hughes remains for a year.

Henrietta Vinton Davis, increasingly alienated from Marcus Garvey, is elected First Assistant President General of the rival UNIA Incorporated, based in Harlem.

Arthur Schomburg is appointed curator of the Negro Division at the 135th Street Branch Library.

The Savage Studio of Arts and Crafts opens at 163 West 143rd Street in Harlem. Founded and owned by Augusta Savage, the studio attracts many young artists, including Norman Lewis, William Artis, and Ernest Crichlow.

Seventeen-year-old violinist Dean Charles Dixon organizes the Dean Dixon Symphony Orchestra. The teenage prodigy studies music and conducting at the Juilliard School of Music.

Lillian Hardin Armstrong organizes the Harlem Harlicans, an all-woman swing band. (She married Louis Armstrong in 1924; the two separated in 1931 and were divorced in 1938.)

The Rockland Palace stages an integrated transvestite costume ball contest. Drag competitions are also held at the Savoy Ballroom. Black competitor Bonnie Clark complains that the judges usually favor the white drag queens.

1933

January 7. The opera version of *The Emperor Jones* opens at the Metropolitan Opera. White baritone Lawrence Tibbett plays Brutus Jones. (The European production in 1934 casts Jules Bledsoe in the title role.)

March 1. Hall Johnson's *Run Little Chillun* opens as Broadway's first production of a black folk opera written by a black composer. The cast of more than two hundred singers, actors, and dancers includes Fredi Washington and Edna Thomas.

March 6. President Franklin Delano Roosevelt launches the New Deal program, leading to broad changes in the monetary system and the creation of federal agencies to regulate private industry and find jobs for millions.

March 8. Actress and dancer Isabel Washington marries the Reverend Adam Clayton Powell Jr. Powell's father opposes his son's marriage to the divorced showgirl, but Powell Jr. prevails.

Adam Clayton Powell Jr. leading picket line, ca. 1940. Demonstrators picket McCrory's on Harlem's 125th Street to protest unfair hiring practices.

Thousands gather inside and outside the Abyssinian Baptist Church on the rainy wedding day. (The couple honeymoons on Martha's Vineyard in Massachusetts.)

April 21. Rev. Adam Clayton Powell Jr. leads several hundred demonstrators to City Hall, demanding more black doctors and nurses, and better health care at Harlem Hospital. The event is Powell Jr.'s inaugural foray as a community leader as he takes the lead in Harlem's "Jobs for Negroes" movement.

June 29. In a Tokyo speech, Langston Hughes declares that African Americans are in sympathy with Japan. Japan, says Hughes, is the "only large group of dark people in the world who are free and independent." The FBI monitors Hughes.

July 22. Caterina Jarboro sings the title role in *Aïda* with the Chicago Opera Company at Manhattan's Hippodrome Theatre. (Reviewers remark on the large number of blacks who attend the two days of performance, including dancer Bill Robinson and singer Paul Robeson. By popular demand, the opera is performed again in September at Brooklyn's Ebbets Field. Born in North Carolina and raised in Brooklyn, Jarboro, a one-time *Shuffle Along* chorus girl, trained for an operatic career in Europe, where she performed through most of the 1930s.)

The Home Owners Loan Corporation (HOLC) is signed into law by President Franklin Roosevelt. Designed to offer low-interest loans to promote home ownership, the program creates a rating system that ranks neighborhoods in one of four color-coded categories: A, B, C, or D. D neighborhoods, physically deteriorated and often predominantly black, are color coded red, or redlined.

Harlem Hospital nurse Salaria Kee leads a demonstration against segregationist policies at the hospital with five other black nurses. The six stage a sit-in at a whites-only table in the hospital dining room to protest overcrowding and the need for more beds so that sick people will no longer be turned away.

Samuel Leibowitz, a white attorney from Brooklyn, becomes the first lawyer to represent the Scottsboro Boys.

Sixteen-year-old Claudia McNeil sings at The Black Cat, a Greenwich Village night club. (A talented actress and singer, McNeil will receive critical acclaim when she plays Lena Younger in Lorraine Hansberry's *A Raisin in the Sun* in 1959.)

Lena Horne, a sixteen-year-old Bronx high school student, is hired as a dancer at Harlem's Cotton Club, performing on stage with Cab Calloway, Count Basie, Ethel Waters, and Billie Holiday.

Repeal of the Volstead Act ends Prohibition, ending the need for many uptown nightclubs.

1934

February 20. The musical *Four Saints in Three Acts* opens on Broadway, running for six weeks before moving on to Chicago. Written by Gertrude Stein and Virgil Thomson, the show is performed by an all-black cast of forty dancers and singers, with Eva Jessye as choral director.

Playbill for Kykunkor *featuring Asadata Dafora, 1934.*

June. W. E. B. DuBois resigns from the national staff of the NAACP in a disagreement over policy and racial strategy. Dissatisfied with the organization's liberal and integrationist programs, DuBois advocates more self-help and black-led initiatives. He calls for blacks "to stand together in united action for their economic emancipation."

December 21. *Kykunkor,* an African dance operetta by Asadata Dafora, opens on Broadway. (Dafora, a native of Sierra Leone, studied voice in Milan and taught dance in Germany before forming his world-renowned dance company.)

The National Housing Act of 1934 adopts the use of color-coded housing survey maps as the basis for loan eligibility. The Federal Housing Administration (FHA) begins redlining massive areas that are inhabited primarily by African Americans, within the nation's cities, discouraging integrated housing. People who wish to purchase homes in redlined areas are routinely refused mortgage loans, charged excessive interest rates, or burdened with high down payments. The loan practices discourage housing investment in black neighborhoods and subsidize white flight from the cities.

A boycott against the A. S. Beck shoe store in Harlem ends as a court injunction rules that since the protestors are not an organized labor union but rather a racial group, they cannot legally stage pickets and boycotts. The ruling bans economic boycotts.

The Citizens' League for Fair Play is formed by a coalition of Harlem organizations. It protests hiring discrimination in area stores. The court decision against race-based boycotts leads to the group's being disbanded. (The state supreme court reverses the decision, and the organization is reborn as the Greater New York Coordinating Committee for Employment in 1938.)

Henrietta Vinton Davis is elected President General of the UNIA Incorporated, becoming the first (and only) woman to hold the post.

Painter Aaron Douglas is commissioned to create "Aspects of Negro Life," a mural at the 135th Street Branch Library. (The Kansas-born artist had illustrated books by several authors including Alain Locke, James Weldon Johnson, Charles S. Johnson, and Claude McKay.)

Aaron Douglas showing mural to Arthur Schomburg. The six-foot-square oil on canvas mural, Song of the Towers, *is part of Douglas's series* Aspects of Negro Life, *created under the sponsorship of the WPA, 1934.*

Aspiring author and journalist Dorothy West publishes *Challenge,* a literary magazine devoted to black writers.

Hurtig and Seamon's Music Hall on 125th Street between Seventh and Eighth Avenues in Harlem is purchased by Frank Schiffman and Leo Brecher, who rename it the Apollo Theatre. Opening night features Ralph Cooper and Benny Carter's orchestra.

WORLD WAR II AND THE STRUGGLE FOR CIVIL RIGHTS

1935–1964

Overleaf:

Double V for Victory rally, West 119th Street, Harlem, 1942.

George E. C. Haynes, Thurgood Marshall, and James Nabrit after Supreme Court victory, 1954. The Brown v. Board *decision orders schools to be desegregated "with all deliberate speed."*

WORLD WAR II MADE THE GREAT WAR KILLING SPREE OF 1914–1918 look almost modest in retrospect. The 35 million men, women, and children who were either killed in battle or victimized dwarfed the 10 million casualties of World War I. Tens of millions of others were wounded. Nearly every country on the globe was eventually drawn into this conflict and every country was affected by it in some way.

World War II ushered in the beginning of the end of European colonial rule in Africa, Asia, and the Americas. The war also brought with it the beginning of the end of Jim Crow, America's unique system of racial segregation that determined the lives of American blacks in the South, and significantly influenced them throughout the nation. And the war ended the Great Depression. All of these global and national events and phenomena defined the context in which black New Yorkers fashioned their struggles for freedom and human dignity in the era between the Harlem riots of 1935 and the passage of the Civil Rights Act of 1964.

The Struggle Against Fascism

By the time the United States entered the war in December 1941, Germany, Italy, and Japan (the Axis powers) controlled most of Europe as well as much of China, Asia, and northern Africa. The war ended with the defeat of German and Italian fascism and Japanese militarism, and the retaking of most of these territories by Allied powers (including the United States). It also ushered in the nuclear age and the emergence of the United States and the Soviet Union as the two dominant political forces on the planet.

Italy had missed out on the Berlin Conference of 1885 when the European powers divided up Africa. As a consequence, Italy, the seat of Europe's first great empire (the Roman Empire), found itself a marginal player in the European empire-building games of the late nineteenth century. Seeking a place among the European imperial elite in 1896, Italy invaded Ethiopia, one of the three remaining self-governing black nations and the oldest independent African nation. To the delight of the entire African world, Italy was soundly defeated by the Ethiopian imperial army. Italians were devastated by the defeat at the hands of "a country without a trace of civilization." For the next forty years, Italians looked for an opportunity to avenge this blight on their national dignity and sense of national pride. In 1935 Italian dictator Benito Mussolini took it upon himself to lead Italy back to its former imperial glory. Avenging the 1896 defeat in Ethiopia was seen as a means of restoring the country's dignity and affirming Italy's right to sit among Europe's imperial elite.

In October 1935 Italian troops based in neighboring Eritrea invaded Ethiopia. For most of the African world, this invasion marked the beginning of World War II. Black people throughout the African world voiced their opposition to the invasion. In Harlem, London, Kingston, and other parts of the African world, African peoples organized defense funds and occasionally raised troops to help defend Ethiopia, a global symbol of pride and dignity. Black New Yorker Perry Julien, for instance, went to Ethiopia to help organize and train Haile Selassie's Ethiopian air force. By May 1936, however, Italy had conquered the ancient African kingdom and joined forces with Germany's Adolf Hitler to make fascism an alternative to Europe's competing democratic and communist/socialist political systems.

By 1935 Germany was in the full control of Adolf Hitler and his Nazi Party. The racism and antisemitism that would become the foundation of Hitler's policy of Aryan supremacy had already taken root in German cultural and social practice. The Nuremberg Laws, signed by Hitler on September 15, 1935, rescinded the civil rights of Germany's 600,000 Jews, stripped them of German citizenship, barred them from practicing a profession, and prohibited sex or marriage between Jews and non-Jews. (Comparable statutes had governed the relations between black Americans and American society since the latter decades of the nineteenth century.) Nazi doctrine proclaimed "the Aryan race" to be superior to all people in all spheres of human endeavor.

When Adolf Hitler and Germany hosted the 1936 Olympic Games in Berlin, it was with the expectation that German athletes would showcase the superiority of "Aryan blood." African American athletes, headed by Ohio State track star Jesse Owens, shattered Hitler's claims of Aryan superiority. Owens won four gold medals and the title Athlete of the Games. Collectively, ten African Americans won thirteen medals, including eight golds. Defeated at the Games, Hitler eventually took his ideology and program onto the battlefields of Europe.

Meanwhile, Japanese military leaders were primed to redouble their efforts to conquer China. On July 7, 1937, Japanese troops crossed the Yongding River about ten miles west of Beijing and launched the second Sino-Japanese War. By October, Japan had captured Beijing, Nanjing, and Shanghai, and established Japanese rule in mainland China. In November 1935 Germany, Japan, and Italy signed an Anti-Comintern Pact—a pledge of mutual support against the Soviets that extended the "Rome-Berlin Axis" to Tokyo.

Adolf Hitler's vision of Aryan world supremacy began to take form in 1936 when he remilitarized the Rhineland. Two years later he annexed Austria and the Czechoslovakian Sudetenland. In 1939 his troops took the rest of Czechoslovakia and divided up Poland with the Soviet Union. France and Britain finally declared war on Germany during the invasion of Poland, and their declaration marked the official beginning of World War II. By the summer of 1942, Hitler's Third Reich European empire was larger than any since the ancient Roman Empire.

Meanwhile, Japan's imperial visions had expanded from China to Pearl Harbor, Malaya, Burma, and Australia. The bombing of U.S. bases on Pearl Harbor, Hawaii, on December 7, 1941, forced the United States to enter the global war on the side of the Allies.

The African Freedom Struggle

During World War II, colonized African peoples from the continent and the diaspora were once again called upon to come to the aid and defense of their European colonial overlords. Once again, as in World War I, they were drafted into colonial armies and asked to risk their lives on the battlefields of Europe to defend freedoms that they themselves did not enjoy. Most were willing to join forces in the struggle against Hitler's racism and Nazism and Mussolini's fascism, but, like their African American counterparts, they expected the rewards of freedom in return for their service and sacrifices.

Like sectors of the African American community, African peoples viewed the Japanese as people of color and as the advance guard of the global struggle against European domination and imperialism. As a consequence, they frequently defended and celebrated Japanese victories over European colonial powers. They were less clear about their position on Japanese aggression against the Chinese and other people of color. Fighting and dying on the battlefields of Europe, colonized African soldiers once again reaffirmed the fact that whites were as vulnerable as they were and that the myths of white racial supremacy were unfounded. By the end of the war they were also clear that, given the weakness and fragility of the major European colonial powers, the era of European colonial domination of the world was ending.

Their assessments proved to be correct. Europe's modern colonial system, which was at its peak and appeared to be invincible in 1939, was for all practical purposes ended by 1965. Colonized people in Africa, Asia, and Latin America, like their African American counterparts, organized during the war and emerged from it seeking self-government and national independence. The Philippines became a sovereign state in 1946, and India and Pakistan became independent members of the British Commonwealth in 1947. Ceylon and Burma followed in 1948; Indonesia, Laos, Cambodia, and Vietnam became sovereign nations in 1949; and Libya gained its freedom in 1951.

In 1954 representatives of the colonized and formerly colonized peoples of Africa, Asia, and Latin America met in Bandung, Indonesia, to explore the feasibility of creating an independent political agenda, rooted in their collective interests rather than those of the democratic West or the Communist East. To the chagrin and outright opposition of the U.S. government, Congressman Adam Clayton Powell Jr. represented African Americans at this international gathering of the "wretched of the earth," who collectively dubbed themselves the "third world." Morocco, Tunisia, Malaysia, Ghana, and French Guiana were among the leaders of the post-Bandung independence surge during the 1950s, but 1960 was the most important year of decolonization. In Africa alone, eighteen colonies gained their independence. By 1964 the process was almost complete. Portugal, which had not been drawn into the war, held onto her colonies in southern Africa into the 1970s. And South Africa's system of racial segregation was not toppled until the 1990s. But for all intents and purposes, the former British, French, and Dutch colonial regimes were history by 1964.

The African American Struggle for Democracy

Almost 700,000 black Americans served in the nation's armed forces during World War II. A nondiscrimination clause in the Selective Service Act of 1940 ensured the presence of one black for every nine men inducted into the service. But virtually all black inductees served in segregated all-black units, usually under white leadership. Black American leaders and civil rights activists urged blacks to make their participation in the war effort a Double V campaign: victory against fascism and discrimination abroad, and against segregation and discrimination at home.

A March on Washington Movement, organized by black New Yorker A. Philip Randolph, challenged the Roosevelt administration to ensure that blacks gained access to the jobs being created in the war industries. On June 25, 1941, President Roosevelt signed Executive Order No. 8802, which stated that "there shall be no discrimination in the employment of workers in defense industries or government because of race, creed, color or national origin." A Fair Employment Practices Committee (FEPC) was established to investigate complaints and redress grievances. The FEPC and Executive Order No. 8802 put the domestic aspect of the Double V campaign on the national agenda and provided a vehicle for challenging racial segregation in employment. Never fully effective, they nevertheless laid the foundations for the modern Civil Rights Movement.

Victories over discrimination in the military and on the domestic front during the war heightened black expectations and renewed their commitment to dismantle America's entire system of racial segregation once the war ended. The NAACP and its Legal Defense and Educational Fund took the lead after the war, prosecuting cases that challenged racial segregation in education, public accommodations, housing, and employment. Harlem Congressman Adam Clayton Powell Jr., who entered the U.S. House of Representatives during the war, brought a new focus of attention on discriminatory practices in the nation's capital as well as its Congress.

The Congress of Racial Equality (CORE) organized the first "freedom ride" to integrate public transportation facilities in the southern states in 1947, the same year in which Jackie Robinson broke the color bar in major league baseball. The 1954 Supreme Court decision in *Brown v. Board of Education of Topeka, Kansas* outlawed the "separate but equal" doctrine and made racial segregation in public educational facilities unconstitutional. It inaugurated the modern Civil Rights Movement, which, spurred on by the Montgomery Bus Boycott of 1955, announced the imminent demise of Jim Crow and the birth of the civil rights revolution of the 1950s and 1960s.

The Civil Rights Acts of 1957, 1960, and 1964 reaffirmed the rights of blacks to full citizenship and equal protection before the law—rights that had been denied them for most of the twentieth century. A. Philip Randolph and Bayard Rustin's 1963 March on Washington attracted more than 250,000 men, women, and children of all races and creeds who subscribed to the nation's founding principle that "all men [and women] are created equal."

The Struggle for Economic Opportunity

Fiorello LaGuardia's tenure as mayor did for the City of New York what Franklin D. Roosevelt's New Deal did for the nation as a whole. Aided by former New York Governor Roosevelt and by the Second World War, LaGuardia and his associates wrested the nation's largest and hardest-hit city from the depths of depression and set it on the road to recovery. When LaGuardia took office in 1934, the city debt of $1.9 billion was greater than that of the forty-eight states combined. More than 142,600 families were on relief and the city's budget deficit totaled $30 million. Between 1933 and 1939 the city received more than $1 billion in federal aid. By 1936 one-seventh of all Works Progress Administration (WPA) spending was flowing into New York City. That same year, President Roosevelt organized key black leaders to ensure that blacks got a fair share of the available funds. The Harlem Race Riot of 1935, an African American protest against the entrenched racial discrimination that had plagued black New Yorkers' existence for centuries, had focused local and national attention on the black plight during the Depression and served as a catalyst for improving black access to jobs, programs, and welfare services.

Generally speaking, the outbreak of the war in Europe in 1939 ended the Depression and breathed new life into the American economy. Even before the United States entered the war, however, LaGuardia's administration was well on the way to revamping the city's infrastructure. The West Side Highway had opened in 1937. LaGuardia Airport opened in 1939 and construction was begun on Idlewild [later John F. Kennedy] Airport. The Triboro, Whitestone, and Henry Hudson Bridges were completed by 1940, as were the Midtown Tunnel and the new Sixth Avenue Subway line. Three subway lines (two of them bankrupt) were consolidated into a single unified system.

During World War II jobs in the war industries of the city, especially at the Brooklyn Navy Yard, were opened to blacks. Black New York women took advantage of opportunities in shipbuilding and other industrial trades. Black New York men experienced improved employment opportunities during the war as well. The G.I. Bill offered black New Yorkers who had fought in the armed services unprecedented opportunities to purchase housing and pursue college and university degrees. The abolition of restrictive covenants and discrimination in housing, coupled with the G.I. Bill, opened housing opportunities for black New Yorkers in the outer boroughs. There was a downside, however, to this prosperity. Over the next two decades, the dispersal of the black middle and upper classes from Harlem, among other factors, would leave the former capital of the black world a mere shadow of its former self. Upwardly mobile residents of Harlem took advantage of the new housing opportunities. Many moved to Brooklyn or Queens, taking with them their economic resources and social power. The decline continued and spread.

Between 1958 and 1964, factory jobs in metropolitan New York fell by 87,000. Between 1960 and 1964, 800,000 white residents fled New York City for the suburbs. The building boom continued, however, and between 1947 and 1963 more than 58 million square feet of new office space was created—more than in the next twenty-two largest cities combined. But the boom was to create a new, service-based economy in which job opportunities for blacks were limited. Thus a foundation was laid for a postwar depression among black New Yorkers who were still seeking access to the American economy.

1935

February. In an interview with Claude McKay in the *Nation,* Father Divine asserts that if he represented race, creed, color, or nation, he could not be "omnipotent."

February 25. At Madison Square Garden, Jesse Owens sets a new world record in the 60 meters at 6.5 seconds during a semifinal run but is beaten in the finals by Ben Johnson, who ties the mark.

March 19. Long-simmering charges of police brutality boil over when Lino Rivera, a black high school student, is arrested for allegedly stealing a pocketknife at the S. H. Kress Five and Dime store on 125th Street in Harlem. False rumors spread that Rivera has been beaten to death by police. By nightfall more than ten thousand angry black residents are protesting in the 125th Street main shopping area. Some in the crowd break the windows of white-owned businesses and rampage through the streets. Five hundred police and white merchants demand that Governor Herbert Lehman send in the National Guard. Lehman refuses. About two hundred stores are destroyed, with property losses of over $2 million. A hundred blacks are arrested, three are killed, and thirty more are injured.

March 22. New York newspapers debate the role of the Communist Party in the Harlem unrest. The *New York Herald Tribune* reports, "The Communists have long regarded [Harlem] as an ideal ground for agitation. They easily set down the American Negro as the Achilles' heel of our social system and they have been unwearied in their efforts, both in Harlem and elsewhere, to exploit him to their own ends. Their success has been almost nil. In the depression, as in the World War, the country's Negro citizens have shown themselves as loyal, as patient, and as sensible as those of any other group, and often much more so than some groups."

March 23. At Madison Square Garden, Jesse Owens equals the world record in the 60-yard dash, running the distance in 6.1 seconds. Owens shares the record with Ralph Metcalf.

March 27. Responding to the Harlem riot, Adam Clayton Powell Jr., an assistant pastor at Abyssinian Baptist Church, writes the first of three articles for the *New York Post*. He describes the unrest as a "protest against empty stomachs, overcrowded tenements, filthy sanitation, rotten foodstuffs, chiseling landlords and merchants, discrimination in relief, disfranchisement, and against disinterested administration."

April. Following the Harlem uprising, Mayor Fiorello LaGuardia names a study commission headed by Howard University sociologist E. Franklin Frazier to investigate the unrest. The commission draws angry crowds to its hearings.

After the Harlem disturbance, **Dorothy Height,** a caseworker for the New York City Department of Welfare, is appointed the agency's first black personnel supervisor. (A graduate of New York University, she earned her bachelor's and master's degrees in four years. The Virginia-born student worked in restaurants, a laundry, and as a proofreader for Marcus Garvey's newspaper, *Negro World*.)

June 25. Boxer Joe Louis from Lafayette, Alabama, makes his New York City debut at Yankee Stadium against six-foot-seven, 275-pound Primo Carnera, "the Italian Giant." The fight occurs as news headlines predict an invasion of Ethiopia by Italy's fascist dictator, Benito Mussolini. Social commentators see the bout as a battle between American democracy and Italian fascism. Louis knocks Carnera out in the sixth round.

July. Charles Hamilton Houston is hired as the NAACP's first full-time paid special counsel. (**Thurgood Marshall,** *his former student, serves as special assistant counsel from 1936 to 1938.*)

September 24. At Yankee Stadium Joe Louis knocks out former heavyweight champ Max Baer in the fourth round. Earlier in the day Louis married nineteen-year-old Marva Trotter.

October 10. The folk opera *Porgy and Bess* opens on Broadway at the Alvin Theatre. Based on the 1928 play *Porgy,* the show stars Todd Duncan and Anne Wiggins Brown in the title roles. The musical's book is by DuBose Heyward, with lyrics by Heyward and Ira Gershwin, and music by George Gershwin.

December 5. The National Council of Negro Women (NCNW) is founded in New York City at the 137th Street YWCA. The Council is the culmination of a five-year effort led by Mary McLeod Bethune to convince the National Association of Colored Women that a new organization was needed to enable the voices of black women to be heard more fully in every economic, social, and political sphere. Fourteen black women's organizations are convened to form the NCNW.

Herbert L. Bruce, a businessman, becomes the first black district leader in the Democratic Party.

Police Sergeant Samuel J. Battle is named police lieutenant.

More than one thousand black New York men sign up to fight for Emperor Haile Selassie in Ethiopia's battle against invading Italy. Nationwide, more than seventeen thousand promise to fight for the Ethiopian cause. By U.S. law, Americans who fight for Ethiopia face a three-year jail term, a $2,000 fine, and loss of citizenship.

Bishop Arthur Matthew changes the name of the Commandment Keepers of the Living God to the Falashas of America, following the coronation of Emperor Haile Selassie in Ethiopia. The denomination associates itself with Jewish traditions as observed by the Ethiopian Hebrew rabbinate. Elements traditionally associated with the African American religious experience, such as gospel hymns, remain a part of the religion.

(Left) *Anne Wiggins Brown and Todd Duncan in* Porgy and Bess, *1935.*

(Right) *Louis Armstrong and Billie Holiday.*

From his church headquarters at 455 Lenox Avenue in Harlem, Father Divine boasts an interracial membership of over two million nationally, of which about half a million are verifiable. Divine's Peace Mission calls for an end to the "mistreatment of the Jews in Germany and all other countries."

W. E. B. DuBois's *Black Reconstruction* is published by Harcourt, Brace and Company. He writes the book "to refute aspersions cast on the Negro" during the post–Civil War era. (DuBois updates the book for re-issue in 1963.)

Zora Neale Hurston's *Mules and Men* is published by Lippincott. Based on Hurston's field studies in Louisiana, the book is regarded as the first collection of African American folklore to be compiled and published by an African American.

A Citizen's Committee of the 135th Street Branch Library is formed to obtain more adequate quarters for the library and the Negro Division.

Billie Holiday makes her first appearance at Harlem's Apollo Theatre. She also records with Teddy Wilson's orchestra and appears in the short film *Symphony in Black* with Duke Ellington.

Rose McClendon and Dick Campbell found the Negro People's Theater in Harlem. (Following McClendon's death in 1936, Campbell and Muriel Rahn organize the Rose McClendon Players to keep her artistic dreams alive.)

Painter and educator Aaron Douglas is named president of the Harlem Artists' Guild.

Federal Arts Project field director Charles Henry Alston oversees thirty-five artists on the Harlem Hospital mural project. A DeWitt Clinton High School and Columbia University graduate, Alston has

The *"306 Group," 1933.* Artists working on the WPA Mural Project are pictured in front of project director Charles Alston's studio at 306 West 141st Street in Harlem. Front row, left to right: *Gwen Knight, Edgar Evans, Francisco Lord, James Yeargans, and Fred Coleman.* Back row: *Add Bates, Grace Richardson, Richard Lindsay, Vertis Hayes, Charles H. Alston, Cecil Gaylord, Sollace Glenn, Elba Lightfoot, Selma Day, Ronald Joseph, Georgette Seabrooke, and Donald Reid.*

won acclaim from art critics for his earlier oil studies of "Negro types." Alston's students include **Romare Bearden,** Robert Blackburn, **Jacob Lawrence,** and Charles White.

The Harlem Art Workshop is created in the auditorium of the 135th Street Branch of the New York Public Library. Directed by James L. Wells, a Howard University art professor, the workshop conducts classes in painting, sculpture, photography, woodworking, and other arts and crafts.

1936

The Black Cabinet is organized. The informal network of black leaders, also known as the Black Brain Trust and the Federal Council on Negro Affairs, plans strategies to secure a fair share for blacks under Franklin D. Roosevelt's New Deal program. Members include **Robert C. Weaver,** *Mary McLeod Bethune, Lawrence Augustus Oxley, William Johnson Trent Jr., Eugene Kinckle Jones, and Frank S. Horne, all of whom work in various federal agencies.*

Indian pacifist Mohandas K. Gandhi, declaring his support for the American civil rights struggle, says, "it may be through the Negroes that the unadulterated message of nonviolence will be delivered to the world."

March 19. One year after the Kress riot, the biracial commission that investigated the unrest presents Mayor LaGuardia with its findings. The commission concludes that the riot occured because of the "Jim Crowism" and pervasive "oppression" within New York City's African American community. The report calls for an end to employment discrimination; new schools and more teachers in Harlem; more black staff at city hospitals, especially at Harlem Hospital; and an end to police brutality against blacks. The commission concludes, "Lack of confidence in the police and even hostility towards these representatives of the law were evident at every stage of the riot. This attitude of the people of Harlem has been built up over many years of experience with the police in this section." LaGuardia suppresses the commission's report as inflammatory.

April 27. The 1936 edition of the *Ziegfeld Follies* opens at the Winter Garden featuring Josephine Baker and the Nicholas Brothers.

June 19. At Yankee Stadium, young heavyweight boxer Joe Louis is knocked out in the twelfth round by German heavyweight Max Schmeling. Langston Hughes observes, "I walked down Seventh Avenue and saw grown men weeping like children, and women sitting on the curbs with their heads in their hands. All across the country that night when the news came that Joe was knocked out, people cried."

July 11. The completion of the Triborough Bridge links Harlem to Corona, Queens, and the African American population of Corona begins to grow.

July 11–12. At Randall's Island stadium, Jesse Owens qualifies for the Olympics in the 100 meters, winning in 10.4 seconds; the broad jump, leaping 26 feet, 3 inches; and the 200 meters, winning in the world record time of 21 seconds.

July 18. The *Amsterdam News* obtains a copy of the report of Mayor LaGuardia's commission on the Harlem riot. Publishing the document in full, the paper is critical of the mayor for withholding the report, which it says reached conclusions that Harlem residents had known long before the riot.

July 28. The Sigma Gamma Rho sorority's Kappa Sigma alumnae chapter is organized in New York City.

August. Jesse Owens wins four gold medals at the Olympic games in Berlin, Germany, debunking Adolf Hitler's notion of a superior Aryan race.

A voter referendum changes the governance of New York City from a Board of Aldermen to a City Council with proportional representation. The new system further erodes Tammany Hall's power, making it necessary for the Democratic Party to consider the black vote.

The Communist Party again selects James Ford as its vice presidential candidate. The communist platform makes a strong appeal to black voters: "The Negro people suffer doubly. Most exploited of working people, they are also victims of Jim-Crowism and lynching. They are denied the right to live as human beings." The party targets Harlem, with white members holding frequent rallies on

Lenox and Seventh Avenues. A rallying cry heard often is "Black and white, unite and fight!"

Audley Moore joins the Communist Party, campaigning on behalf of black vice presidential candidate Ford. Other women in the Harlem Communist Party include Bonita Williams, Claudia Jones, and Louise Thompson. Thompson and artist Augusta Savage organize the Vanguard, a left-wing social club from which a chapter of the Friends of the Soviet Union develops. Bayard Rustin joins the Young Communist League.

Ethiopian support groups in Harlem include the Provisional Committee for the Defense of Ethiopia, the Ethiopian World Federation, and the Black Legion. Black nurses, led by Salaria Kee, raise enough money to transport medical supplies and a seventy-five-bed hospital to Ethiopia.

The Central Harlem Health Center is constructed on Fifth Avenue, between 136th and 137th Streets, at a cost of $250,000. Dr. John West, its director, is selected primarily because of his medical accomplishments as a volunteer in Ethiopia.

The Harlem River Houses, one of the first two federally funded housing projects in New York City, is constructed from 151st to 153rd Street along Harlem River Drive. Built to provide high-quality housing for African American working people, the project is an outcome of the 1935 riots. Among the projects' seven architects is John Louis Wilson Jr.

Harlem Sidewalk Athletic Teams are organized by Robert Douglas, William Culbreath, and Joseph Yancey Jr. (Known later as the Pioneer Club, the teams provide sports opportunities for Harlem boys and girls.)

The Penguin Club is organized in Harlem "to break down the social ostracism extended to interracial couples."

Benny Goodman's trio, a unit within Goodman's band that includes pianist Teddy Wilson and drummer Gene Krupa, becomes a quartet with the addition of vibraharpist Lionel Hampton.

The Cotton Club closes in Harlem and reopens downtown at 48th Street and Broadway.

Orson Welles directs the Federal Theatre Project's Harlem production of *Haitian Macbeth*. Performers include former Lafayette Players' member Edna Thomas as Lady Macbeth and Rosetta LeNoire as the First Witch.

1937

The U.S. Supreme Court frees Communist Party member Angelo Herndon from a Georgia prison, reversing its 1935 ruling that Herndon was guilty of violating the state's 1861 law against insurrections and slave revolts, finding the statute unconstitutional.

June 22. Joe Louis knocks out James J. Braddock in the eighth round in Chicago, becoming the first black heavyweight champion since Jack Johnson.

July 19. Langston Hughes tells Spanish Loyalist supporters in Paris that, "In America, Negroes do not have to be told what fascism is in action. We know. Its theories of Nordic supremacy and economic suppression have long been realities to us."

August. *The African*, the official organ of the Universal Ethiopian Students Association, issues a directive outlining acceptable words and terms—"African-American" instead of "Afro-American," and "Black" instead of "Negro," for example.

September 26. Bessie Smith dies of injuries sustained in a car accident in Clarksdale, Mississippi, after a white hospital refuses her treatment.

October 9. Tenor Roland Hayes performs at Town Hall in a fundraiser for the New York Committee to Aid the Southern Negro Youth Congress.

October 29. Henry "Hank" Armstrong wins the featherweight title with a sixth-round knockout over Pete Sarron at Madison Square Garden.

November 1. Reverend Adam Clayton Powell Jr. becomes the new senior minister of Abyssinian Baptist Church, succeeding his father.

November 7. At a National Council of Negro Women (NCNW) function attended by Eleanor Roosevelt, NCNW president Mary McLeod Bethune enlists Dorothy Height's involvement in the council's work for equal rights in employment and education, marking the start of Height's role as an NCNW volunteer.

November 21. The American Negro Ballet presents its inaugural performance at the Lafayette Theater at 2225 Seventh Avenue. The ballet is accompanied by the New York Negro Symphony Orchestra directed by Wen Talbert.

Richard Wright moves to Harlem to work as a writer for the Communist Party's *Daily Worker.*

Theodore "Ted" Poston is hired by the *New York Post.* Poston is the first black columnist to work full time for a New York daily newspaper. A former *Amsterdam News* city editor, Poston served as chief of the Negro News Desk in the Office of War Information during World War II.

Oscar Garcia Rivera, a Puerto Rican of African descent, is elected to the New York State Assembly in the Seventeenth Assembly District.

Anna Arnold Hedgeman is appointed head of the black branch of the Brooklyn YWCA. Hedgeman organizes picket lines to advocate the employment of black clerks in Brooklyn department stores.

Dorothy Height leaves the New York City Department of Welfare to become assistant director of the Harlem YWCA. (She later credits her welfare department and Y experience for helping her understand the problems confronting women in domestic labor and the necessity for community-based organizations.)

The Harlem Community Art Center opens with Augusta Savage as its first director.

Count Basie, a Kansas City musician and orchestra leader, brings his band to New York City.

Dominated by black entertainers, 52nd Street between Fifth and Sixth Avenues is termed "Harlem Downtown." Appearing at clubs in the area are Fats Waller, **Dizzy Gillespie,** and Billie Holiday.

The Harlem Suitcase Theatre, founded by Louise Thompson, Hilary Phillips, and Langston Hughes, presents productions in a second-floor loft at 317 West 125th Street. The organization includes actress Edith Jones and her husband, actor Robert Earl Jones. Supported financially by the Communist-linked International Workers Order, the theater earns the record during its 1936–1937 season for the longest run to date of a single play in the community: 135 performances of Hughes's *Don't You Want to Be Free?: A Poetry Play, From Slavery Through the Blues to Now—and Then Some!—with Singing, Music and Dancing.*

Dorothy West founds a second black literary magazine, called *New Challenge.* Richard Wright serves as associate editor for the journal, which publishes only one issue.

1938

The NAACP Legal Defense and Educational Fund is established to challenge segregated education. (Thurgood Marshall is named director the following year.)

March. In *New Negro Alliance vs. Sanitary Grocery Company,* the U.S. Supreme Court overrules the 1934 A. S. Beck's Harlem shoe store case that prohibited the mounting of pickets and boycotts. The new verdict clears the way for blacks to participate in boycott activities to protest racial discrimination. The Supreme Court's boycott ruling sparks Adam Clayton Powell Jr.'s. formation of the Greater New York Coordinating Committee for Employment (GNYCC). The group plans an assault on job discrimination practiced throughout the city, not just by Harlem merchants. Believing Powell's group is Communist-influenced, A. Philip Randolph forms the Harlem Jobs Committee (HJC). Both groups stage pickets at stores and utility company outlets throughout the city.

It was Minton's where a musician *really* cut his teeth and *then* went downtown to The Street. Fifty-second Street was easy compared to what was happening up at Minton's. You went to 52nd Street to make money and be seen by the white music critics and white people. But you came uptown to Minton's if you wanted to make a reputation among the musicians.

—Miles Davis with Quincy Troupe,
*Miles: The Autobiography of
Miles Davis*

Spring. "Tuesday is 'black-out night,' " declares Rev. Adam Clayton Powell Jr. in a campaign to force Consolidated Edison to hire black workers. Every Tuesday night, GNYCC supporters forgo electric lights for two-cent candles, which flicker from many Harlem apartment windows. The campaign climaxes with a "Bill-Payers' Parade" at Con Ed's office at 32 West 125th Street. Hundreds of bill-payers pay their bills with nickels and dimes. Con Ed reaches agreement with Powell to hire black trainees. The pact is hailed by Powell and Mayor Fiorello LaGuardia.

April 25. Over three thousand people attend a rally at Harlem's Rockland Palace where Rev. Adam Clayton Powell Jr. declares, "Harlem is sick and tired of promises. The hour has struck to march!" Other Harlem ministers join Powell's activism. Rev. Lorenzo King, of St. Mark's Protestant Episcopal Church, proclaims, "We're tired of religion that puts us to sleep. We've got to put religion to work—for us!"

May 31. Hank Armstrong wins a fifteen-round decision over Barney Ross to capture the welterweight title at Long Island City, N.Y. (In August, he defeats lightweight Lou Ambers at Madison Square Garden, becoming the only boxer in history to hold three titles simultaneously: lightweight, welterweight, and featherweight.)

June 22. Joe Louis defeats Max Schmeling in two minutes, four seconds of the first round in Yankee Stadium to retain the heavyweight championship title. African Americans celebrate this victory at a time when Hitler's Nazism is on the rise.

Juvenile arrests of African American boys rise from twelve percent of the city total of juvenile arrests in 1930 to twenty-five percent in 1938.

Col. Benjamin O. Davis Sr. is appointed Commander of the National Guard 369th Regiment in Harlem. (Davis becomes the first black promoted to the rank of general in the U.S. military.)

Carlos Cooks obtains a charter from Marcus Garvey to form and lead the Advance Division of the UNIA in Harlem. With the fragmentation of the organization since Garvey's deportation, the Advance

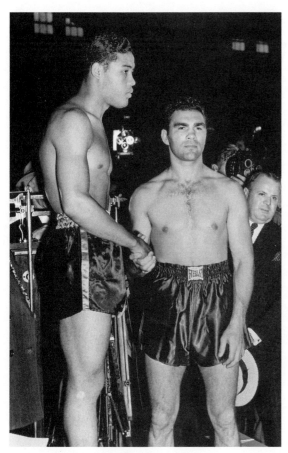

Joe Louis and Max Schmeling weighing in.

From "High Tide in Harlem: Joe Louis as a Symbol of Freedom"

In Harlem, that area of a few square blocks in upper Manhattan where a quarter of a million Negroes are forced to live through an elaborate contrivance among landlords, merchants, and politicians, a hundred thousand black people surged out of taprooms, flats, restaurants, and filled the streets and sidewalks like the Mississippi River overflowing in flood time. With their faces to the night sky, they filled their lungs with air and let out a scream of joy that it seemed would never end, and a scream that seemed to come from untold reserves of strength. They wanted to make a noise comparable to the happiness bubbling in their hearts, but they were poor and had nothing. So they went to the garbage pails and got tin cans; they went to their kitchens and got tin pots, pans, washboards, wooden boxes, and took possession of the streets. They shouted, sang, laughed, yelled, blew paper horns, clasped hands, and formed weaving snake-lines, whistled, sounded sirens, and honked auto horns. From the windows of the tall, dreary tenements torn scraps of newspaper floated down. With the reiteration that evoked a hypnotic atmosphere, they chanted with eyes half-closed, heads lilting in unison, legs and shoulders moving and touching:

"Ain't you glad? Ain't you glad?"

—Richard Wright, *New Masses,* July 5, 1938

Division is considered a reaffirmation of Garvey's founding ideals. (Cooks, a native of the Dominican Republic, is a former member of New York Juvenile Division and the UNIA African Legion.)

A. Philip Randolph is elected president of the National Negro Congress at a meeting attended by over 800 delegates representing 585 black organizations.

Amsterdam News reporter Henry Lee Moon is fired for attempting to form a union. Moon is hired by the Federal Public Housing Authority as a "race relations advisor."

The Negro Actors Guild is founded in New York City by Leigh Whipper and Noble Sissle as a benevolent guild for black actors and actresses. Sissle serves as its first president, Ethel Waters and Marian Anderson are vice presidents, and W. C. Handy is treasurer. Fredi Washington, who starred in the 1934 film *Imitation of Life,* serves as the guild's first executive secretary. (Washington also works as a columnist and theater editor for the *People's Voice,* a weekly newspaper published by her brother-in-law, Adam Clayton Powell Jr.)

The New York Chamber Orchestra is founded by Dean Dixon.

Howard University instructor Dr. Charles Drew receives a Rockefeller Foundation research grant to continue his blood plasma studies at Columbia-Presbyterian Hospital. Drew establishes an experimental blood bank at the hospital.

Opportunity magazine focuses on anti-Semitism in Nazi Germany. Editor Elmer A. Carter urges African American newspapers, magazines, and social and civic organizations to stop anti-Semitism from spreading among black Americans.

Haiti, by W. E. B. DuBois, plays at the New Federal Theatre. The production stars Rex Ingram. Ingram has appeared in several Hollywood films, including *King Kong* and the original *Tarzan.*

Gospel singer and guitarist Sister Rosetta Tharpe gains national prominence after performing at the Cotton Club with bandleader Cab Calloway. Although criticized by some for performing in secu-

OFFICERS
of the
Negro Actors Guild of America

ETHEL WATERS
Vice-President

MARIAN ANDERSON
Vice-President

WILLIAM C. HANDY
Treasurer

NOBLE SISSLE
President

ROBERT P. BRADDICKS
Assistant Treasurer

DUKE ELLINGTON
Vice-President

FREDI WASHINGTON
Executive Director & Sec'y

EDNA THOMAS
Vice-President

PAUL ROBESON
Vice-President

LOUIS ARMSTRONG
Vice-President

Rev. A. C. POWELL, Jr.
Chaplain

FRANK WILSON
Vice-President

J. ROSEMOND JOHNSON
Vice-President

Negro Actors Guild of America officers, 1938.

lar arenas, Tharpe becomes the first gospel singer to record for a major label when her show-stopping routine attracts the attention of Decca records executives.

1939

January 25. Boxer John Henry Lewis battles Joe Louis for the heavyweight title at Madison Square Garden. The bout is the first time two black fighters have fought for the heavyweight championship since Jack Johnson fought Jim Johnson in Paris in 1913. Louis wins the fight with a first-round knockout.

April 9. Marian Anderson draws a crowd of 75,000 blacks and whites to an Easter Sunday concert at the Lincoln Memorial in Washington, D.C., after the Daughters of the American Revolution refuse to permit her to sing in Constitution Hall, which they own, because of race.

July 22. Jane Mathilda Bolin is appointed Justice of the Domestic Relations Court of the City of New York by Mayor LaGuardia. Born in Poughkeepsie, New York, she is the first black woman judge in the United States.

October 2. Musical compositions by W. C. Handy, William Grant Still, Harry T. Burleigh, James Weldon Johnson, and Nathaniel Dett highlight the "NYC Festival of American Music," sponsored by the American Society of Composers, Authors and Publishers (ASCAP). Performers include singer Minto Cato, Juanita Hall, the Southernaires, the Wen Talbert Choir, and the Abyssinian Choir.

November. The Harlem Suitcase Theatre opens its season with satirical skits by Langston Hughes. Among them are: *Limitations of Life,* which satirizes the film *Imitation of Life* by reversing the Claudette Colbert (white employer) and Louise Beavers (black maid) roles; and *Em-Fuehrer Jones,* a satirical view of Adolf Hitler lost in the Black Forest. Also on the bill is the theater's first-season hit *Don't You Want to Be Free.* (During a trip to Los Angeles the following spring to work on a script for the musical *St. Louis Woman,* Hughes forms a West Coast counterpart to the Suitcase Theatre, calling it the New Negro Theater.)

J. Raymond Jones makes his first attempt to become district leader of the Nineteenth Assembly District in Harlem. Though Jones determines that blacks are the largest group within the district, Tammany leaders keep it from black control. (Threatened by Harlem's large black population, Tammany leaders had carefully divided Harlem among four assembly districts so that in each district blacks were a minority.)

Judge Jane Mathilda Bolin.

Bertram Baker is appointed deputy collector of Internal Revenue.

Marian Anderson performs at the Lincoln Memorial, 1939.

Daniel Burrows, a Harlem realtor, is elected district leader of Harlem's Nineteenth Assembly District.

Harlem boxer Walker Smith Jr. (Sugar Ray Robinson) wins the *New York Daily News* Golden Gloves featherweight title. In order to be eligible for the Amateur Athletic Union sanctioned bout, Smith uses the AAU card of a fighter named Ray Robinson, whose name he adopts.

Lawrence Reddick is named curator of the Negro Division of the 135th Street Branch Library, replacing Arthur Schomburg, who died the previous year.

Augusta Savage completes *Lift Every Voice and Sing,* a sculpture commissioned for the 1939 New York World's Fair.

The Salon of Contemporary Negro Art opens in Harlem. Founded by Augusta Savage, the salon is the city's first black-owned gallery devoted to the work of black artists, among them Meta Warrick Fuller, Selma Burke, Gwendolyn Knight, and Grace Mott Johnson. (The salon, though critically successful, cannot support itself financially and closes within a year.)

Augusta Savage working on Lift Every Voice and Sing.

Way Down South, by Langston Hughes and Clarence Muse, is the first Hollywood film with a script by black writers.

Katherine Dunham forms her first professional dance company, performing in New York City and Chicago. Dunham, a dancer-choreographer and anthropologist, emphasizes serious research in developing artistic expressions.

Dorothy Maynor debuts at Town Hall.

Hats by New York milliner Mildred E. Blount are exhibited at the New York World's Fair. Based on hat designs from 1690 to 1900, the collection is critically acclaimed. Blount's reputation leads to her designing hats for many Hollywood films, including *Gone With the Wind* and *Easter Parade*. Her clients include Joan Crawford,

"Rara Tonga," from the musical Tropical Revue, *ca. 1944. Choreographer Katherine Dunham performing in her work with Laverne French and Tommy Gomez.*

Hat designer Mildred Blount, 1946.

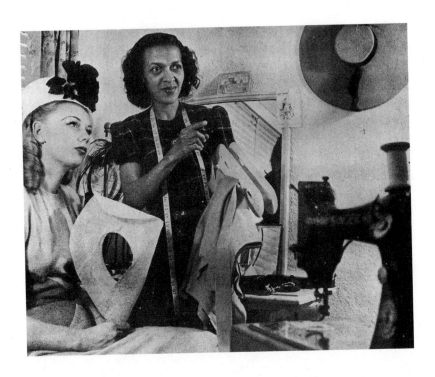

Rosalind Russell, Gloria Vanderbilt, and Marian Anderson. (In the 1940s Blount opens a shop in Beverly Hills.)

A chapter of Jack and Jill of America is formed in New York City. Founded in Philadelphia a year earlier, the club sponsors social and cultural activities for the children of black professional men and women.

1940

New York City's black population is 458,444 or 6.15% of the total, 7,454,995. The city's black population ranks first in the nation, ahead of Chicago, Philadelphia, the District of Columbia, and Baltimore.

February. Richard Wright's *Native Son*, a portrait of the life of a black youth in the ghetto, is published.

April 7. The Booker T. Washington stamp, the first U.S. postage stamp to honor an African American, is issued.

June 5. Frederick O'Neal and Abram Hill found the American Negro Theatre (ANT). The company, based at the 135th Street Branch Library in Harlem, provides training for blacks interested in playwrighting, acting, directing, and the technical aspects of play production.

September. Bessye Bearden is elected chair of the executive board of the Harlem Community Art Center. A journalist, and mother of painter Romare Bearden, she is also the founder of the Colored Women's Democratic League and the treasurer of the National Council of Negro Women.

September 6. Richard Wright and Paul Robeson headline "An Evening with Two of America's Most Distinguished Artists," at the Golden Gate Ballroom at 142nd Street and Lenox Avenue. The program benefits the Negro Playwrights Company, founded by Theodore Ward.

October 4. "Sugar" Ray Robinson makes his professional boxing debut at Madison Square Garden, knocking out Joe Echeverria in the second round.

November. John H. Johnson publishes the first issue of Negro Digest. *(Ebony magazine follows in 1945.)*

The American Negro Theatre production Days of Our Youth, *1946. Pictured among the cast is Harry Belafonte (seated left).*

The Blood Transfusion Association in New York City makes an emergency request to Dr. Charles Drew at Howard University to return to New York to oversee a massive blood plasma project to aid wounded soldiers on the battlefields of Europe. Drew accepts the assignment, serving as Medical Director of the Blood for Britain Program. (When the United States enters the war, Drew serves as medical director of the American Red Cross blood program. However, Drew differs strongly with the American military policy of separating white blood from blood donated by blacks. Asked to resign over the issue, Drew does and returns to teach at Howard University for the remainder of the war.)

Eunice Hunton Carter is appointed the first black woman district attorney in New York State by Governor Thomas E. Dewey. (Born in Atlanta, Georgia, the Fordham University School of Law graduate was one of the "twenty against the underworld," as Dewey had called his team when he was special prosecutor. Carter's investigative skills helped trigger the biggest organized crime prosecution in the nation's history in the late 1930s.)

Claudia Jones is elected chair of the Young Communist League. Jones, born in Port of Spain, Trinidad, is editor of the League's *Weekly Review* and the *Spotlight*. She is also a supporter of the Communist-controlled National Negro Congress.

A. Philip Randolph refuses re-election as head of the National Negro Congress, believing that Communist influence is clearly behind the organization.

Audley Moore runs unsuccessfully for a City Council seat on the Communist Party ticket.

The Negro Division of the 135th Street Branch Library is renamed in honor of Arthur Schomburg.

Philippa Duke Schuyler, eight-year-old prodigy, is placed on the Distinguished Students List by the National Piano Teachers' Guild for the fifth consecutive year. A day at the New York World's Fair is named in her honor.

Music by Philippa Schuyler, 1938. Schuyler composed "The Wolf," her first piece for piano, at the age of five.

The Katherine Dunham Dance Company appears in the Broadway production of *Cabin in the Sky*. Dunham collaborates with George Balanchine on the show's choreography.

Singer Ruth Brown wins amateur night at the Apollo Theater, singing "It Could Happen to You."

1941

March 21. The Harlem Community Arts Center, directed by Gwendolyn Bennett, sponsors a "Beaux Arts Ball" at the Savoy Ballroom. An interracial crowd enjoys the festive costume ball, which features benefit chairwoman Mollie Lewis Moon as Marie Antoinette.

March 30. The National Urban League sponsors a one-hour national radio program to promote equal employment opportunities for blacks in the defense program. Among the participants are Marian Anderson, Eugene Kinckle Jones, Joe Louis, Bill "Bojangles" Robinson, and Ethel Waters. A National Urban League survey of defense plants in Brooklyn conducted during the year finds only

WPA Harlem Community Arts Center instructors. Front row, left to right: *Zell Ingram, Pemberton West, Augusta Savage, Robert Pious, Sarah West,* and *Gwendolyn Bennett.* Back row: *Elton Fax, Rex Goreleigh, Fred Perry, William Artis, Francisco Lord, Louise Jefferson,* and *Norman Lewis.*

234 blacks employed in a total work force of 13,840. Almost half of the plants exclude blacks entirely.

April 16. Gwendolyn Bennett is suspended from her job as director of the Harlem Community Arts Center because of accusations that she is a Communist. New York City Art Project director Audrey McMahon charges Bennett with violating Section 15-F of the Emergency Relief Appropriation Act, which stipulates that no Communist can be employed on any WPA project. Bennett denies the accusation, stating: "I am not a Communist and have never been one. I am perfectly innocent of any charge." Though Bennett is supported by the Citizen's Sponsoring Committee of the Center, she is dismissed from the post. Among the Committee's members are Regina Andrews, Bessye Bearden, E. Simms Campbell, Alta Douglas, Mollie Lewis Moon, and Eslanda G. Robeson.

June. Clarence Cameron White and John F. Mathews present their opera *Ouanga* with an all-black cast at the New School for Social Research in Manhattan. Anne Wiggins Brown stars in the opera, which is about the brief reign of Jean Jacques Dessalines, emperor of Haiti in 1804.

June 16. Twenty-two thousand blacks rally at Madison Square Garden in support of A. Philip Randolph's demand that the federal government act to end employment discrimination. Randolph threatens to stage a March on Washington, D.C., that will attract more than a hundred thousand people. Brooklyn activist Anna Hedgeman joins A. Philip Randolph's March on Washington Committee. Hedgeman's history of support for the picketing of defense plants that refuse to hire black workers becomes a key element in the planned national march against racism in the defense industries and military.

June 23. The African Nationalist Pioneer Movement is founded by Carlos Cooks. (The organization conducts an annual Marcus Garvey Day Parade on August 17th, Garvey's birthday, and forms, as Garvey did, an African Legion and a Women's Auxiliary. They also organize a Universal African Relief program that sends clothing to Southwest Africa, and promote an ongoing "Buy Black!" campaign.)

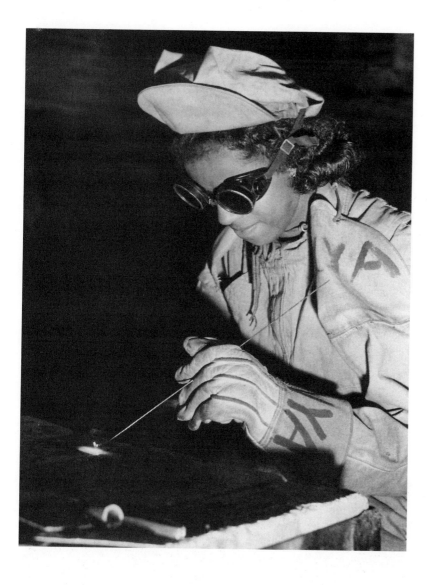

A welder at the Brooklyn Navy Yard.

June 25. Following A. Philip Randolph's threat in May to lead a hundred thousand African Americans in a March on Washington, President Franklin Roosevelt issues Executive Order 8802 prohibiting racial discrimination in federal government employment and establishing the Fair Employment Practices Committee (FEPC).

November. Sculptor Selma Burke receives her first major exhibition at McMillen Galleries in New York City. (A graduate of Columbia University, Burke works as a truck driver at the Brooklyn Navy Yard following the outbreak of World War II.)

WAKE UP, NEGRO AMERICA!

DO WE WANT WORK?
DO WE WANT OUR FULL RIGHTS?
DO WE WANT JUSTICE?

WHAT IS IT?

It is a Negro mass movement to get the full benefits of this democracy.

WHO IS ITS LEADER?

A. Philip Randolph, International President of the Brotherhood of Sleeping Car Porters, founder of the MARCH-ON-WASHINGTON MOVEMENT.

WHAT HAS THE MOVEMENT DONE?

Won Presidential Order barring discrimination in war industries and governmental agencies.

Won the appointment of the Fair Employment Practice Committee to enforce this Order.

As a result, won a change from the Jim Crow hiring policy of some firms and governmental agencies.

But more important, has built a nation-wide unity of Negroes as never before.

WHAT NEEDS TO BE DONE?

Demand more enforcing power for the Fair Employment Practice Committee.

Demand the opening of the Army, Navy, Marine and Air Corps to Negroes on the basis of equality.

Abolish all economic and political discriminations against the Negro.

WHAT CAN I DO?

Join the MOVEMENT and help swell its ranks 13,000,000 strong by paying ten cents membership fee at its offices, 2084 Seventh Avenue, or at a regular Wednesday night meeting, 8:30 at the Harlem Y. M. C. A.

Volunteer for some branch of work.

Support the MADISON SQUARE GARDEN RALLY of the MOVEMENT to be held June 16th by selling tickets, soliciting contributions, distributing publicity, speaking before groups or doing such work as you think will aid in the cause of the MOVEMENT.

"Winning Democracy for the Negro Is Winning the War for Democracy"

Headquarters:
NEW YORK DIVISION "MARCH-ON-WASHINGTON MOVEMENT"

HOTEL THERESA

Phone: MOnument 2-3350   2084 Seventh Avenue

440

March on Washington Movement broadside, 1941.

Moving from his political support base in the Nineteenth Assembly District, Daniel Burrows is elected District Leader of Harlem's Twenty-second Assembly District.

Lester Granger becomes executive director of the National Urban League. Granger works to get the federal government to withhold funding from any public or private housing development that practices discrimination.

East Harlem Houses are constructed with federal, state, and city government subsidies. Social and architectural critics deplore the advent of spartan high-rise buildings as functioning more like warehouses than like neighborhoods or communities.

Richard Wright's book, *Native Son,* is adapted as a play and produced on Broadway. Wright breaks from the Communist party.

Musician Valaida Snow is arrested and interned in a Nazi concentration camp while touring in Denmark. (Severe weight loss during her incarceration leaves her in poor health, but she resumes performing after the war. Better known overseas than she is in the United States, she is called "Little Louis" by her European fans because her trumpet style is influenced by Louis Armstrong.)

Dean Dixon is guest conductor of Arturo Toscanini's NBC Symphony Orchestra. (Dixon is guest conductor of the New York Philharmonic Orchestra in 1942 and of the Philadelphia Orchestra in 1943.)

December 7. Dorie Miller of Waco, Texas, messman on the USS Arizona, *mans a machine gun during the Pearl Harbor attack and downs four planes. (He is later awarded the Navy Cross.)*

1942

January 9. Joe Louis scores a first-round knockout over Buddy Baer at Madison Square Garden. Louis donates his full share of the fight proceeds, $89,092, to the Navy relief fund. (Louis learns later that the money is still considered income by the federal government.)

March 13. The Harlem Community Art Center's second annual Beaux Arts Ball is held at the Savoy Ballroom. Proceeds of the dance benefit the Center, a Harlem servicemen's agency, and Allied war relief organizations.

Summer. The National Urban League Guild is organized under the leadership of Mollie Lewis Moon, who states that the new group will "further the activities of the Urban League." The Guild is an outgrowth of the Citizens' Sponsoring Committee of the Harlem Community Art Center, formed in 1940 to help finance the Center.

August. A hat created by New York designer Mildred Blount is featured on the cover of *Ladies' Home Journal.*

October 2. Welterweight Sugar Ray Robinson defeats Jake LaMotta in a ten-round decision at Madison Square Garden. (The match is the first of six pitting Robinson against LaMotta.)

Audley Moore is elected secretary of the New York State Communist Party.

Louis Armstrong purchases a home in Corona, Queens, where he resides with his wife, Lucille.

Harlem teenage tennis sensation **Althea Gibson** wins the New York State girls' singles title. A star at the Harlem River Tennis Courts, Gibson is supported by the Harlem Cosmopolitan Tennis Club, which took up a collection to pay for her court membership and tennis lessons.

1943

January. Duke Ellington's orchestra performs *Black, Brown and Beige* at Carnegie Hall. The composition pays homage to spirituals, blues, and jazz.

February 5. The National Urban League Guild sponsors its first Beaux Arts Ball. The affair, organized by Guild president Mollie Moon, attracts three thousand people to the Savoy Ballroom. The extravagant evening features pianist and singer Hazel Scott, actor

National Urban League Guild president Mollie Moon at a Beaux Arts Ball.

African Ceremonial, *1943. Choreographer Pearl Primus performs in her own dance work.*

Canada Lee, and a horse-and-carriage ride from subway entrances at 135th Street to the Savoy for the elaborately costumed attendees.

February 14. *African Ceremonial,* the first work choreographed by dancer Pearl Primus, premieres at the 92nd Street Young Women's Hebrew Association. The Trinidad-born choreographer becomes known for projects with social and cultural relevance.

April. Nineteen-year-old Sarah Vaughn wins the $100 first prize in the Apollo Theatre's amateur night contest singing "Body and Soul." Vaughn also wins a week's engagement at the Apollo. During her run, Billy Eckstein, singer for Earl "Fatha" Hines's band, hears Vaughn and recommends her to Hines, who hires her as his female vocalist. (Eckstein later forms his own band and takes Vaughn with him.

Sarah Vaughn and Billy Eckstein, ca. 1946. The jazz stylists perform together with Earl "Fatha" Hines, later with the Eckstein band.

Influenced by Eckstein band members Charlie Parker and Dizzy Gillespie, Vaughn works extensively on her improvisational style.)

June 20. Blacks and whites in Detroit battle in America's worst race riot of the World War II period. Police kill seventeen blacks but no whites.

The Congress of Racial Equality (CORE) stages the first successful sit-in demonstration at a Chicago restaurant.

August. A Kings County grand jury reports on social conditions in the Bedford-Stuyvesant section of Brooklyn. The jury blames Mayor LaGuardia and the city's other top officials, including the police chief, for neglecting the area and allowing gangs, crime, and physical decay to go unchecked. The grand jury denies that the problems are racial. LaGuardia and his officials win the battle for public opinion by blaming the district's growing number of black residents for its decline.

August 1. Six people are killed and 185 injured in Harlem race rioting. The disturbance is caused when a white policeman attempts to arrest a black woman in the company of a black soldier. (The NAACP's Walter White and Roy Wilkins demand an investigation into the incident. Elsewhere in the United States, racial disturbances occur in Detroit, Mobile, and Beaumont, Texas.)

December. The House Un-American Activities Committee targets two alternative community-based Harlem schools, the Jefferson School for Democracy and the George Washington Carver School, as hotbeds of communism. Poet Gwendolyn Bennett, director of the Carver school, is ousted from her post. NAACP Executive Secretary Walter White, distancing his own organization from any possible charges of communist influence, characterizes the schools as among "a group of similar institutions with which the communists were seeking to increase their influence among Negroes."

J. Raymond Jones forms a political club in Harlem, naming it the George Washington Carver Democratic Club. The club is racially integrated, and unique in that its leader is black.

The Katherine Dunham School of Arts and Research opens in New York City. Students study world culture as part of their training as artists. (Among the artists who later study at the school are Marlon Brando, James Dean, and Arthur Mitchell.)

James Baldwin leaves Harlem and moves downtown to Greenwich Village to write. He rents an apartment for twenty-five dollars a month and works at Calypso, a restaurant on Sullivan Street frequented by Richard Wright.

1944

The United Negro College Fund (UNCF) is established in New York City.

An American Dilemma, the report of the Carnegie-Myrdal study of the Negro in America, 1937–1941, is published. Directed by Swedish social scientist Gunnar Myrdal, the research team includes African American scholars Ralph Bunche, Allison Davis, St. Clair Drake, E. Franklin Frazier, and Charles Johnson, among others.

August 30. *Anna Lucasta* opens on Broadway, transferring from the American Negro Theatre. Hilda Simms and Canada Lee star in the play by Philip Yourdan, adapted by Abram Hill and Harry Wagstaff Gribble. (The play runs on Broadway for almost three years.)

September 11. The American Negro Opera Company debuts at Carnegie Hall.

Communist Party leader Benjamin Davis wins the City Council seat vacated by Adam Clayton Powell Jr., running at Powell's request. (Davis joined the Communist Party after encountering extreme hostility in an Atlanta courtroom during his defense of Angelo Herndon. The presiding judge reportedly addressed Davis in his initial appearance by saying, "Well, nigger, go ahead and say what you have to say." Davis moved to New York in 1935.)

Assembly districts in Manhattan are reduced from twenty-three to sixteen. As a result, Harlem's Twenty-second Assembly District is incorporated into the Thirteenth Assembly District. Leadership of the enlarged Thirteenth District is split in two, with the leadership of its majority black eastern half given to J. Raymond Jones.

The American Negro Theatre production of Anna Lucasta, *1944. Pictured are Canada Lee, Hilda Simms, Alice Childress, and Alvin Childress.*

A federally subsidized apartment complex is built in Fort Greene for shipyard workers and navy dependents in the area surrounding the Brooklyn Navy Yard.

Paul Robeson stars in the Theatre Guild's Broadway production of *Othello.* The cast also features Uta Hagen as Desdemona and Jose Ferrer as Iago. The show sets a Broadway record for a Shakespearean production, with 296 performances. The production tours nationwide after its New York City run.

1945

February 23. Sugar Ray Robinson battles Jake LaMotta at Madison Square Garden in their fourth bout. Robinson wins with a tenth-

Paul Robeson as Othello, 1943–1944.

round decision. (Fights two, won by LaMotta, and three, won by Robinson, were held in Detroit in 1943.)

April. Protesters against major league baseball's segregationist policies picket outside Yankee Stadium on the Yankees' opening day.

April 7. Joe Bostic, a reporter for *The People's Voice*, Congressman Adam Clayton Powell's newspaper, challenges Brooklyn Dodgers president Branch Rickey to give tryouts to two black ballplayers. Bostic confronts Rickey at the Dodgers' upstate Bear Mountain training camp, bringing two black players, pitcher Terris McDuffie and infielder Dave "Showboat" Thomas. They are denied tryouts.

April 25. Black American consultants attending the founding meeting of the United Nations in San Francisco include W. E. B. DuBois, Mary McLeod Bethune, Ralph J. Bunche, and Walter White.

May 1. Manhattan City Councilman Benjamin Davis calls for an investigation of major league baseball's discriminatory policy against African Americans.

July 1. The Ives-Quinn Law goes into effect in New York State, prohibiting employment discrimination. Councilman Benjamin Davis notes that the national offices of both of baseball's major leagues are in New York City and should abide by the new law by admitting black players into the major leagues.

August 1. Adam Clayton Powell Jr., following his divorce from wife Isabel, marries Hazel Scott, the Trinidad-born jazz pianist and popular nightclub singer. The ceremony is held in Stamford, Connecticut, with a reception at Manhattan's Café Society.

August 11. Mayor LaGuardia convenes a panel to investigate discrimination in professional baseball. The panel includes Yankee president Lawrence McPhail, Dodgers president Branch Rickey, St. Martin's Church pastor Dr. John H. Johnson, and dancer Bill "Bojangles" Robinson.

August 27. Brooklyn Dodgers president Branch Rickey meets with **Jackie Robinson** for the first time. He discusses with Robinson the possibility of becoming the first black player in white organized baseball since 1889.

September 2. World War II ends on V-J Day as the Japanese surrender. (A total of 1,154,720 blacks were inducted or drafted; 7,768 black commissioned officers were listed in official records in August 1945; and at the height of the conflict, 3,902 black women were enrolled in the Women's Army Auxiliary Corps [WACS], and 68 in the Navy auxiliary [WAVES].)

September 24. A bronze plaque of Franklin Roosevelt by Selma Burke is unveiled at the White House by President Harry Truman. (Many historians believe the image on the dime is from Burke's work, though credited to mint engraver John R. Sinnock.)

October 20. Mayor LaGuardia's committee on discrimination in baseball issues its findings. The committee concludes that prejudice and tradition are the fundamental reasons for the continuation of segregated baseball teams.

October 23. Branch Rickey announces the signing of Jackie Robinson as a player for the Montreal Royals, the Brooklyn Dodgers' minor league affiliate.

Former Brooklyn District Attorney William O'Dwyer runs against LaGuardia for mayor. Needing the black vote, O'Dwyer hires J. Raymond Jones as his personal secretary. O'Dwyer declares Jones "my eyes and ears in Harlem."

The Stuyvesant Community Center opens in a three-story building in Bedford-Stuyvesant, Brooklyn. Directed by Albert Edwards, the center offers services to the growing black population of the area.

The Daughters of the American Revolution refuse to allow Hazel Scott to perform in Constitution Hall. Scott's husband, U.S. Representative Adam Clayton Powell Jr., publicly criticizes First Lady Bess Truman for her continued ties to the D.A.R. (Powell's remarks so anger President Truman that the congressman is never again invited to the Truman White House.)

Nora Douglas Holt is the first black person accepted into the Music Critics Circle of New York.

Writer Dorothy West leaves Harlem and moves to Massachusetts, where she writes a weekly column for the *Martha's Vineyard Gazette.*

Richard Wright moves to 82 Washington Place in Greenwich Village. (Following protests by white neighbors, Wright moves his family to Paris in 1947.)

Printmaker and sculptor Elizabeth Catlett receives a Julius Rosenwald Foundation award to do compositions on African American women. Catlett uses the award to begin work on her graphic series, *Negro Woman,* while serving as director of Manhattan's George Washington Carver School.

1946

June 3. The U.S. Supreme Court bans segregation in interstate bus travel.

Paul Robeson leads a delegation from the American Crusade to End Lynching to see President Harry Truman, demanding that he sponsor antilynching legislation.

The U.S. Justice Department sues the Mortgage Conference of New York, a coalition of banks, for discriminating against black and Latino residents of the city. The suit claims that the Conference has mapped each borough demographically and conspired to deny loans to nonwhite people and in nonwhite areas.

Ella J. Baker is elected president of the New York branch of the NAACP. She is the first woman to hold the position.

Constance Baker Motley becomes a law clerk for Thurgood Marshall at the NAACP's Legal Defense Fund after graduating from Columbia Law School. Motley, whose parents were immigrants from Nevis, was born in New Haven, Connecticut.

The National Urban League reports that there are only twenty-two licensed black electricians in New York City. Only six black electricians have been admitted to the International Brotherhood of Electrical Workers. Only six black men are in the plumbers' local, and only two black men belong to the plasterers' union.

Psychologists Kenneth and Mamie Clark create the Northside Center for Child Development, the first comprehensive agency to deal with the psychological and social needs of black children.

Compositions from the *Zodiac Suite,* by Mary Lou Williams, are performed at Carnegie Hall by the New York Philharmonic Orchestra— the first time the orchestra has performed works by a black woman jazz composer. Williams, who has written music for Louis Armstrong, Duke Ellington, Tommy Dorsey, and Benny Goodman, presents three pieces: "Aquarius," "Pisces," and "Scorpio."

Sugar Ray Robinson beats Tommy Bell in a fifteen-round decision at Madison Square Garden to win the vacant welterweight championship.

Camilla Williams is the first black woman to perform with the New York City Opera.

Pearl Bailey makes her Broadway debut as Butterfly in *St. Louis Woman,* which also features the tap-dancing Nicholas Brothers. Bailey wins the 1946 Donaldson Award for most promising newcomer of the year. The show's book is by Arna Bontemps and Countee Cullen, lyrics by Johnny Mercer, and music by Harold Arlen.

Elizabeth Catlett is awarded a second Rosenwald Fellowship. She and her husband, painter Charles White, leave New York and travel to Mexico, where they work with Taller de Grafica Popular, a collective of socially active artists. (Catlett's activism eventually gets her labeled an "undesirable" by the U.S. State Department. She divorces White, marries Mexican painter Francisco Mora, and eventually becomes chair of the sculpture department at the National School of Fine Arts at the Universidad Nacional Autonoma de Mexico.)

1947

April. The House Committee on Un-American Activities cites Paul Robeson as "supporting the Communist Party and its front organizations."

Elizabeth Catlett's Political Prisoner, *1971.*

Broadway cast of St. Louis Woman, *1946. Left to right: Harold Nicholas, Ruby Hill, Fayard Nicholas, and Pearl Bailey.*

April 10. Jackie Robinson plays his first game for the Brooklyn Dodgers at Ebbets Field, breaking the major league color barrier.

August 21. Lena Horne is greeted by 200,000 fans and admirers in Brooklyn as the borough celebrates Lena Horne Day. A motorcade accompanies her as she is driven through the streets where she played during her childhood. At Borough Hall she is presented with the key to Brooklyn. A singer and actress, Horne makes many films in the 1940s, including *Panama Hattie, Cabin in the Sky, Stormy Weather, I Dood It, Swing Fever, Thousands Cheer, Broadway Rhythm,* and *Two Girls and a Sailor.*

October 23. The NAACP files "An Appeal to the World" with the United Nations, requesting intervention in U.S. domestic affairs on behalf of a suffering and persecuted minority.

Jackie Robinson and teammate Dan Bankhead are the first black players in a World Series in the playoff against the Yankees. Robinson is named Rookie of the Year.

Mayor William O'Dwyer appoints J. Raymond Jones Deputy Commissioner of Housing and Buildings, making Jones the city's highest-

Jackie Robinson at Ebbets Field.

ranking and highest-paid black political appointee. Jones's new job, along with his membership on the New York County Democratic Executive Committee and his position as District Leader of the Thirteenth Assembly District East, makes him the most powerful black politician in Harlem—Congressman Adam Clayton Powell Jr. notwithstanding. But more so than Powell, Jones is regarded as a genius with campaign strategies, petitions, and election laws.

Urban planner Robert Moses uses eminent domain to help Metropolitan Life build the 8,756-unit Stuyvesant Town on the Lower East Side. The development is for whites only.

Marie M. Daly becomes the first black woman to receive a Ph.D. in chemistry, earning a degree from Columbia University.

Trinidad emigrant Jesse Wattle organizes the first Caribbean street carnival along Seventh Avenue in Harlem.

The nation's oldest black college, Wilberforce University, defeats Bergen College of New Jersey 40–12 at Madison Square Garden in the first basketball game ever between black and white colleges.

Two New York professional football teams, the New York Yankees and the Brooklyn Dodgers, both members of the All American Football Conference, sign black players to their squads. The Yankees acquire running back Buddy Young, and the Dodgers hire running back Elmore Harris.

1948

June 25. Joe Louis knocks out Jersey Joe Walcott in the eleventh round of their bout at Madison Square Garden to retain his heavyweight title.

The U.S. Supreme Court rules in favor of the NAACP in *Shelley v. Kraemer,* declaring restrictive housing covenants "unenforceable as law." (Despite the ruling, covenants denying blacks the right of rental or home ownership are regularly approved by the Federal Housing Authority until 1968.)

Harry Haywood, a leader of the Harlem Communist Party, publishes *Negro Liberation,* a study of the social and economic conditions of African Americans. He finished the work with financial support from Paul Robeson.

Henry Lee Moon's *Balance of Power: The Negro Vote*, a study of black voting patterns after Reconstruction, is published. He argues that the black voting bloc is crucial in presidential elections. Moon is hired as public relations director of the NAACP.

Claudia Jones and other New York City Communist Party leaders are arrested on charges of sedition. Jones is nearly deported before a protest campaign persuades the federal government to free her on bail.

Jean Blackwell Hutson is named curator of the Schomburg Collection of Negro Literature and History at the New York Public Library's 135th Street Branch.

Gordon Parks becomes a photojournalist with *Life* magazine. (He completes more than three hundred assignments during nearly a quarter of a century.)

Communist Party leaders Claudia Jones and Benjamin Davis at party headquarters in Harlem, 1948.

Jean Blackwell Hutson and Langston Hughes, pictured at the Schomburg Collection with Pietro Calvi's bust of Ira Aldridge as Othello.

The Beaux Arts Ball breaks the color line at Rockefeller Center's Rainbow Room. To ensure desegregation of the elegant nightclub, ball organizer Mollie Moon names Winthrop Rockefeller a co-host for the annual dance. (She says later that she chose a Rockefeller because "nobody was going to buck the landlord.")

The National Football League's New York Giants sign safety Emlen Tunnell from the University of Iowa. (Tunnell, a World War II veteran, is named All-Pro four times and sets an NFL record of seventy-nine interceptions.)

Billie Holiday returns to New York City after serving nine and one-half months at the Federal Reformatory for Women in Alderson, West Virginia, for illegal narcotics possession. Upon her arrival in New York, Holiday learns that her cabaret card has been revoked and she is barred from performing in local clubs.

1949

March 1. Heavyweight champion Joe Louis announces he is retiring from boxing.

May 21. The first New York chapter of The Links, Inc. is organized by Dorothy Reed and Bernia L. Austin at the invitation of Links' co-founders Margaret Hawkins and Sarah S. Scott of Philadelphia. The eight-member chapter, which focuses on the educational, civic, and cultural interests of African American women, elects Reed as its first president.

August 8. Dr. Peter Marshall Murray is elected to the American Medical Association's (AMA) House of Delegates. The first black member of the AMA body, Murray is a former president of the all-black National Medical Association.

September 23. New York City Councilman Benjamin Davis Jr. is one of eleven Communist leaders convicted in federal court of conspiring to overthrow the United States government. (Despite the conviction, Davis's name remains on the November election ballot, though he loses to a coalition candidate representing the Republican, Democratic, and Liberal parties. In 1951 he is sent to federal prison in Indiana, where he serves three years and four months. At the end of his sentence, he serves an additional two months at the Allegheny County Jail in Pittsburgh, Pennsylvania, for having refused, in 1953, to reveal the names of people belonging to the Communist Party's Commission on Negro Work. In prison, Davis begins work on his unpublished autobiography.)

Bertram Baker wins a seat in the state assembly.

Title I of the Housing Act of 1949 provides "slum clearance" funds. Using the federal money, Robert Moses constructs low-income projects in the South Bronx and the Brownsville section of Brooklyn. (Historians later determine that Moses made secret deals with real-estate agents for the development of middle- and upper-middle-class white communities such as Kew Gardens, Fresh Meadows, Brighton Beach, and Lefrak City, without regard for comprehensive planning for the black and Hispanic tenants who were displaced.)

The New York City–based National Association of Colored Graduate Nurses dissolves itself, closing its offices at Rockefeller Center, where it has been located since the mid-1930s. The black nurses take the action as the all-white American Nurses Association ends its segregationist policies.

The New York Giants baseball team signs Henry Thompson as the team's first black player.

Brooklyn Dodger pitcher Don Newcombe is named the National League's Rookie of the Year.

Conductor Dean Dixon, unable to secure a permanent position with a major American orchestra, leaves for Europe. (Dixon works abroad until 1970, when he returns to the United States following engagements with Sweden's Göteborg Symphony Orchestra, Germany's Hessian Radio Symphony Orchestra, and the Sydney Symphony Orchestra in Australia.)

Carol Diann Johnson, a fourteen-year-old singer raised in Harlem and the Bronx, wins first prize on Arthur Godfrey's *Talent Scouts*. (A student at New York City's High School of Music and Art, she later assumes the stage name Diahann Carroll.)

1950

January 15. New Yorkers are among the more than four thousand delegates from one hundred national organizations attending the National Emergency Civil Rights Conference in Washington, D.C.

May 1. Gwendolyn Brooks is the first black recipient of a Pulitzer Prize, winning the award for her book of poetry, Annie Allen.

June 28. Paul Robeson, speaking at a Civil Rights Congress rally at Madison Square Garden, calls on President Truman to stop sending troops to Korea. Robeson is particularly incensed that black soldiers are being sent to fight Koreans: "I have said it before and I say it again, that the place for the Negro people to fight for their freedom is here at home."

July. The U.S. State Department revokes Paul Robeson's passport. (Robeson's career and income plummet as he refuses to denounce the Soviet Union. Robeson is criticized by many black leaders, including Walter White, Roy Wilkins, and Jackie Robinson, but his "inalienable right to speak and sing to all who wish to hear him" is endorsed in a joint statement by Mary Church Terrell, Adam Clayton Powell Jr., and other black leaders despite their disagreements with his position on Russia and Communism.)

Ralph Bunche wins the Nobel Peace Prize for successfully negotiating the 1949 armistice between Egypt and Israel.

September 27. Joe Louis comes out of retirement to fight Ezzard Charles at Madison Square Garden for the heavyweight title. Charles scores a fifteen-round decision over Louis.

United Nations diplomat Ralph Bunche.

U.S. Representative Adam Clayton Powell Jr. proposes the "Powell Amendment" in the U.S. House of Representatives. The bill, offered with the backing of the NAACP, would eliminate federal funding to any segregated facility or institution. (Powell brings the proposal before Congress annually until its implementation in the 1964 Civil Rights Act.)

Claudia Jones and fifteen other New York City Communist Party leaders are arrested under the Smith Act, for "teaching and advocating Marxism." She is convicted and sent to federal prison for one year.

The city housing authority plans construction of spartan high-rise (ten- to sixteen-story) projects in low-income communities. (During the 1950s, about one third of East Harlem is leveled to create the Wagner, Taft, and Jefferson complexes. More than 75,000 austerely designed low-income units are constructed, housing more than 500,000 low-income tenants.)

Dr. Muriel Petioni opens a medical practice at 114 West 131st Street. The Trinidad-born daughter of a Harlem physician, Petioni pioneers in the successful treatment of drug addiction.

Charles Alston sells a painting to the Metropolitan Museum of Art. He also becomes the first black instructor at the Art Students League in Manhattan.

Four black players are on the Brooklyn Dodgers roster: Jackie Robinson, Roy Campanella, Dan Bankhead, and Don Newcombe. With only nine black players in the major leagues, many fans consider the Dodgers to be black America's team.

The New York Knickerbockers sign Nathaniel "Sweetwater" Clifton from Xavier University as their first black player. (In the 1950–1951 season Clifton plays in sixty-five games, averaging 7.5 rebounds and 8.6 points per game.)

Elayne Jones joins the New York City Opera and Ballet as a percussionist after graduating from Juilliard. She is a native New Yorker of Barbadian ancestry.

1951

Governor Adlai Stevenson orders the National Guard to suppress rioting by four thousand whites protesting the attempt by a black family to occupy a home in all-white Cicero, Illinois.

May 25. Willie Howard Mays joins the New York Giants. (The Giants, in fifth place when Mays joins the team, go on to win the pennant.)

June 21. Pfc. William Thompson of Brooklyn is awarded the Congressional Medal of Honor posthumously for heroism in Korea. It is the first grant of the medal to an African American since the Spanish-American War.

October. Appearing in *Aïda*, Janet Collins is the first black ballerina to perform at the Metropolitan Opera. (She is a former member of the Katherine Dunham dance troupe.)

October 26. Joe Louis is knocked out by Rocky Marciano in the eighth round at Madison Square Garden. The bout is Louis's last.

Civil rights attorney William L. Patterson's Civil Rights Congress presents the United Nations with a "We Charge Genocide" petition listing hundreds of acts of genocidal violence against African Americans.

Ella Baker runs unsuccessfully as a Liberal party candidate for city council.

Dodger catcher Roy Campanella is named the National League's Most Valuable Player of the year.

Tennis star Althea Gibson becomes the first African American to play in England's Wimbledon tennis tournament.

1952

Charlotta Bass resigns as editor of the California Eagle *and runs for vice president of the United States on the Progressive Party ticket.*

Congressman Adam Clayton Powell Jr. supports Averill Harriman for the Democratic presidential nomination. Harriman loses to

Adlai Stevenson, who infuriates Powell by selecting Senator John Sparkman of Alabama as his vice-presidential running mate.

The City Council passes the Sharkey-Brown-Isaacs Bill, which bars discrimination against children in agencies receiving city funds, and gives the commissioner of welfare the right to terminate funding if discrimination exists. Some white agencies go out of business rather than accept black children.

Choreographer and dancer Cholly Atkins teaches tap at the Katherine Dunham School of Arts and Research. Regularly partnered with Charles "Honi" Coles, Atkins also begins teaching choreography to vocal groups. (Among the groups Atkins will coach are the Cadillacs and Frankie Lymon and the Teenagers. In the 1960s Atkins becomes staff choreographer for Motown Records, coaching the Supremes, the Temptations, and Gladys Knight and the Pips.)

John Oliver Killens, novelist, teacher, and civil rights activist, establishes the Harlem Writers Guild.

Chicago-born **Lorraine Hansberry,** a recent graduate of the University of Wisconsin, joins the staff of *Freedom* as associate editor. Hansberry writes the pageant that commemorates the first anniversary of the Harlem-based newspaper founded by Paul Robeson.

Eartha Kitt stars on Broadway in *New Faces of 1952*. (Born in South Carolina, Kitt moved to New York City to live with an aunt, and became a dancer and singer with the Katherine Dunham troupe.)

1953

March 24. Langston Hughes is summoned to Washington, D.C., to testify before the Senate Permanent Sub-Committee on Investigations chaired by Senator Joseph McCarthy. Questioned by Roy Cohn and McCarthy, Hughes admits past sympathy for the Communist party but states flatly, "I am not a member of the Communist Party now and have never been a member of the Communist Party." (Prior to the Senate hearing, gossip columnist Walter Winchell had several times listed Hughes as a known communist.)

November 3. Bronx Assistant District Attorney Walter Gladwin is elected to the New York State Assembly. The British Guiana–born Gladwin wins in the predominantly black and Puerto Rican Seventh District, becoming the borough's first black Assemblyman.

November 3. Hulan Jack wins election as Manhattan Borough President. The borough's first black president, Jack is the first African American to hold a major elective office in a major American city.

Percy E. Sutton opens a law office in Harlem with his brother, Oliver, and George Covington, and begins working on cases for the NAACP.

Manhattan Borough President Hulan Jack at tree planting ceremony, March 16, 1959.

Ann Lowe is chosen as dress designer for the wedding of Jacqueline Bouvier and John Fitzgerald Kennedy. Lowe creates gowns for the bride, the bridesmaids, and the mother of the bride.

Amsterdam News senior music critic Nora Holt is musical director-producer of *Concert Showcase,* a program airing on radio station WLIB. A founding member of the National Association of Negro Musicians, Holt is former music critic for the *Chicago Defender.*

Brooklyn Dodger catcher Roy Campanella is named the National League's Most Valuable Player of the year.

1954

January 1. Anna Arnold Hedgeman, named mayoral assistant by Mayor Robert Wagner, is the first black woman in a mayor's cabinet.

May 17. The U.S. Supreme Court rules that segregation is unconstitutional in Brown v. Board of Education of Topeka, Kansas.

June 1. Emperor Haile Selassie of Ethiopia is honored with a ticker-tape parade in lower Manhattan. President William V. S. Tubman of Liberia receives the same honor in October.

The Federal Housing Act of 1954 makes low-interest loans available for urban renewal and redevelopment. Critics argue that slum clearance is used to control the city's racial geography, raze black neighborhoods for white private development, and buffer white neighborhoods from blacks.

Dr. Peter Marshall Murray is elected president of the Medical Society of the County of New York. (Murray will also serve as vice president of the Hospital Council of Greater New York from 1954 to 1961.)

Bessie Allison Buchanan is elected to the New York State Assembly from Harlem. The first black woman to serve in the assembly, Buchanan is a native New Yorker.

Youngblood, by John Oliver Killens, is the first book published by a member of the Harlem Writers Guild. Members, who include Rosa Guy, Walter Christmas, and **John Henrik Clarke,** meet regularly to critique each other's work. (Later Guild members include Maya

Emperor Haile Selassie of Ethiopia with Adam Clayton Powell Jr., 1954. The Emperor presents a coptic cross to the Abyssinian Baptist Church.

Angelou, Chester Himes, Ossie Davis, Louise Meriwether, Walter Mosley, Walter Dean Myers, and Terry McMillan.)

Paule Marshall graduates cum laude and Phi Beta Kappa from Brooklyn College. Working as a researcher for *Our World* magazine, Marshall, raised in Brooklyn's West Indian community, begins to write short stories, including her first, "The Valley Between."

Norma Merrick becomes the first black woman to be licensed as an architect in New York State. Born in New York City, the Barnard College graduate is employed at the prestigious firm of Skidmore, Owings and Merrill, and as an instructor at the City College of New York. (In 1962 she becomes the first black woman to be licensed as an architect in California.)

1955

January 7. Marian Anderson makes her debut at the Metropolitan Opera House as Ulrica in Verdi's *Masked Ball*. She is the first African American singer in the company's history.

January 31. Paul Eugène Maloire, President of Haiti, is honored with a ticker-tape parade in lower Manhattan.

April. Elston Howard signs a contract with the New York Yankees. Howard, a catcher who formerly played with the Kansas City Monarchs in the Negro Leagues, is the Yankees' first black player.

April 18. The Bandung Conference of leaders of nations of Africa and Asia opens in Indonesia.

May 31. The U.S. Supreme Court, attempting to reach full compliance with its 1954 ruling, orders school districts to use "all deliberate speed" to achieve the Court's mandate.

August 27. The body of fourteen-year-old Emmett Till of Chicago is found floating in the Tallahatchie River in Leflore County, Mississippi. He was allegedly killed for whistling at a white woman. (Two men charged with the murder are found not guilty by an all-white Mississippi jury.)

Robert C. Weaver, a Harvard-trained housing specialist, becomes commissioner of the New York State Rent Administration. He is the first black member of the New York State cabinet.

Roy Wilkins becomes the third executive secretary of the NAACP following the death of Walter White. Wilkins is a strong opponent of segregation and an advocate of protection of voting rights and equality in housing, jobs, and public accommodations.

Claudia Jones is arrested again for her activities with the Communist Party. This time she is deported and relocates to London, where she continues her work with the party. (In England, Jones becomes editor of the *West Indian Gazette* and works with the Caribbean Labour Congress.)

Author and playwright Alice Childress is the first black woman to win an Obie Award. She wins for her off-Broadway play, *Trouble in Mind*, a play about white directors who insist on presenting black stereotypes.

The Coordinating Council for Negro Performers leads a boycott against television to stress the desire for more black performers in the medium. Actress Rosetta LeNoire is among the council's organizers.

Roy Campanella is named National League Most Valuable Player for the third time.

December 1. Rosa Parks, a seamstress and civic leader, ignites the Montgomery, Alabama, bus boycott by refusing to give up her bus seat to a white man. Reverend Martin Luther King Jr. is elected as leader of the protest.

1956

March. The **Rev. Dr. Gardner C. Taylor,** pastor of Concord Baptist Church in Brooklyn, hosts Dr. Martin Luther King Jr. at a fundraiser. Ella J. Baker, Bayard Rustin, and white civil rights supporter Stanley Levinson form In Friendship, which works as a fundraising arm for the southern civil rights movement.

May 26. Althea Gibson wins the women's singles title at the French Open.

June 12. Subpoenaed by the House Un-American Activities Committee, Paul Robeson travels from his home at 16 Jumel Terrace in Harlem to Washington, D.C. Asked by a Congressional inquisitor why, if he liked Russia so much, he did not stay there, Robeson replied, "Because my father was a slave, and my people died to build this country, and I'm going to stay right here and have a part

Labor Day I felt happy,
Because I played Carnival in New York
    City
Seventh Avenue was jumpin'
Everybody was shakin'

From 110 to 142,
We had bands of every description . . .
This is the first time New York ever had
Carnival on the streets like Trinidad.

    —Calypso singer Lord Invader, 1956

of it, just like you. And no fascist-minded people like you will drive me from it. Is that clear?"

November 9. Coloratura soprano Mattiwilda Dobbs appears as Gilda in the Metropolitan Opera production of Verdi's *Rigoletto*. Dobbs is the second black woman to perform at the Met, following Marian Anderson; and the third African American, following Robert McFerrin.

Congressman Adam Clayton Powell Jr. endorses Republican President Dwight D. Eisenhower for re-election, angering Tammany Hall. Democratic Party leader Carmine DeSapio exiles Powell from party support.

Historian John Hope Franklin joins the faculty at Brooklyn College.

1957

Eighty-six percent of all black Brooklynites live in the Bedford-Stuyvesant section. Bedford-Stuyvesant is also the district with the lowest median income in the borough.

February 13. Martin Luther King Jr. forms the Southern Christian Leadership Conference (SCLC) in New Orleans.

Martin Luther King Jr. and Harry Belafonte being interviewed by George Goodman of WLIB Radio, 1962.

March. Ghana becomes an independent African state.

April. The Broadway opening of Alice Childress's play, *So Early Monday Morning,* is canceled, as the playwright refuses to make changes suggested by a white director. The play, an adaptation of her 1956 off-Broadway hit, *Trouble in Mind,* centers on tensions that arise among a group of black and white actors and a white director in presenting a story about a Southern lynching.

July 6. Althea Gibson becomes the first black woman to win the Wimbledon singles tennis championship. Gibson also wins the doubles with partner Darlene Hard. Several days later she is honored with a ticker-tape parade in lower Manhattan.

August 29. The Civil Rights Act of 1957, the first federal civil rights legislation since 1875, establishes a Civil Rights Commission and a Civil Rights Division of the U.S. Department of Justice.

President Dwight D. Eisenhower sends one thousand paratroopers from the 101st Airborne Division to intervene in Little Rock, Arkansas, after Governor Orval Faubus orders units of the National Guard to block desegregation of Central High School by the "Little Rock Nine."

September 8. Althea Gibson wins the women's singles title at Forest Hills, Queens, defeating Louise Brough to become the first African American to win a major U.S. national championship.

December 5. New York becomes the first city to legislate against racial or religious discrimination in the housing market with the adoption of a Fair Housing Practices Law.

December 9. King Mohammed V of Morocco is honored with a ticker-tape parade in lower Manhattan.

Malcolm X assembles the city's first major Muslim protest and negotiates a release to the hospital for Johnson Hinton, a member of his mosque who was arrested and brutally beaten for intervening with a police officer who had beaten a black woman and man. The group marches in formation behind the ambulance and remains at the hospital until doctors pronounce Hinton out of danger.

J. Daniel Diggs becomes Brooklyn's first African American city councilman.

Tennis champion Althea Gibson.

Daniel Fignold is provisional president of Haiti for nineteen days. He emigrates to Brooklyn immediately after his term, establishes himself among the Haitian community, and continues his political activism.

James Allen becomes director of the Addicts Rehabilitation Center (ARC), an outgrowth of a program founded by Rev. Eugene Callendar.

Langston Hughes's musical *Simply Heavenly* opens in New York City.

Cicely Tyson stars in the Harlem YMCA's Little Theatre production of *Dark of the Moon,* directed by Vinnette Carroll. Born in Harlem to an immigrant couple from Nevis, West Indies, Tyson is an actress and a model.

Harlem-born actor Ivan Dixon III makes his Broadway debut in *The Cave Dwellers,* by William Saroyan. (Dixon's film career begins the following year in *The Defiant Ones* as a stunt double for Sidney Poitier.)

1958

January 23. Althea Gibson is the first African American voted Woman Athlete of the Year by the Associated Press.

June. Elijah Muhammad appoints Malcolm X minister of Harlem's Temple Number 7. In the temple and on Harlem street corners, Malcolm lectures on his black nationalist doctrine, "We are black first and everything else second." (Malcolm later writes about the impact of Harlem on his own Nebraska family and upbringing.)

September 20. Martin Luther King Jr. is stabbed in the chest by Izola Curry, a black woman, while autographing copies of *Stride Toward Freedom,* the story of the Montgomery bus boycott, in a Harlem store. (Curry is later ruled insane.)

Adam Clayton Powell Jr. seeks re-election without support from Tammany Hall. Opposed by Carmine DeSapio and Manhattan Borough President Hulan Jack, Powell enlists the support of J. Raymond Jones, who helps the incumbent easily defeat Tammany candidate Earl Brown. Jones, out of city politics since 1950, re-emerges as the preeminent local black political leader.

Clifford L. Alexander graduates from Yale Law School and is appointed assistant district attorney for New York County. (Alexander's undergraduate years were at Harvard University, where he served as the student council's first black president.)

LeRoi Jones (later **Amiri Baraka**) publishes the first issue of *Zazen,* a magazine devoted to "A New Consciousness in Arts & Letters."

Adam's [Clayton Powell Jr.] year might be 1958, but 1959 was mine and I knew that, with the Presidential election coming up the next year, sooner or later somebody would be in touch with me. Negroes were on the move throughout the U.S. They were registering in increasing numbers, and a large part of the white population had now come to its senses and were supporting us. The election for the presidency could not be won by any white person without the Negro vote.

—J. Raymond Jones,
The Harlem Fox, 1989

My father, the Reverend Earl Little, was a Baptist minister, a dedicated organizer for Marcus Garvey's UNIA. With the help of such disciples as my father, Garvey, from his headquarters in New York City's Harlem was raising the banner of black race purity and exhorting the Negro masses to return to their ancestral African homeland—a cause which had made Garvey the most controversial black man on earth.

—Malcolm X,
The Autobiography of Malcolm X, 1965

285

Malcolm X addressing a Harlem rally in front of the Hotel Theresa.

(The first and subsequent *Zazen* issues include work by Jones, Allen Ginsberg, and Jack Kerouac. A year earlier, Jones had moved to Greenwich Village from Newark following a stint in the U.S. Air Force. Later he recalls the education he received interacting with new schools of writers—Beat and Black Mountain—and watching Langston Hughes reading to the music of Charles Mingus at the Five Spot.)

Caryn Johnson, an eight-year-old child from a New York City housing project, begins acting at the Helena Rubinstein Children's Theatre at the Hudson Guild. (As an adult she will change her name to **Whoopi Goldberg.**)

Harlem's Savoy Ballroom at 596 Lenox Avenue is demolished to make way for a housing project. (Famous dances developed there through the years include the Lindy Hop, Peckin', Truckin', the Suzy Q, and the Congeroo.)

Texas-born dancer **Alvin Ailey** forms his own dance company. The Alvin Ailey American Dance Theater begins as a repertory company of seven dancers dedicated to new works and modern dance classics.

Band leader Machito and vocalist Graciela at the Savoy.

The Alvin Ailey American Dance
Theater performing its signature piece,
Revelations, ca. 1965.

1959

March 1. Playwright Lorraine Hansberry delivers a speech, "The Negro Writer and His Roots," at a writer's conference sponsored by the American Society of African Culture in New York. Hansberry declares that "all art is ultimately social."

March 11. Lorraine Hansberry's *A Raisin in the Sun* opens at the Ethel Barrymore Theater, with **Sidney Poitier,** Claudia McNeil, **Ruby Dee,** and Diana Sands. At twenty-nine, Hansberry is the youngest American, the fifth woman, and the first black playwright to win the New York Drama Critics Circle Award for Best Play of the Year. For her performance as Beneatha, Diana Sands wins the Variety Critic's Award for most promising young actress and the Outer Critics Circle Award as best supporting actress. (Bronx-born Sands is a graduate of Manhattan's High School of Performing Arts.)

November 4. Sékou Touré, Premier of Guinea, is honored with a ticker-tape parade in lower Manhattan.

The Negro American Labor Council is formed by black workers within the AFL-CIO who feel that they will continually be denied the rights afforded to white workers. James Haughton, chief organizer for the council, notes that its goal is to "build a black workers' movement, independent of any political party . . . that would be conscious of its historical mission and not impeded and divided by racism."

James Dumpson is named the first black to head a department of public welfare in a major American city. He urges the city to develop programs that will help black families and youth.

Paule Marshall's novel *Brown Girl, Brownstones* is published. It is the compassionate story of a black immigrant family's struggles in Brooklyn.

Author and social critic Lorraine Hansberry.

Rehearsal for A Raisin in the Sun, *1959. Director Lloyd Richards with cast members Sidney Poitier, Ruby Dee, Claudia McNeil, and Diana Sands.*

Glancing down the interminable Brooklyn street you thought of those joined brownstones as one house reflected through a train of mirrors, with no walls between the houses but only vast rooms yawning endlessly one into the other. Yet, looking close, you saw that under the thick ivy each house had something distinctively its own. Some touch that was Gothic, Romanesque, baroque or Greek triumphed amid the Victorian clutter.

—Paule Marshall
Brown Girl, Brownstones

New York City's black population is 1,087,931, or 13.98% of the total, 7,781,984. The city's black population ranks first in the nation, ahead of Chicago, Philadelphia, Detroit, and the District of Columbia.

Harry Belafonte's *Odds Against Tomorrow* is the first modern film produced by an African American.

November 29. South Africa–born singer Miriam Makeba comes to New York to pursue her entertainment career at the urging of Harry Belafonte. (In New York, Makeba records South African music, featuring songs in her native Xhosa, with its distinctive clicking sounds.)

The Harlem Y production of *Dark of the Moon* moves downtown to the Equity Library Theater. The play's cast includes James Earl Jones, Isabel Sandford, and Cicely Tyson, with choreography by Alvin Ailey.

1960

February 1. Four North Carolina A&T College students trigger a sit-in movement when they refuse to leave a "whites-only" Woolworth's lunch counter in Greensboro, North Carolina, after being denied service.

May 6. The Civil Rights Act of 1960 makes it unlawful to flee to avoid prosecution for bombing offenses.

June 20. Mayor Robert Wagner proclaims "World Championship Day" in New York City, awarding boxer Floyd Patterson the city's medallion for regaining his heavyweight title from Ingmar Johansson a week earlier.

December. The marriage of Adam Clayton Powell Jr. and Hazel Scott ends with a divorce in Juarez, Mexico. Powell then travels to Puerto Rico, where he marries Yvette Diago, his twenty-nine-year-old Puerto Rican secretary.

Sam Rayburn, Speaker of the U.S. House of Representatives, invites J. Raymond Jones to Capitol Hill, where he enlists Jones to support Texas senator Lyndon Baines Johnson's nomination for president at the Democratic National Convention. Jones, following consultation with Congressman Adam Clayton Powell Jr., strikes a deal committing support for Johnson on the first two ballots, in exchange for Rayburn's commitment to arrange for Powell to become chairman of the powerful House Education and Labor Committee.

Democratic presidential hopeful John Kennedy's campaign allegedly attempts to bribe J. Raymond Jones to back off from his support for Lyndon Johnson. (Years later, Jones brings the claimed payoff to light in his autobiography, *The Harlem Fox*.)

Jackie Robinson appears at Brooklyn's Concord Baptist Church to appeal for support for Republican presidential candidate Richard M. Nixon.

World and national leaders in New York for the opening of the United Nations General Assembly visit Harlem. They include Soviet Premier Nikita Khrushchev; Cuban Prime Minister Fidel Castro;

Fidel Castro dining with employees at the Hotel Theresa, 1960.

President Kwame Nkrumah of Ghana; Sam Nnujoma, leader of the Southwest Africa Peoples Organization (SWAPO); and Nation of Islam leader Elijah Muhammad. Castro and his delegates stay at the Hotel Theresa in Harlem.

The Negro American Labor Council is organized with A. Philip Randolph as president. (In 1972 it is replaced by the Coalition of Black Trade Unionists.)

The newspaper *Muhammad Speaks* is founded by Nation of Islam leader Elijah Muhammad and run by New York Temple leader Malcolm X. Under Malcolm's direction it evolves from a monthly to a weekly paper.

A Puerto Rican in New York, and Other Sketches, a book by **Jesus Colon,** a journalist and political activist, is published by Mainstream Publishers.

Afro-Cuban singer **Celia Cruz** leaves Cuba and debuts in New York City. (During the 1960s Cruz tours with orchestra leader Tito Puento and becomes known as the "Queen of Salsa.")

1961

January. Congressman Adam Clayton Powell Jr. is elected Chairman of the House Education and Labor Committee.

January 31. Diplomat and lawyer Edward R. Dudley is elected by the City Council to finish Hulan Jack's term as Manhattan borough president. Dudley, a Carver Democratic Club member and a former Ambassador to Liberia, replaces Jack, who resigned after being convicted of accepting an illegal gift of $4,500.

May 4. CORE leader James Farmer heads a group of thirteen Freedom Riders departing from Washington, D.C., for Anniston, Alabama, in a move to desegregate bus terminals. After attacks in Anniston, Birmingham, and Montgomery, Attorney General Robert F. Kennedy dispatches four hundred U.S. marshals to Montgomery to keep order.

May 11. Tunisian president Habib Bourguiba is honored with a ticker-tape parade in lower Manhattan. Ibrahim Abboud, president of the Sudan, is accorded the same honor in October.

September 28. **Ossie Davis**'s *Purlie Victorious* opens on Broadway.

November. The Interstate Commerce Commission prohibits segregated hotel and motel accommodations.

November 7. Incumbent Edward Dudley, running as a Democrat-Liberal, wins the general election for Manhattan borough president. (In 1962, Dudley is the first black nominated by either major political party for a high-ranking state office: attorney general. Dudley edges out Republican opponent Louis J. Lefkowitz among New York City voters, but is defeated by a wide margin upstate and in the suburbs. Dudley continues as borough president until January 1, 1965. In 1970 he is appointed administrative judge of the New York State Supreme Court.)

Mayor Robert F. Wagner Jr., fighting for his political life, turns to J. Raymond Jones to run his campaign. All five Democratic County leaders, led by Tammany's Carmine DeSapio, oppose Wagner's reelection. Jones's petition expertise overcomes DeSapio's drive to keep Wagner off the ballot. Wagner wins with an overwhelming percentage of black votes.

Charles Rangel is appointed assistant U.S. Attorney for the Southern District of New York.

Percy Sutton is elected branch president of the New York City Chapter of the NAACP. During his two-year term, Sutton participates in demonstrations and freedom rides throughout the South.

Whitney M. Young Jr. replaces Lester Granger as executive director of the National Urban League. Under Young's leadership the League becomes an active participant in the civil rights movement.

Clifford Alexander is named executive director of the Manhattanville–Hamilton Grange Neighborhood Conservation Project. The project enforces housing code standards for landlords in an effort to improve housing.

The first issue of *Freedomways: A Quarterly Review of the Black Freedom Movement* is published with Shirley Graham as editor; W.

Alphaeus Hunton, associate editor; Margaret G. Burroughs, art editor; and Esther Jackson, managing editor.

Opera star **Leontyne Price** makes her debut at the Metropolitan Opera as Leonora in *Il Trovatore*. It is the Met's first opening night with a black woman singing a major role. Price receives a forty-two minute ovation, among the longest in Met history.

Ellen Stewart rents a basement space at 321 East Ninth Street to form a café-theater, Cafe La MaMa (later the La MaMa ETC—Experimental Theatre Company).

The Blacks by Jean Genet opens off-Broadway, starring **Maya Angelou**, Roscoe Lee Browne, Godfrey Cambridge, Louis Gossett Jr., James Earl Jones, Helen Martin, and Cicely Tyson.

Lewis Ferdinand Alcindor, a graduate of a parochial elementary school, enrolls at Power Memorial Academy. (Alcindor, later known as **Kareem Abdul-Jabbar,** leads his high school to two national basketball championships.)

1962

January 16. A suit accusing the New York City Board of Education of using "racial quotas" is filed in U.S. District Court on behalf of black and Puerto Rican children.

May 25. Félix Houphouët-Boigny, president of the Ivory Coast, is honored with a ticker-tape parade in lower Manhattan.

July. The Umbra Writers Workshop is founded at Tom Dent's apartment at 242 East Second Street on Manhattan's Lower East Side. Members include David Henderson, Nora Hicks, Askia Muhammad Touré, Lorenzo Thomas, Ishmael Reed, and Brenda Walcott.

August. The African Nationalist Pioneer Movement (ANPM) announces plans to construct a "Marcus Garvey Memorial Building" in Harlem at 141st Street and Eighth Avenue. ANPM founder Carlos Cooks says the structure will be built using a black architect, black labor, and with money raised by blacks. Cooks says the building will pay tribute "to the greatest leader that our race has pro-

Carlos Cooks reviews members of the African Legion, followed by Lt. Charles Nuokeogi Peaker, 1963.

duced this century." (The building is about two-thirds constructed when the city issues several code violations. In 1970 the city takes ownership of the property for non-payment of taxes and destroys the partially completed structure.)

August 6. Jamaica is proclaimed independent.

James Meredith integrates the University of Mississippi, following an order by the U.S. Supreme Court thwarting Governor Ross Barnett's attempt to block his entry.

October 22. Katherine Dunham stars in *Bamboche* at the 54th Street Theatre. The musical, directed by Dunham, co-stars Robert Guillaume.

Congressman Adam Clayton Powell Jr. conducts hearings on racism in the garment industry. Florence Rice, chairperson of her union shop, testifies about extensive racism in the International Ladies Garment Workers Union (ILGWU). She reports that because of her testimony she was forced out of her job and black-balled by the union.

Charles Rangel resigns from his post as assistant U.S. attorney to become legal counsel to the New York City Housing and Redevelopment Board. (Months later Rangel takes a post as an associate counsel to the New York State Assembly.)

The Harlem Neighborhood Association, Inc., founded in 1958, receives $250,000 from the City of New York and $230,000 from the federal government to implement Harlem Youth Opportunities Unlimited (HARYOU), its multifaceted program designed to address the needs of black youth. Clifford Alexander is named program and executive director.

Audley Moore forms the Reparations Committee of Descendants of U.S. Slaves to demand federal reparations for all African Americans as partial compensation for slavery and its continuous and lingering effects.

1963

National Urban League Executive Director Whitney Young proposes a domestic Marshall Plan to help black Americans achieve overall equality.

January 29. An exploratory meeting of black public officials, businessmen, lawyers, retailers, and government employees is arranged by Robert Mangum, H. Floyd Britton, and William Simms. Meeting participant Livingston Wingate states: "It is time the fleeing middle classes stopped fleeing and take a definite stand. It is time that Negroes got hold of themselves and began helping their institutions. Negroes are being constantly displaced from skilled and semi-skilled occupations. High dropouts in high schools are resulting in our young people being unprepared to enter into American industry. Negro economy is in crisis." (The group later calls itself One Hundred Men. At the peak of the 1960s Civil Rights movement, the group changes its name to One Hundred Black Men, Inc. The organization engages in a variety of activities to assist black males, including mentoring programs, adoption of a Harlem school, and advocacy for business development.)

February. Anna Hedgeman, working with A. Philip Randolph on plans for an October March on Washington, suggests combining

Randolph's jobs march with Martin Luther King Jr.'s proposed July March on Washington for a strong civil rights bill. The joint march is agreed upon and set for August. Hedgeman serves as the only woman on the organizing committee.

April 1. King Hassan II of Morocco is honored with a ticker-tape parade in lower Manhattan.

April 21. A Chattanooga Freedom Walk, from Chattanooga, Tennessee, to Jackson, Mississippi, is initiated by William Moore, a lone white postman. Moore is murdered two days later in Gadsden, Alabama. Members of SNCC (Student Nonviolent Coordinating Committee) and CORE are physically assaulted and arrested as they complete his pilgrimage.

Civil Rights demonstrators led by Martin Luther King Jr. are attacked by the Birmingham, Alabama, police, led by Commissioner Eugene "Bull" Connor, who authorizes the use of dogs and high-powered fire hoses.

Medgar Evers, an NAACP field secretary, is killed outside his home in Jackson, Mississippi.

May. Playwright Lorraine Hansberry hosts a SNCC fundraiser at her Croton-on-Hudson home. Harry Belafonte, Lena Horne, and James Baldwin attend the gathering to support the southern freedom movement.

May 1. Emlen Tunnell becomes the first black assistant coach in the National Football League—for the New York Giants.

August 28. More than two hundred thousand protesters from across the nation, including thousands of black New Yorkers, join in the March on Washington for Jobs and Freedom. Martin Luther King Jr. delivers his "I Have A Dream" speech at the Lincoln Memorial.

Four young girls—Addie Mae Collins, Denise McNair, Carole Robertson, and Cynthia Wesley—are killed when the Sixteenth Street Baptist Church in Birmingham, Alabama, is bombed during a Sunday School service.

Two black students accompanied by a U.S. deputy attorney are denied entry to the University of Alabama when Governor George Wallace physically blocks the doorway. The students, accompanied by National Guardsmen, are admitted later.

To me, the March on Washington, which happened the same year that JFK was assassinated, marks the end of the second phase of the civil rights movement, in which SNCC and the students had come to center stage, even though King was still seen as the maximum leader. Malcolm's cold class analysis at Selma, talking about the House Slave and the Field Slaves and how the House Slave identified with his white Master so completely that when the Master got sick, the House Nigger did too, and when the Master's house caught on fire the House Nigger would scream, 'Boss, our house on fire!' But the Field Slave would fan the flames. That bit of class analysis dug into me.

—Amiri Baraka,
The Autobiography of LeRoi Jones

Sally's Special Freedom Bus, August 28, 1963. This is one of the many locations taking bus reservations for New Yorkers traveling to the March on Washington for Jobs and Freedom.

October 4. Emperor Haile Selassie is honored a second time with a ticker-tape parade in lower Manhattan.

Percy Sutton and Charles Rangel co-found the John F. Kennedy Democratic Club in Harlem (later the Martin Luther King Jr. Club).

Oliver Tambo, co-leader with Nelson Mandela of the African National Congress, visits Harlem.

President John Kennedy selects HARYOU Executive Director Clifford Alexander to serve as foreign affairs officer of the National Security Council.

The Allen Committee is created by Mayor Robert F. Wagner to prepare proposals for desegregating the city's public schools.

Trumpets of the Lord opens off-Broadway. Directed by Donald McKayle and starring Cicely Tyson, the production is Vinnette Carroll's adaptation of James Weldon Johnson's *God's Trombones.*

Yankee catcher Elston Howard is named the American League's Most Valuable Player. Howard is the American League's first black to receive the honor.

1964

President Lyndon B. Johnson, who assumed office after President Kennedy's assasination the previous year, declares a War on Poverty.

February. James Baldwin's *Blues for Mister Charlie* opens on Broadway. Directed by Burgess Meredith, the play stars Al Freeman Jr. and Diana Sands.

March. LeRoi Jones's *The Dutchman* opens off-Broadway at the Cherry Lane Theatre. The Obie award–winning play stars Robert Hooks. (Jones's *The Toilet* and *The Slave* are also produced off-Broadway during the year.)

March 12. Malcolm X resigns from the Nation of Islam. He leaves for Mecca in April.

April 13. Sidney Poitier wins the Academy Award for Best Actor for his performance in the film *Lilies of the Field*.

April 22. James Farmer, director of the Congress of Racial Equality (CORE), leads a demonstration at the New York World's Fair protesting discrimination and racism. Police arrest 294 demonstrators.

June 22. Three civil rights workers—James Earl Chaney, Andrew Goodman, and Michael Schwerner—are murdered in Mississippi at the start of the Mississippi Summer Project sponsored by the Council of Federated Organizations (COFO).

June 26. Franklin H. Williams, the first black ambassador in the U.S. delegation to the United Nations, is appointed to the Economic and Social Council by President Lyndon B. Johnson.

July 2. The Civil Rights Act of 1964, the century's most comprehensive civil rights legislation, is signed by President Johnson. The bill, which passes despite a Senate filibuster lasting more than three months, includes public accommodation and fair employment sections.

July 18. Demanding an end to police brutality, CORE marches on a Harlem police station. CORE leaders are arrested, and central Harlem erupts in four days of rioting and racial unrest. Traditional leaders Roy Wilkins, A. Philip Randolph, Bayard Rustin, and James

Farmer attempt to quell the violence but are unsuccessful. The unrest spreads to the Bedford-Stuyvesant section of Brooklyn.

July 24. Over 600 blacks are arrested in Rochester, New York, following racial violence sparked by the arrest of a black teenager by white police. Four people die and more than 350 are injured.

August 20. President Johnson signs an Economic Opportunity Act.

December 3. J. Raymond Jones is elected chief of Tammany Hall, making him its first black leader. Jones replaces Edward Costikyan as leader of the New York County Executive Committee. Jones, a compromise leader to broker the battle between Regular and Reform Democrats, takes the post at a time when the Democratic Party is trying to prevent a Republican takeover of the city. (In 1992 Costikyan serves as a chief strategist for Rudolph Giuliani.)

December 10. Martin Luther King Jr. receives the Nobel Peace Prize.

President Johnson's domestic agenda maximizes Representative Adam Clayton Powell Jr.'s influence in the U.S. House of Representatives. Powell, chairman of the powerful House Education and Labor Committee, marshals increased federal aid for school programs and Head Start, and support for an increased minimum wage. Powell, in collaboration with President Johnson, is instrumental in the passage of almost every element of the War on Poverty campaign.

Brooklyn schoolteacher **Shirley Chisholm** is elected to the state assembly, representing Bedford-Stuyvesant.

Constance Baker Motley becomes the first African American woman elected to the New York State Senate.

Percy Sutton is elected to the New York State Assembly.

Kenneth Brown is elected from Queens to the New York State Assembly.

A commission appointed by Mayor Robert Wagner finds that blacks are concentrated in low-wage clerical jobs in a limited number of city government agencies. (A significant change occurs when the American Federation of State, County, and Municipal Employees [AFSCME], which has many black members, wins the right to collective bargaining in 1965.)

The City Wide Committee for Integrated Schools, chaired by Rev. Milton Galamison of Brooklyn, wages a campaign of black student boycotts and strikes to achieve full school integration.

Malcolm X assumes the name El-Hajj Malik El-Shabazz following his pilgrimage to Mecca, and creates the Organization of Afro-American Unity (OAAU), seeking to unite all African and African-descended people.

The first African Day Parade is held in Harlem.

Jazzmobile, Inc. is founded by jazz pianist/composer/educator **Billy Taylor** to present, propagate, and preserve jazz—America's classical music. The organization pioneers in using experienced professionals as artist/instructors and role models to provide high quality arts education and job training through workshops, master classes, lecture demonstrations, arts enrichment programs, outdoor summer concerts, special indoor concerts, and audiovisual documentation.

Actress Diana Sands is cast in the Broadway play *The Owl and the Pussycat*. Controversy surrounds the production as Sands plays love interest to white actor Alan Alda. (Sands receives a Tony nomination for her performance, but the film version of the play casts Barbra Streisand in her role.)

MOBILIZING BLACK POWER FOR THE NEW MILLENNIUM

1965–1998

Overleaf:

Howard Beach protest demonstration on behalf of Michael Griffith, 1987.

African National Congress President Nelson Mandela and Mayor David N. Dinkins at City Hall, 1990.

BY 1965, AMERICA'S COLD WAR WITH THE SOVIET UNION HAD TURNED into a hot, armed conflict in Vietnam. War had also broken out in the streets of America's cities. The southern-based, nonviolent civil rights movement suddenly had to compete for media attention with the social unrest in northern urban centers. Nonviolence gave way to urban rebellions, and integrationist goals were challenged by nationalist ones. Black power, the ideological expression of this change, emerged as the driving political force in the lives of black New Yorkers in the closing decades of the twentieth century.

Wars in Vietnam and Urban America

The era of European colonial domination was rapidly coming to a close. But the United States had not learned the lessons of its European allies. Flush with pride from its emergence as the number one superpower in the world, the United States was intent on defending its global leadership position against challenges from the Soviet Union and its communist allies.

When North Vietnam invaded South Vietnam in 1965, the United States, sensing that a North Vietnamese victory would result in the expansion of communist influence in Asia, joined the fray, siding with an outmanned, outgunned, "democratic" South Vietnam. African Americans were disproportionate participants in and casualties of this war. They were drafted at a higher rate than whites (thirty percent to eighteen percent) and in 1966, for instance, they constituted 22.4 percent of all army troops killed in action. Black New Yorkers were counted among both groups.

War took its toll on the streets of American cities by 1965 as well. In 1964, for instance, black New Yorkers rioted in Harlem, East Harlem, Bedford-Stuyvesant, Brownsville, and South Jamaica after a white police officer shot and killed a fifteen-year-old black student. A year later, the Watts (Los Angeles) riot became the symbol of the wave of revolts that would sweep urban black America through the end of the decade and the beginning of the next. Some thirty-four people were killed and four thousand arrested as more than ten thousand people rioted in Watts.

Subsequent urban uprisings would have the same general profile—confrontations between predominantly white "peacekeeping" police forces and the predominantly black citizenry who lived there.

It took the killing of white students by white forces at Kent State University in Ohio to bring this phase of black resistance to a halt. Black urban dwellers seemingly surmised that if the government was willing to kill its own young white citizens for protesting against its policies and practices, it just might be willing to exterminate its black rebels to "keep the peace." J. Edgar Hoover and the FBI's counterintelligence program (COINTELPRO) had already declared war on black revolutionaries and civil rights leaders alike.

Meanwhile, President Lyndon Baines Johnson had launched a War on Poverty, the most elaborate federal social and human services program since the presidency of Franklin D. Roosevelt. New York Congressman Adam Clayton Powell Jr. became Johnson's principal collaborator. Powell, as chairman of the powerful House Education and Labor Committee, came close to setting the nation's social policy agenda as he led the fight to pass legislation establishing Medicare and Medicaid programs, food stamps, Head Start, the Job Corps, and other human development-focused initiatives.

Under Johnson's leadership, Congress also passed the Voting Rights Act of 1965, and Johnson himself appointed black New Yorkers Robert Weaver and Thurgood Marshall, the first black Cabinet member and the first black Supreme Court Justice, respectively. Johnson's human-centered domestic agenda was effectively undermined economically, politically, and morally, however, by his continuing efforts to bomb the Vietnamese "back to hell." The bombing campaigns and the antiwar protests they engendered led to Johnson's political demise, and the war in Vietnam siphoned off the money needed to wage a full-fledged nationwide assault on poverty.

The Vietnam War compounded economic problems for black New Yorkers. For the first time, New York City was not strategically positioned to play a major role in an overseas conflict involving the United States. Benefits that had accrued to the New York economy during most previous wars simply were not by-products of the Vietnam conflict. The Great Blackout of November 9, 1965, was perhaps a harbinger of the next decade and a half. Eighty thousand square miles, including all of New York City, were without electrical power for thirteen hours.

By 1965 the lights were going out on the New York economy as well. Between 1952 and 1965, the manufacturing sector, the strength of its economy, suffered a net loss of 87,000 jobs. Over the same period, 800,000 white residents left the city for the suburbs and a virtually permanent welfare class began to emerge throughout the five boroughs. John Lindsay, elected in 1965 to lead New York out of this crisis, was hit with even more challenges when he took office in January 1966. First, there was a twelve-day transit strike. This was followed by a twenty-five-day newspaper blackout, a thirty-three-day dock strike, and a seventy-five-day hiatus on shipping deliveries. The rate of serious felonies tripled in the 1960s, welfare expenditures doubled in five years, and by 1969, the city's annual operating expense budget had tripled to $6.1 billion in a mere decade. The city's population peaked at 7,984,862 in 1970. Then the economic decline came in earnest.

The 1970s saw the South Bronx transformed into a national symbol of urban decay. The welfare rolls increased to one million clients. Of the 125 Fortune 500 companies who made New York City their headquarters in 1970, only ninety-four remained by 1975, thereby further eroding the city's economic base. Transit fares rose and sales taxes increased. Even though the city budget increased to over $6.6 billion, services remained uneven and increasingly unreliable. Lindsay left office with an estimated $1.5 billion budget gap in 1974 and by 1975, the city's indebtedness exceeded $13 billion.

Reviving the Spirit of Nationalism

The Johnson-Powell initiatives had been driven by the demands of the Civil Rights movement under the leadership of Martin Luther King Jr., which had been challenged, in turn, by the separatist ideology of Malcolm X, Elijah Muhammad, and the Nation of Islam. By 1965 Malcolm X's nationalist ideas had begun to gain a foothold. Black New Yorker Stokely Carmichael, Chairman of the Student Nonviolent Coordinating Committee (SNCC), and fellow SNCC worker Willie Ricks raised the call for "Black Power" in 1966. Mere mention of the words became rallying cries for new forces of black economic, political, religious, and cultural mobilization and action. Reflecting both a rejection of the integrationist political and social philosophy of Martin Luther King Jr. and the Civil Rights Movement, as well as an assertion of a newly found black identity, the Black Power Movement of the late 1960s and early 1970s was more northern than southern, more urban than rural, and more militant black nationalist than universal integrationist. The concept "Black Power" had been proposed by Adam Clayton Powell Jr. in the early 1960s, and many of its evolving tenets and practices were rooted in the teachings of New Yorkers Marcus Garvey, Carlos Cooks, and Malcolm X.

It is not surprising, then, that New York was the place where some of the most developed organized expressions of black power concepts and ideas emerged. James Cone and the National Conference of Black Churchmen spearheaded the religious expression of black power in the Black Theology Movement. Amiri Baraka was on point in the development of the Black Arts Movement. Harlemites Vincent Harding and John Henrik Clarke were in the forefront of the development of the Black Studies Movement. The Ocean Hill–Brownsville struggle for community control of black education (a century-old struggle in New York) was fueled by the energy, ideas, and ideology of the Black Power Movement.

New York was one of the first cities in the country to pass laws banning restrictive racial covenants in housing. Passage of these laws did not immediately change the social attitudes and practices of white New Yorkers who had grown accustomed to the city's systems of de facto racial segregation in the housing industry. Some of the major civil rights battles in New York City were waged by courageous black New Yorkers who were seeking to purchase or rent housing in previously all-white enclaves. White residents of these communities responded to these efforts to integrate them in harsh, sometimes violent ways. Some black New Yorkers lost their newly purchased property to arson and racially inspired vandalism. Others lost their lives or those of their loved ones. These struggles underscored the fact that racial discrimination and segregation were as much northern and national as they were southern and regional phenomena.

Exercising Voting Power

The most enduring impact of black power concepts on New York City was in the electoral political arena. In 1965 only one black New Yorker (Adam Clayton Powell Jr.) had ever been elected to the U.S. Congress. The number of blacks in city and state government was negligible. Fueled by the urban rebellions and a newly found sense of blacks' right to participate in political affairs, black New Yorkers began electing more and more blacks to higher and higher political offices. Over the next two and a half decades, Charles Rangel, Shirley Chisholm, Major Owens, Edolphus Towns, and Floyd Flake would be elected to multiple terms in the U.S. Congress. The New York State Black and Puerto Rican Legislative Caucus, organized in 1966 with twelve members, would have thirty-one members by 1998. Black New York membership on the City Council increased from only a few in 1965 to seventeen in 1998. Between 1965 and 1998, Percy Sutton, David Dinkins, and C. Virginia Fields were elected president of the Borough of Manhattan.

The 1984 and 1988 presidential campaigns of Reverend Jesse Jackson had a significant impact on electoral politics in New York City. Black New Yorkers in unprecedented numbers registered and voted for Reverend Jackson in what many considered to be the first serious attempt by an African American to make a run for the presidency. (Black New Yorker Shirley Chisholm had made history when she became the first black woman presidential candidate in 1972.) The political mobilization the Jackson campaigns engendered paid off in 1989 with the election of David Dinkins as the city's 106th—and first African American—mayor. Four years later, Dinkins was narrowly defeated by Republican candidate Rudolph Giuliani. Meanwhile, political activist Reverend Al Sharpton threw his hat in the ring and made an impressive run for the U.S. Senate in 1994. And New Yorker H. Carl McCall, who had been appointed state comptroller in 1993, was elected to the office in 1994. He was the top vote-getter in the state in his reelection bid in 1998.

A City in Transition

By 1980, signs of economic recovery were in the air, along with signs of dramatic gains in the struggle for black access to the city's institutions of higher learning, government, and corporate life. The passage of national affirmative action legislation opened the doors of opportunity for thousands of black New Yorkers who had previously had limited opportunities to enroll in the city's colleges and universities. State-funded programs helped eliminate the economic barriers and compensate for the failures of the city's public schools. During the 1970s and 1980s black and Hispanic enrollments increased dramatically. By the 1990s the white backlash had transformed the formerly free City University (when it served a predominantly white student body) into one that charged constantly increasing tuition fees for its now predominantly black and Hispanic student body.

The 1990 census indicated that for the first time in its more than three-hundred-year history, the majority of New York City residents were people of color. Of the 7,322,564, 3.4 million were blacks, nonwhite Hispanics, and Asians, of whom 2.3 million were people of African descent.

Even more ethnically and culturally diverse than ever, the newest black New Yorkers were no longer mainly southern migrants. The Hart-Cellar Act of 1965 opened the doors to immigrants from the Caribbean, Latin America, and Africa. After 1965, immigration from Jamaica, Trinidad and Tobago, St. Vincent, Grenada, Barbados, Panama, and Guyana increased. Nearly one half of all immigrants from these islands settled in New York City, as did more than three quarters of all Dominican immigrants. A large influx of Haitians also came, as did growing numbers of Ethiopians, Nigerians, Senegalese, and South Africans. By the 1990s upwards of eighty thousand continental-African born immigrants lived in New York City.

The black population of New York City in 1990 would rank as the fourth largest city in the nation if it were organized as an independent municipality. Entering the new millennium, New York City's people-of-color majority is projected to increase.

1965

February 15. Malcolm X accuses the Nation of Islam of bombing his home. (He had left the Nation the previous year after a split with its leader, Elijah Muhammad.)

February 21. Malcolm X is assassinated while delivering a speech at a meeting of the Organization of Afro-American Unity at the Audubon Ballroom in Harlem. Ella Collins, his sister, replaces him as head of the organization.

He was and is a Prince—our own black shining Prince—who didn't hesitate to die, because he loved us so.

—Ossie Davis, eulogy for Malcolm X, 1965

February 23. State senator Constance Baker Motley is elected by unanimous vote of the New York City Council to fill a one-year vacancy as Manhattan borough president, the first black woman to hold that office. (She wins the general election for the position nine months later with Democratic, Republican, and Liberal party support.)

March. Judith Jamison makes her New York debut with the American Ballet Theatre in Agnes de Mille's *The Four Marys*. Alvin Ailey invites her to join his company later that year. She becomes a star in May 1971 with the premiere of *Cry*, which Ailey dedicates "For all black women everywhere—especially our mothers."

Constance Baker Motley being sworn in as Manhattan borough president by Mayor Robert Wagner.

April. Joan Murray becomes the first black woman reporter at a New York City television station, reporting light news and features on WCBS-TV.

April. The Harlem Writers Guild hosts a conference at the New School for Social Research. Participants include John O. Killens, John Henrik Clarke, Lofton Mitchell, Wiliam Branch, Ossie Davis, and Sylvester Leaks. Allan Morrison of *Ebony* magazine presides.

August 6. The Voting Rights Bill is signed by President Lyndon Johnson. It authorizes the suspension of literacy tests and the sending of federal examiners into the South.

August 11. Thurgood Marshall is confirmed by the Senate as solicitor general of the United States.

August 13. The National Guard is mobilized to quell a major uprising in the Watts section of Los Angeles. (Lasting six days, the rebellion toll includes 34 killed, 1,032 injured, 4,000 arrested, and $35 million in property damage. The National Guard is placed on stand-by alert the following day to subdue rioting on the West Side of Chicago.)

September. New York City comptroller Abraham Beame proposes that the city use its pension fund to extend mortgages to non-white home buyers to counteract the racial bias of private banks.

October 15. Lorraine Hansberry's play *The Sign in Sidney Brustein's Window* opens on Broadway. (In ill health when the play began rehearsals, Hansberry dies at the age of thirty-four on the day that it closes.)

November 2. Republican mayoral candidate John Lindsay receives a surprising forty percent of the black vote as he defeats Democrat Abe Beame. In Brooklyn, black candidates James H. Shaw and incumbent William C. Thompson win state senate seats, and Samuel Wright and incumbents Bertram Baker and Shirley Chisholm win state assembly seats. In Harlem, Basil Paterson wins a state senate contest, filling the seat vacated by Constance Baker Motley, as attorney **David N. Dinkins,** and incumbents Mark T. Southall and Percy E. Sutton, win state assembly seats. Dennis Coleman wins a state senate seat in the Bronx, and Kenneth Brown is the victor in a Queens assembly race.

November 15. At the invitation of Adam Clayton Powell Jr., Martin Luther King Jr. preaches to overflow audiences at two successive Sunday morning services at the Abyssinian Baptist Church.

Adam Clayton Powell Jr. raises the issue of Black Power at a rally in Chicago.

Freedom National Bank is founded at 275 West 125th Street in Harlem, with assets of over $10 million. Jackie Robinson is the first chairman of the board, and William Hudgins is the first president.

Brooklyn CORE and the Reverend Milton A. Galamison form the Brooklyn Freedom Democratic Party, modeled on the Mississippi Freedom Democratic Party (MFDP), in another grassroots attack on the white power structure of the Brooklyn Democratic machine.

R. C. Collier, leader of the Black Liberation Front, is arrested in New York on charges that he is planning to bomb the Statue of Liberty, the Washington Monument, and the Liberty Bell.

White residents of Queens and Brooklyn form SPONGE: the Society for the Prevention of Negroes Getting Everything. The organization is their response to the increase of civil rights protests in New York City.

The U.S. Court of Appeals rules that demonstrators arrested during civil rights protests are not entitled to federal court trial of state charges.

The Hart-Cellar Immigration Act opens an immigrant flow from the Caribbean to the United States, with New York City as a major destination.

The New York State Housing Financing Agency announces a subsidy program for six hundred low-income families to enter middle-income housing projects in New York City. The program is mild given the extent of housing segregation in the city.

The New York City Planning Commission reports that seventy percent of families who cannot find housing of reasonable size and price are black or Puerto Rican.

John B. King is the first African American appointed executive deputy superintendent of the New York City schools. (He joins the faculty of the school of education at Fordham University in 1967.)

The Citywide Coordinating Commission establishes a summer jobs program for youths in Harlem and Bedford-Stuyvesant. The half-million-dollar commitment seeks to avoid a repetition of the previous summer's disturbances.

Samuel Riley Pierce Jr. is named to the board of directors of U.S. Industries, Inc. (A judge in the New York Court of General Sessions and former faculty member at New York University Law School, Pierce later becomes the first African American to serve on the board of a major insurance company, the Prudential Insurance Company of America.)

Dark Ghetto: Dilemmas of Social Power, by Kenneth B. Clark, is published. Based on Clark's experience as founder, and chairman from

1962 to 1964, of Harlem Youth Opportunities Unlimited (HARYOU), the book calls for immediate action by government and business leaders to provide better education for inner-city youths.

James Baldwin's play *The Amen Corner* opens in New York, produced by Maria Cole, the widow of Nat King Cole. His short story collection, *Going to Meet the Man,* is published.

The Autobiography of Malcolm X is published. The book is written with the assistance of Alex Haley.

Claude Brown's *Manchild in the Promised Land* is published.

1966

January 3. Floyd McKissick replaces James Farmer as national director of the Congress of Racial Equality (CORE).

January 10. Julian Bond, communications director of the Student Nonviolent Coordinating Committee (SNCC) and a critic of the Vietnam War, is denied his seat in the Georgia legislature. (Bowing to national pressure and legal decisions, the legislature seats him in January 1967.)

January 18. Robert C. Weaver is sworn in as secretary of the new United States Department of Housing and Urban Development, the first black person to serve as a cabinet member.

February. Mayor John Lindsay awards the New York Urban League $136,250 in antipoverty funds to fight bias.

March. Three Black Muslims—Norman 3X Butler, Thomas 15X Johnson, and Talmadge X Hayer—are convicted of murdering Malcolm X. (In April they are given life sentences.)

July 31. A "Black Power" statement by the National Committee of Negro Churchmen is published as a full-page advertisement in the *New York Times.* Led by Dr. Benjamin Payton, the executive director of the Commission on Religion and Race of the National Council of Churches, the clergymen support the Black Power ideology, asserting, "The fundamental distortion facing us in the controversy about 'black power' is rooted in a gross imbalance of power and

Author James Baldwin at the Selma-to-Montgomery voting rights march, Alabama, 1965.

Where does one run when he is already in the promised land?

—Claude Brown,
Manchild in the Promised Land,
1965

conscience between Negroes and white Americans. It is this distortion, mainly, which is responsible for the widespread, though often inarticulate, assumption that white people are justified in getting what they want through the use of power, but that Negro Americans must, either by nature or by circumstance, make their appeal only through conscience. As a result, the power of white men and the conscience of black men have both been corrupted." (Soon afterwards the group changes its name to the National Committee of Black Churchmen.)

July–September. The National Guard is mobilized to subdue uprisings in Omaha, Chicago, Cleveland, Milwaukee, Dayton, and San Francisco. (Racial violence is reported in forty-three cities during the year, with 11 killed, more than 400 injured, and 3,000 arrested.)

August 30. Constance Baker Motley is confirmed as a federal district judge over fierce opposition by Senator James Eastland of Mississippi.

November 8. Manhattan Borough President Percy Sutton defeats his Republican challenger Nicholas Tsoucalas by a better than two-to-one margin. Harlem State Senator Basil Paterson is re-elected, as is Brooklyn State Senator William C. Thompson. Former Bronx State Senator Ivan Warner, who had quit the senate to make an unsuccessful bid in 1965 for the Bronx borough presidency, is returned to office. In assembly races, six black Democratic incumbents are returned to office, including newcomer Charles Rangel, a former assistant U.S. attorney, who was elected to the post formerly held by Borough President Sutton. In the governor's race, incumbent Nelson Rockefeller credits his black supporters with helping him make a strong showing among black voters. Rockefeller's backers include labor leader Fred O'Neal, Rev. Wyatt Tee Walker, and Bessie Buchanan.

Lisle C. Carter is appointed assistant secretary of the U.S. Department of Health, Education and Welfare by President Johnson.

Elliot P. Skinner, a professor of sociology at Columbia University, is named ambassador to Upper Volta, West Africa.

The New York State Black and Puerto Rican Legislative Caucus is organized with twelve members.

Robert Magnum is appointed Commissioner of the State Division of Human Rights, and James Hicks is appointed assistant commissioner.

Robert D. Lowery is the first African American to be appointed commissioner of the New York City Fire Department.

James Colston is selected as president of Bronx Community College of the City University of New York (CUNY), the first black person to head a college in New York State.

James R. Dumpson is named head of the Fordham University School of Social Work. (Dumpson had served as associate dean of the Hunter College School of Social Welfare.)

Hundreds of people from Bedford-Stuyvesant, Harlem, the South Bronx, and the Lower East Side stage a sit-in at City Hall, demanding the continuation of federal slum repair programs.

Whitney M. Young Jr., executive director of the National Urban League, is elected president of the ninety-three-year-old National Conference on Social Welfare.

Rev. Eugene Callendar succeeds Alexander J. Allen as executive director of the New York Urban League. (While at the league, Callendar establishes the Street Academy Program and Harlem Prep.)

Father Rodrigue Auguste of Haiti comes to St. Teresa Roman Catholic Church in Brooklyn to minister to the borough's growing Haitian community. Father Auguste establishes the Christian Organization of the Haitian Community.

Curator Jean Hutson calls attention to the plight of the Schomburg Collection in her speech accepting a citation from the New York Branch of the Association for the Study of Negro Life and History. The address triggers efforts by concerned individuals and organizations to raise funds, and to improve the collection's status within the New York Public Library. (The Ford Foundation awards a grant of $15,000 the following year for the initiation of an archival preservation program.)

Amiri Baraka launches the Black Arts Movement in Harlem.

Langston Hughes's autobiography, *The Big Sea,* is the primary resource for the hour-long CBS-TV special *Strolling Twenties.* Harry Belafonte is producer of the show, and cast members include George Kirby, Sidney Poitier, Nipsey Russell, Diahann Carroll, Joe Williams, and Sammy Davis Jr.

Micki Grant plays attorney Peggy Nolan on the soap opera *Another World.* She is the first black person to receive a daytime story line.

1967

January 3. The Metropolitan Applied Research Center (MARC) is founded, with offices at City College. Kenneth B. Clark is named president.

January 9. Congressman Adam Clayton Powell Jr., removed as chairman of the House Education and Labor Committee on a

Black Arts Movement leader Amiri Baraka.

charge of wrongfully appropriating congressional funds, accuses the House of Representatives of racism.

March 1. Adam Clayton Powell Jr. is expelled from the House of Representatives by a vote of 307 to 116.

March 13. A boycott begins at Manhattan's Public School 125 by black parents who are unhappy over the educational system and the ethnic composition of New York City schools. (The boycott lasts nine days.)

April 4. Martin Luther King Jr. declares his opposition to the Vietnam War during a press conference in New York City. Later in the day he again denounces the war at Riverside Church in Harlem.

April 11. Harlem voters reelect Adam Clayton Powell Jr., defying Congress.

April 15. Journalist and concert pianist Philippa Duke Schuyler gives a concert on South Vietnamese television. (On May 9, she is killed in a helicopter accident while helping to transport children from a Catholic orphanage in the Hue war zone to the relative safety of Da Nang.)

April 26. *Hallelujah Baby* opens on Broadway. Leslie Uggams and Robert Hooks star in the musical about the history of race relations in the United States.

April 28. Following Muhammad Ali's refusal to report to a U.S. army induction center in Houston, the New York State Athletic Commission and the World Boxing Association withdraw recognition of Ali as heavyweight champion. (Ali's last bout occurred at Madison Square Garden on March 22, when he successfully defended his title against challenger Zora Folley. Ali does not regain sanction to fight again until 1970.)

May 12. H. Rap Brown replaces Stokely Carmichael as chairman of SNCC.

June. The American Museum of Natural History opens its Hall of Man in Africa.

America *is* fighting a racist war, which is what the young people know, and is why they are so enraged. America is simply continuing, as it was bound to do, the history of Europe, and is fighting in Southeast Asia to protect the material interests of the Western world. This world, from Berlin to Washington, is bound together by military treaties, by trade, by habit, by what they dare to call religion. . . . I would like to point this out as cogently as I can. I would like to make it as clear as I can that this course is not only criminal, it is also inevitably doomed to failure.

—James Baldwin,
Palm Springs, 1968

Muhammad Ali debating with Iona College students about his Vietnam stand, 1968.

June 13. Thurgood Marshall is named to the U.S. Supreme Court by President Lyndon B. Johnson.

June 20. Muhammad Ali is convicted in federal court in Houston of violating the Selective Service Act by refusing induction into the armed services on the grounds that he is a Muslim minister.

July. The National Urban Coalition is organized to advocate for the reordering of national priorities by the American people and Congress; and for expanded efforts in both the public and private sectors to provide jobs, housing, education, and other needs. The New York Urban Coalition is organized as an affiliate of the national organization.

July 20. More than a thousand people attend the first Black Power Conference in Newark, New Jersey.

August. Naomi Sims makes a breakthrough in the fashion world as the first black model to appear on the cover of the *New York Times* supplement, *Fashions of the Times*. (A sketch of model Donyale Luna on the cover of *Harper's Bazaar* in January 1965, was the first image of a black woman ever featured on a major American fashion magazine.)

September 6. Walter E. Washington, chairman of the New York City Housing Authority, is appointed by President Lyndon Johnson to head the newly reorganized municipal government of Washington, D.C. Washington is the first black to govern a major American city. (He is elected mayor in 1974.)

November 7. Carl B. Stokes is elected mayor of Cleveland, Ohio, and Richard G. Hatcher of Gary, Indiana. Sworn in on November 13, Stokes becomes the first black mayor of a major American city.

November. A Senate permanent investigating committee reports that there have been seventy-five major urban rebellions in 1967, compared with twenty-one in 1966. In 1967 eighty-three people have been killed, compared with eleven in 1966 and thirty-six in 1965.

Ersa Hines Poston becomes president of the New York State Civil Service Commission.

Cyril Tyson is named deputy administrator of the New York City Human Resources Administration and head of the Office of Minority Economic Development.

The Bedford-Stuyvesant Restoration Corporation, the first non-profit community development corporation in the United States, is founded through the bipartisan efforts of Senators Robert F. Kennedy and Jacob K. Javits, working with community residents. Governed by a twenty-six-member community board, and assisted by a business advisory board of nine members from the greater metropolitan area, the corporation uses a combination of public and private funds to improve the quality of life and the economy

Committee for Racial Pride picketing Wigs Parisian on 125th Street, Harlem, mid-1960s.

Restoration
VOL. 3, NO. 2 • AFFILIATED WITH BEDFORD-STUYVESANT D&S CORP. • 1368 FULTON ST. • BROOKLYN, N.Y. 11216 • FEB. 1975

Spotlight on Scattered Rehabilitation — Part 1

Bedford-Stuyvesant Restoration Corporation newsletter, February 1975.

of the area. Franklin A. Thomas, a Brooklyn native, is chosen as president and CEO of the Bedford-Stuyvesant Restoration Corporation.

Columbia University announces a $2.7 million fund to improve social conditions in Harlem.

The Harlem Commonwealth Council, a newly formed community development corporation, cites employment and housing problems, the population decline, and decreasing business activity as major barriers to development in Harlem. Among those involved in the council are Isaiah Robinson, Roy Innis, Preston Wilcox, and James Dowdy.

Operation Crossroads Africa, organized by Rev. James Robinson of the Church of the Master, celebrates its tenth anniversary. (The program serves as a model for the Peace Corps.)

James T. Whitehead Jr. becomes a flight engineer for TWA at John F. Kennedy International Airport. (During his earlier U.S. Air Force career, Whitehead was the first black U-2 pilot.)

Black Power: The Politics of Liberation in America, a collaborative work by Stokely Carmichael (later Kwame Ture) and Charles Hamilton, is published.

Science fiction writer Samuel R. Delany wins the Nebula Award for his novel *The Einstein Intersection* and his short story "Aye and Gomorrah."

Romare Bearden and Carroll Greene Jr. are co-curators of an exhibition in the Great Hall of City College that features works by African American artists from 1800 to 1950. Among the artists are Charles Alston, Jacob Lawrence, Norman Lewis, and Ernest Crichlow.

Manhattan-born Bill McCreary becomes a newscaster with WNEW-TV. (In 1970, McCreary anchors *The 10 O'Clock News*, and in 1987 he is named executive producer of the *McCreary Report*.)

Black Power advocate Stokely Carmichael (Kwame Ture).

The Urban Arts Corporation of New York City is founded by Vinnette J. Carroll, who serves as artistic director.

Robert Macbeth and Ed Bullins organize the New Lafayette Theatre company in Harlem.

In the Heat of the Night, *starring Sidney Poitier and Rod Steiger, wins an Academy Award for best motion picture. The film explores interracial male bonding. Another of the year's top films,* Guess Who's Coming to Dinner, *starring Poitier, Spencer Tracy, and Katherine Hepburn, examines interracial marriage.*

Pearl Bailey, starring in *Hello Dolly,* is named entertainer of the year by *Cue* magazine.

1968

March 1. The National Advisory Commission on Civil Disorders (the Kerner Commission) says that white racism was the fundamental cause of the uprisings in American cities. The commission says that America is "moving toward two societies, one black, one white—separate and unequal."

March 27. Martin Luther King Jr. visits Harlem and Queens to raise support for a planned march on Washington, D.C., as part of his Poor People's Campaign.

Rev. William A. Jones Jr., pastor of Bethany Baptist Church in Brooklyn, founds Operation Breadbasket of the Greater New York SCLC. The organization advocates black economic development and community involvement in local schools. (In 1969, Alfred Sharpton becomes the organization's youth director. As a child, Sharpton was a popular preacher known as "The Wonderboy.")

The Fair Housing Act of 1968 promotes loans for home buyers in low-income communities. The act makes it unlawful to refuse to sell or rent a home to any person because of race.

April 4. Dr. Martin Luther King Jr. is assassinated in Memphis, Tennessee, triggering uprisings in more than a hundred cities. Forty-six people are killed; 20,000 federal troops and 34,000 National Guardsmen are mobilized to subdue the disturbances.

April 5. Crowds reacting to the assassination of Martin Luther King Jr. gather in the streets and damage property in Harlem, Queens, and Central Brooklyn.

April. Black students stage a protest at Columbia University to stop the construction of a large gymnasium in Morningside Park. The students say the gym would dominate the park, preventing its use by local residents. Columbia, Harlem's largest landowner, stops construction of the facility.

May. Adam Clayton Powell Jr. calls for a protest in front of 1270 Fifth Avenue, an apartment complex purchased by Columbia University, claiming that Columbia has raised rents there to force out black and Latino residents. Columbia denies the charges.

May 11. Nine Poor People's Campaign caravans arrive in Washington, D.C., from various parts of the country, and Resurrection City is created near the Lincoln Memorial to house them.

June. Fourteen tenants who conducted a rent strike to protest the lack of security at the Lillian Wald Houses in Manhattan lose a case brought by the New York City Housing Authority. The judge rules that the "Housing Authority is not required to provide protection."

July. The New York City Housing Authority rejects a proposal that the name of the Kingsborough Houses in Brooklyn be changed to the Malcolm X Houses.

July 3. Father Harold A. Salmon becomes the first black Roman Catholic priest in the New York City Archdiocese, installed by Archbishop Cooke as vicar delegate for Harlem.

September 5. One hundred fifty white off-duty police officers attack three members of the Black Panther Party outside the Brooklyn Criminal Court.

September 9. **Arthur Ashe** becomes the first African American man to win a major tennis championship when he wins the men's singles at the first United States Open at Forest Hills, New York.

Tennis champion Arthur Ashe.

October. Melba Tolliver becomes a reporter at WABC-TV. New York editor of *Ebony* and Johnson Publishing Company bureau chief Ponchitta Pierce is hired as special television correspondent for *CBS News*.

October 16. Tommie Smith and John Carlos protest racism by raising their fists in black power salutes on the victory stand after coming in first and third in the 200-meter race at the Olympics in Mexico City.

October 18. **Bob Beamon** leaps 29 feet 2½ inches—nearly two feet beyond the existing world record—and establishes world and Olympic long jump records.

Bob Beamon sets long jump record at 1968 Olympics, Mexico City.

November 5. Shirley Chisholm defeats James Farmer, former CORE director, to become U.S. Representative for the Twelfth Congressional District, which includes the Bedford-Stuyvesant section of Brooklyn. One of the younger and more militant politicians in Brooklyn's Unity Democratic Club, she is the nation's first black Congresswoman.

Barbara M. Watson is appointed director of security and consular affairs at the U.S. Department of State.

Ruth V. Washington is appointed by Governor Nelson Rockefeller to serve on the Workmen's Compensation Board.

Rev. Eugene Callender is named deputy administrator of the city's Housing and Development Administration. (He served as a member of President Lyndon Johnson's Task Force on Manpower and Unemployment the previous year.)

Mayor John Lindsay establishes a commission to study racial hatred and tension in New York City.

In the wake of school disruptions, the Board of Education, with financial assistance from the Ford Foundation, establishes I.S. 201 in Harlem, along with experimental districts in lower Manhattan and Ocean Hill-Brownsville in Brooklyn. The People's Board of Education is created by ministers, parents, and teachers in Ocean Hill–Brownsville. Their goal is to decentralize the administration of the local schools in order to improve the quality of education available to nonwhite children. The People's Board begins making personnel decisions in the local schools. As a result, the community finds itself at odds with the United Federation of Teachers. The unified experiment collapses because of a teachers' strike in the fall. Ocean Hill-Brownsville introduces one of the early rifts in black-Jewish relations in New York City. The New York Civil Liberties Union issues a report on the Ocean Hill–Brownsville controversy entitled "Burden of Blame." Commenting on the chaos created by the experiment, it concludes that the "major burden of blame must fall on the central Board of Education and, lamentably, on the United Federation of Teachers."

> We will build a democratic America in spite of undemocratic Americans. We have rarely worried about the odds or the obstacles before—we will not start worrying now. We will have both of our goals—Peace and Power!
>
> —Shirley Chisholm,
> speech at Federal City College,
> Washington, D.C., 1969

Frank S. Horne is named assistant administrator for Equal Opportunity in Housing. (A Brooklyn resident, he has been involved in housing since being a part of the "Black Cabinet" during Roosevelt's New Deal administration.)

The Mitchell-Lama Act subsidizes Co-op City, a middle-income project in the Bronx. Units rent for $20 a room. (More than 138,000 units are added by the 1970s.)

The Urban Development Corporation is formed to construct new housing in urban communities. The agency builds thirty-two housing projects, including Twin Parks in the Bronx and cooperative apartments on Roosevelt Island.

The Government National Mortgage Association (Ginnie Mae) is established, ostensibly to provide loans for low-income areas.

Cyril D. Tyson is named commissioner of the Manpower Career and Development Agency, which controls hundreds of training and job placement centers throughout greater New York.

Lillian Roberts is named associate director for organization for District Council 37 of the American Federation of State, County and Municipal Workers (AFSCME) of the AFL-CIO, which represents over 125,000 New Yorkers.

Franklin H. Williams, former Ambassador to Ghana, is selected to head the Urban Minorities Center established at Columbia University. The university is awarded $10 million by the Ford Foundation to "effect solutions of urban and minority problems, $2.7 million to be involved in Harlem."

Rev. Milton Galamison, a Brooklyn community leader, is elected vice president of the New York City Board of Education.

The *Amsterdam News* establishes an editorial policy that replaces the term "Negro" with "African American" and "Black."

The Haitian-American Citizens Society, a political organization, is established in New York. Its goal is to channel the power of the Haitian community for political gain.

Richard Moore (later Dhoruba bin-Wahad), with Lumumba and Afeni Shakur, run the Black Panther headquarters in Harlem. (The Shakurs are the parents of rap artist Tupac Shakur.)

The Studio Museum in Harlem is founded to provide work and exhibition space for African American artists.

The Negro Ensemble Company (NEC), headed by Douglas Turner Ward, Robert Hooks, and Gerald S. Krone, begins operations with the goal of developing black actors, playwrights, technicians, and managers. (After Douglas Turner Ward wrote an article in the *New York Times* in 1966 calling for the establishment of a black theater group, the Ford Foundation invited him to submit a proposal and provided initial funding for the new company.)

The Schomburg Corporation, a coalition of individuals and organization representatives, is formed to coordinate support activities for the Schomburg Collection.

Black Fire: An Anthology of Afro-American Writing, edited by Amiri Baraka and Larry Neal, is published. A handbook of theory, criticism, and creative writing, the book captures the spirit of the Black Arts Movement.

The Studio Museum in Harlem.

A scene from the Negro Ensemble Company's first production, Song of the Lusitanian Bogey, *1968.*

Black Art is the aesthetic and spiritual sister of the Black Power concept. As such, it envisions an art that speaks directly to the needs and aspirations of Black America. . . . One is concerned with the relationship between art and politics; the other with the art of politics.

—Larry Neal,
"The Black Arts Movement,"
*Black Fire: An Anthology of
Afro-American Writing,* 1968

A Negro History Tour of Manhattan by Middleton A. ("Spike") Harris, president of Negro History Associates, is published.

William Branch produces the ninety-minute documentary *Still a Brother: Inside the Negro Middle Class* for National Educational Television.

James Booker, *Amsterdam News* columnist and political editor, organizes the first national conference of black elected officials in Chicago. (Booker had previously served as the chief information consultant for the National Advisory Committee on Civil Disorders, and consultant and director of information for the 1966 White House Conference on Civil Rights.)

Brooklyn native and resident Charles Blagrove Hobson, a producer with ABC-TV, wins Emmy and Capital Press Club awards.

The Boys Choir of Harlem is founded by **Walter J. Turnbull** as the Ephesus Church Choir of Central Harlem. (The Choir Academy of Harlem is established in 1986, and graduates its first twelfth grade class in 1996. Students are required to maintain a B average in order to remain in the choir, and ninety-eight percent go on to college. The choir contributes to film soundtracks, records, tours nationally and internationally, and has a sensational two-week run on Broadway in 1994.)

Shirley Verrett opens the Metropolitan Opera season with her debut in *Carmen*.

Actor and director Barbara Ann Teer, dissatisfied with the lack of respect for black culture in American professional theater, founds the National Black Theatre (NBT) in Harlem. (In 1983 NBT purchases property on 125th Street and Fifth Avenue to develop the National Black Institute of Communication through Theater Arts, a

The Boys Choir of Harlem performs at the Schomburg Center's annual Heritage Weekend Celebration, 1997.

block-long complex that combines commercial retail businesses with theater and arts activities.)

James Earl Jones wins the Tony award for best actor of the year in a drama for his performance in the play *The Great White Hope*.

Diahann Carroll stars in the television series *Julia* as a single mother, the widow of an American killed in the Vietnam War. She is the first African American to play a leading role in a television situation comedy.

1969

January 6. The WCBS-TV *Black Heritage* series, with John Henrik Clarke and Vincent Harding as co-directors, expands. The series, co-produced by Columbia University, ultimately includes 120 half-hour telecasts featured on stations across the country.

January. The exhibition *Harlem on My Mind* opens at the Metropolitan Museum of Art, funded by a $250,000 grant from the Henry Luce Foundation. Artists Romare Bearden and Norman Lewis object to the exhibition, noting that if the Met wanted to open its doors to Harlem, works of black artists should be shown there. (Among the African Americans who worked with exhibition coordinator and book editor Allon Schoener were Donald Harper, A'Leila Walker Nelson, and Reginald McGhee. McGhee brought to light the highly acclaimed photographs of Harlem photographer James VanDerZee.)

April 19. One hundred black students, carrying rifles and shotguns, seize the Student Union Building at Cornell University, protesting racism.

April 26. The Langston Hughes Community Library and Cultural Center is founded in Queens at 102-09 Northern Boulevard. Created through the effort of the Library Action Committee of Corona–East Elmhurst, the new library is renovated from an old Woolworth store. (In 1987, the Hughes Center becomes an official branch of the Queens Borough Public Library. In the fall of 1999, the library, under the leadership of its executive director, Andrew P. Jackson, will move to a new and larger facility a block away.)

May 4. Former SNCC Executive Secretary James Forman interrupts a Sunday service at Riverside Church to present the National Black Economic Development Conference's "Black Manifesto." The document supports the development of black businesses but criticizes "black capitalism." Taking aim at religious institutions, the Black Manifesto demands of "white Christian churches and Jewish synagogues, which are part and parcel of the system of capitalism, that they begin to pay reparations to black people in this country. We are demanding $500,000,000."

May 21–23. At North Carolina A&T College, one student is killed and five policemen are injured when police and National Guardsmen fire on demonstrators.

June. National Educational Television's *Black Journal* begins airing with William Greaves as executive producer and James McDonald as associate producer. One of the show's objectives is to train and develop new black television reporters, editors, producers, and technicians. (The show receives the Golden TV Award from the National Association of Radio and Television Announcers.)

September 5. Rock star Jimi Hendrix performs at a Friday night Harlem block party on 139th Street between Lenox and Fifth Avenues. Conceding that his fans are far more white than black, the Seattle-born Hendrix says, following his rare uptown appearance, "I was glad to be able to come home." Other performers at the WLIB-sponsored concert include Maxine Brown, Big Maybell, La Rocque Bey, and Love Men Ltd. (Formerly a guitarist for James Brown, Little Richard, Tina Turner, Wilson Pickett, and the Isley Brothers, Hendrix performed extensively in New York in the mid-1960s, using the name Jimmy James.)

September 6. The new Harlem Hospital building opens.

September 23. Afro-American Day in Harlem is proclaimed by Mayor John Lindsay. In a parade sponsored by the United Federation of Black Community Organizations, hundreds of paraders and pedestrians pass in review on Seventh Avenue before Manhattan Borough President Percy Sutton, Livingston Wingate, Father Harold A. Salmon, and Ossie Davis.

September. The New York City Police Department reports a 142% increase in the number of summonses given to nonmedallion, or gypsy, cabs. Most of the illegal cabs are operated by minority and immigrant drivers. Gypsy operators say they cannot afford the high cost of legal medallion taxis. (Medallions, or official taxicab licenses, were introduced in 1937 at a price of ten dollars. Because their number is limited—frozen since the 1930s at 11,787—individual medallions are valued at over $100,000 by the 1980s.)

September. A community coalition including Representative Adam Clayton Powell Jr. begins protests at the Harlem site of a proposed state office building. The coalition demands housing during a meeting with Governor Nelson Rockefeller. (The building is later named for Powell.)

November 4. Manhattan Borough President Percy Sutton is re-elected to a full-term, gaining more than eighty percent of the total vote. Black voters help Mayor John V. Lindsay gain a second four-year term. Running on the Liberal-Independent ticket, Lindsay receives more than seventy-five percent of the black vote in defeating Democrat Mario Procaccino. Among the mayor's supporters are Sutton, U.S. Representatives Adam Clayton Powell Jr. and Shirley Chisholm, and Assemblyman Charles Rangel.

November. The new Dr. Louis T. Wright Wing is dedicated at Harlem Hospital, with Dr. Arthur Logan officiating.

December 4. Black Panther leaders Fred Hampton and Mark Clark are killed in a Chicago police raid.

In a seven-to-one decision written by Chief Justice Earl Warren, the U.S. Supreme Court invalidates the ruling that expelled Congressman Adam Clayton Powell Jr. from the House of Representatives in March 1967.

Roy Wilkins and former U.N. Ambassador Arthur Goldberg head an unofficial commission organized to win the release of thirteen Black Panthers confined in New York City jails. Attorneys for the NAACP Legal Defense and Educational Fund take the case to the U.S. Supreme Court.

James Farmer is appointed assistant secretary of the Department of Health, Education and Welfare by President Richard Nixon.

The Martin Luther King Jr. Center for Nonviolent Social Change is established in Atlanta. (The Institute of the Black World, the center's research arm, becomes independent in 1970.)

The New York State Insurance Department takes action against insurance companies for racial discrimination in canceling fire insurance policies in slum areas.

Oliver Sutton is sworn in as a civil court judge. He is president of the Harlem Civic Association and vice president of the Harlem NAACP.

Ivan A. Michael is the first African American appointed to the New York City Planning Commission. A Harlem lawyer, Michael is general counsel for the United Block Association and a board member of the New York Urban League.

Robert B. Speaks is appointed as the first African American director of the newly created office of Professional Resources of the City Planning Commission.

Rhody McCoy, Ocean Hill-Brownsville School District Administrator, is appointed to the New York City Interim Board of Education. Isaiah Robinson is appointed as Manhattan's representative.

Jessie L. Behagan is appointed as the nation's first black superintendent of a woman's prison, taking charge of the Rikers Island facility, which has over five hundred inmates. (A graduate of City College, Behagan rose through the ranks in the New York City Department of Correction, with thirty-one years of service.)

Charles Alston is appointed to the eleven-member Art Commission of the City of New York, which approves the designs for all city buildings and all works of art on city property.

Robert C. Weaver is appointed president of Baruch College, CUNY. Weaver is also named to the boards of the Metropolitan Life Insurance Company and the Bowery Savings Bank.

John Henrik Clarke is appointed professor of Black Studies at Hunter College. An associate editor of *Freedomways,* Clarke is also the editor of the books *Malcolm X: The Man and His Times* and *William Styron's Nat Turner: Ten Black Writers Respond.*

Medgar Evers College, CUNY, opens in the Crown Heights section of Brooklyn.

The Metropolitan Applied Research Center (MARC), the first black think-tank in the nation, is established in Manhattan under the

Historian John Henrik Clarke.

leadership of Kenneth Clark to analyze and advocate for solutions to the problems confronting blacks, particularly those dealing with education.

Minister Louis Farrakhan announces the opening of the University of Islam in Mosque No. 7 at 116th Street and Lenox Avenue in Harlem. The redesigned burned-out building also houses classrooms for children, a restaurant, a clothing store, and a bookstore. Farrakhan advocates an independent school system to "properly provide Black people with a knowledge of themselves."

Franklin H. Williams is named president of the Phelps-Stokes Fund, a fifty-eight-year-old organization specializing in education and housing in the United States and Africa. The fund assists African postgraduate students in the United States and is also concerned with Native American affairs.

Stephen Wright is appointed president of the College Entrance Examination Board.

The Center for Urban Education initiates leadership training programs in the South Bronx and Brooklyn. Workshops are held in cooperation with the Puerto Rican Forum, and the center cooperates with the Eugenio Maria De Hostos Community College in the Bronx.

Barbara Scott Preiskel is elected president of the board, and T. George Silcott is named executive director of the interfaith, interracial Wiltwyck School for Boys in Yorktown Heights. (The school was founded in 1939 by individuals concerned that the city had no facilities for delinquent black Protestant boys under the age of twelve. Eleanor Roosevelt, Justine Wise Polier, Mrs. Marshall Field, and Marion E. Kenworthy were among the founders.)

Harlem-Dowling Children's Services, established as a satellite of Spence-Chapin Services to Children, is the city's first black-staffed agency devoted to black and Latino children and families. It is created because of the unwillingness of black teenage girls to respond

The Weeksville Lady. The nineteenth-century tintype image found at the dig site is the symbol of the Society for the Preservation of Weeksville.

to agencies outside their communities, and because of the growing number of "boarder babies" remaining in hospitals beyond the time they are medically ready for discharge.

Oliver D. Williams and Pauline Williams host the first meeting of the Weeksville Society in their home in Brooklyn. The society's goal is to restore the nineteenth-century buildings still existing from the historic African American community in the Bedford-Stuyvesant section. An archeological dig unearths significant documents and items, including the constitution and by-laws of the Abyssinian Benevolent Daughters of Esther printed in 1853 by a black printer, tintype photographs, pottery, children's clothing, and toys. (The dig was initiated the previous year by historian James Hurley and former Weeksville resident William T. Harley after it was discovered that the houses were about to be cleared for the construction of new city housing.)

The Beth Shalom Ethiopian Hebrew Congregation dedicates its new synagogue at 730 Willoughby Avenue in Brooklyn. Chief Rabbi W. A. Matthew of the Ethiopian Hebrew Congregation of

Brooklyn Scout Troop #342 participates in the Weeksville archeological dig, 1969.

America and the West Indies conducts a special service for the congregation of five hundred.

Whitney Young's *Beyond Racism* is published. It is distributed by Henry Ford II as "a book that should be read by every citizen who wonders whether there is anything he can do or should do to help eliminate racial injustice and build respect and understanding between Black and white Americans."

J. Bruce Llewellyn purchases Fedco Food Stores, a ten-store supermarket chain. (By the early 1980s, Fedco expands to twenty-seven stores grossing $85 million annually. Together with basketball star Julius Erving and comedian Bill Cosby, Llewellyn purchases a thirty-six percent share of the Coca-Cola Bottling Company of New York, which is traded in 1985 for ownership of the Philadelphia Coca-Cola Bottling Company, one of the country's largest. Other corporate ventures include investments in cable television.)

Homecoming, a collection of poems by Sonia Sanchez, is published by Broadside Press with an introduction by Don L. Lee (Haki Madhubuti). (Recognized as one of the most influential writers and proponents of black nationalism, Sanchez is also an advocate for university-level black studies programs. Her next book of poetry, *We a BaddDDD People,* is published in 1970.)

New York native **Arthur Mitchell,** moved by the assassination of Martin Luther King Jr., founds the Dance Theatre of Harlem to provide African American youth with the opportunity to learn and perform classical ballet.

Byron E. Lewis founds Uniworld Group Inc., an advertising and marketing company.

Moneta Sleet Jr., a staff photographer for Johnson Publishing Company, Inc., becomes the first African American to win a Pulitzer Prize for photography for his portrait of Coretta Scott King and her daughter at the funeral of Martin Luther King Jr.

Bronx natives Edward T. Lewis and Clarence O. Smith found the Hollingsworth Group, a magazine publishing house in New York.

Dance Theatre of Harlem poster for the company's highly acclaimed production of Firebird.

The National Newspaper Publishers Association endorses *Black Journal* in an effort to prevent the Channel 13 production from being cut. Funding for the NET show is cut from $100,000 to $10,000.

Elmore Tee Collins, one of the nation's few black animators, helps bring the new *Sesame Street* show to 170 television stations across the country. Harry Belafonte and James Earl Jones are among the special guests on the children's show hosted by Willie Lee and Loretta Long.

Charlayne Hunter-Gault, a reporter with the *New York Times,* is the first black woman inducted into the National Professional Journalism Society. (She first gained national attention when, as Charlayne Hunter, she was the first black woman admitted to the University of Georgia in 1961.)

The film *Cotton Comes to Harlem,* directed by Ossie Davis, opens, starring Raymond St. Jacques, Godfrey Cambridge, and Calvin Lockhart.

Muhammad Ali makes his Broadway acting debut in the musical *Buck White,* playing a Black Power leader. The music and lyrics are by Oscar Brown Jr., who adapted the book from the original play *Big Time Buck White* by Joseph Dolan Twotti. It is staged by Brown and Jean Pace.

Vinnie Burroughs opens her one-woman show, *Walk Together Children,* at the Greenwich Mews Theatre. She is acclaimed as a "good impersonator and a resourceful and appealing actress."

The NAACP Legal Defense and Educational Fund files suit in U.S. District Court on behalf of Muhammad Ali, asserting his right to box in New York State.

Lenny Wilkens begins his basketball coaching career as player-coach of the struggling Seattle SuperSonics.

Confined to a wheelchair because of a 1958 automobile accident, Roy Campanella is inducted into the Baseball Hall of Fame, with Casey Stengel and Stan Musial on hand for the swearing-in.

An extravagantly costumed participant in the Brooklyn West Indian Day Parade.

Carlos Lezama organizes the first Caribbean Carnival along Eastern Parkway in Brooklyn. Lezama becomes the head of the West Indian American Day Carnival Association and makes Brooklyn's Labor Day event the largest public parade in New York City.

1970

February 17. Dick Gregory and Ossie Davis lead a group of black and Puerto Rican citizens in an appeal to the United Nations to censure the United States for genocidal policies toward racial minorities.

February. A Rand Corporation study urges the city to turn over slum properties to black tenants and end the reign of white slumlords.

March. At a meeting of black Protestant clergy, Bishop W. L. Bonner urges suburban black professionals to return to Harlem and help the less fortunate.

April. The Federation of Black Community Organizations of Staten Island is formed.

June 16. Kenneth Gibson is elected mayor of Newark, New Jersey.

June 22. President Richard Nixon signs a bill extending the Voting Rights Act of 1965 to 1975.

June 23. Assemblyman Charles B. Rangel defeats incumbent Congressman Adam Clayton Powell Jr. in the Democratic primary.

June. Residents of the Brownsville section of Brooklyn protest the lack of sanitation services in the area by burning garbage in the streets.

July 4. The "Black Declaration of Independence" is published as a full-page ad in the *New York Times*. Issued by the National Committee of Black Churchmen, the document declares in part, "When in the course of Human Events, it becomes necessary for a People who were stolen from lands of their Fathers, transported under the most ruthless and brutal circumstances 5,000 miles to a strange land, sold into dehumanizing slavery, emasculated, subjugated, exploited, and discriminated against for 351 years, to call, with finality, a halt to such indignities and genocidal prac-tices—by virtue of the Laws of Nature and of Nature's God, a decent respect to the Opinions of Mankind requires that they should declare their just grievances and the urgent and necessary redress thereof."

July. After white youths attack black teenagers attending a night school program in the Flatbush section of Brooklyn, a major row occurs involving hundreds of youths.

August 3–7. Two thousand people attend the Congress of African Peoples convention in Atlanta.

August 14. The City University of New York inaugurates an open admissions policy designed to increase the number of poor and minority students.

August. The Department of Justice investigates the Lefrak building firm—developers of Lefrak City—for discriminating against non-white applicants. Black and Latino civil rights organizations expose Lefrak's racist policies. (A year later the New York Urban League announces that two hundred black and Latino families have found apartments in Lefrak-owned buildings.)

October 13. UCLA professor and political activist Angela Davis is arrested in New York City and charged with unlawful flight to avoid prosecution for her alleged role in a shootout at the Marin County courthouse in San Rafael, California, on August 7. Police charge that she helped supply the guns for the shootout, which left four people dead, including the presiding judge. (Davis is acquitted in June 1974 by a white jury in the Superior Court of San Jose.)

November 2. More than eight thousand people gather for a Black Solidarity Day rally at the Manhattan Center. Four minutes of cheering greets the mention of Angela Davis's name by attorney Haywood Burns. Burns says that the U.S. system of justice is "more criminal than just." Several organizations participate in the "soli-darity" rally, including the National Urban League, the Black Pan-thers, SNCC, and the Nation of Islam.

November. The Black Panthers and the Young Lords organize rent strikes in Bedford-Stuyvesant, Brooklyn.

Daniel Patrick Moynihan, presidential policy advisor from New York, suggests a policy of "benign neglect" of African Americans. (He is elected U.S. Senator from New York in 1976.)

The Federal National Mortgage Association (Fannie Mae) is created to provide loans in needy areas. (As with Ginnie Mae, it is discovered that much of the funding is used to provide mortgages in middle-class suburbs in the South and West rather than in the urban Northeast.)

Eleanor Holmes Norton becomes chair of the New York City Commission on Human Rights. (In 1977 she leaves that post to head the federal Equal Employment Opportunity Commission.)

Arthur Lewis becomes the first black appointed as an assistant district attorney on Staten Island.

Richard Darrell Trent becomes president of Medgar Evers College, CUNY.

William Oscar Allen becomes executive director of the Arthur C. Logan Memorial Hospital in New York.

Clara McBride Hale drops her retirement plans and opens Hale House in Manhattan to care for drug-addicted infants and children after her daughter Lorraine, a doctor, sends a young drug-addicted mother and baby to her home in Harlem.

The Coalition of 100 Black Women is established in New York City to assess and act upon issues that directly or indirectly affect the black family. The founders are concerned with the fragmentation of groups within the race and the lack of a mechanism to mobilize quickly to deal with issues confronting the community. The founding members include Edna Beach, Cathy Connor, Evelyn Cunningham, Corien Davies-Drew, Evelyn Payne-Davis, Dorothy West Gordon, Lovette Harper, Hermenia Jackson, Yvonne Jones Reid, Muriel Kellogg, Mary Burke Washington, Dorothy Orr, Elizabeth Peacock, Arden B. Shelton, Juanita Sleet, Virginia Smit, Tracey

Clara "Mother" Hale, founder of Hale House.

Tyler, Joyce Wein, Delores Wright, Laverne Usry, Martha Lewis, and Jan Yates Norton.

The Black Academy of Arts and Letters, headquartered in New York City, holds its first annual awards banquet with Harry Belafonte as master of ceremonies. A Hall of Fame is established, and Carter G. Woodson, Henry O. Tanner, W. E. B. DuBois, Paul Robeson, C. L. R. James, Lena Horne, Diana Sands, and Amiri Baraka are inducted. (The organization was founded in Boston in 1969 in the tradition of the American Negro Academy [1897–1916] to "define, reserve, cultivate, promote, foster and develop the arts and letters of black people." C. Eric Lincoln, a historian of black religion, is elected president; author John O. Killens, vice president; psychiatrist Alvin Poussaint, treasurer; and author Doris Saunders, secretary.)

I Know Why the Caged Bird Sings, by Maya Angelou, is published. With its publication she becomes the first black woman to have a nonfiction work on the best-seller list.

Toni Morrison's novel *The Bluest Eye* is published.

Charles Gordone wins a Pulitzer Prize for his play *No Place to Be Somebody.*

The Black Woman: An Anthology, compiled by Toni Cade (Bambara), is published. The anthology—which includes writings by Audre Lorde, Bambara's mother Helen Cade Brehon, Abbey Lincoln, and Alice Walker—brings women's issues to the black political agenda.

Actor, director, and writer Woodie King Jr. founds the New Federal Theatre, housed at the Henry Street Settlement on Manhattan's Lower East Side. (In 1965 King became cultural arts director of Mobilization for Youth, an antipoverty program that helped provide training for minority youth. In 1980 he creates the National Black Touring Circuit, a program to cultivate an international black theater audience.)

Men have got to develop some heart and some sound analysis to realize that when sisters get passionate about themselves and their direction, it does not mean they're readying up to kick men's ass. They're readying up for honesty. And women have got to develop some heart and some sound analysis so they can resist the temptation of buying peace with their man with self-sacrifice and posturing.

—Toni Cade (Bambara),
"On the Issue of Roles,"
The Black Woman: An Anthology

Denzel Washington and Kirk Kirksey in the New Federal Theater production of Laurence Holder's When the Chickens Come Home to Roost, *1981.*

Albert Murray's book *The Omni-Americans: New Perspectives on Black Experience and American Culture* is published. Murray maintains that what is called "black" culture is really American culture.

Louise Meriwether's *Daddy Was a Numbers Runner,* a novel about a young girl growing up in Harlem in the 1930s, is published.

The first issue of *Essence* magazine is published, with **Edward T. Lewis** as financial manager.

It is not a coincidence that the history of Black business in this country is a history of wave after wave of Black accomplishment being blocked by wall after wall of racism and backlash.

—Earl Graves, "Black Reflections: Visions of the Future," *Negro History Bulletin,* June 1981

Earl G. Graves establishes the magazine publishing house Earl G. Graves Ltd. in New York City and becomes the publisher and editor of *Black Enterprise,* the first African American business magazine.

Joseph Nelson Boyce becomes a correspondent and, later, a bureau chief for *Time* magazine.

Dr. Chester Redhead is elected the first black president of the Eastern Dental Society.

Advisory board from the inaugural issue of Black Enterprise, *1970. Seated: Edward W. Brooke, Shirley Chisholm, and Charles Evers. Standing: Earl G. Graves, John Lewis, William R. Hudgins, Julian Bond, Thomas A. Johnson, and Henry G. Parks, Jr.*

Kareem Abdul-Jabbar, playing for the Milwaukee Bucks, wins the NBA Rookie of the Year Award.

1971

January. The Congressional Black Caucus is founded.

April 6. Rev. Ralph Abernathy, chairman of SCLC, leads a march down Wall Street. Organizers accuse President Nixon, Governor Rockefeller, and Mayor Lindsay of fostering racism.

April 20. The Supreme Court rules that busing is an acceptable method of integrating public schools.

May. Anger toward city officials increases after city officials close the National Economic Growth and Reconstruction Organization (NEGRO) Harlem job-training center and factory, alleging hazardous conditions.

May 5. A protest in the Brownsville and East New York sections of Brooklyn against Governor Nelson Rockefeller's signing of legislation to cut social services begins peacefully but ends in vandalism and arson.

NBA basketball star Kareem Abdul-Jabbar.

June. Latimer Gardens, a 423-unit public housing project in Flushing, Queens, is dedicated. It is named for inventor Lewis H. Latimer, a black New Yorker.

June. WABC-TV news reporter Melba Tolliver changes her hair from straightened to natural. Tolliver, who takes on the new look the day before she is to cover Tricia Nixon's wedding at the White House, is told by studio executives to change her hair back. Advised that she looks less attractive and less feminine with her Afro, Tolliver refuses to alter her hair. Public support for Tolliver prompts the station to relent, allowing her to wear her hair as she desires.

July 23. The *Haiti Observateur* is founded in Manhattan by brothers Leopold and Raymond Joseph. The weekly newspaper's motto is "Where there is no vision, the people perish." Articles are in English and French. (The paper is now based in Brooklyn.)

July. City Commission on Human Rights Chairman Eleanor Holmes Norton investigates block-busting real estate agencies and finds "ample circumstantial evidence to indicate that unscrupulous realtors are deliberately fomenting fear and racial bigotry." New York's Secretary of State investigates the illegal practice and proposes a moratorium on realty sales in the East Flatbush and Crown Heights sections of Brooklyn, and the Laurelton and Cambria Heights areas of Queens.

July. Black residents of Jamaica and St. Albans, Queens, protest plans to build additional high-rise public housing in an already underserved neighborhood.

September 9. Inmates seize the Attica State Correctional Facility and hold several guards hostage. Their demands include coverage by the state minimum wage law, better food, and no reprisals. (Thirty-one inmates and eleven prison employees are killed during two days of rioting. Among the twenty-four-man team of negotiators are Clarence Jones, publisher of the Amsterdam News; *Assemblyman Arthur O. Eve of Buffalo; State Senator Sidney Von Luther of Harlem; and Rev. Wyatt Tee Walker, pastor of the Canaan Baptist Church and special assistant for urban affairs to Governor Rockefeller.)*

December. A dialogue by James Baldwin and Nikki Giovanni is broadcast on the television program *Soul*, on WNET-TV. (It is published as a book in 1973 with foreword by Ida Lewis and afterword by Orde Coombs.)

December 18. Jesse Jackson founds People United to Serve Humanity (PUSH) in Chicago.

A *New York Times* survey reveals a reversal in trends: more blacks are migrating south than north.

Georgia L. McMurray is appointed commissioner of the newly formed Agency for Child Development by Mayor John Lindsay.

Carmel Carrington Marr is appointed commissioner of the New York State Public Service Commission.

The Black Aesthetic, edited by Addison Gayle, is published. A manifesto of the Black Arts Movement, this collection of essays by prominent black artists repudiates white aesthetics as a valid basis for judging black art.

Camille Billops, a visual artist and instructor at Rutgers University, and her husband, James Hatch, a writer and professor of English at the City College of New York, start the Hatch-Billops Collection to answer "the need to document the lives and art of African Americans." The private research library includes theater memorabilia, manuscripts, taped interviews, slides, books, and other materials documenting black American cultural history.

Raisin, a musical based on Lorraine Hansberry's *A Raisin in the Sun,* opens on Broadway.

African American jazz musicians—including David Murray, Sam Rivers, Henry Threadgill, Craig Harris, Julius Hemphill, and Olu Dara—are developing their avant-garde expressions in the jazz loft scene.

1972

January 25. Congresswoman Shirley Chisholm launches a bid to be the presidential nominee of the Democratic party, the first black person to run for the presidency in one of the major parties. Chisholm reflects on the period that brought her to national power: "No political history of the years from 1962 to 1972 can be a faithful one unless it pays close attention to the unprecedented fact that a new generation during those years decided, almost en masse, to lay hands on their society and change it."

March 10–12. Three thousand delegates and five thousand observers attend the national black political convention in Gary, Indiana.

Congresswoman Shirley Chisholm campaigns in New York with Congressman Ed Koch.

March. The steering committee of the New York delegation to the National Black Congress calls for self-determination, self-government, and reparations.

November 17. Andrew Young of Atlanta becomes the first black congressman from the South since Reconstruction.

Benjamin J. Malcolm is appointed commissioner of the New York City Department of Corrections. He is the first black man to head the department.

Miracle Makers, a multifaceted social service organization, is developed at a day-care center founded by members of Freewill Church of God in Christ in Brooklyn. (With more than five hundred employees, Miracle Makers programs include early childhood education, support services for grandparent caregivers, child welfare services, family programs, services for the disabled, dropout prevention, homeless assistance, a SRO facility, and a training institute.)

Jerome Heartwell Holland is the first African American to serve on the board of the New York Stock Exchange.

Percy Sutton forms the Inner City Broadcasting Corporation and negotiates the purchase of WLIB-AM for $2.5 million and WLIB-FM for $600,000. Sutton fulfills a forty-year dream to own a New

Entrepreneur and civic leader Percy E. Sutton.

York City radio station. (By the end of the 1970s, Inner City Broadcasting is the most profitable black business in Harlem, with a net worth of $15 million.)

Richard D. Gidron opens Dick Gidron Cadillac Inc. in the Bronx. It is the first major black-owned automobile dealership in the city. (Today Gidron's car dealerships are among the largest in New York City.)

The Schomburg Collection is transferred by the New York Public Library from the Branch Libraries to the Research Libraries and renamed the Schomburg Center for Research in Black Culture. The library and the Schomburg Corporation secure a National Endowment Grant for the Humanities Award of $200,000 in outright and matching funds to inventory the collection for the first time in twenty-five years.

Lincoln Center holds a two-week black arts festival produced by Ellis Haizlip.

Henry Lewis becomes the first black conductor of the Metropolitan Opera with its production of *La Bohème*. (In 1968, Lewis was named conductor of the New Jersey Symphony Orchestra, becoming the first black conductor of a leading American symphony orchestra.)

Harlem-born producer and writer Suzanne de Passe co-authors the screenplay for *Lady Sings the Blues*, which becomes a successful motion picture starring Diana Ross and Billy Dee Williams. De Passe is of West Indian ancestry.

President Richard Nixon orders a moratorium on new public housing development.

1973

March. The New York Civil Liberties Union sues the New York City Housing Authority for its policy of targeting people in low-income housing projects for eviction because of the criminal activities of their nonresident adult children.

May 29. Thomas Bradley becomes mayor of Los Angeles.

July. The nation's first black-owned radio news network, National Black Network (NBN), is launched with midtown offices at 1350 Avenue of the Americas. Founded by businessmen Eugene Jackson and Sidney Small, NBN produces five-minute newscasts, a nightly sports and business report, and a news commentary program. Featured among NBN's highly regarded broadcast team is Mal Goode, who was the first black network television reporter when he joined ABC News in 1962.

August–September. An investigation is launched into the firebombing of a house in the Oakwood section of Staten Island. The bombing occurred shortly before a West Indian-American family was to take ownership.

October. The Trump Management Corporation is sued by the Justice Department in federal court for violating the Fair Housing Act by refusing to rent to nonwhite applicants.

November 6. Coleman Young is elected mayor of Detroit.

November 6. Percy Sutton wins a third term as Manhattan borough president, and City Comptroller Abraham Beame, receiving strong black voter support, becomes the city's first Jewish mayor. City Council seats are won in Brooklyn by former Assemblyman Samuel D. Wright and Mary Pinkett, president of the Social Services Employees Union, Local 371; in Harlem by Frederick Samuels; and in Queens by Archie Spigner.

New York City–born lawyer Gloria E. A. Toote is appointed by President Nixon as assistant secretary for equal opportunity of the U.S. Department of Housing and Urban Development. The appointment makes Toote the highest-ranking black woman during the Nixon and Ford administrations. (At the 1980 Republican National Convention, Toote gives a nominating speech for candidate Ronald Reagan.)

Mount Morris Park on Fifth Avenue between 122nd and 124th Streets is renamed Marcus Garvey Park.

George Washington Carver, the renowned Tuskegee Institute scientist, is inducted into New York University's Hall of Fame of Great Americans.

The Black Child: A Parents' Guide, by Phyllis Harrison-Ross and Barbara Wyden, is published. (Harrison-Ross, founder and director of the Community Mental Health Center at Metropolitan Hospital, moderates the nationally syndicated television show *All About Parents.*)

Stephen Burrows receives the Coty Award, America's highest fashion honor. (A native of New Jersey, Burrows graduated from the Fashion Institute of Technology. Henri Bendel opened a boutique called Stephen Burrows World in 1970. Burrows's second Coty Award comes in 1977.)

AUDELCO (Audience Development Committee, Inc.) is established with Vivian Robinson as president/director. The organization attempts to provide better public relations and build new audiences for nonprofit theater and dance companies. The annual AUDELCO Awards recognize excellence in black theater.

Retiring New York Mets centerfielder Willie Mays is honored by Mayor John Lindsay at Shea Stadium, Queens. (Mays began his professional career in 1948 with the Birmingham Black Barons of the Negro Leagues. In 1950 he came into major league baseball through the New York [later San Francisco] Giants' system and ended his career with the New York Mets. Mays made twenty-four All Star appearances.)

1974

January. The Renegades, a youth gang, and fifteen families use a city loan and their own labor to renovate an abandoned building in East Harlem.

April 8. Henry "Hank" Aaron, of the Atlanta Braves, breaks Babe Ruth's home run record when he hits his 715th home run.

August. Harlem businessman Lloyd Williams launches Harlem Week. (The celebration grows to an annual two-week celebration of cultural, economic, and sports achievements sponsored by the Uptown Chamber of Commerce.)

October. Police sergeant Anthony Vivelo, corrections officer Nicholas Lombardi, housing police sergeant Robert Barbieri, and real estate broker Albert Anzalone are indicted by a federal grand jury for conspiracy to vandalize a house to keep a black family out of a predominantly white neighborhood.

President Nixon signs the Housing Act of 1974 into law. No longer will the federal government be a builder of low-income housing. Instead, Section 8 of the new law provides tax and other incentives for the private sector to furnish housing for low-income residents.

Representative Charles B. Rangel becomes chair of the Congressional Black Caucus.

Paul Gibson becomes deputy mayor of New York City, the first black person to hold that position.

Dell Realty Co., Deane Realty Co., and Price Realty Co. are charged with "racial steering"—manipulating black and Latino renters and buyers through a policy of not showing them apartments and houses in predominantly white areas in Brooklyn and Queens.

A suit filed by the NAACP results in a sweeping decision by U.S. District Court Judge Jack Weinstein ordering city and federal officials to desegregate a Brooklyn high school by correcting the demographic imbalance in a local housing project, providing parks and playgrounds, and insuring the safety of the area. He also demanded that busing to integrate the school begin immediately, and gave the officials two months to submit a plan and eight months to begin its implementation.

William Aiken of Aiken & Wilson CPAs becomes the first black person appointed to the New York State Board for Public Accountancy.

The Adam Clayton Powell Jr. State Office Building is dedicated at the corner of 125th Street and Adam Clayton Powell Jr. Boulevard (Seventh Avenue).

Working from his midtown Manhattan office, boxing promoter **Don King** orchestrates the "Rumble in the Jungle" between Muhammad Ali and George Foreman in Zaire, his first major fight production.

Brooklyn-born singer and actress Stephanie Mills stars as Dorothy in the Broadway opening of the musical *The Wiz,* directed by Geoffrey Holder.

1975

January. The Rosedale, Queens, home of Mr. and Mrs. Ormistan Spencer, a black couple, is firebombed. (In June 1975, Arthur Lanoni and Michael Biggio, the two white men arrested for the January bombing, are acquitted. Another pipe bomb explodes at the Spencer residence in July. In August Spencer is confronted by a "white rights" group outside his home. Spencer, brandishing a gun, and his wife are shot when the gun fires as police attempt to disarm him. He is charged with criminal possession of a firearm. In December a bomb arrives with a note from the Ku Klux Klan. In April 1976 Spencer is cleared of the criminal possession charges.)

May. The Schomburg Center's fiftieth anniversary is celebrated with a reception at the 135th Street building. (An exhibition opens at the Library's Central Building in November with a reception and a screening of the documentary film *From These Roots,* co-produced by William Greaves and the Center.)

July 5. Arthur Ashe becomes the first African American man to win the Wimbledon singles title.

October. Black off-duty policemen begin patrolling in Rosedale, Queens, to stop the harassment of black residents. The patrols are an immediate response to the September firebombing of the home of another black family, the Wynders.

Puerto Rico–born Brooklyn lawyer Gilbert Ramirez, a long-time activist and politician in the Bedford-Stuyvesant area, becomes a justice of the New York State Supreme Court.

The Bedford Stuyvesant Restoration Commercial Center is opened at Fulton and Herkimer Streets in Brooklyn. Constructed at a cost of $6 million, it offers office and commercial space and a skating rink.

A ten-acre park at Broadway and Richmond Terrace on Staten Island is dedicated to Laurence C. Thompson, the first black serviceman killed in the Vietnam War.

Black women doctors in New York City establish the Susan Smith McKinney Medical Association.

Award-winning singer and producer Roberta Flack establishes her production company, Magic Lady Inc., in New York.

1976

March 2. *Bubbling Brown Sugar,* by Loften Mitchell, opens on Broadway. The musical charts the history of African American entertainment in Harlem from 1910 to 1940.

July. The Democratic National Convention is held in New York City. Former Georgia governor James Earl Carter is nominated for the presidency with strong black support. Former Texas Congresswoman Barbara Jordan delivers the keynote address, and Rev. Martin Luther King Sr. closes the convention.

September 28. Muhammad Ali defeats Ken Norton at Madison Square Garden.

The Home Mortgage Disclosure Act becomes law, strengthening laws against redlining.

The New York Police Department takes almost two hours to respond to a report that a group of white youths has broken into the Staten Island house of a black family. The police are accused of failing to protect black residents.

Vernon Jordan becomes head of the National Urban League.

Benjamin Hooks replaces Roy Wilkins as executive secretary of the National NAACP.

Civil rights leader Vernon E. Jordan Jr.

Black Agency Executives is organized to support the emerging group of "first" black managers who head social service agencies that were previously administered by whites but now service predominantly black constituencies.

Ntozake Shange's choreopoem *for colored girls who have considered suicide, when the rainbow is enuf* opens on Broadway. The play wins an Obie Award, as well as Emmy, Tony, and Grammy Award nominations.

Designer Willi Smith launches his own clothing label, WilliWear Ltd. (Smith's first business attempt was in 1973 with his sister, actress Toukie Smith, who often modeled his clothes. By 1982 WilliWear has an annual gross topping $5 million. Smith introduces WilliWear Men in 1978. His awards include Designer of the Year, International Mannequins, 1978; Coty American Fashion Critic's Award for Women's Fashions, 1983; and the Cutty Sark Award, 1986, for menswear design.)

Vinnette J. Carroll becomes the first black woman to direct a Broadway musical with the opening of *Your Arms Too Short to Box With God.* She collaborates with New York-based actress and songwriter Micki Grant.

1977

President Jimmy Carter tours the South Bronx. He pledges to rebuild the devastated Charlotte Street neighborhood.

Andrew Young is named by President Jimmy Carter as America's first black Ambassador to the United Nations.

January. The television miniseries based on Alex Haley's novel Roots *is broadcast on ABC television and is viewed by 130 million viewers over eight consecutive evenings. Haley wins a special Pulitzer Prize. The series also captures nine Emmy awards, the largest number ever awarded to a single television series.*

February 11. Clifford Alexander Jr. is nominated and confirmed as the first black Secretary of the United States Army.

July 10. Hundreds of black residents demonstrate at the 71st Precinct, Crown Heights, Brooklyn, against the Lubavitch Hasidic civilian anticrime patrol that operates in the neighborhood. They accuse the patrol of indiscriminately targeting black people.

July 13–14. An electrical power blackout brings massive looting and vandalism in New York City's commercial districts. Especially hard hit are black neighborhoods like Harlem and Bedford-Stuyvesant. Mayoral candidates Edward Koch and Herman Badillo use the unrest to attack Mayor Abraham Beame. President Jimmy Carter rejects the city's bid for federal disaster funds.

August. Clerk of the City of New York David N. Dinkins, chairman of the Council of Black Elected Democrats, asks its members to condemn President Carter for failing to grant disaster-area status to sections of the city affected by looting.

October 18. Reggie Jackson hits three home runs in the last game of the World Series to lead the Yankees' triumph over the Los Angeles Dodgers.

October. Three hundred members of the Allah Nation of Five Percenters attend a City Planning Commission meeting to protest plans for building housing on the Harlem site where they have run a school since 1967.

October. A coalition of black leaders accuses the Tri-State United Way of neglecting African American and Latino citizens. The United Way takes their criticisms under consideration.

November 8. Former U.S. Representative Ed Koch, a Democrat, is elected mayor, defeating Liberal party candidate Mario Cuomo and Republican Roy Goodman. Manhattan Borough President Percy Sutton says that Koch has promised to appoint more blacks to key positions than three of his predecessors—Beame, Lindsay, and Wagner—combined. In the Bronx, Rev. Wendell Foster wins a seat on the City Council. Brooklyn City Council incumbents Samuel D. Wright and Mary Pinckett are re-elected, as is Archie Spigner in Queens.

Diplomat Barbara M. Watson.

Barbara Watson is named assistant secretary of state for consular affairs, the first woman to hold this diplomatic rank.

Manhattan Borough President Percy Sutton makes an unsuccessful bid to be the Democratic nominee for mayor of New York. In addition to being supported by his Manhattan constituency, Sutton is supported by a West Indian political club organized by Dr. Lamuel Stanislaus, a Grenadian immigrant and a community leader in Crown Heights, Brooklyn.

Lucille Mason Rose becomes deputy mayor of New York City, the first black woman to hold that position.

Brooklyn activist Rev. Herbert Daniel Daughtry founds the Commission on African Solidarity and the Coalition of Concerned Leaders & Citizens to Save Our Children. (He becomes a board member of the United African-American Churches of New York State, the National Rainbow Coalition, and the Randolph Evans Memorial Scholarship Fund.)

Roscoe C. Brown Jr., an educator and former Tuskegee Airmen squadron commander, is named president of Bronx Community College.

Everybody's: The Caribbean-American Magazine is established by Grenadian immigrant Herman Hall to cover Caribbean and Caribbean New York politics and culture.

William Anthony "Tony" Brown establishes Tony Brown Productions in New York City. (The following year he begins the popular syndicated television show *Tony Brown's Journal*. Brown had earlier founded and served as the first dean of the School of Communications at Howard University.)

1978

January 9. Gordon J. Davis is appointed Commissioner of Parks and Recreation by Mayor Koch. (Formerly a member of the City Planning Commission, Davis restores the Sheep Meadow in Central Park and co-founds the Central Park Conservancy. He later becomes a member of the Board of Trustees of the New York Public Library and helped found Jazz at Lincoln Center, serving as chairman of its board of directors.)

January 16. Three black astronauts are named: Maj. Frederick G. Gregory, Maj. Guion S. Bluford, and Dr. Ronald E. McNair.

March. The Justice Department charges that Trump Management, owners of fifteen thousand apartments in New York City, continues to discriminate against black applicants. (Trump had earlier stipulated with the court that it would cease its discriminatory practices.)

March. The Black Community Congress of Central Brooklyn is founded during a three-day convention. It is intended to be a watchdog for organizations affecting the district.

June 17. Arthur Miller, a community leader in Crown Heights, Brooklyn, is choked to death by police officers during the arrest of his brother, Samuel Miller, for driving without a license. In response, Mayor Edward Koch names Deputy Mayor Herman Badillo to head a Commission on Intergroup Relations. (Later that year a Brooklyn grand jury clears the police of wrongdoing. The United States Justice Department agrees to investigate the death.)

June. The Men of Crown Heights, a black civilian patrol group, is founded in Brooklyn. It begins with three hundred members.

June 28. The Supreme Court orders the University of California Medical School to admit Allan P. Bakke, a white man, in a "reverse" discrimination suit.

July. A Black United Front protest in Crown Heights, Brooklyn, in response to the death of Arthur Miller, attracts two thousand participants. The Policemen's Benevolent Association holds a simultaneous and antagonistic march remembering the eleven officers killed in Brooklyn over the prior sixteen years.

August. Brooklyn minister Rev. Herbert Daughtry leads a group to protest the killing of Arthur Miller during President Carter's signing of a bill granting federal aid to New York City.

November. A thousand people march from Crown Heights, Brooklyn, to Manhattan's financial district during a Black United Front protest against racial violence and police brutality. They condemn the low quality of policing in Crown Heights.

The National Urban League declares the state of race relations in New York City to be at a twenty-year low. The League pays special attention to the relationship between the New York Police Department and African Americans.

Eighth Avenue in Harlem is renamed Frederick Douglass Boulevard.

Clifton R. Wharton Jr., former president of Michigan State University, becomes the first African American chancellor of the State University of New York.

Warrington Hudlin establishes the Black Filmmaker Foundation in New York City. (Hudlin releases a feature film, *Street Corner Stories,* in 1979. He goes on to release films in a joint venture with his brother Reginald Alan Hudlin, including *House Party,* 1990; *Boomerang,* 1992; and *BeBe's Kids,* 1992.)

Quincy Thomas Troupe Jr. wins the American Book Award of the Association of American Publishers for *Snake-back Solos: Selected Poems, 1969–1977.*

The Brooklyn Museum opens the exhibition "Two Centuries of Black American Art."

Jeanne Moutoussamy-Ashe's photography exhibition tours the Soviet Union. (Moutoussamy-Ashe studied at Cooper Union and New York University. In 1982 she publishes *Daufuskie Island,* a photo essay on a South Carolina culture. She is married to tennis star and sports historian Arthur Ashe.)

1979

Marcus Alexis is appointed chairman of the Interstate Commerce Commission.

January 30. **Franklin A. Thomas** is named president of the Ford Foundation, the first African American to head a major American foundation.

February. The NAACP wins a court case to stop Staten Island officials from placing a low-income housing project in an area largely occupied by minorities and the poor.

April. Governor Hugh Carey signs a bill that allows groups of tenants, rather than just individuals, to file suits in New York City Housing Court for unsatisfactory living conditions.

May. The Council of Churches of New York City reports that 133 congregations have formed 84 nonprofit housing organizations and constructed over 33,000 apartments in the previous four years. A *New York Times* article on the report features Harlem's St. Philip's Episcopal Church.

August 22. Two hundred black leaders, meeting in New York City, express support for former U.N. Ambassador Andrew Young, who resigned under pressure after an unauthorized meeting with representatives of the Palestine Liberation Organization. The group demands that blacks be given a voice in shaping American foreign policy. (Young is succeeded by career diplomat Donald McHenry.)

August. White residents firebomb the house of David Sicard and Renee Burwell, a black couple living in Rosedale, Queens.

August. The Harlem Urban Development Corporation announces a $122 million project to redevelop the northern section of Central Park.

September. A cross is burned outside the Flatbush, Brooklyn, house of Jocelyn Morgan, a black woman.

Bennet Simon and P. Anthony Keating are held for burning a cross outside the house of Wayne Quamina, a black man living in Borough Park, Brooklyn.

Crosses are burned outside the homes of two black families on Garibaldi Avenue, New Dorp Beach, Staten Island. (Several hundred people march through the neighborhood to protest violence against black residents. Later that month three thirteen-year-old white boys are arrested for the cross burning.)

November. A march from Harlem to the United Nations is one of the events during Black Solidarity Day. Dr. Carlos Russell and Gene Adams lead the procession. They demand an opportunity to present a list of grievances to U.N. Secretary General Kurt Waldheim.

December. The Open Housing Center of the NAACP Metropolitan Council and Columbia University Law School's Fair Housing Clinic file suit against the Starrett City housing complex in Brooklyn for discriminating against black applicants.

Amalya Lyle Kearse is appointed to the United States Court of Appeals, Second Circuit, New York City. She is the first woman justice in the Second Circuit.

Haskell G. Ward is appointed deputy mayor for human services. (Ward had previously been deputy administrator of program operations at the Human Resources Administration.)

Mayor Edward Koch appoints Gloria M. Allen, a pediatrician from Queens, to head the Commission on the Status of Women in New York City.

North General Hospital opens in an eight-story building at Madison Avenue and 124th Street, formerly occupied by the Hospital for Joint Diseases, which moved downtown. (North General's founder and president, Eugene L. McCabe, leads a $150 million fund-raising effort to build a new facility. In 1991 a new 200-bed community hospital is constructed at 1879 Madison Avenue.)

The Valley is created by the Cathedral of St. John the Divine on the Upper West Side of Manhattan to deal with the problems of black and Latino youth between the ages of fourteen and twenty-four. Executive director John Bess develops educational, job services, arts, recreation, counseling, and leadership development programs. (By 1998 the organization serves over 100,000 youth.)

The Sandy Ground Historical Society is formed in an attempt to preserve and publicize the existence of the oldest "surviving free black community in the United States." (The Staten Island neighborhood is later included in the National Register for Historic Places, and the Moses K. Harris House becomes a National Landmark. The community was founded in the early 1800s by free black people, largely strawberry farmers, from New York and New Jersey, and freed oystermen from Maryland and Virginia.)

Ella Fitzgerald.

Ella Fitzgerald receives a Kennedy Center Medal of Honor from President Jimmy Carter for her lifetime achievements.

Lois Alexander opens the Black Fashion Museum on West 126th Street in Harlem.

The Sugar Hill Gang releases one of the first recorded rap albums, *Rapper's Delight,* which sells over two million copies in the United States and eight million worldwide. The group stars Guy "Master

Gee" O'Brien of New York, Michael "Wonder Mike" Wright of Montclair, New Jersey, and Henry "Big Bank Hank" Jackson of the Bronx. Sugar Hill Records, founded in Englewood, New Jersey, handles the group and is the first company dedicated to rap music. (Sugar Hill goes on to introduce such pioneering artists as Grandmaster Flash, Kurtis Blow, and Sequence—the first women's rap group.)

Betty Allen becomes executive director of the Harlem School of the Arts. An accomplished opera singer and teacher, Allen also chairs the voice department.

Willie Mays, former All Star player with the Giants and Mets, is elected to the Baseball Hall of Fame.

1980

January 12. The New York Police Department loses a discrimination case when a local court rules that fifty percent of all newly hired police officers must be black or Latino. At the time the department is almost ninety percent white. (Later in the year the Court of Appeals amends the January 12 ruling, deciding that until a new police examination is developed, a third of all newly hired officers must be black or Latino.)

January. A cross is burned on the front lawn of the house of an interracial couple in the East Bronx.

May 29. Vernon Jordan, president of the National Urban League, is shot outside his Fort Wayne, Indiana, motel room. He survives a rifle shot that leaves a fist-sized hole in his back.

June. The National Black United Front hosts one thousand delegates from thirty-four states at a national conference convened in Brooklyn. Rev. Herbert Daughtry is chairman and national organizer.

July. A U.S. District Court judge forbids Bedford Gardens, a Brooklyn housing development, to implement a quota system that would favor Hasidic Jewish applicants over black and Puerto Rican renters.

August. President Jimmy Carter and presidential candidate Ronald Reagan address the National Urban League during its convention in New York City.

August. Prime Minister Robert Mugabe of Zimbabwe is the featured speaker during the Harlem Week celebration. The prime minister advocates racial pride.

September. The *New York Times* pays a group of nonwhite employees $685,000 to settle a racial discrimination suit.

With a $15,000 personal loan, Robert L. Johnson begins operating Black Entertainment Television (BET), the first black-owned cable satellite television network.

Haitian Creole is second only to Spanish as the native language of immigrant children in the New York City public school system.

The Caribbean Action Lobby, a national political organization, is founded. Among the organizers are former New York State Senator Waldaba Stewart and *Carib News* writer Colin Moore.

F. Donnie Forde, an immigrant from Aruba, establishes Caribbean American Media Studies to collect and distribute information on West Indians in New York City.

Artist Romare Bearden opens an exhibit at the Brooklyn Museum.

Gil Noble, host of *Like It Is* on WABC-TV, wins two Emmy awards.

Toni Cade Bambara wins the American Book Award for her novel *The Salt Eaters*. (Her earlier works include two collections of short stories, *Gorilla, My Love* [1972] and *The Sea Birds Are Still Alive* [1977]. Bambara was born in New York and raised in Harlem, Bedford-Stuyvesant, Queens, and Jersey City, New Jersey.)

William Greaves is inducted into the Black Filmmakers Hall of Fame, and is an honoree at the first Retrospective of Black American Films in Paris. (A director, producer, and writer, Greaves's work behind the camera earns over sixty international film festival awards. In addition to *From These Roots,* on the Harlem Renaissance period, his documentary film subjects include Ida B. Wells, Booker T. Washington, Frederick Douglass, and Ralph Bunche. He is executive producer for Universal's feature film *Bustin' Loose,* starring Richard Pryor and Cicely Tyson.)

Stephanie Mills wins a Grammy award for her million-selling single "Never Knew Love Like This Before." The following year the song wins her an American Music Award.

1981

January 22. Samuel Riley Pierce Jr. is named Secretary of Housing and Urban Development.

March. Five white youths from Far Rockaway, Queens, are arrested after they use an automobile in an attempt to kill three young black women.

May 12. *Lena Horne: The Lady and Her Music* opens on Broadway. (The show wins Tony, Drama Desk, Drama Critics Circle, and Grammy awards, and becomes the longest running one-woman show on Broadway.)

July. Mayor Edward Koch announces an end to the city's policy of giving preference to neighborhood residents when selling off city-owned property in Harlem. Community leaders fear that the change will lead to gentrification. (Those fears are fanned again in August 1982, when Koch announces his housing and economic redevelopment plan for Harlem.)

September. U.S. policy regarding the Haitian "boat people" hardens. President Ronald Reagan orders the Coast Guard to stop and search all Haitian vessels in waters between the United States and Haiti. Ships are directed back to Haiti, and refugees who complete the voyage to the United States are held in detention camps. The Catholic bishops of the United States, the Congressional Black Caucus, NAACP, labor unions, and other organizations protest the President's policy toward Haitians. (Between October 1981 and September 1991, more than 23,000 Haitian immigrants are intercepted by the Coast Guard. Only twenty-four are judged to have credible claims of political per-

Lena Horne.

secution allowing them to be paroled into the United States to pursue asylum claims.)

October 27. Andrew Young is elected mayor of Atlanta.

Lillian Roberts is appointed commissioner of the New York State Department of Labor.

Carlos Cardozo Campbell is named assistant secretary of commerce.

Walter Nobles becomes the first black brigade commander, the highest ranking midshipman, at the U.S. Naval Academy. (Born and raised in New York City, Nobles majored in physical science.)

Roy Emile Alfredo Innis, born in St. Croix, becomes national chairman of the Congress of Racial Equality (CORE). Innis looks to recharge the failing civil rights organization. (He had been national director of CORE since 1968.)

The National Coalition of 100 Black Women (NCBW) is founded as an expansion of the Coalition of 100 Black Women. The organization presents an annual Candace Award to recognize black women of achievement. (By 1991, under the leadership of president Jewel Jackson McCabe, NCBW grows to fifty-nine chapters in twenty-two states and the District of Columbia.)

Suzanne de Passe becomes president of Motown Productions, the film division of Motown Records. (In 1992 she forms her own company, de Passe Entertainment.)

Susan L. Taylor, beauty editor, succeeds Marcia Ann Gillespie as editor-in-chief of *Essence* magazine. (Taylor's inspirational books include *Lessons in Living,* 1995; *In the Spirit: The Inspirational Writings of Susan L. Taylor,* 1993; and *Confirmation: The Spiritual Wisdom That Has Shaped Our Lives,* 1997, with her husband, writer Khephra Burns.)

Award-winning journalist Edward R. Bradley leaves *CBS Reports* to become a correspondent on CBS's *60 Minutes.*

St. Clair Bourne Jr. produces a major segment of an NBC-TV *White Paper Special,* "America: Black and White." He is the only independent producer on the project, which wins the Monte Carlo Film Festival's Best Documentary Award. (Documentary films produced by Bourne include *In Motion: Amiri Baraka, The Black and the Green,* and *Langston Hughes: The Dream Keeper.*)

Composer, arranger, and music executive Quincy Jones.

Award-winning musician and producer **Quincy Delight Jones Jr.** founds Quest Records in New York City.

Giancarlo Esposito wins an Obie award for his performance in *Zooman and the Sign.*

Brooklynite Bernard King is named the NBA's first-ever Comeback Player of the Year.

1982

January 1. John E. Jacob, executive vice president of the National Urban League, succeeds Vernon Jordan as president of the League.

June 29. President Reagan signs a bill extending provisions of the 1965 Voting Rights Act for twenty-five years.

Rev. Jesse Jackson travels to the Vatican to meet with Pope John Paul II. He discusses United States policies toward Haitian refugees.

June 29. Karl B. Rodney begins publishing *The New York Carib News,* a weekly newspaper covering Caribbean affairs in New York and the Caribbean. Rodney is former president of the Jamaican Progressive League. (By 1999 circulation reaches 67,000.)

July. **Rev. Emerson J. Moore** becomes auxiliary bishop in the Catholic Archdiocese of New York.

Bishop Emerson Moore with Pope John Paul II, St. Charles Borromeo Church, Harlem, 1979.

Representative Shirley Chisholm announces that she will not seek re-election after thirteen years in the House. She cites the difficulty of serving her district and the damage being done to it by Ronald Reagan's presidency.

November 2. Former state senator **Major R. Owens** succeeds Shirley Chisholm as the U.S. Representative from the Eleventh Congressional District in Brooklyn.

Constance Baker Motley becomes chief judge of the Southern District of New York.

Associated Black Charities (ABC), a human service federation, is founded by Black Agency Executives to promote the delivery of quality health and human services to African Americans through a system of voluntary community-based organizations. Member agencies throughout New York City address community needs through day care, senior care, foster care, preventive services, emergency food and shelter, youth employment training, medical and mental health care, and substance abuse prevention and rehabilitation services. ABC provides the agencies with financial, managerial, and technical assistance.

Seventeen hundred people participate in a New York City Black Convention at City College in Harlem, seeking to solve issues facing the black community and to find ways to hold elected officials accountable. The event, organized by the Harlem Commonwealth Council, results in the formation of a network of two thousand people.

The Association of Community Organizations for Reform Now (ACORN) holds a rally at which it demands that city officials begin a homesteading program for abandoned houses in the East New York and Brownsville sections of Brooklyn.

Bryant Charles Gumbel becomes the co-host of NBC-TV's *Today* show, the top-rated and most widely watched morning news program on national network television.

Presidential candidate Gov. Bill Clinton being interviewed by Today *host Bryant Gumbel, 1992.*

Spike (Shelton Jackson) Lee wins the Academy of Motion Picture Arts & Sciences' Student Academy Award for *Joe's Bed-Stuy Barber Shop: We Cut Heads.*

Dr. Dial Hewlett Jr. becomes chief of infectious diseases at Lincoln Medical and Mental Health Center in the Bronx.

Charles Fuller wins a Pulitzer Prize for *A Soldier's Play,* produced by the Negro Ensemble Company. (The play is made into the motion picture *A Soldier's Story* in 1984.)

John A. Williams wins an American Book Award for his novel *!Click Song.*

Gloria Naylor publishes her first novel, *The Women of Brewster Place,* a year after graduating from Brooklyn College. The book receives an American Book Award in 1983.

The New Renaissance Writers Guild is formed with founding members Arthur R. Flowers, Joyce L. Dukes, Martin Simmons, Brenda Connor-Bey, Wesley Brown, Rachel Christmas, Walter Dean Myers, Doris Jean Austin, Terry McMillan, Jackie Johnson, and Stephanie Williams.

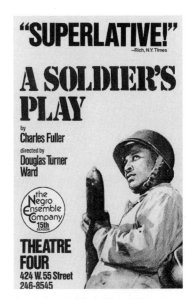

Poster for A Soldier's Play, *1982.*

*Director Spike Lee and cinemato-
grapher Ernest Dickerson on the set
of* Malcom X.

1983

January. Mayor Edward Koch announces plans to sell sixteen city-owned brownstones in Harlem. The buildings will be converted into condominiums and sold to Harlem residents.

March. The New York Appellate Division of the State Supreme Court rules that the city can continue to publish notices of public hearings only in English. The ruling comes in spite of the rapid growth of the Latino, Haitian, Chinese, and Korean immigrant communities.

April 29. Harold Washington is sworn in as the first black mayor of Chicago.

June. Black picnickers at Miller Field in New Dorp, Staten Island, are attacked by a gang of white teenagers.

July. Governor Mario Cuomo meets with the leaders of East Brooklyn Churches to discuss their Nehemiah Plan, a housing and commercial redevelopment strategy to build low-rise, single-family houses and bring middle- and working-class families back to the area. The state promises $7.5 million in support. (In November a plan to build a thousand Nehemiah houses on twenty vacant blocks in Brownsville, Brooklyn, is announced.)

July. The groundbreaking is held for a $14 million housing project, the Hunterfly Estates, in Bedford-Stuyvesant, Brooklyn.

July. The Audubon Apartments open in Harlem. (The Harlem Commonwealth Council sponsored the rehabilitation using federal funds.)

September 17. Vanessa Williams, born in the Bronx, wins the 1984 Miss America pageant. (Forced to resign the title during her reign, Williams later becomes a successful actress and singer.)

September. Twenty-five-year-old Michael Stewart of Brooklyn slips into a coma and dies in police custody after being arrested for painting graffiti on a subway wall. (The Stewart family and their advisors insist that the young man was choked and beaten by the police. New York City chief medical examiner Dr. Elliot Gross issues an autopsy report that confirms that Stewart suffered bodily injuries and facial bruises but pinpoints the cause of death as unrelated heart failure. The Stewart family demands that Gross be removed from office for destroying evidence by removing the victim's eyes without permission. Black civil rights advocates protest outside the offices of Manhattan district attorney Robert Morgenthau.)

September. State health commissioner David Axelrod charges that most of the children being housed in the welfare hotels that the city rents for the homeless are suffering from malnutrition. Mayor Koch responds that an examination of over two thousand children disclosed no cases of malnutrition but many other health issues.

October. Black families bring a class action lawsuit against the Starrett City housing complex in Brooklyn, challenging its thirty-five percent black residency ceiling. (The struggle for space in Starrett City underscores the tightly restricted housing market for black renters and buyers. Starrett remains a prime location for black apartment seekers, although the same month that the suit was filed a New York Public Interest Research Group [NYPIRG] report found a disproportionate number of respiratory illness cases among residents at Starrett City, which sits near a large city landfill. A settlement reached with Starrett City in May of the following year is then challenged by the Reagan administration. In April 1985 a federal judge approves a plan according to which Starrett City will continue to rent the majority of its apartments to white people in order to "maintain racial balance." In May 1987 a federal court bars racial quotas that limit nonwhite residency.)

October 25. U.S. Marines invade the Caribbean island of Grenada.

November 2. President Reagan signs a bill designating the third Monday of January as a federal holiday in honor of Martin Luther King Jr.

November. The NAACP Legal Defense Fund files a class action suit charging that the Helmsley-Spear realty company is discriminating against black people.

Black leaders from New York City ask Congress to investigate brutality and misconduct in the New York Police Department.

Richard L. Rowe becomes general manager of John F. Kennedy International Airport.

Jessye Norman makes her Metropolitan Opera debut in the role of Cassandre in Berlioz's *Les Troyens.*

Under the direction of Walter Turnbull, the Boys Choir of Harlem makes its first national tour.

Wild Style, one of the first films generated by the success of rap music, is released.

1984
Bishop Desmond Tutu of South Africa receives the Nobel Peace Prize for his opposition to apartheid.

W. Wilson Goode is elected mayor of Philadelphia.

June 6. Andrew W. Cooper begins publishing *The City Sun* in Brooklyn. (The paper reaches a circulation of 64,000 before its demise in 1997.)

August. Diane L. Dixon of the Brooklyn-based Atoms Track Club wins an Olympic gold medal with the U.S. 4 × 400-meter relay

Jessye Norman.

team. (In 1988 Dixon is on the silver medal 4 × 400-meter relay Olympic team. In 1991 she sets the American indoor record for 400 meters and the world indoor record for 440 yards. From 1982 to 1992 she reigns as U.S. National Indoor Champion at 400 meters.)

August. Patrick Aloysius Ewing of the New York Knicks wins a gold medal with the U.S. basketball team at the Olympics. (Ewing repeats as a gold medalist with the 1992 team.)

October 29. Sixty-six-year-old Eleanor Bumpurs is slain in her Bronx apartment by two shotgun blasts fired by a white police officer during an eviction proceeding. The shots are fired by Officer Stephen Sullivan at almost point-blank range. (Although Bumpurs had a history of mental problems, a city medical consultant had examined her four days earlier and found her to be no danger to herself or others. Tried for manslaughter in 1987, Sullivan contends that the shooting was necessary because Bumpurs attacked a fellow officer with a ten-inch kitchen knife. The prosecution maintains that the second blast, which killed her, was unnecessary because the first had badly injured the hand in which she was holding the knife. Justice Fred W. Eggert, who presided over the six-week nonjury trial in State Supreme Court in the Bronx, finds Sullivan not guilty.)

Benjamin Ward is appointed by Mayor Edward Koch as the first black person to serve as commissioner of the New York City Police Department. (Ward resigns in 1989 because of health problems related to asthma.)

The Nehemiah Plan constructs more than fifteen hundred houses on vacant land. The plan is declared a national model for low-income home ownership.

Congressmen Major Owens and Charles Schumer of Brooklyn make a joint appeal for African Americans and Jews to "re-establish the kinship that served them in the past."

Arthur Ashe and Harry Belafonte organize Artists and Athletes Against Apartheid to support the South African liberation movement.

Racism can't be overcome. It will be there for the rest of your life. There will always be people who don't like you because you're Black, Hispanic, Jewish. You have to figure out how to deal with it. Racism is not an excuse to not do the best you can.

—Arthur Ashe,
Sports Illustrated, July 1991

Howard Dodson Jr. is named chief of the Schomburg Center for Research in Black Culture of the New York Public Library. (Dodson guides the Schomburg Center through a successful $15.2 million capital campaign and an $8.8 million construction and renovation project. He also institutes a scholars-in-residence program and expands the agenda of public cultural and educational programs.)

Jane Morgan Lyons becomes the first African American woman to serve as the Chief Executive Officer of the Sea View Hospital Rehabilitation Center and Home in Staten Island. She assumes responsibility for administering the 304-bed institution, including its adult day care and respite programs, and oversees a $26 million budget and seventy acres of land with over forty buildings.

Poster for The Piano Lesson, 1990.

August Wilson wins the New York Drama Critics Circle Award for his play *Ma Rainey's Black Bottom*. (Wilson wins Pulitzer Prizes for *Fences* in 1987 and *The Piano Lesson* in 1990. The plays are directed by Lloyd Richards, artistic director of the Yale Drama School.)

The Cosby Show airs on NBC-TV. Filmed in NBC's Brooklyn studios, the show intentionally avoids many of the racial stereotypes that have long burdened black performance and enjoys an eight-year run as the most popular situation comedy on television. The cast includes comedian and actor **William "Bill" Cosby Jr.** and Phylicia Ayers Allen (Rashad), Malcolm-Jamal Warner, and Tempestt Bledsoe.

Def Jam Records is organized in New York City by Rick Rubin and DJ Jazzy Jay. (Under Russell Simmons's leadership, Def Jam becomes the most powerful label in rap music, ending the early dominance of Sugar Hill Records.)

Peter Westbrook wins an Olympic bronze medal in the saber competition. (Westbrook was the first black NCAA saber champion in 1974 while a student at New York University [NYU].)

1985

February. Stephen Sullivan, the policeman who shot Eleanor Bumpurs, is indicted for manslaughter. (In April the indictment is dismissed and Sullivan returns to work on full status. The case is reopened in 1987 but Sullivan is again cleared. In March 1991, under Mayor David Dinkins, the city agrees to pay $200,000 to the Bumpurs estate.)

February. A bomb explodes at the offices of the Patrolmen's Benevolent Association. A group calling itself the Red Guerrilla Defense claims responsibility and suggests that the bomb is to avenge the PBA's support for the police killings of Eleanor Bumpurs and Michael Stewart.

February. Harry Belafonte wins the ABAA Music Award and a Grammy for his efforts to aid Ethiopian famine victims and for conceiving and giving leadership to USA for Africa with the production of the award-winning *We Are the World* album and video.

February. Herman "Denny" Farrell, state assemblyman from Manhattan, announces his candidacy for the mayoralty against incumbent Edward I. Koch. (Farrell's entry into the race deflates the campaign of Herman Badillo, the most recognizable challenger, by dividing black and Latino voters. Both bids are unsuccessful.)

Assemblyman Al Vann unsuccessfully challenges incumbent Howard Golden for the borough presidency of Brooklyn. Vann and a number of black politicians in Brooklyn are seeking to restructure borough politics through the Coalition for Community Empowerment.

Medgar Evers College establishes the Center for Law and Social Justice on its Brooklyn campus to address major policy issues related to public and private discrimination in New York City. It monitors and develops studies on police brutality, provides legal expertise on redistricting and mortgage discrimination, and operates a parent education program to encourage parental involvement in public schools. Attorney Esmeralda Simmons becomes director of the new Center. (A Brooklyn native, Simmons has served with the New York State Division of Human Rights, the New York State Attorney General's office, and the Office of Civil Rights of the U.S. Department of Education.)

Lamuel Stanislaus becomes Grenada's ambassador to the United Nations. Although born in Grenada, Dr. Stanislaus is a U.S. citizen who resides in Crown Heights, Brooklyn.

Bill Cosby.

Herman "Denny" Farrell announces his candidacy for mayor on the steps of City Hall.

Wardell R. Lazard begins the Wall Street investment banking firm W. R. Lazard & Co.

Amaziah Howell III establishes Howell Petroleum Products Inc. at the Brooklyn Navy Yard.

Sonia Sanchez receives an American Book Award for *homegirls & handgrenades*, a book of poetry and prose.

The Apollo Theatre's fiftieth anniversary is marked with a gala celebration. (The Apollo's revival began when it was purchased by an investment group headed by Percy Sutton in 1981. Declared a national historic landmark, the theater continues its commitment to black entertainment as the nonprofit Apollo Theatre Foundation, chaired by Representative Charles Rangel.)

LL Cool J, born James Todd Smith in Queens, signs with Def Jam Records and releases *Radio*. (The album goes platinum. The movie *Krush Groove* opens, starring New York rappers Run DMC and LL

From "Reflections After the June 12th March for Disarmament"

I have come to you tonite because there are
inhumanitarians in the world. they are not
new. they are old. they go back into history.
they were called explorers, soldiers, mercenaries,
imperialists, missionaries, adventurers,
but they looked at the world for what
it would give up to them and they violated
the land and the people, they looked
at the land and they sectioned it up for
private ownership, they looked at the
people and decided how to manipulate
them thru fear and ignorance, they looked
at the gold and began to hoard and
worship it.

—Sonia Sanchez,
homegirls & handgrenades, 1985

Cool J. In 1992 LL Cool J wins a Grammy for his single "Mama Said Knock You Out.")

Debbie Allen and the Apollo Dancers at the theater's fiftieth anniversary celebration, 1985.

Dorothy Rudd Moore's opera, *Frederick Douglass,* opens in New York City.

1986

January 20. The first Martin Luther King Jr. federal holiday is observed.

February. Haitian Americans celebrate in the snow-covered streets of New York when President Jean-Claude Duvalier flees Haiti for France. Duvalier's fall comes after months of civil unrest and international pressure. Duvalier leaves aboard a U.S. Air Force jet.

April 22. Adelaide L. Sanford is honored at a community tribute at P.S. 21 in Brooklyn's Bedford-Stuyvesant following her recent election by the state legislature to a seven-year term as a member of the Board of Regents of the University of the State of New York. The Regents oversee all public and nonpublic elementary and secondary schools; all postsecondary institutions including the State University and the City University of New York; all museums, libraries and historical societies; and have jurisdiction over thirty-one major professions. A former New York City elementary school teacher and principal, Sanford, who "never saw a child who could not learn," says, "Read history and you'll see what happened to American Indians, Chicanos and Blacks. You'll see that America lacks the will and wisdom to educate her oppressed. It is for us to read between the lines and understand that we must establish a program for liberating education." (In April 1993 she is re-elected to a second seven-year term.)

June. Daniel Garrett organizes Other Countries, a community of gay and lesbian writers of African descent in New York City. (Taking their name from James Baldwin's 1960 novel *Another Country*, which broke gender and racial limitations, the group conducts a writers' workshop at the New York Lesbian and Gay Community Services Center and publishes anthologies of poetry and prose, including *Other Countries: Black Gay Voices*, 1988; *Sojourner: Black Gay Voices in the Age of Aids*, 1993; and *Voices Rising*, 1998.)

September 7. The opera *X*, about the life of Malcolm X, by Anthony Davis, is presented by the New York City Opera. The libretto is by Thulani Davis. (The cousins also collaborate on the opera *Amistad*, which premieres in 1997.)

October 7. George C. Wolfe's *The Colored Museum*, a satire on the black American experience, opens at the Joseph Papp Public Theatre. Playwright Wolfe wins awards from the Dramatists Guild, AUDELCO, and the HBO/Theatre Communication's Group.

November 5. **Rev. Floyd H. Flake**, pastor of the Allen A.M.E. Church in Queens, is elected to the United States Congress.

November 22. Brooklynite Mike Tyson defeats thirty-three-year-old Trevor Berbick in Las Vegas to win the World Boxing Council's heavyweight championship, making him the youngest boxer to hold the title. (A year later, he wins the World Boxing Association and International Boxing Federation titles.)

December 3. The *New York Times* estimates that 20,000 community car service vehicles are operating in the city, with many functioning as gypsy cabs that pick up people on the street. More than 10,000 gypsies operate in minority neighborhoods, the majority of them owned and/or operated by Caribbean and African immigrants. Many immigrants operate illegal jitney-style bus routes along major thoroughfares. Some accept subway tokens as payment.

December 20. Michael Griffith, of Trinidadian ancestry, is struck and killed by an automobile while being chased by a white mob along Shore Parkway in Howard Beach, Queens. (Griffith, Cedric Sandiford, and Timothy Grimes had car trouble while passing through Howard Beach. They entered a neighborhood pizza parlor to use the phone and were confronted by a gang of white people. The black men were followed from the shop and chased by white residents carrying weapons. Mayor Edward Koch later compares Griffith's murder to a Deep South lynching. A year after the killing, Jason Ladone, Jon Lester, and Scott Kern, the three leaders of the attack, are convicted of manslaughter. Lester and Kern are acquitted of murder charges. Michael Pirone is acquitted of all charges.)

December 28. Twelve hundred people march through Howard Beach to protest the death of Michael Griffith.

The NAACP moves its national headquarters from New York City to Baltimore, Maryland.

Mayor Edward Koch appoints a Commission on Black New Yorkers.

Le Critique, an English-language magazine, is founded by Haitian immigrant Joe Florestan and edited by Raymond Joseph to cover Haitian affairs on the island and in the United States.

A National Black Writers Conference is held at Medgar Evers College in Brooklyn, with presentations by Maya Angelou and Margaret Walker Alexander. Novelist and professor Elizabeth Nunez is director of the conference.

Hockey player Tony McKegney is traded to the New York Rangers. The son of a Nigerian father and a Canadian mother, he is the team's first black player.

1987

February. An interracial group of South Queens residents forms in response to the Howard Beach attack. They request city support for programs to ease racial tensions.

April 16. The *New York Daily News* is found guilty by a federal judge of discriminating against four black reporters regarding promotions, salaries, and assignments.

April. An additional seven hundred Nehemiah houses are completed in the Brownsville section of Brooklyn. The brick row houses are sold to low- and middle-income families.

April. Columbia University again finds itself in a dispute over attempts to evict black and Latino residents from university-owned apartments.

November. A decline in the white population of the Co-op City complex in the Bronx creates a nonwhite majority. Co-op City announces a marketing plan to attract more white applicants.

November 3. Kurt Schmoke is elected the first black mayor of Baltimore.

December. The New York Police Department admits that undercover officers have infiltrated the meetings of the Civil Rights Coalition without departmental approval. The department is under investigation for keeping a "Black List," a catalog of black people and organizations believed to be radical. A federal district court judge enjoins the Police Department from destroying or altering any records related to that list.

Representative Charles Rangel moves to have Congress exonerate the late Marcus M. Garvey of mail fraud charges.

Representative Charles Rangel and Manhattan Borough President David Dinkins campaign for Democratic presidential candidate Jesse Jackson.

David R. Jones is named the first African American president of the Community Service Society of New York (CSS), a nonprofit research, advocacy, and social service organization. (An advocate in behalf of the poor for 150 years, CSS addresses issues such as inequitable education, inadequate health care, and the scarcity of low-income housing.)

The Black Leadership Commission on AIDS (BLCA) is founded by Debra Fraser-Howze to inform, coordinate, and organize strategies for indigenous black leadership to respond to HIV and AIDS at the national and local levels. (In 1995 Fraser-Howze is appointed by President Bill Clinton to his Presidential Advisory Committee on HIV/AIDS. By 1998 BLCA has affiliates in seventeen cities across the country, each governed by a locally based Board of Commissioners comprising clergymen, elected officials, business, legal, and medical professionals, members of the media, and social policy experts. The organization provides consultation to national organizations and helps to raise more than $35 million in funds for HIV and AIDS programs.)

Reginald Lewis masterminds and negotiates the deal that brings together the billion-dollar TLC Beatrice International Holdings Inc., in New York, with himself as chief executive officer.

Johnnetta B. Cole, Hunter College professor of anthropology and Afro-American Studies, is named the first black woman president of Spelman College in Atlanta.

W. Haywood Burns is named dean and professor of law at the CUNY Law School at Queens College, the first African American to head a law school in New York State.

Savion Glover co-stars with Gregory Hines and **Sammy Davis Jr.** in the film *Tap.* (Glover appeared in the Broadway production *Black and Blue,* and at the age of twelve was the youngest male ever nominated for a Tony Award. The 1995 Broadway musical *Bring in 'da Noise, Bring in 'da Funk,* choreographed by Glover and conceived and directed by George C. Wolfe, chronicles the history of black America through tap dance.)

Joseph Nelson Boyce becomes a senior editor at the *Wall Street Journal*.

1988

January. A coalition of black labor leaders, ministers, and organization executives meets at Brown Memorial Baptist Church in Brooklyn to plan an economic boycott against racism in New York City for February 19.

January. Police Commissioner Benjamin Ward says that race relations have deteriorated significantly and blames the policies of the Reagan administration.

March. Richard R. Green is named chancellor of the New York City school system. (Green, the former head of schools in Minneapolis, is the first African American to lead New York's schools. Green dies of asthma only fourteen months after taking office.)

November 4. Bill and Camille Cosby donate $20 million to Spelman College in Atlanta, the largest single gift to a black college by black Americans.

Lenora Fulani, a candidate of the New Alliance Party, becomes the first African American woman to qualify for federal matching funds in a presidential campaign. Her campaign receives $600,000.

The New York Police Department's uniformed personnel is seventy-seven percent white. The New York Fire Department's uniformed personnel is ninety-three percent white.

Harlem Congregations for Community Improvement launches the Bradhurst Project in Harlem. (HCCI in partnership with the Consortium for Harlem Development, Inc., creates over one thousand apartments.)

Concord Baptist Church's Christfund, the only foundation among black churches, awards grants ranging from $1,000 to $50,000 derived from the interest of an endowment. The primary grant recipients are Bedford-Stuyvesant social service agencies, but grants are given outside the area as well.

West Harlem Environmental Action (WHE Act) is organized by political club colleagues Peggy Shepard, Vernice Miller, and Chuck Sutton to address black environmental issues. The group cites the North River Sewage Treatment Plant and Harlem's six bus depots as contributors to the community's ecological and health problems. The area has one of the city's highest rates of asthma, particularly among children.

W. Don Cornwell begins Granite Broadcasting Corporation, an affiliation of television networks.

Bernard Beal leaves a senior vice presidency with Shearson Lehman to begin his own investment banking firm, M. R. Beal & Co.

Arnold Rampersad wins the Clarence L. Holte Prize for *I, Too, Sing America* (1986), the first volume of his biography *The Life of Langston Hughes*. (He wins an American Book Award for *I Dream A World* [1988], the second volume of the biography.)

Max Roach is awarded a MacArthur Foundation "genius award," the first awarded to a jazz musician.

New York City native Mark Jackson, of the New York Knicks, is named NBA Rookie of the Year.

1989

January. The NAACP and the New York Open Housing Center file suit against the *New York Times* for running racially discriminatory housing advertisements. (The NAACP drops the suit when the *Times* submits to negotiations. In August 1993 the paper agrees to a policy requiring pictures of people in housing advertisements to reflect the demographic makeup of the metropolitan area. Developers were manipulating racial images in advertisements to attract and discourage renters by race.)

February 10. **Ronald Brown,** who guided Jesse Jackson's historic presidential campaign, becomes head of the Democratic National Committee, the first African American to assume that post.

Max Roach.

National Democratic Committee Chairman Ron Brown at 1992 Democratic Convention. Convention executive Alexis Herman (sworn in as Secretary of Labor May 1997) is at left.

July. Manhattan Borough President David Dinkins's Advisory Council on Child Welfare reports that there are 33,000 children in foster care, an increase of nearly 100 percent since 1985. The report states that 56 percent of the children in foster care are black. It cites that a black male has a 33 out of 1000 chance of entering foster care once in his life time; a black female, a 28 out of 1000 chance; a white male 4 out of 1000; and a white female 3 out of 1000.

New York State Assemblyman Al Vann establishes the Children's Braintrust in response to reports that an alarming number of black children are being placed in foster care. The racially mixed group of officials from labor, social service agencies, and education outlines a comprehensive set of principles and rights for children and families, including the right to economic support from the state, and to services that are culturally sensitive.

August 23. Yusuf Hawkins is killed by a gang of white youths in the Bensonhurst section of Brooklyn. Hawkins and three friends, in Bensonhurst to look at a used car, are attacked by the gang, who are out to catch black or Latino men who are dating white women from the area. Hawkins and his friends are beaten, and Hawkins is shot. (The police search for weeks for the suspects and fear that one may have absconded to Italy. Eventually the suspects are captured and tried. Joseph Fama, the trigger man, is convicted of murder and other charges. Keith Mondello is acquitted of murder but convicted of lesser charges. Fama receives a sentence of thirty-two years to life. Mondello gets five to fifteen years. Al Sharpton leads a series of demonstrations against the verdict and light sentence that Mondello has received.)

August 31. More than 7,500 people create a mile-long protest march across the Brooklyn Bridge. The demonstration, billed as a "Day of Outrage and Mourning" to protest the killing of Yusef Hawkins, ends in violence as police clash with protesters. Four people, including two photographers, are arrested and twenty police officers are injured.

September 21. **Colin R. Powell** is named by President George Bush to be chairman of the Joint Chiefs of Staff, the highest appointed military command in the nation. At the age of fifty-two, he is the youngest man and the first black to hold the position.

November 7. Lieutenant Governor L. Douglas Wilder is elected governor of the state of Virginia, the first African American to serve as governor of any state since Reconstruction, and the only African American ever elected governor.

General Colin Powell, chairman of the Joint Chiefs of Staff.

Harlem political rally, 1989.

November 7. David N. Dinkins becomes the first African American elected mayor of New York City, defeating Republican nominee Rudolph W. Giuliani.

Mayor Edward Koch announces a plan to finally end the housing of homeless people in welfare hotels by using federal Section 8 funds in a voucher program to provide rent subsidies.

The Financial Institutions Reform, Recovery, and Enforcement Act (FIRREA) becomes national law, providing funds to private lenders helping to finance low-income housing projects.

The Abyssinian Development Corporation is incorporated as a nonprofit community-based organization by the Abyssinian Baptist Church.

Robert T. Johnson is elected district attorney of Bronx County. He is the first black person to win that seat in New York City.

The Balm in Gilead is founded by Pernessa Seele to work through black churches to stop the spread of HIV and AIDS in African American communities and to support individuals infected with and affected by AIDS. (National in scope by 1998, the organization is endorsed by over ten black church denominations and caucuses that provide potential outreach to over 20 million black Americans. The Balm in Gilead provides churches with opportunities for training, networking, and education, including its annual Black Church Week of Prayer for the Healing of AIDS, and the production of educational and training products.)

Kenneth Chenault is named president of the American Express Consumer Card Group. (In 1993 Chenault is appointed president of the Travel Related Services division; and in 1995 is promoted to vice chairman of American Express.)

Percy Allen II becomes CEO and vice president for hospital affairs at the University Hospital of Brooklyn, SUNY Health Science Center.

William "Bill" White, once a baseball star with the New York Giants, is named president of the National League, headquartered in New York City. (White was a six-time All Star and seven-time Gold Glove winner.)

Judith Jamison is named artistic director of the Alvin Ailey Dance Company.

The South African musical *Sarafina!* opens on Broadway. It is written and directed by Mbongeni Ngema, with music by Ngema and Hugh Masekela.

William Edwards "Bill" Lee III wins the L.A. Critics Award for the score to his son Spike Lee's film *Do the Right Thing*. Included on the soundtrack is "Fight the Power" by Rapper Chuck D (Carleton Douglass Ridenhour) and his group, Public Enemy.

1990

January 1. David Dinkins is sworn in as mayor of New York City in a private ceremony. Harry Belafonte, Jesse Jackson, and Nobel Prize–winner Bishop Desmond Tutu of South Africa are in attendance. (During the official celebration the following day, Dinkins refers to New York's population as a "gorgeous mosaic.")

Lee Patrick Brown is sworn in as commissioner of the New York City Police Department. Brown, former chief of police in Houston, Texas, is brought in to implement David Dinkins's plan to increase police patrols, consolidate the New York Police Department with the housing and transit police, reduce police brutality and corruption, and impose a residency requirement on new officers.

February. The home of Wilfred and Agnes Phillips, a black couple, is partially burned by white residents in Canarsie, Brooklyn.

March. New York State Supreme Court justice Peter J. McQuillan throws out the 1973 conviction of Richard Moore, a Black Panther accused of a 1971 machine-gun attack on two police officers assigned to protect the home of Manhattan district attorney Frank Hogan. Moore is freed on bail. He was serving a sentence of twenty-five years to life.

May 6. *Once on This Island*, a musical based on the novel *My Love, My Love* by Rosa Guy opens off broadway at Playwrights Horizon. The critically acclaimed show moves to Broadway in 1991. (Guy has written seventeen novels, including *The Friends*, which was included on the 1973 *New York Times* "Best of the Best" list.)

May. While shopping, Giselaine Fetissainte, a Haitian American, is harassed by the employees of a Korean-owned market in the Flatbush section of Brooklyn. Activist Sonny Carson organizes a boycott and causes a firestorm of controversy when he expands

the protest to target all Korean-owned stores in black neighbor-hoods. The South Korean government expresses its concern over racial and ethnic tensions in New York City. As the protest drags on, Mayor David Dinkins, under pressure to condemn the boy-cott, attempts to personally mediate the dispute. The Guardian Angels, a citywide safety patrol, begins guarding local Korean-owned stores.

David Dinkins turns in petitions, 1989, meeting the qualification to run for Mayor of the City of New York.

May. Mayor David Dinkins and Governor Mario Cuomo hold a town meeting on race relations at the Episcopalian Cathedral of St. John the Divine in Manhattan. John Cardinal O'Connor of the Roman Catholic Archdiocese of New York is also in attendance.

June 20. Nelson Mandela, freed leader of the South African National Congress, visits the United States to thunderous greetings in New York, Boston, Atlanta, and Los Angeles. In New York City, he speaks at the United Nations and is honored with a ticker-tape parade in lower Manhattan, parades in Brooklyn and Harlem, and a gala at Yankee Stadium.

October. Mayor Dinkins imposes a five percent pay cut on himself and 700 senior city officials, while ordering a salary freeze for 3,800 managerial-level employees. The move is made to demonstrate his administration's commitment to making the city fiscally sound.

November 9. Freedom National Bank, one of the nation's largest black-owned banks, is declared insolvent by federal regulators. Founded in 1965, the bank has 22,000 depositors and $91 million in deposits. (The Federal Deposit Insurance Corp. issues refunds to the depositors.)

According to census data, Caribbean immigrants to New York City live within well-defined geographic boundaries in communities that they share primarily with other people of color, both native and foreign born. They are primarily in the Crown Heights/East Flatbush, Bedford-Stuyvesant, and Brownsville/East New York sections of central Brooklyn; Cambria Heights, Jamaica, Queens Village, Springfield Gardens, Laurelton, Jackson Heights, and Rosedale in Queens; central Harlem and Washington Heights in Manhattan; and the northeast and south Bronx. Central Brooklyn is the heart of the Caribbean community in the city.

Gwendolyn Calvert Baker becomes president of the New York City Board of Education.

Patricia Polson Satterfield becomes the first black woman elected to a judgeship in Queens County. Satterfield sits on the Civil Court.

Hazel Dukes, a well-known civil rights activist on Long Island, is appointed president of the New York City Off-Track Betting Corporation. She is also New York State president of the NAACP.

Paul Edward Gates becomes director of the department of dentistry at Bronx-Lebanon Hospital. Dr. Gates is also an associate professor at the Albert Einstein School of Medicine.

Conrad Harper is elected president of the New York City Bar Association, the first African American to head the 120-year-old organization.

The Christian Times begins publishing. Editor Rev. Dennis Dillon advises readers to refrain from buying what they cannot afford, and fosters economic empowerment through selective patronage and business development. (By 1998 the paper reaches a circulation of more than 42,000.)

Walter Mosley's first novel, *Devil in a Blue Dress,* is published. It wins the Private Eye Writers of America's Shamus Award and is nominated for the Mystery Writers of America's Edgar Award. (The book, featuring detective Ezekiel "Easy" Rawlins, begins a series that continues with *A Red Death* in 1991, *White Butterfly* in 1992, and *Black Betty* in 1994.)

Whoopi Goldberg wins an Oscar for her role in the film *Ghost.*

Wesley Snipes, raised in New York, plays the lead role in the film *New Jack City.* (Snipes, who attended SUNY at Purchase on the Victor Borge scholarship, goes on to starring roles in *Jungle Fever,* 1991; *White Men Can't Jump* and *Passenger 57,* 1992; *The Rising Sun* and *Demolition Man,* 1993; *Drop Zone,* 1994; *Murder at 1600,* 1997; and *Blade,* 1998. In 1991 he forms Amen Ra Films, his own independent production company, to develop projects for film and television.)

1991

Motorist Rodney King is beaten by members of the Los Angeles Police Department after being stopped for an alleged speeding violation.

January 12. Accompanied by the parents of Yusuf Hawkins, Rev. Al Sharpton is leading a demonstration against racial violence through Bensonhurst, Brooklyn, when he is stabbed in the chest by Michael Riccardi, a twenty-seven-year-old white man.

February 1. A ceremony is held at the Schomburg Center (beginning at midnight, January 31, the eve of Langston Hughes's birthday) to celebrate the return of Hughes's cremains to Harlem. The ceremony, written by the late George Houston Bass, former secretary to

Langston Hughes and guardian of the cremains, includes the pouring of libations, readings, and musical performances. Among the participants are Maya Angelou, Amiri Baraka, Toni Morrison, Hughes's biographer Arnold Rampersad, Howard Dodson, Jean Blackwell Hutson, and jazz pianist Randy Weston, who also played at Hughes's funeral. (The ashes of the noted poet were interred in fall 1990 in a specially designed container that was sealed beneath the floor cosmogram entitled "Rivers," designed by New York artist Houston Conwill, and dedicated to Hughes. The Center's new auditorium slated to open in April 1991 is also named in Hughes's honor.)

February. Andrew Cuomo and the Housing Enterprise for the Less Privileged (HELP) announce that they will provide housing for 150 families in East New York, Brooklyn.

March. Mayor Dinkins endorses Ujamaa Institute, an experimental public high school for black and Hispanic young men. Sociologist Kenneth B. Clark condemns the project as completely out of line with the 1954 *Brown v. Topeka Board of Education* Supreme Court decision.

May. Workmen begin unearthing human remains from the African Burial Ground during the preconstruction phase of a federal office building in lower Manhattan. (Following the discovery of fully intact burials in late September, archaeologists recognize it as the largest and only known urban pre–Revolutionary War cemetery in America. Believed to have encompassed five to six acres, including what is now City Hall Park, the burial ground was in use mainly during the 1700s, when Africans represented 14.4 percent to 20.9 percent of the population. Consistent with the status of Africans during the period, the burial ground was located outside the city limits. According to city maps, parts of it were being covered over by development by the late 1700s.)

May. The New York City Partnership begins selling homes in Stuyvesant Mews, a group of sixty-six two-family townhouses for low- and middle-income families in Bedford-Stuyvesant, Brooklyn.

June. A 1976 suit against the New York City Housing Authority over racial discrimination is finally settled. The Housing Authority

Schomburg Center chief Howard Dodson and former curator Jean Blackwell Hutson pour libation honoring Langston Hughes, 1991. Hughes's cremains are interred beneath the cosmogram, which was created by artist Houston Conwill.

Libation ceremony for the ancestors being removed from the seventeenth-century African Burial Ground, 1992.

confesses to giving fifteen years of preferential treatment to Hasidic Jewish families applying to the Independence Towers, Jonathan Williams Plaza, and Taylor-Wythe projects in Williamsburg, Brooklyn, while discriminating against black and Latino families during that same period. The Housing Authority agrees to accept only black and Latino applicants to the three Williamsburg complexes for several years.

June. During a Brooklyn speech, Mayor David Dinkins announces that the city will evict owners of illegal firearms from public housing projects. Ironically, the speech is interrupted by gunfire.

July. A firebomb destroys the Fillmore Real Estate Office in Canarsie, Brooklyn, as white residents fear the growing number of black homeowners in the area. A month later, Mayor David Dinkins meets with forty clergy and community leaders to discuss the new tensions in a neighborhood known for racial intolerance. An inter-racial group of Canarsie residents calls for an end to the firebomb-ing and intimidation.

July 1. President George Bush nominates Judge Clarence Thomas to fill the seat vacated by Supreme Court Justice Thurgood Marshall.

August 19. Crowds of black people gather in Crown Heights, Brooklyn, after a seven-year-old black child, Gavin Cato, is struck and killed by a car from the motorcade of the leader of the Lubavitch Hasidic movement. Fighting breaks out between members of the two communities, and Yankel Rosenbaum, a twenty-nine-year-old Hasidic man from Australia, is fatally stabbed. A sixteen-year-old black youth, Lemrick Nelson Jr., is arrested by police and charged with the attack. (Later, a Brooklyn grand jury decides not to indict Josef Lifsh, the unlicensed driver of the car that killed Gavin Cato. The Cato family, immigrants from Guyana, files an unlawful death and negligence suit against Lifsh. On August 27 Rev. Al Sharpton delivers the eulogy at Gavin Cato's funeral and declares that his death was caused by "the social accident of apartheid." Outside, activist/organizer Sonny Carson tussles with the police.)

Leonard Jeffries Jr., a professor at the City College of the City University of New York, comes under attack for a speech given at a state conference in Albany. Jeffries is accused of anti-Semitism. Governor Mario Cuomo urges CUNY to discipline Jeffries. A CUNY faculty panel recommends that no action be taken against Dr. Jeffries.

August. Five hundred people march through Harlem in support of Leonard Jeffries.

September 30. A military coup ousts Haitian President Jean-Bertrand Aris-tide and refugee boat departures from Haiti increase rapidly. President George Bush orders U.S. Coast Guard vessels to intercept boats and transport refugees to detention facilities at the United States Naval Base in Guantanamo Bay, Cuba. (Between October 1991 and May 1992, 34,000 Haitians are interdicted at sea and taken to Guantanamo. About 10,500 are found to have a plausible claim to asylum and are flown to the United States. The remaining 23,500 are returned to Haiti.)

September. Alphonse "Buddy" Fletcher founds Fletcher Asset Management, Inc. (Trading on the open market for its own account and on behalf of clients, the firm has accounted on some days for more than five percent of the trading volume at the New York Stock Exchange. A graduate of Harvard, Fletcher becomes a member of the university's Board of Overseers, and a professorship is established in his name at the W. E. B. DuBois Institute for Afro-American Research in recognition of his support.)

October 30. Black Entertainment Television (BET) becomes the first African American company to be listed on the New York Stock Exchange, when president Robert L. Johnson announces the sale of 4.2 million shares of BET stock.

November 21. President Bush reverses himself and signs the Compromise Civil Rights Act of 1991, making it easier for workers to sue in job discrimination cases.

December. ACORN issues a report that charges the city's major mortgage lenders with continuing to discriminate against black and Latino applicants. (In 1990 thirty-six percent of all black applicants, twenty-five percent of Latino applicants, and eighteen percent of white applicants were rejected.)

A Federal Reserve Bank study reveals that thirty-four percent of blacks requesting mortgage loans are rejected, compared to fourteen percent among whites.

Alan Bond forms Bond, Procope Capital Management with the backing of Ernesta Procope, president of E. G. Bowman Co., Wall Street's first black-owned insurance brokerage firm. (By 1996 the firm has $320 million under management from public funds, labor unions, and corporations.)

The Central Brooklyn Credit Union is opened by the Brooklyn Central Partnership, a coalition of fifteen community organizations.

As a result of a strike by workers of Legal Services of New York, hundreds of tenants are evicted and thousands find themselves in Housing Court without representation.

Audre Lorde is named New York State's Poet Laureate by Governor Mario Cuomo. (An international spokesperson for women's issues and gay and lesbian rights, Lorde is a founder of the Kitchen Table: Women of Color Press and the Sisterhood in Support of Sisters in South Africa.)

The music collection of the late Louis "Satchmo" Armstrong is moved from his home in Corona, Queens, to Queens College. (In 1994 the catalogued Armstrong Archives, which include 5,000 photographs and 650 home-made tape recordings, are made available to the public. In August 2001, at a ceremony that will mark Armstrong's 100th birthday, the renovated Louis Armstrong House at 34-56 107th Street will be opened to the public.)

Russell Simmons, CEO of Def Jam Productions, begins Rush Communications, the parent company of a conglomerate that includes music, film, television, fashion, and radio businesses.

Sylvia Rhone, raised in Harlem, becomes president and chief executive officer of her own label—EastWest—under Atlantic Records. She also heads the Acto EastWest label in New York City.

Mule Bone, by Langston Hughes and Zora Neale Hurston, is produced at the Ethel Barrymore Theatre. Directed by Gregory Mosher, the play includes a prologue and an epilogue by George Houston Bass, music by Taj Mahal, and choreography by Dianne McIntyre.

Michael Jordan, born in Brooklyn, wins the NBA championship with the Chicago Bulls. (Jordan and the Bulls go on to win in 1992, 1993, 1996, 1997, and 1998.)

1992

March 23. Leonard Jeffries is removed as chairman of City College's Department of African-American studies because of alleged anti-Jewish remarks made in 1991. (A federal court ruling that the college violated Jeffries's First Amendment rights of free speech is followed by an appeals court reversal. In 1995 college trustees move not to re-elect Jeffries as chairman. Allowed to remain as a tenured professor, Jeffries is replaced as department chairman by Professor Moyibi Amoda, a specialist in African politics.)

Audre Lorde.

When we are loved we are afraid
love will vanish
when we are alone we are afraid
love will never return
and when we speak we are afraid
our words will not be heard
nor welcomed
but when we are silent
we are still afraid.

So it is better to speak
remembering
we were never meant to survive.

—Audre Lorde,
from "A Litany for Survival,"
The Black Unicorn, 1978

April 26. *Jelly's Last Jam* opens on Broadway. Directed by George C. Wolfe and starring Gregory Hines, the musical celebrates the life of jazz legend Jelly Roll Morton.

May 19. On the 67th birthday of Malcolm X, film director Spike Lee announces that a group of prominent blacks have donated money to help him complete his forthcoming film, rescuing him from a financial dispute with Warner Brothers. At a news conference at the Schomburg Center for Research in Black Culture attended by Malcolm's widow, Betty Shabazz, Lee says contributors for the film *Mal-*

Marquee for Malcolm X, *Apollo Theatre, 1992.*

colm X are Bill Cosby, Michael Jordan, Oprah Winfrey, Magic John-son, Janet Jackson, Prince, and Peggy Cooper Cafritz, founder of the Duke Ellington School of the Arts in Washington, D.C.

May. A march through Manhattan to commemorate the birthday of Malcolm X results in the arrest of sixty-five demonstrators.

June. Firecrackers explode in front of the home of Gilberto and Gladys Faria in the Throgs Neck section of The Bronx. "No Blacks" is spray-painted on their sidewalk as neighbors warn them not to sell their house to a black family.

July. Former Texas Congresswoman Barbara Jordan delivers the Democratic National Convention's keynote address at Madison Square Garden. (In 1976 Jordan became the first black keynote speaker at a national political convention, when she first addressed the national Democratic party.)

Former Representative Barbara Jordan addressing the Democratic National Convention, Madison Square Garden, 1992.

July. In a discrimination suit settlement, the New York City Housing Authority admits that it "steered" black and Latino applicants away from certain housing projects, and publicly states that it has agreed to a major integration program.

July. The death of Jose Garcia, a 24-year-old Dominican immigrant shot by a police officer, sparks several nights of rampage and protests in Washington Heights. Thousands of protesters stage a peaceful demonstration outside the 34th Police Precinct on 183rd Street and Broadway. The loudest crowd response is for senatorial candidate Rev. Al Sharpton, who joins Dominican community leaders at the rally. Sharpton asks, "Why are people of color always the victims of police brutality?"

Lemrick Nelson Jr., the black teenager accused of murdering Yankel Rosenbaum in Crown Heights in 1991, is acquitted by a jury. Jurors find the varying police accounts of Nelson's arrest and identification incredible. Passions are again inflamed in the central Brooklyn neighborhood. Over four thousand Hasidic residents gather to protest the verdict. Rosenbaum's brother declares that Mayor David Dinkins is responsible for the turmoil and the jury verdict. The Justice Department decides to investigate the incident.

September. Rudolph W. Giuliani appears at a rally sponsored by the Policemen's Benevolent Association to protest Mayor Dinkins's call for an all-civilian agency for investigating police misconduct. The Grand Council of Guardians, an organization of black police officers, supports the establishment of a civilian review board. Giuliani—attempting to crystallize his tough-on-crime, politically conservative, and police-friendly image—uses a bullhorn to condemn the mayor and the proposed board before thousands of off-duty police officers. However, the off-duty officers in his audience turn rowdy, tie up traffic on the Brooklyn Bridge, and then riot in front of City Hall. Off-duty cops jump up and down on cars and shout racial epithets about the mayor at City Hall. Several on-duty officers assigned to crowd control participate in the melee. Acting police commissioner Raymond W. Kelly later orders that forty-two officers be disciplined, including a captain and several sergeants on crowd control and an on-duty officer who shouted racial slurs as

he ushered protesters past the police barricades. Black leaders seek an investigation into Rudolph Giuliani's and PBA president Phil Caruso's roles in inciting the riot.

September. Rev. Al Sharpton receives a stunning 166,000 votes in the Democratic primary for the United States Senate.

November. Derwin Pannell, a black police officer working undercover, is shot by white uniformed officers while arresting a subway fare beater in Canarsie, Brooklyn. The white officers assume that Pannell is the criminal. Pannell, who never fires a shot, is shot at twenty-one times, including a bullet that hit him in the throat.

Mayor David N. Dinkins, Rosaura Olivares (right), the aunt of Jose Garcia, and John Cardinal O'Connor issue a call for peace in Washington Heights, Gracie Mansion, 1992.

Rep. Floyd H. Flake introducing Eric Adams of the Guardians Association, a black police officers' organization, to his congregation at the Allen A.M.E. Church, Jamaica, Queens. Rev. Al Sharpton (right rear) says that off-duty black police guarded him during his senate campaign.

Undercover operations are suspended as the Police Department reexamines its procedures, such as special wrist bands that enable undercover officers to identify each other.

November 3. Carol Moseley-Braun of Illinois becomes the first black woman elected to the U.S. Senate.

November 6. President-elect Bill Clinton names Vernon Jordan to head his transition team.

Rev. Jesse Jackson and the African-American Clergy Council of New York attend the New York Board of Rabbis' annual Thanksgiving luncheon. Jackson uses the opportunity to defend Mayor David Dinkins against political attacks in response to his administration's handling of Crown Heights, some of which go so far as to call the mayor a murderer.

December. Ralph Nimmons, a homeless black man, is beaten by a gang of Hasidic men behind the Lubavitch headquarters on Eastern Parkway in Brooklyn. The Lubavitch men claim that Nimmons is a burglar, but police file assault and other charges against one of them, Moshe Katzman. Mayor David Dinkins denounces the assault and is himself denounced by many in the Lubavitch community. Dinkins is heckled and called a "Jew hater" while attempting to defend his statements. (Within a couple of weeks a Lubavitch man is robbed and threatened with a knife by two black men who allegedly state "this is for Nimmons." While painting a mural at the Ebbets Field Houses in Crown Heights, a Hasidic artist is attacked by a group of black men.)

West Indian poet and dramatist Derek Walcott wins the Nobel Prize for literature.

Mae Jemison is the first black woman to become an astronaut, serving on the space shuttle Endeavor.

A study of inequality in the awarding of city contracts leads Mayor David Dinkins to announce the New York City Minority and Women-Owned Business Enterprise Program. Firms owned by minorities and women are receiving only seven percent of the city's multibillion-dollar spending budget although they are a quarter of the eligible business community.

Following an assault in Oneonta, Dr. Leif Hartmark of SUNY-Oneonta gives the state police a list of 125 black men in the student body so that they can each be interrogated. (In November 1996 the New York State Court of Appeals rules that the black men can sue the university and the state police. In February of the following year a U.S. Appeals Court rules that Dr. Hartmark acted within his official capacity.)

Thomas Jefferson High School in East New York, Brooklyn, holds a cotillion honoring the top ten girls and the top ten boys.

American Urban Radio Networks is established in New York City. Sydney L. Smalls and Ronald R. Davenport head up the multimillion-dollar firm.

John Utendahl establishes Utendahl Capital Partners, a Wall Street investment banking firm.

Daymond John (chief executive officer) creates a factory in his mother's Hollis, Queens, home and is joined by neighbors J. Alexander Martin (designer), Keith Perrin (manager of celebrity relations), and Carl Brown (manager of licensees) in developing FUBU (For Us, By Us), a line of clothing by and for young urban

Cotillion, Thomas Jefferson High School, East New York, Brooklyn, 1992.

men. (The fashion line is endorsed by a former neighbor, rap star LL Cool J, who appears in the company's first advertising campaign in 1993. As the company's gross sales escalate from $40 million in 1997 to $350 million in 1998, FUBU begins to explore reaching a broader constituency by producing more mainstream styles—everything from backpacks to men's suits.)

The film *Daughters of the Dust,* by Julie Dash, wins first prize in cinematography at the Sundance Film Festival. Cinematography is by Arthur Jaffa. The film airs on the PBS American Playhouse series. (Dash begins her own company, Geechee Girl Productions, in 1988.)

In the Tradition, an anthology of young black writers, is published by Harlem River Press. Edited by Kevin Powell and Ras Baraka, the introduction proclaims, "We can't help ourselves. We must yell. We must write. It keeps us sane and our enemies in check. It is chanting for our people. This is for the people. Our people. Word."

Actress Anna Deavere Smith opens a one-woman show, *Fires in the Mirror: Crown Heights, Brooklyn, and Other Identities,* at the Joseph Papp Public Theater. (In her highly-acclaimed performance, Smith portrays twenty-six people drawn from interviews conducted in Crown Heights.)

Bronx-born actor, musician, and activist Abdul-Malik Kashie Yoba is musical co-director on the Emmy-nominated television show, *City Kids.* Yoba has an extensive background in outreach and advocacy with inner city youth. (Malik Yoba becomes a co-star on *New York Undercover* in 1994.)

Brooklyn's Riddick Bowe wins the heavyweight boxing championship.

1993

January. Maya Angelou becomes the first black poet to participate in a presidential inauguration. She reads "On the Pulse of Morning" at the swearing-in of President Bill Clinton.

Here, root yourselves beside me.
I am that Tree planted by the River,
Which will not be moved.
I, the Rock, I, the River, I, the Tree
I am yours—your passages have been
   paid.
Lift up your faces, you have a piercing
   need
For this bright morning dawning for
   you.
History, despite its wrenching pain,
Cannot be unlived, but if faced
With courage, need not be lived again.

   —Maya Angelou,
   On the Pulse of Morning

Maya Angelou.

411

February. The New York City Consumer Affairs Department accuses local contractors of targeting low-income black and Latino homeowners, pressuring them to take second mortgages to pay for home improvements, and then making unnecessary and/or shabby repairs and improvements to the properties.

March. George C. Wolfe is named head of the New York Shakespeare Festival, including the Joseph Papp Public Theatre, one of the nation's most influential theater projects.

May. **H. Carl McCall** is elected by the New York State Legislature to fill an unexpired term as the state's comptroller.

September. The National Baptist Convention draws eight thousand delegates from across the country to Madison Square Garden for its annual meeting. A survey by the organization's New York host committee indicates that some six hundred churches in the New York metropolitan area deposit $152 million annually in twenty-one banks, and have $40 million in loans. Each Monday morning the churches deposit over $3 million in New York City banks.

October. Toni Morrison becomes the first African American woman to win the Nobel Prize for literature.

October. Two hundred fifty Latino residents of Williamsburg, Brooklyn, take over a housing project as it nears completion. They fear that Hasidic Jewish families will get preferential treatment when the project opens.

Senate Republicans lead an attack on Lani Guinier, President Bill Clinton's nominee to head the Civil Rights Division of the Department of Justice. After her record has been distorted by Republicans, Guinier is kept from officially defending herself when Clinton withdraws her nomination. The following year she publishes The Tyranny of the Majority.

Yolanda T. Moses, a cultural anthropologist from California State University, becomes the tenth president of the City College of New York.

Robert Erik Pipkins, a resident of Staten Island, is a member of the U.S. National Championship men's luge team. He is a member of the U.S. Olympic teams in 1992 and 1994.

1994

January. Worshippers at Muhammad's Mosque No. 7 in Harlem fight with police officers who enter the sanctuary on reports of a robbery in progress. Eight officers are injured.

January. Shortly after taking office, Mayor Rudolph Giuliani is booed during a speech at a tribute to Martin Luther King Jr. at the Brooklyn Academy of Music.

February. An interracial jury in Mississippi finds Byron de la Beckwith, who was twice freed by all-white hung juries, guilty of the 1963 murder of Medgar Evers.

March. A police department sting operation videotapes three police officers from the 30th Precinct in Harlem breaking into an apartment, beating the occupant, and stealing drugs and money. In April fourteen officers are taken from the station in handcuffs for participating in a protection racket in which drug dealers paid them in exchange for safe passage. A month later eleven other officers are arrested and Police Commissioner William J. Bratton targets thirty-five officers from the 30th for arrest or disciplinary action. Many people arrested by officers in the precinct or convicted on their testimony begin to have their cases dismissed or reopened. By the end of 1996 about 125 cases are thrown out because of corruption at the 30th Precinct.

April. The Mollen Commission, investigating police corruption in New York City, accuses the New York Police Department's Internal Affairs Division of burying corruption cases. The commission also reports that police officers regularly make false arrests, tamper with evidence, and commit perjury, which the officers euphemistically call "testifying."

August. Two black undercover transit police officers are shot by an off-duty white officer who mistakes them for criminals. (Police offi-

Toni Morrison.

If anything I do, in the way of writing novels or whatever I write, isn't about the village or the community or about you, then it isn't about anything. I am not interested in indulging myself in some private exercise of my imagination . . . which is to say yes, the work must be political.

—Toni Morrison,
"Rootedness:
The Ancestors as Foundation,"
Black Women Writers (1950–1980),
1984

cers Desmond Robinson and David Thompson were arresting a suspect when off-duty officer Peter Del-Debbio began shooting at them. Robinson is critically wounded. Thompson accuses Del-Debbio of continuing to fire after Robinson was shot and had fallen face down on the ground, hitting Robinson two additional times in the back. Police Commissioner Bratton reexamines the undercover guidelines. Del-Debbio is among the 4,450 transit police officers who saw the department's twenty-minute video about the danger of racial profiling, filmed after white officers shot officer Derwin Pannell in 1992. In March 1996, Del-Debbio is found guilty of second-degree assault. Officer Desmond Robinson asks that Del-Debbio be given leniency. Del-Debbio is sentenced to five years probation and two hundred hours of community service.)

August. A study of thirty cities, including New York and its suburbs, shows that black homeowners are taxed more than white homeowners.

December. The U.S. Department of Housing and Urban Development designates Harlem as one of six sites for an Empowerment Zone (EZ). The ten-year designation is accompanied by a federal grant of $100 million and $250 million in federal tax credit. The Upper Manhattan Empowerment Zone (UMEZ) administers the EZ in Central, East, and West Harlem, and in Washington Heights and Inwood.

The Board of Education adopts a resolution sponsored by African American members Esmeralda Simmons and Dennis Walcott (executive director of the New York Urban League) to create the Commission on Children of African Descent. Led by African American educator Donald Smith, the commission holds hearings and produces a policy paper addressing the high drop-out rate and low achievement of black students, and curriculum reform.

Patricia S. Cowings delivers the eleventh annual lecture for the Society of Nuclear Medicine. Cowings, a native of the Bronx, is a pioneer in the field of biofeedback. She is a research psychologist and director of the Psychological Research Laboratory at NASA's Ames Research Center.

Congressman Charles B. Rangel and Percy E. Sutton at an Empowerment Zone meeting in the Adam Clayton Powell Jr. State Office Building.

Harry Belafonte is honored at the White House with the National Medal of Arts.

Edwidge Danticat's first novel, *Breath, Eyes, Memory,* is published. (Born in Haiti, her short stories have appeared in over twenty periodicals, and she has won awards from *Seventeen* and *Essence* magazines, as well as a James Michener Fellowship.)

Max Rodriguez launches the *Quarterly Black Review of Books.*

Brooklyn's Michael Moorer wins the heavyweight boxing championship.

1995

January. **Richard Parsons** becomes president of Time Warner Inc.

August. The city government faces massive liability from nearly a thousand claims filed on behalf of children—overwhelmingly black and Latino—poisoned by lead paint and pipes in city-owned apartments.

October. Thousands of black men from New York City purchase tickets for the Million Man March in Washington, D.C. Sixteen hundred buses are reserved despite media attacks on Minister Louis Farrakhan, who issued the call for a national day of atonement and prayer for black men to rededicate themselves to each other and their communities.

Rudolph F. Crew, former superintendent of schools in Tacoma, Washington, is named chancellor of the New York City Board of Education.

Qubilah Shabazz, the daughter of Malcolm X and Betty Shabazz, is arrested, charged with conspiracy to kill Minister Louis Farrakhan. Dr. Shabazz meets with Farrakhan at the Apollo Theater in Harlem.

The New York Human Rights Commission fines Brooklyn's Park West Realty firm for failing to show available apartments to black and Latino customers.

Outside, gunshots crack the uptown frost and I think to myself how lucky I am to be young, Black, male, and alive at twenty-five. But that of course doesn't mean I don't think about the precariousness of my life, because I do: each and everyday before I leave my apartment I brace myself for some humiliation (the ultimate would be dying a senseless, meaningless death) at the hands of a racist cop, a condescending employer, an overly watchful store owner, or even another young Black male. Ghetto culture keeps its children on the edge.

—Kevin Powell,
from "Ghetto Bastard,"
Brotherman: The Odyssey of Black Men in America, 1995

Brotherman: The Odyssey of Black Men in America, an anthology of black male authors edited by Herb Boyd and Robert L. Allen, is published by Ballantine Books.

LL Cool J stars with Debbie Allen in the television series *In the House.*

Brooklyn's Riddick Bowe regains the heavyweight boxing title.

1996

March. Ernest Campbell, a black freelance news reporter for NBC-TV, is assaulted in Manhattan by off-duty officer Robert Clarke of the Yonkers Police Department and his brother Thomas Clarke. (In August 1997 Clarke pleads guilty to assault and agrees to resign from the Yonkers Police Department and to never seek employment as a police officer anywhere. He and his brother receive three years probation and two hundred hours of community service.)

June. The Audre Lorde Project (ALP), a gay and lesbian organization for people of color, is organized in Fort Greene, Brooklyn. The group serves people of "African/Black/Caribbean, Arab, Asian and Pacific Islander, Latina/o, and Native/Indigenous descent." ALP forms the GRIOT (Gay Reunion in Our Time) Circle to assist elderly members with a variety of services including education, recreation, telephone reassurance, and home visits.

September. Harlem-born rapper Tupac Amaru Shakur dies from wounds received in a West Coast drive-by shooting.

December 18. Ghanaian diplomat Kofi Annan is named Secretary-General of the United Nations, culminating thirty-five years of UN service.

Charles C. Kidd Sr. becomes president of York College, CUNY.

Assemblyman Jules Polonetsky wins in his attempt to have the city rescind its contract for the X-Men, a Nation of Islam security firm, to patrol the Ocean Towers in Coney Island, Brooklyn, although the Nation of Islam has proven quite effective at reducing violence and crime in public housing projects.

Harlem street shrine in memory of rap stars Notorious B.I.G. and Tupac Shakur.

Amnesty International issues a report warning against the New York Police Department's alarming pattern of excessive force. Mayor Giuliani and Police Commissioner Howard Safir dismiss the report. Police brutality cases in 1996 cost the city a record $27.3 million in judgments and settlements.

Documentary filmmaker Kathe Sandler is awarded a Guggenheim Fellowship. Her films include *Remembering Thelma* and *A Question of Color.*

Renee Brown becomes director of player personnel for the newly formed Women's National Basketball Association (WNBA).

1997

February. Lemrick Nelson Jr. and Charles Price are convicted on federal charges for the murder of Yankel Rosenbaum during the 1991 Crown Heights disturbance.

June 1. The New York premiere of *John Henrik Clarke: A Great and Mighty Walk* is the centerpiece of a tribute to Clarke presented by

United Nations Secretary-General Kofi Annan.

the Schomburg Center. The film, directed by St. Clair Bourne, is the first of a series of documentaries on great African scholars to be produced by Wesley Snipes.

June. Attallah Shabazz, the first child of Malcolm X, delivers a eulogy in behalf of her sisters during a memorial service at Manhattan's Riverside Church for her mother, Dr. Betty Shabazz, who died three weeks after being severely burned by a fire in her Yonkers apartment. The *Amsterdam News* and *Carver Federal Savings Bank* organized blood drives in Harlem during her hospitalization. Malcolm Shabazz, the twelve-year-old grandson of Betty Shabazz and Malcolm X, is charged with setting the fire. (Represented by Percy Sutton and David Dinkins, who arrange for him to plead to second-degree manslaughter as a juvenile, he is sentenced to eighteen months, with possible annual extensions until the age of eighteen years, to be served at the Hillcrest Center in Lenox, Massachusetts.)

August 9. Abner Louima, a Haitian American, is arrested after fighting outside a nightclub in Flatbush, Brooklyn. Four police officers take Louima to a deserted street and beat him. Louima is then tortured in the bathroom of the 70th Precinct. According to reports, police officer Charles Schwartz holds Louima while officer Justin Volpe shoves a toilet plunger into his rectum. Dr. Jean-Claude Comas of Coney Island Hospital reports that Louima suffered a perforated colon, bruised bladder, the loss of two teeth, and a jaw fracture. Radio Soleil D'Haiti is flooded with calls. (Thousands of people, many carrying plungers and Haitian flags, march through Brooklyn demanding action from the mayor. Several hundred people demonstrate before the U.S. Department of Justice in Washington, D.C. Police Commissioner Howard Safir reassigns all of the supervisors at the 70th Precinct and suspends its desk sergeant. Volpe pleads guilty in May 1999.)

August. In Queens, the newly constructed tennis stadium for the U.S. Open is named in honor of the late Arthur Ashe.

September. Kevin Teague, a twenty-seven-year-old black man, is assaulted with baseball bats and a steering-wheel lock by Alfonse

Russo, Andrew Russo, Anthony Mascuzzo, and Ralph Mazzatto, all white, in Carroll Gardens, Brooklyn. The four men are tried for attempted murder and other charges but found guilty only of assault.

October 26. Thousands of black women from New York City attend the Million Woman March in Philadelphia.

November. The Girls Choir of Harlem makes a highly acclaimed debut at Lincoln Center.

November. In Brooklyn, federal judge Frederick Block dismisses a lawsuit seeking to hold former Mayor David Dinkins and former Police Commissioner Lee P. Brown personally liable for damages suffered during the 1991 violence in Crown Heights.

December. South Bronx Churches, a neighborhood housing organization that has built 512 units, announces plans to build 240 additional low- and middle-income Nehemiah houses.

A federal study reports that black people are rejected for home loans at twice the rate of white applicants.

Manhattan Borough President Ruth Messinger's Black Family Task Force reports that while the median income for black families nearly doubled between 1980 and 1990, it was still only sixty percent of white median family income. The report also states that thirty-three percent of all black families lived in poverty in 1990, compared to twenty-nine percent in 1979.

Wynton Marsalis wins a Pulitzer Prize for music for his jazz opera *Blood on the Fields,* the first ever awarded to a jazz artist.

Best-selling novelist Walter Mosley advocates support of black publishers by placing *Gone Fishin'*—the first book in his Easy Rawlins series—with Black Classic Press, owned by Paul Coates of Baltimore. (Mosley also founds the Open Book Committee of PEN, an international writers' association, to help secure more positions for people of color in publishing, and co-founds the certificate program in publishing at City College.)

Musician and composer Wynton Marsalis, director of Jazz at Lincoln Center.

419

Teresa Weatherspoon of the New York Liberty wins the defensive player of the year award for the first season of the Women's National Basketball Association (WNBA). (Weatherspoon repeats in 1998.)

1998

February. Puff Daddy (Sean Combs) wins Grammy awards for best rap album for his LP "No Way Out," and for best rap performance by a duo or group for "I'll Be Missing You." (Combs's recording label, Bad Boy Entertainment, launched in the early 1990s, has signed artists such as Mary J. Blige, Jodeci, Craig Mack, and the Notorious B.I.G.)

April. A centennial exhibition on the life of Paul Robeson, *Paul Robeson: Bearer of a Culture,* opens at the New-York Historical Society. It is organized by the Paul Robeson Foundation as part of the year-long international centennial celebration.

April. In a press conference with the family of Yankel Rosenbaum, Mayor Rudolph Giuliani apologizes on behalf of New York City for the handling of the 1991 unrest in Crown Heights. The administration agrees to pay $1.1 million to the twenty-nine plaintiffs—Lubavitch individuals and institutions—who filed a federal suit against the city, charging that the police did nothing to protect them during the disturbances. David Dinkins and Lee P. Brown, now the mayor of Houston, accuse Giuliani of grandstanding and attempting to draw political benefits from the tragic events of 1991. Some black leaders criticize Giuliani's complete disinterest in the family of Gavin Cato, the child whose death sparked the turmoil in Crown Heights.

September. Thousands of black youths line Malcolm X Boulevard in Harlem for the Million Youth March. (Earlier, Khalid Muhammad, the organizer, engaged in a protracted public argument with Mayor Rudolph Giuliani. Giuliani attempted to prevent the march but was himself thwarted by the courts. The march ends in violence as thousands of police in riot gear storm the stage.)

October 5. The exhibition *The New York Black 100* opens at the Schomburg Center, followed by a ceremony honoring the group at the Abyssinian Baptist Church. Celebrating the lives and achievements of the one hundred most significant black New York history-makers of the twentieth century, the exhibition provides clear evidence that some of black America's most outstanding history-makers trace their roots to or through New York City. *The New York Black 100* exhibition is one of a series of exhibits and programs in a city-wide project entitled *Black New Yorkers/Black New York,* organized to commemorate the centennial of the merger of New York's five boroughs in 1898. The *Black New Yorkers/Black New York* Project is organized by the Schomburg Center for Research in Black Culture in collaboration with twenty cultural organizations and institutions throughout the city. In addition to commemorating the centennial of the city, the project attempts to focus public attention on the role of people of African descent—from the continent of Africa, the Caribbean, and throughout the United States—in the making of New York's history and culture.

November. H. Carl McCall is the top vote-recipient in the state in his reelection bid to serve another term as comptroller of the State of New York.

November 17. The exhibition *Black New York Artists of the 20th Century: Selections from the Schomburg Center Collections* opens as part of the center's Black New Yorkers/Black New York initiative.

December. Ossie Davis and Ruby Dee observe their fiftieth wedding anniversary with a celebration event to benefit twelve local black theater companies. Davis and Dee hope to revitalize the type of black theater activity that gave them their starts in the 1940s.

New York State Comptroller H. Carl McCall.

Congressman Charles Rangel travels with President Clinton on a mission to six countries in Africa, the first such visit to the continent by a sitting American president. Rangel tells the press that, "For the first time a high-level delegation of Americans is visiting Africa on a mission aimed at the positive transformation of the continent in terms of trade and development." (A visitor to Africa during the previous year, Rangel is responsible for the African Growth and Opportunity Act.)

Nearly two thousand participants attend the Fifteenth Annual Ancient Kemetic Studies Conference at City College. The event is

Actors and activists Ossie Davis and Ruby Dee.

hosted by the Association for the Study of Classical African Civilizations (ASCAC), founded by Leonard Jeffries. Forty-nine scholars and experts speak at the conference, focusing on language, education, science and technology, spiritual development, and black culture.

AFTERWORD

Black New Yorkers, whose saga is chronicled in this excellent illustrated volume compiled by the Schomburg Center for Research in Black Culture, are heir to an especially rich vein of the African American experience. We have lived and worked amidst what is arguably the most richly textured cultural quilt in the world—borough to borough, river to river, high-rise to tenement. A part of everything colorful in this world resides in New York City, and every branch of our vast family tree has shed a leaf or two in its neighborhoods. We are part of a gorgeous mosaic.

However representative of the diaspora black New Yorkers are, we are also a unique people. The music, the politics, the landscape—nothing is more uniquely New York than the people themselves. Black New Yorkers are challenged to venture daily into uncharted territory, pursue excellence, and embrace differences. The city demands that we be part of it, and that demand is non-negotiable.

We came to this city, as did millions of others, seeking the means to improve our lots in life and seize opportunities we had been denied elsewhere. Too often, however, instead of finding its streets "paved with gold," we have found what many now term its "mean streets." We have struggled to create neighborhoods from inferior housing, to educate our children in the hallways of over-crowded schools, to compete for a living wage from the end of an unemployment line, to seek health care from a hospital emergency room for lack of adequate insurance.

Nonetheless, we are still here. We are more than two million strong, and we are here to stay. We have built strong institutions on the solid foundations laid brick by brick by successive generations of African American scholars and educators, entrepreneurs, writers and artists, doctors and lawyers, and political leaders. And each generation has stood on the shoulders of those who came before us. They paved and paid the way that we might succeed.

When I arrived in New York City in 1950, intent upon getting a law degree and pursuing a political career, the way had been paved by talented and dedicated men and women who have become legendary within both professions. Nearly forty years later, due in no small measure to the lessons and efforts of such folks, the people of the City of New York elected me to serve as its 106th mayor and the first African American to take on the mantle of its highest office. That same year, Colin Powell became the first African American to head the Joint Chiefs of Staff of the United States Armed Forces, and Bill White became the first black president of baseball's National League. Black New Yorkers both.

The talents, perseverance, and genius of these and many more African Americans who have called New York home are a source of great pride for the rest of us. We all understand well, however, that the ultimate measure of our individual successes is not to be found in the heights to which we may have risen in our respective fields. It is to be found in the contributions we have been able to make to enabling our black New York family to enjoy full and productive lives. Our victories have been hard-won, by those past and present, and have belonged to our entire community. We have been heirs to a remarkable heritage, and each of us hopes to perpetuate that tradition by passing our torch to the next generation of black New Yorkers.

As *The Black New Yorkers* takes a backward glance in documenting the investment we have made in New York and the city's debt to its African American citizens, let us look ahead to the next century of our participation—our *full* participation—in the gorgeous mosaic that is New York.

David Dinkins

SELECTED BIOGRAPHIES

EARLY BLACK NEW YORK LEADERS

Ira Aldridge (1807?–1867). Born in New York City, Aldridge attended the African Free School and received early acting experience in the African Grove Theater. Moving to England in 1824, he gained wide acclaim as one of the greatest Shakespearean tragedians of his time. Aldridge was billed as a native of Senegal and dubbed "The African Roscius" when he made his debut in the role of Othello at The Theatre Royal in Covent Garden in 1833. With his first continental tour in 1852, he became one of the most famous actors on the European stage.

Samuel Cornish (1796–1858). Born free in Delaware, Cornish moved to New York City in 1819. An advocate of black self-help and an abolitionist, Cornish and John Russwurm founded *Freedom's Journal* in 1827. In 1837 Cornish founded the *Colored American,* one of the nation's most successful early black newspapers.

Frederick Douglass (1818–1895). Born into slavery in Maryland, in 1838 Douglass disguised himself as a sailor and escaped to New York City. One of the country's greatest orators, he is regarded by many as the century's leading abolitionist spokesman. Douglass also distinguished himself as a journalist, founding his first newspaper, the *North Star,* in 1847; and as a public official and diplomat in his federal government appointments.

Henry Highland Garnet (1815–1882). Born into slavery in Maryland, Garnet fled as a child with his family to New York City, where he later attended the African Free School. As an anti-slavery clergyman, Garnet gained a statewide and national reputation as a powerful voice for freedom.

J. W. C. Pennington (1807–1870). Born a Maryland slave named James Pembroke, Pennington escaped to freedom in 1827. Residing in Brooklyn, he worked as an abolitionist, teacher, and minister. Pennington opposed black immigration to West Africa and Haiti; instead he advocated voting rights for blacks and urged black enlistment in the Union Army.

Charles Lewis Reason (1818–1893). The son of Haitian immigrants, Reason was born in New York City. Educated along with his brothers, Patrick and Elmer, at the African Free School, he became a teacher and was active in promoting education for black children.

David Ruggles (1810–1849). Born to free parents in Connecticut, Ruggles owned a boarding house and a bookstore in Manhattan. As an abolitionist leader, he aided in the escape of more than six hundred fugitives through his Underground Railroad station on Lispenard Street in lower Manhattan.

John Russwurm (1799–1851). Born in Jamaica, Russwurm was the son of a slave woman and an English merchant. With Samuel Cornish, he founded *Freedom's Journal*, the nation's first black newspaper. A colonization advocate, Russwurm later migrated to West Africa, helping to found Liberia.

Amanda Berry Smith (1837–1915). Born a slave in Maryland, Berry moved from Philadelphia to Greenwich Village with her husband, AME Church deacon James Henry Smith. She began conducting revivals at AME churches in New York and New Jersey in 1869, and became a leader in the Women's Christian Temperance Union (WCTU), pursuing missionary work in England, Scotland, India, and West Africa.

Susan Maria Smith McKinney Steward (1847–1918). Born in Brooklyn, one of eleven children, Steward was the first African American woman doctor in New York State and the third in the nation. In addition to maintaining a full medical practice and surgical rounds, she was a community activist involved in Bridge Street Church missionary work, suffragist activities, and serving as president of the Women's Christian Temperance Union Number 6 in Brooklyn.

Sojourner Truth (Belle, Isabell, or Isabella Baumfree?, ca. 1787–1883). Born a slave in Ulster County, New York, Sojourner Truth arrived in New York City in 1829, where she worked as a domestic. Transformed by a mystical experience in 1843, she changed her name and began traveling as a preacher and abolitionist. Truth was also a staunch champion of the women's rights movement.

James Varick (1750–1827). Born in Orange County, near Newburgh, New York, Varick grew up in New York City, possibly attending the Free School opened for blacks in 1760, and later opening a shoemaking shop in his home on Orange Street. Encountering racial prejudice at John Street Methodist Church, Varick led a group of some thirty black members that withdrew and formed Zion Church, the first black church in New York. He became the first bishop of the African Methodist Episcopal Zion denomination.

Samuel Ringgold Ward (1817–ca. 1866). Born into slavery in Maryland, Ward and his family escaped bondage by fleeing to New Jersey. His family later moved to New York City, where he was educated at the African Free School. A clergyman and abolitionist, Ward toured nationally and abroad as an outspoken opponent of slavery.

THE NEW YORK BLACK 100

The following listing of the 100 most significant black New York history-makers of the twentieth century was selected as part of the Schomburg Center's Black New Yorkers/Black New York project by a citywide consortium of cultural institutions, the project advisory committee, and nominations from the general public gleaned from the distribution throughout the city of over 40,000 nomination forms.

Kareem Abdul-Jabbar (Ferdinand Lewis Alcindor Jr., 1947–). Born in New York City, Abdul-Jabbar began his athletic career at Power Memorial High School, where he earned three All-America selections and led his team to a 95–6 record. He changed his name upon adopting the Islamic faith in 1971. A star player at the University of California at Los Angeles, he went on to become a professional basketball legend, being named the National Basketball Association (NBA) Most Valuable Player six times and leading his teams to six championships. He was inducted into the Basketball Hall of Fame in 1995.

Alvin Ailey (1931–1989). Born in Rogers, Texas, Ailey moved to New York City to study dance in 1954, and formed his own dance company in 1958. From its first version in 1960, Ailey's *Revelations* has been the signature piece of the company, which has gained world renown with performances blending modern, jazz, and ethnic dance. Its productions of more than 150 works have showcased the talents of Ailey and many other noted black choreographers. Ailey was named a Distinguished Professor at the City College of New York in 1985, the first choreographer to receive that designation.

James Allen (1925–). Encouraged to seek treatment for his drug addiction, Allen rediscovered God and kicked his habit. After he earned a degree in social work, he and his wife joined the Christian Reform Church in New York City, pastored by Eugene Callendar, who had started a drug program that became the Addicts Rehabilitation Center (ARC) in 1957. As executive director of ARC, Allen runs a treatment facility for nearly 500 recovering addicts, one of the largest in New York State. The ARC Gospel Choir has earned national and international acclaim.

Marian Anderson (1902–1993). Born in Philadelphia, Anderson first performed in public at the age of ten as "the baby contralto." She won first place and critical acclaim in a singing competition sponsored by the New York Philharmonic at Lewissohn Stadium in 1925, leading to more engagements. A Rosenwald Fellowship made it possible for her to study abroad in 1929, and her career flourished in Europe during the 1930s. After the Daughters of the American Revolution blocked a scheduled performance in Constitution Hall in Washington, D.C., in 1939, Anderson appeared on the steps of the Lincoln Memorial for an Easter morning concert that drew 75,000 people. In 1955 she became the first African American soloist to sing with New York's Metropolitan Opera. She was appointed a member of the U.S. delegation to the United Nations in 1958, and received the Congressional Medal of Honor in 1978.

Maya Angelou (Marguerite Johnson, 1928–). Born in St. Louis, Angelou spent her early childhood in Arkansas. Arriving in New York in the early 1950s to pursue an artistic career, she studied dance with Pearl Primus, and in 1954 toured Europe and Africa in *Porgy and Bess.* She wrote *Cabaret for Freedom* with Godfrey Cambridge to raise funds for SCLC, and served as the organization's northern coordinator from 1960 to 1961. With the publication in 1970 of her autobiographical *I Know Why the Caged Bird Sings,* she became the first black woman to have a nonfiction work on the best-seller list. She has sustained her acclaimed author status with her later autobiographical works and books of poetry.

Louis Armstrong (1901–1971). Born in New Orleans, Armstrong began his musical career singing on the street for pennies. Moving to New York City in 1924, he performed as a cornet soloist with leading jazz bands before forming his own big band and ultimately becoming known as "the Ambassador of Jazz." As a recording star, he was one of the first to popularize "scat singing," and during his long performance career he appeared in more than fifty motion pictures and documentaries. Armstrong was a multiple Grammy winner, including a posthumous Grammy Lifetime Achievement Award in 1972, and two Hall of Fame Grammy Awards in 1974 and 1993. His home in Queens County, New York, has been converted into a museum in his honor by the City University of New

York's Queens College, the institution that also houses his archives.

Arthur Ashe (1943–1993). Ashe, a native of Richmond, Virginia, became the first African American man to win the U.S. Open singles title in Forest Hills, New York, in 1968. He was the first black man to win the Wimbledon singles title in 1975, the first black captain of the American Davis Cup team (champions in 1980, 1981, and 1982), and the first black man inducted into the International Tennis Hall of Fame, in 1985. The author of the three-volume series *A Hard Road to Glory* and an avid anti-apartheid crusader and civil rights activist, Ashe also worked to enlighten public awareness about AIDS. He was honored posthumously with the Presidential Medal of Freedom.

Ella Baker (1903–1986). A native of Norfolk, Virginia, Baker graduated from Shaw University. She was outraged at the poverty and despair she found in New York's black community during the Depression, and became involved with organizing consumer cooperatives and with the Works Progress Administration (WPA) literacy program. She began working with the NAACP as a field secretary in 1940, and became director of branches in 1943. In 1958, she moved to Atlanta to work with the Southern Christian Leadership Conference (SCLC). Leaving in 1960 to work for the Young Women's Christian Association, she became an advisor to the student sit-in movement, focusing on the development of the Student Nonviolent Coordinating Committee (SNCC) and later helping to launch the Mississippi Freedom Democratic Party. Throughout her work, she maintained her residence in Harlem.

James Baldwin (1924–1987). Born in Harlem, Baldwin was encouraged to write by Harlem Renaissance poet Countee Cullen, his junior high school French teacher. Beginning with his first novel, *Go Tell It on the Mountain,* published in 1953, he produced a prolific body of literary works that both exposed and challenged readers to confront and resolve racial and sexual biases in American society. Baldwin received critical acclaim for the collected essays in *Notes of a Native Son, Nobody Knows My Name,* and *The Price of the Ticket,* and the nonfiction work *The Fire Next Time.* His plays *The Amen Corner* and *Blues for Mister Charlie* had successful Broadway runs and numerous revivals.

Amiri Baraka (LeRoi Jones, 1934–). Arriving in New York City after his discharge from the Army in 1957, Baraka, born in Newark, New Jersey, became part of the Beat generation, writing poetry and pieces on jazz. He gained fame as a playwright with the 1964 Obie award–winning production of *The Dutchman,* and has gone on to write in a variety of forms including drama, poetry, music criticism, fiction, autobiography, and the essay. Founder of the Black Arts Repertory Theatre/School in Harlem in 1964, Baraka was the major architect of the Black Arts Movement of the mid-1960s to the mid-1970s, advocating the essential relationship between art and politics. He became a professor of Africana Studies at the State University of New York at Stony Brook in 1979.

Bob Beamon (1946–). The war counselor in his gang in the South Jamaica, New York, projects where he grew up, Beamon could not read or write at the age of fourteen. His promising performance at a high school track meet attracted the attention of Jamaica High track coach Larry Ellis, whose guidance led Beamon to set New York State High School track records in 1965 that still stand. He was the NCAA long jump and triple jump champion in 1967. In one of the most remarkable individual athletic performances of all time, Beamon's leap of 29 feet 2½ inches, nearly two feet beyond the existing world record, established world and Olympic long jump records. He was inducted into the United States Olympic Committee Hall of Fame in 1992.

Romare Bearden (1911–1988). Brought to New York from Charlotte, North Carolina, as a child, Bearden attended the Art Students League and graduated from New York University. He was employed by the city as a social worker for twenty-one years between 1938 and 1966, while he painted. Perhaps the most well-known of African American artists, Bearden explored various styles moving from American Scene to abstract figurative, abstract expressionist, water color, and photomontage collages, which he popularized, and for which he is best known. The author of essays and a book on African American artists, he organized exhibitions highlighting the work of black artists, and was one of the founders of "Spiral" in 1963, and the Cinque Gallery in 1969. He was named to the American Academy of Arts and Letters in 1966, and received the President's National Medal of Arts in 1987.

Harry Belafonte (Harold George Belafonte, 1927–). Born in Harlem, Belafonte spent part of his childhood with family in Jamaica. He began acting studies with the American Negro Theatre, going on to win critical acclaim for roles in theater and film, and becoming the first black to produce a major show for television. His first album, *Calypso,* produced in 1956, was the first album to go platinum. His concert tours have introduced audiences around the world to the music of Africa and the diaspora. A civil rights activist and humanitarian, Belafonte received the National Medal of Arts in 1994. He received a Grammy Award for his work in organizing the recording of the song "We Are the World."

James Hubert "Eubie" Blake (1883–1983). Playing in Baltimore clubs by the age of sixteen, Blake composed his first rag piece *Charleston Rag,* in 1898. Later moving to New York, he worked with his partner, singer and lyricist Noble Sissle, and Flournoy Miller and Aubrey Lyles to create the 1921 pioneering hit Broadway musical *Shuffle Along.* Blake wrote several other Broadway musicals, some in collaboration with Andy Razaf and Henry Creamer. He wrote more than 350 piano pieces and songs, including *Memories of You* and *You Were Meant for Me.* His life and career were celebrated in the Broadway musical *Eubie* in 1978.

Ronald H. Brown (1941–1996). While growing up at the Hotel Theresa in Harlem where his father was the manager, Brown, a native of Washington, D.C., met many of the leading cultural and political leaders of the day. Following his graduation from Middlebury College and St. John's University Law School, he served as spokesperson and deputy director of the National Urban League's Washington, D.C., operations, and worked in the offices of Senator Edward Kennedy. He became the first African American chief counsel of the Senate Judiciary Committee in 1980, and the first black chairman of the National Democratic Party in 1989. Brown was confirmed as Secretary of Commerce in 1993, the first black to hold the cabinet post.

Ralph J. Bunche (1904–1971). Born in Detroit, Michigan, Bunche was a renowned scholar and statesman when he arrived in New York, transferring from service in the U.S. State Department to the United Nations in 1947. He had been a member of the United States delegation at the founding of the United Nations in 1945. Bunche served as Acting Chief of the Division of Dependent Area Affairs and as Director of the Division of Trusteeship before joining the Permanent Secretariat of the United Nations in 1948 as Principal Director of the Trusteeship Council. The highest ranking African American at the United Nations, his negotiation of the end of the Arab-Israeli War in 1949 earned him the Nobel Peace Prize in 1950.

W. Haywood Burns (1940–1996). Spending his childhood years in Peekskill, New York, Burns, a graduate of Harvard College, received his law degree from Yale University Law School. A founder of the National Conference of Black Lawyers, Burns served as assistant council for the NAACP Legal Defense Fund and general counsel for Dr. Martin Luther King's Poor People's Campaign, represented prison inmates following the 1971 Attica prison uprising, was attorney for Angela Davis, and helped to draft South Africa's interim constitution. He served as vice provost and dean for Urban and Legal Programs at City College and in 1987 was named dean and professor of law at the CUNY Law School at Queens College, becoming the first African American to head a law school in New York State.

Shirley Chisholm (1924–). Born in Brooklyn, Chisholm spent part of her childhood in Barbados with relatives, returning to complete high school in Brooklyn and earn degrees from Brooklyn College and Columbia University. She worked in the fields of education and child welfare before winning a seat in the New York State Assembly in 1964. With her victory as Representative for the 12th Congressional District in Brooklyn in 1968, Chisholm became the first African American woman elected to the U.S. House of Representatives, where she served seven terms. In 1972, she was the first black woman to seek nomination as the Democratic presidential candidate. Following her retirement, Chisholm became a professor at Mount Holyoke College in Massachusetts.

John Henrik Clarke (1915–1998). Born in Union Springs, Alabama, Clarke hopped a freight train in 1933, leaving the South to seek a life of scholarship and activism in New York. He developed his skills as a writer and lecturer with Harlem historical and literary organizations; studied history and world literature at New York University, Columbia University, and the League for Professional Writers, but was most greatly influenced by resources found in libraries and his association with prominent historians and bibliophiles such as Arthur Schomburg. A distinguished authority on African and African American history, he was named Professor Emeritus of African World History at Hunter College, and a Distinguished Visiting Professor of African History at Cornell University.

Jesús Colón (1901–1974). Born into a working-class Afro-Puerto Rican family in Cayey, Puerto Rico, journalist and political activist Colón moved to New York when he was sixteen years old. A founding member of the first Puerto Rican committee of the Socialist Party in New York during the 1920s, he became a full-time labor organizer and was the national head of the thirty Spanish and Portuguese speaking lodges of the International Workers Order (IWO), a multinational fraternal organization founded in 1930. Colón also founded and operated a publishing house, Editorial Hispanica, which published history and library books in Spanish. An active member of the Communist Party, he was a regular columnist for the *Daily Worker*, the Party's national publication. Colón's writings are considered landmarks in the development of Puerto Rican literature in the continental United States. He was a clear forerunner of the Nuyorican writers of the 1960s and 1970s.

William "Bill" Cosby (1937–). Born in Philadelphia, Cosby began performing comedy routines in the fifth grade. His professional career in New York City began at the Gaslight Café during the early 1960s. The first African American to star in a network television series, *I Spy*, Cosby was also the first black actor to win Emmy awards for best actor in a running series. An outspoken critic of black images in television, he has added the roles of writer, director, and producer to his list of achievements. With his wife, Camille, he has become a respected philanthropist, supporting the work of African American educational and cultural organizations working in the African American community.

Celia Cruz (1924–). Leaving her native Cuba in 1960, Cruz arrived in New York, bringing with her the authentic sounds and rhythms of Cuba's African-based secular and religious music. With Tito Puente and his orchestra, and on her own, Cruz has toured the world, and is universally recognized as the "Queen of Salsa." She has collaborated with other recording artists, including David Byrne of The Talking Heads and Patti LaBelle. Her work has earned Grammy and National Medal of Arts awards.

Miles Davis (1926–1991). Born in Alton, Illinois, Davis arrived in New York City in 1945 to attend the Juilliard School of Music. He was soon working the 52nd Street clubs with Charlie Parker and Coleman Hawkins, and touring with the bands of Billy Eckstine and Benny Carter. Forming the first of his own great quintets by the mid-1950s with John Coltrane, Red Garland, Paul Chambers, and Philly Joe Jones, he made his first recording *Miles Ahead*, with arranger Gil Evans, in 1956. This was followed by *Porgy and Bess* and *Sketches of Spain*. *Kind of Blue* in 1958 featured Coltrane with Cannonball Adderley and Bill Evans, and in the mid-1960s he continued his innovative explorations with Wayne Shorter, Herbie Hancock, and Ron Carter. His attraction to electronic instruments led to *Bitches Brew* in 1968, the beginning of the "fusion" style.

Ossie Davis (1917–). Leaving Howard University to study theater, Davis, born in Cogdell, Georgia, joined the Rose McClendon Players based in Harlem. Since debuting on Broadway in *Jeb,* he has appeared in numerous theatrical productions, including his own *Purlie Victorious,* and the Tony Award–winning *I'm Not Rappaport.* He has written additional theater works, and has numerous film and television credits as an actor and director. Through their company, Emmalyn II Productions, he and his wife, Ruby Dee, have produced critically acclaimed television programs. He received the National Medal of Arts Award in 1995 for his artistic skills and his social activism.

Sammy Davis Jr. (1925–1990). A native New Yorker, Davis began performing in vaudeville at the age of three in the Will Mastin Trio with his father, Sam Sr., and his uncle, Will Mastin. He made his film debut in 1931 with Ethel Waters in *Rufus Jones for President.* The versatile singer, dancer, and actor appeared on almost every variety show and comedy series on network television between 1956 and 1980, and starred in his own series in the mid-1960s. He played in two hit productions on Broadway, *Mr. Wonderful* (1956) and *Golden Boy* (1964).

Ruby Dee (1923–). A product of Harlem's American Negro Theater, Dee, born in Cleveland, is well known for her performances in *A Raisin in the Sun* and *Purlie Victorious.* Her television credits include an ACE Award for *Long Day's Journey into Night* and an Emmy for Hallmark Hall of Fame's *Decoration Day.* On film she has appeared in *A Raisin in the Sun, Gone are the Days, Buck and the Preacher, Do the Right Thing,* and *Jungle Fever,* among others. As an author, Dee won the 1989 Literary Guild Award. She was inducted into the Theatre Hall of Fame in 1988; and, with her husband, Ossie Davis, was inducted into the NAACP Image Award Hall of Fame in 1989, and received the National Medal of Arts Award in 1995.

David N. Dinkins (1927–). Born in Trenton, New Jersey, Dinkins became active in politics soon after receiving a degree from Brooklyn Law School in 1956. He was elected to the New York State Assembly in 1965. Named to the New York City Board of Elections in 1972, Dinkins later became the first African American to serve as president of the Board, and served as City Clerk from 1975 to 1985.

Winning election as Manhattan Borough President in 1985, he addressed a broad array of concerns from school decentralization to AIDS treatment and prevention services. Dinkins defeated Rudolph Giuliani in 1989 to become the first African American mayor of New York City.

Robert "Bob" Douglas (1882–1979). Born on the Caribbean island of St. Kitts, Douglas, known as "the father of black basketball," organized Brooklyn's best known black team, the Spartan Five (formerly the Spartan Braves). He moved the team to Harlem in 1923, renaming it the New York Renaissance Big Five (the Rens) for its home court, the Renaissance Casino. The Rens, the first full-salaried black professional basketball team, ran up a record of 1,588 wins and 239 losses during their peak years, 1923 to 1939, and were the first black team in the Basketball Hall of Fame. In 1939 the Rens became the first black team on record to win a professional world championship.

W. E. B. DuBois (1868–1963). Born in Great Barrington, Massachusetts, DuBois left a faculty position at Atlanta University to move to New York in 1910. An eminent scholar and the author of *The Souls of Black Folk* (1903), DuBois was one of the original founders and incorporators of the NAACP in New York City in 1909. He served as its director of publicity and research, a member of its board of directors, and editor of its journal, *The Crisis,* from 1910 to 1934. Leaving to become chairman of the Department of Sociology at Atlanta University, where he wrote *Black Reconstruction in America,* he returned to the NAACP in 1944 as director of special research until 1948. His distinctions as a historian, sociologist, and founder of the Pan African Movement remain unsurpassed in the annals of twentieth-century African American history. At the invitation of President Kwame Nkrumah, he took up residence in Ghana in 1961, where he died on the eve of the 1963 March on Washington.

Katherine Dunham (1910–). Moving from Chicago to New York in the 1930s to choreograph works for the New York Labor Stage, Dunham received a Julius Rosenwald Foundation Fellowship in 1936, which allowed her to travel and study dance in the West Indies, particularly Haiti. She formed an all-black dance troupe in 1940 that toured Europe and the United States, choreographed for motion pictures and Broadway musicals, and directed the Dunham School of Dance in New York City, training dancers in classical ballet, African and Caribbean dance forms, anthropology, and other cultural arts. She was the first black choreographer at the Metropolitan Opera, during the 1963–1964 season. Among numerous awards, she has received the Kennedy Center Honors (1983).

Edward Kennedy "Duke" Ellington (1899–1974). Arriving in New York City from Washington, D.C., in 1923, Ellington was performing at the Cotton Club in Harlem by 1927, shaping an orchestra with outstanding soloists and its own distinct style. His 1932 composition, *It Don't Mean a Thing If It Ain't Got That Swing,* signaled a new style of big band jazz. The orchestra performed at Carnegie Hall in 1943 in the first of what became annual concerts until 1950. Ellington also composed and performed for motion picture soundtracks, and created liturgical works. Creating a legacy of more than two thousand works, he was a multiple Grammy winner, and received the Presidential Medal of Freedom from the United States in 1969 and the Legion of Honor from France in 1973.

James Reese Europe (1881–1919). Born in Mobile, Alabama, Europe, a pianist and violinist, moved to New York in 1903. He organized the Clef Club in 1910, a union comprising many of the best African American musicians in the city. The Club's building served as a booking office, supplying groups of three to thirty musicians virtually day and night. With the Clef Club, and later the Tempo Club, which offered dance orchestras for hire, Europe was the first to bring prestige and some degree of professional order to the lives of black musicians in New York City. In 1912, he took an orchestra of more than 125 African American musicians to Carnegie Hall, introducing black music to much of the city's white cultural elite for the first time. Europe's 369th Regimental Marching Band introduced jazz to Europe during World War I.

Ella Fitzgerald (1918–1996). Born in Newport News, Virginia, Fitzgerald was living in Yonkers when she attracted the attention of noted band leader Chick Webb after winning an amateur night contest at the Apollo at the age of sixteen. She began singing with his orchestra at the Savoy Ballroom in 1935, recording her first hit, "A-Tisket, A-Tasket," with them in 1938. She performed with Dizzy Gillespie, Duke Ellington, and Louis Armstrong, among others, in elegant supper clubs, with symphony orchestras, and in jazz clubs. The recipient of numerous awards since the 1970s, she was a multiple Grammy-winner and received the Kennedy Center Medal of Honor Award in 1979 and the National Medal of Arts in 1987.

Floyd H. Flake (1945–). A native of Los Angeles, Flake attended Houston public schools, and is a graduate of Wilberforce University and Payne Theological Seminary. He received his appointment as pastor of Allen AME Church in Queens in 1976. Under his leadership, the church has successfully undertaken a dynamic revitalization of its neighborhood, initiating and administering a variety of housing and social service projects. Flake won a seat in the U.S. House of Representatives in 1986, where he served until 1997.

T. Thomas Fortune (1856–1928). Born to slave parents in Jackson County, Florida, Fortune came to New York in 1879. He found work as a printer, but soon began his career in journalism as part owner of a weekly tabloid, *Rumor.* The *Freeman,* which he launched as sole owner in 1884, became the *New York Age,* the most influential black newspaper in the city, gaining its reputation from Fortune's fiery editorials. He founded the National Afro-American League in 1890 and the National Afro-American Council in 1898. Their platforms helped shape the goals of the NAACP, and encouraged the use of the term "Afro-American" instead of "Negro." Fortune served as adviser and ghost writer for his friend Booker T. Washington. After Marcus Garvey was sentenced to prison in 1923, Fortune became editor of the Universal Negro Improvement Association's *Negro World.*

Marcus Mosiah Garvey (1887–1940). Shortly after landing in America from the island of Jamaica in March 1916, Garvey traveled around the United States lecturing on the need for unity to advance the race. He quietly organized a chapter of the Universal Negro Improvement Association (U.N.I.A.), began publishing a newspaper, the *Negro World,* in January 1918, and opened Liberty Hall on West 138th Street in 1919. The Black Star Line, incorporated in 1919, was a powerful organizing tool for U.N.I.A. organizers who sold stock. By 1920, the organization had hundreds of divisions worldwide, and Garvey presided over its first international convention, which elected him as the "Provisional President of Africa." Garvey claimed to speak for the "400,000,000 Negroes of the world." Under the duress of internal dissension, opposition from black critics, and government harassment, however, the movement began to unravel. The U.S. government, spurred on by a young J. Edgar Hoover, indicted Garvey on fiscal irregularities and imprisoned him, but later commuted his sentence, and deported him back to Jamaica in 1927.

Althea Gibson (1927–). Growing up in Harlem after moving from Silver, South Carolina, at the age of three, Gibson won Police Athletic League and Parks Department paddle tennis competitions. With support and training from the Cosmopolitan Tennis Club, she won the 1942 girls' singles in the New York State tournament sponsored by the all-black American Tennis Association (ATA). Gibson was invited to Forest Hills in 1949, and became the first African American to play at Wimbledon in 1951. She went on to win Wimbledon singles titles in 1957 and 1958, and national clay court and Forest Hills singles in 1957. She was named to the National Lawn Tennis Hall of Fame in 1971.

John Birks "Dizzy" Gillespie (1917–1993). A native of Cheraw, South Carolina, Gillespie settled in New York City in 1937. Along with Charlie Parker, he became a leader of the group of musicians who gathered after working hours at Minton's Playhouse or Clark Monroe's Uptown House in Harlem for jam sessions where they experimented with new ideas. He became musical director of the band organized by Billy Eckstine at the end of 1943, the first big band to feature the new music that he named "bebop." From the mid-1940s on, he led large and small bands, touring throughout the world. His State Department tour as a goodwill ambassador to Europe, the Near East, and Latin America in 1956 was the first time that the United States gave official recognition to a jazz orchestra. He also was credited with being the first to bring Afro-Cuban rhythms into jazz, and the first to use the electric string bass in a jazz group.

Whoopi Goldberg (Caryn E. Johnson, 1955–). As an eight-year-old child from a New York City housing project, Goldberg began performing in children's theater productions at the Hudson Guild Theater. She changed her name and moved to Berkeley, California, in the late 1970s, joining the Blake Street Hawkeyes Theater, where she developed a repertoire of seventeen characters that was ultimately transformed into a Broadway hit produced by Mike Nichols in 1984. Among her film credits are *The Color Purple, Sister Act, Sarafina,* and *Ghost,* for which she won an Academy Award in 1991. Her honors also include Golden Globe, Grammy, and NAACP Image awards.

Earl G. Graves Sr. (1935–). Born in Brooklyn, Graves attended Morgan State University, where he graduated with a B.A. in economics in 1958. In 1970, Graves became founder, publisher, and editor of *Black Enterprise,* the first African American business magazine. An internationally recognized authority on black business development, Graves also serves as Chairman and CEO of Pepsi-Cola of Washington, D.C. In recognition of his support for entre-

preneurial education, Morgan State University renamed its school of business and management the Earl G. Graves School of Business and Management. Graves sits on several corporate boards.

Bryant Gumbel (1948–). Born in New Orleans and raised in Chicago, Gumbel is a graduate of Bates College in Lewiston, Maine. He began his broadcast career in 1972 as a sportscaster for KNBC-TV in Los Angeles. In 1982, Gumbel moved to New York City, where he became the first black co-host of NBC-TV's *The Today Show,* the top-rated and most widely watched morning news program on national network television. He anchored the two-hour weekday program for fifteen years, covering major world events and hosting some of the world's leading personalities. He is a recipient of the Edward R. Murrow Award for Outstanding Foreign Affairs Work, four Emmy Awards, and NAACP Image Awards.

Clara "Mother" Hale (1905–1992). Born in Philadelphia, Hale moved to Brooklyn after her marriage. She began taking in foster children following her husband's death in the 1940s to support her three children, and reared forty foster children in addition to her own. Her career of caring for babies born addicted to drugs began in 1969 when her daughter Lorraine sent a young drug-addicted mother to her home in Harlem with her baby. Hale dropped her retirement plans, and the program soon expanded from her home to a five-story brownstone on West 122nd Street. Hale House had cared for nearly a thousand infants by the time of her death, maintaining a policy of reuniting children with their families after the parents recover from their addiction. The program is currently run by her daughter, Dr. Lorraine Hale.

W. C. Handy (1873–1958). When he arrived in New York City from Memphis with one of his bands in 1918, Handy, a native of Florence, Alabama, was already established as the "Father of the Blues" with his "St. Louis Blues" and "Beale Street Blues." Remaining in New York, he made his first recordings and, with his Memphis partner, Harry Pace, relocated their music publishing firm. When the partnership dissolved in 1920, Pace founded the Pace Phonograph Company, and Handy continued his work through the Handy Music Company. He produced a major concert at Carnegie Hall in 1928 that featured a wide variety of black music from spirituals to orchestral works. In 1940, NBC broadcast an all-Handy program, the first national network presentation of a program entirely of music by a black composer. Today the Handy Brothers

Music Company is celebrating its eightieth year as publishers.

Lorraine Hansberry (1930–1965). Arriving in New York City from Chicago in 1950, Hansberry became a full-time activist. She worked on Paul Robeson's newspaper *Freedom,* spoke, and marched in picket lines, but eventually decided that she could make her most effective contribution through writing. In 1959 her play, *A Raisin in the Sun,* became the first drama by an African American woman to be produced on Broadway. At twenty-nine, she was the youngest American, the fifth woman, and the first black playwright to win the New York Drama Critics Circle Award for the Best Play of the Year. The play was published and produced in over thirty languages worldwide, and Hansberry's film adaptation won a Cannes Festival Award. Other works before her untimely death at thirty-four included *The Sign in Sidney Brustein's Window, Les Blancs,* and *The Movement.*

Dorothy I. Height (1912–). Born in Richmond, Virginia, Height grew up in Rankin, Pennsylvania, and earned Bachelor's and Master's degrees from New York University. While working for the New York Department of Welfare, she was the first African American named to deal with the Harlem uprising of 1935 and became one of the leaders of the National Youth Movement during the New Deal era. Recruited in 1937 by Mary McLeod Bethune, founder and national president of the National Council of Negro Women (NCNW), Height joined her as a volunteer. Moving through the ranks of the Young Women's Christian Association (YWCA) in her professional career, she was a staff member of the National Board from 1944 until her retirement in 1977. She has worked on family and women's issues nationally and internationally as president of the NCNW from 1957 to 1997.

Matthew Henson (1866–1955). An able-bodied seaman who had traveled throughout the world by the age of nineteen, Henson, born in Charles County, Maryland, met explorer Robert E. Peary in 1887. He traveled on all of Peary's subsequent Arctic expeditions between 1891 and 1909, becoming an expert navigator and translator among the Inuit people. Henson became co-discoverer of the North Pole on April 6, 1909, blazing the trail while Peary, whose toes were frozen, was pulled on the sledge. Although his autobiographical account, *A Negro Explorer at the North Pole,* was published in 1912, he did not gain recognition until the 1930s. A resident of Harlem's Dunbar Apartments, Henson was buried in New York on his death, but was reburied at Arlington National Cemetery next to Robert Peary in 1988.

Lena Horne (1917–). Born in Brooklyn, Horne was enrolled as a member of the NAACP at the age of two by her paternal grandmother. Leaving Brooklyn High School for Girls to help support her family during the Depression, she was hired as a dancer at the Cotton Club and later found work singing with Noble Sissle, then Charlie Barnett. She appeared in films such as *Cabin in the Sky* and *Stormy Weather.* On USO tours during World War II, she refused to perform unless black soldiers were admitted to the audience. By the 1950s, she was making albums, appearing in nightclubs all over the world, and appearing on television. Her first lead role in a Broadway show was in *Jamaica* in 1957. Her 1981 Broadway show *Lena Horne: The Lady and Her Music* earned Tony, Drama Desk, New York Drama Critic's Circle, and Grammy awards.

Langston Hughes (1902–1967). Shortly after the publication of his poem "I've Known Rivers" in *The Crisis* magazine, Hughes, born in Joplin, Missouri, moved to New York City to study at Columbia University because it was near Harlem. The most celebrated of the Harlem Renaissance writers, he was inspired by the community's social and cultural life, becoming known as the "poet laureate of Harlem." Hughes drew on blues and jazz to invent new poetic forms, from his first book of poetry, *The Weary Blues* (1926), to his most successful experiment with jazz, *Montage of a Dream Deferred* (1951). Gospel music inspired the plays *Black Nativity* (1961) and *Tambourines to Glory* (1963). The character Jesse B. Semple, known as "Simple," originally conceived in 1943 and appearing weekly in a Chicago *Defender* column, became nationally recognized as a symbol of race consciousness among ordinary folks.

Zora Neale Hurston (1891–1960). Upon receiving an award for her short story "Spunk" published in *Opportunity* magazine, Hurston, originally from Eatonville, Florida, transferred from Howard University to Barnard. She was the first African American woman to graduate from the college. Her anthropology studies there, and at Columbia University with Franz Boas, led to her fieldwork in collecting African American folklore in her native Florida and other southern states. The most widely published black woman writer emerging from the Harlem Renaissance period, she drew on this rich body of research to create vanguard works such as *Mules and Men,* which included material on voodoo in Louisiana, and *Tell My Horse,* about Jamaica and Haiti. Considered her best work by many, *Their Eyes Were*

Watching God (1937) deals with a black woman's quest for fulfillment and liberation.

Jean Blackwell Hutson (1914–1998). Born in Summerfield, Florida, Hutson became the second African American woman to graduate from Barnard College in 1935 and received an M.A. from the Columbia School of Library Service. During the next twelve years she held positions in The New York Public Library's Branch Libraries, moving on to the Schomburg Collection in 1948. Her original assignment of six months stretched into thirty-two years. The Dictionary Catalogue of the Schomburg Collection, published under her leadership in 1962, was put on microfilm and made holdings known to libraries in Europe, Africa, and the Americas. Hutson was named chief when the collection was transferred from The Branch Libraries to The Research Libraries in 1972 and renamed the Schomburg Center for Research in Black Culture. She led the fundraising and lobbying efforts for the new building that opened in 1980.

James Weldon Johnson (1871–1938). A native of Jacksonville, Florida, Johnson earned a B.A. and an M.A. from Atlanta University. He moved to New York City with his brother, J. Rosamond Johnson, in 1901 to write songs for musical theater. Partnering with Bob Cole, they composed more than two hundred songs for Broadway and burlesque shows over the next five years. In 1904 Johnson helped found the Colored Republican Club and in 1906 was appointed U.S. Consul to Venezuela. He was promoted to a post in Nicaragua in 1909. On his return to New York City in 1913, he served as an editorial writer for the *New York Age*. He joined the staff of the NAACP in 1916, and from 1920 to 1930 served as its first black executive secretary, leading the fight against lynching and racial segregation. Johnson wrote the lyrics to "Lift Ev'ry Voice and Sing," the black national anthem.

Quincy Jones (1933–). Born in Chicago, Illinois, Jones grew up in Seattle, Washington, where he started his career as a trumpeter and jazz prodigy under the tutelage of Ray Charles. He played with Lionel Hampton as a teenager. After a stint in Paris, he moved to New York City in 1960, where he became a vice president at Mercury Records, one of the industry's first black executives. An arranger for such musical greats as Count Basie, Frank Sinatra, and Sarah Vaughn, among others, he also produced Michael Jackson's *Thriller,* the biggest selling album of all time. The recipient of twenty-five Grammy Awards,

the second highest number in history, Jones has also scored for television and films such as *In Cold Blood, The Wiz,* and *The Color Purple.*

Vernon E. Jordan Jr. (1935–). Born and raised in Georgia, Jordan earned degrees from De Pauw University and Howard University Law School. He came to New York City after working as the NAACP's Georgia field secretary in the 1960s and helping to register approximately two million black voters as head of the Southern Regional Council's Voter Education Project. He served as Executive Director of the United Negro College Fund (UNCF) and the National Urban League, substantially increasing UNCF funding and doubling the amount of corporate contributions and federal grants to the League. A partner in the Washington, D.C.–based law firm Akin, Gump, Strauss, Hauer & Feld, and a close advisor to President Bill Clinton, Jordan sits on several corporate boards.

Don King (1931–). A native of Cleveland, Ohio, King was dealing in illegal "numbers" by the time he was twenty. In 1966, he was convicted of manslaughter and served four years in the Marion Correctional Institution in Ohio before he started his career as a boxing promoter. The main architect of the famous "Rumble in the Jungle" between Muhammad Ali and George Forman in 1974, he was named the World Boxing Council Promoter of the Decade, 1974 to 1984. The only long-term black promoter in the business, King has wielded more power in the big-money sport over the last twenty years than any other individual. During that time, he has had a hand in virtually every major championship fight.

Lewis H. Latimer (1848–1928). Born in Chelsea, Massachusetts, Latimer learned mechanical drawing in the office of patent solicitors Crosby and Gould in Boston, and prepared the drawings for Alexander Graham Bell's patent application for the telephone. While working for the United States Electric Lighting Company in Bridgeport, Connecticut, Latimer invented carbon filaments for the Maxim incandescent lamp, obtaining a patent in 1881. He supervised the installation of electric lights in New York, Philadelphia, and London. He began working with Thomas Edison in 1883, serving as engineer, chief draftsman, and expert witness on the Board of Patent Control, and was the only black member of the Edison Pioneers. His pioneering work, *Incandescent Electric Lighting: A Practical Description of the Edison System,* was published in 1890.

Jacob Lawrence (1917–). Born in Atlantic City, New Jersey, Lawrence moved from Philadelphia to New York with his family in 1930. He attended public schools and Utopia House, a settlement house where his teacher, painter Charles Alston, recognized his gift as an artist. During the 1930s he worked on the Works Projects Administration (WPA) Federal Art Project, had work space in Alston's "306" studio, and had his first one-man exhibition in 1938 at the Harlem YMCA. Lawrence became the first black artist to be represented by a New York gallery with the highly acclaimed 1941 exhibition of his "Migration of the Negro" series. Famed for his narrative series depicting black historical events and figures (Toussaint L'Ouverture, Frederick Douglass, Harriet Tubman), Lawrence has called his style of painting "dynamic cubism." The Whitney Museum of American Art held a major retrospective exhibition of his work in 1974, and he was elected to the American Academy of Arts and Letters in 1983. He is Professor Emeritus of Art, University of Washington, Seattle.

Spike Lee (Shelton Jackson Lee, 1957–). Born in Atlanta, Georgia, on the eve of the civil rights era, Lee grew up in Brooklyn. He graduated from Morehouse College and New York University's Tisch School of Arts graduate film program. A screenwriter, director, and actor, Lee created an industry-wide awareness of the African American movie-going public with his provocative early films. The box office success of *She's Gotta Have It, School Daze, Do the Right Thing, Mo' Better Blues,* and *Jungle Fever* opened Hollywood's gates for a new generation of young African American filmmakers and actors. An astute businessman, Lee established a film production company, 40 Acres and a Mule Filmworks, and Spike's Joint, a retail outlet. Lee also produces and directs music videos and commercials.

Edward Lewis (1940–). Bronx-born Lewis is a graduate of DeWitt Clinton High school, where he was a New York All-City fullback. After attending the University of New Mexico and Harvard University Business School, Lewis became co-founder and financial manager of a magazine for black women called *Essence.* As publisher and Chief Executive Officer of Essence Communications, Inc., Lewis today heads one of the nation's most successful and diverse African American owned communications companies. He is chairman of the Magazine Publishers of America, and the first recipient of the Media Bridge-Builder Award from the Tanenbaum Center for Interreligious Understanding.

Reginald Lewis (1942–1993). Born in Baltimore, Lewis graduated from Virginia State University and Harvard Law School. He moved to New York City to join the law firm of Paul, Weiss, Rifkind, Wharton & Garrison, moving two years later to Murphy, Thorpe & Lewis as a partner. In 1973 he reorganized his firm with a new partner, Charles Clarkson, and concentrated on corporate law and the venture capital business. In 1983, he formed the TLC Group, an investment firm, of which he was chairman and chief executive officer, and became the first black to enter the billion-dollar takeover business when he purchased the McCall Pattern Company in 1984. His purchase of Beatrice International in 1987 was the largest off-shore leveraged buyout in the history of American business. By 1990, the trimmed-down company boasted $1.1 billion in annual sales from fifteen operating units employing some 7,000 people. Lewis, a generous philanthropist, contributed to several universities and educational and urban renewal programs.

Jane Morgan Lyons (1928–). A native of Williamstown, Massachusetts, Lyons earned degrees from Long Island University and Wagner College, and completed graduate programs at Harvard and New York University. Her work in hospital administration began at the City Hospital Center in Elmhurst, Queens, in 1971. Moving to the Sea View Hospital Rehabilitation Center and Home in Staten Island in 1978, Lyons served as associate executive director in several departments before becoming chief financial officer in 1983. In 1984 she became the first African American woman to serve as the Center's Chief Executive Officer, assuming responsibility, until her retirement in 1997, for administering the 304-bed institution, with adult day care and respite programs, and overseeing a $26 million budget and seventy acres of land with over forty buildings.

Malcolm X (Malcolm Little, 1925–1965). Born in Omaha, Nebraska, Malcolm X dropped out of school in the eighth grade. He moved to Boston, then Harlem, becoming a hustler and a pimp. Forming a burglary ring in Boston, he was arrested and sentenced to prison in 1946. While incarcerated, he was converted to the teachings of Elijah Muhammad, leader of the Lost-Found Nation of Islam. Following his parole in 1952, Malcolm became a minister and the Nation's most effective evangelist. He headed its Harlem mosque and organized temples from coast to coast, recruiting thousands of members and gaining additional sympathizers. Amid growing tension within the Nation's hierarchy and the evolution of his own spiritual beliefs, he resigned from the Nation in 1964 and formed his own Muslim Mosque, Inc., in Harlem. He made a pilgrimage to Mecca the same year, changed his name to El-Hajj Malik El-Shabazz, and embraced the traditional Islamic faith. He was assassinated at the Audubon Ballroom in Harlem in 1965, shortly after he founded the Organization of Afro-American Unity.

Wynton Marsalis (1961–). Born into a musical New Orleans family, Wynton Marsalis was a trumpet soloist with the New Orleans Philharmonic Orchestra by the time he was fourteen. He moved to New York City to study at the Juilliard School of Music. While there, he joined Art Blakey's Jazz Messengers and toured with Herbie Hancock. In 1981 he formed his own quintet and by 1992 was the most celebrated jazz musician of his generation. Downbeat's Jazz Musician of the Year in 1982, 1984, and 1985, Marsalis is also an eight-time Grammy winner. In 1994, he became the first musician to win Grammy awards in both jazz and classical recording. His jazz opera, *Blood on the Fields,* earned him a Pulitzer Prize for music in 1997, the first ever awarded to a jazz artist. Marsalis is the cofounder and Artistic Director of Jazz at Lincoln Center.

Thurgood Marshall (1908–1993). Born in Baltimore and educated at Lincoln University and Howard University Law School, Marshall left a private law practice in Baltimore and moved to New York City to become staff attorney for the NAACP. As director and chief counsel of the NAACP Legal Defense and Education Fund from 1939 to 1961, he was pivotal in the development of strategies to fight racial segregation throughout the country, arguing numerous cases before local, state, and federal courts. Marshall represented the plaintiff in *Brown v. Board of Education of Topeka* before the U.S. Supreme Court, which ruled racial segregation in the public schools unconstitutional. In 1962 he was appointed a judge of the Second Circuit Court of Appeals, and in 1965 he was appointed U.S. Solicitor General, at the time the highest law enforcement position ever held by an African American. In 1967, President Lyndon B. Johnson named Marshall the first black associate justice of the U.S. Supreme Court. In 1946 Marshall was awarded the NAACP's Spingarn Medal.

Victoria Earle Matthews (1861–1907). Arriving in New York City from her native Georgia around 1873, Matthews, primarily self-taught, began writing short stories and essays for *Waverly* magazine and other publications. Her most ambitious work, *Aunt Lindy,* was published in 1893. She did freelance writing for the *New York Times,* the *New York Her-*

ald, and the *Brooklyn Eagle,* and for the *New York Age* and other leading black newspapers. Influenced by anti-lynching crusader and writer Ida B. Wells, she was a founder and the first president of the Woman's Loyal Union of New York City and Brooklyn. A participant in the first national conference of black women in 1895, she was appointed to the executive board of the National Federation of Afro-American Women. When the Federation united with the National Colored Women's League of Washington, she became the first national organizer of the new National Association of Colored Women. A resident of Brooklyn, she was a member of St. Phillips Episcopal Church.

H. Carl McCall (1935–). A native of the Roxbury section of Boston, McCall attended Dartmouth College, Andover Newton Theological School, and the University of Edinburgh in Scotland. An ordained minister in the United Church of Christ, McCall moved to New York City in the 1960s to work in various antipoverty programs. He was elected to the State Senate from Harlem in 1975 and has served as an ambassador to the United Nations and from 1991 to 1993 as President of the New York City Board of Education. He was a vice-president of Citicorp/Citibank from 1985 to 1993. McCall became the first African American elected by popular vote to a statewide office when he was elected to his first full term as Comptroller of the State of New York in November 1994, responsible for governmental financial oversight and managing the state's $105 billion pension fund.

Oscar Micheaux (1884–1951). Born on a farm near Metropolis, Illinois, Micheaux settled in South Dakota, where, by the age of twenty-four, he was worth $20,000 and decided to become a writer. His third book, *The Homesteader* (1917), lured him into filmmaking. When the Lincoln Motion Picture Company refused to let him direct a film based on the book, Micheaux sold stock to his book customers, raising enough money to produce the movie himself. Over the course of his thirty-year filmmaking career, he wrote, produced, directed, and marketed more than forty movies, most of them from his own production company in New York City. While only two of an estimated twenty-seven silent films, and a dozen or so talking films, survive, Micheaux is recognized as the pioneer African American filmmaker of the twentieth century.

Arthur Mitchell (1934–). Born and raised in Harlem, Mitchell graduated from New York's High School for the Performing Arts. In 1955, he joined the New York City Ballet at the invitation of renowned choreographer George

Balanchine as a principal dancer. In 1966, he founded the National Ballet Company of Brazil. Moved by the assassination of Martin Luther King Jr., he founded the Dance Theater of Harlem in 1969 to provide African American youth with the opportunity to learn and perform classical ballet. The organization now includes a school for over five hundred dance students and a company of professionals composed of graduates. It has forged a reputation as an exemplar of American classicism.

Audley "Queen Mother" Moore (1898–1997). Born in New Iberia, Louisiana, Moore joined Marcus Garvey's Universal Negro Improvement Association (UNIA) in New Orleans. Moving to Harlem in the 1920s, she organized domestic workers in the Bronx and helped black tenants to defy evictions by white landlords. During the 1930s she joined the International Labor Defense and became a leading organizer for the Communist party, running as its candidate for the New York State Assembly in 1938 and alderman in 1940. She was the manager of Benjamin Davis's successful 1943 campaign for City Council. Leaving the Communist Party in 1950, she was a co-founder of the Universal Association of Ethiopian Women, and in the 1960s organized the Reparations Committee of Descendants of U.S. Slaves. During a trip to Africa in 1972 to attend Kwame Nkrumah's funeral, she was honored with the title "Queen Mother."

Bishop Emerson Moore (1938–1995). Born into a Baptist family in Harlem, Moore was a convert to Catholicism. A graduate of St. Joseph's Seminary in Yonkers, he was ordained a priest in 1964. In the early 1970s, Moore served as director of the Joseph Kennedy Jr. Memorial Community Center in Harlem and director of the central Harlem Office of Catholic Charities. In 1975, he was appointed pastor of St. Charles Borromeo Church, where, four years later, he greeted Pope John Paul II upon the Pontiff's arrival in Harlem. After returning to Rome, the Pope named Father Moore a monsignor. In July 1982, the Pope elevated him to auxiliary bishop. The Bishop was a leading advocate for equal rights inside and outside the church.

Toni Morrison (Chloe Anthony Wofford, 1931–). A native of Lorain, Ohio, Morrison changed her name to Toni while a student at Howard University. After attending graduate school at Cornell University, she returned to Howard to teach. She became a textbook editor with a subsidiary of Random House in Syracuse, New York, in 1966, and worked on her first novel, *The Bluest Eye* (1970). She moved to New York City in 1968 to become a trade book editor with Random House, rising over the next sixteen years to the position of senior editor. Her second novel, *Sula* (1973), was followed by *Song of Solomon* (1977), which won both the National Book Critics' Circle Award and the American Academy and Institute of Arts and Letters Award. She was appointed to the National Council on the Arts by President Jimmy Carter in 1980. *Beloved* won the 1988 Pulitzer Prize, and in 1993 Morrison became the first African American woman to win the Nobel Prize for literature. Currently the Robert F. Goheen Professor in the Council of the Humanities at Princeton University, she is a Trustee of The New York Public Library.

Constance Baker Motley (1921–). The daughter of West Indian immigrants, Motley was born in New Haven, Connecticut. Following her graduation from Columbia University Law School, she worked with the NAACP Legal Defense and Education Fund from 1945 to 1965. She helped write the briefs filed in the U.S. Supreme Court in Brown v. Board of Education, and tried notable cases against the Universities of Mississippi, Georgia, and Alabama, and Clemson College in South Carolina that broke significant barriers of segregation in the South. She argued ten civil rights cases in the Supreme Court, winning nine. In 1964 Motley became the first African American woman elected to the New York State Senate, and in 1965 she became the first woman elected Manhattan Borough President. Over fierce opposition by Senator James Eastland of Mississippi, she was confirmed as a federal district judge in 1966, and became Chief Judge of the Southern District of New York in 1982.

Gil Noble (1932–). Born and raised in Harlem, Noble graduated from DeWitt Clinton High School in the Bronx, attended City College, and became one of the leading jazz pianists in the city. He began his media career in 1962 as a part-time announcer for WLIB-Radio. At WABC-TV he became the first African American newsman to anchor the weekend news in New York City. As producer and host of *Like It Is,* the longest running African American–produced television program in the country, Noble interviews heads of state, as well as performing arts, political, and sports legends and documents historic figures. Noble has garnered over 650 community awards and numerous industry awards, including seven Emmys.

Jessye Norman (1945–). Born in Augusta, Georgia, Norman received her musical education from Howard University, the Peabody Conservatory of Music in Baltimore, and the University of Michigan, and studied privately with Alice Duschak and Pierre Bernac. She won the 1968 International Music Competition in Munich, and began her professional career singing with the Deutsche Oper in Berlin. She made her recital debut in New York in 1973, and her Metropolitan Opera debut in 1983 in the role of Cassandre in Berlioz's *Les Troyens*. She has appeared in numerous concert performances with philharmonic orchestras around the world, including Los Angeles, London, Israel, Paris, Stockholm, Vienna, and Berlin; and numerous festival performances, including Tanglewood, Aix-en-Provence, and Salzburg. A prolific recording artist, she has made over forty albums and is a multiple Grammy winner. She was a 1997 Kennedy Center Honors recipient. Well-known for her charitable activities, she is also a Trustee of The New York Public Library.

Major R. Owens (1936–). A graduate of Morehouse College and Atlanta University, Tennessee native Owens earned a master's degree in library science at Brooklyn College, settling in Prospect Heights. Working as a librarian at the Brooklyn Public Library, Owens became active in civic and political affairs. Formerly the executive director of the Brownsville Community Council, a New York State Senator, and New York City Deputy Administrator of Community Development, Owens was elected to the United States House of Representatives in 1983 and is a senior member of the Committee on Economic and Educational Opportunities and the Committee on Government Reform and Oversight.

Gordon Parks (1912–). Born in Fort Scot, Kansas, Parks became interested in photography while working on the railroad, taking his first pictures in 1937. He moved to Washington, D.C., to work for the Farm Security Administration as a documentary photographer and eventually headed to Harlem while looking for a job with a major fashion magazine. By the end of 1944, his photographs were appearing in both *Vogue* and *Glamour* magazines. Parks joined *Life* magazine as a photojournalist in 1948, completing over three hundred assignments during nearly a quarter of a century. The first black to produce and direct a film for a major studio in 1968, his creative output over the last three decades has included films, television programs, a musical score and libretto for a ballet, and books of poetry. He received the National Medal of Arts in 1998.

Richard Parsons (1948–). A native of the Bedford-Stuyvesant section of Brooklyn, Parsons was raised in Queens. He graduated from high school at the age of six-

teen, excelled at the University of Hawaii, graduated first in his class from the Union University of the University of Albany Law School, and scored the highest marks among 3,600 lawyers on the state bar exam. He began his legal career as an aide on New York Governor Nelson Rockefeller's legal staff at the age of twenty-three, a position he retained when Rockefeller became Vice President under Gerald Ford in 1974. He joined the law firm Patterson, Belknap, Webb & Tyler in 1977, becoming a partner in two years. In 1988, he was appointed Chief Operating Officer of the Dime Savings Bank of New York, the first black to manage a leading company of that size. He engineered the merger of the bank with the Anchor Savings Bank to create Dime Bancorp. In January 1995, Parsons became President of Time Warner Inc. Recently elected the first African American Chairman of the New York City Partnership and Chamber of Commerce, Parsons is Chairman of the Board of the Upper Manhattan Empowerment Zone.

Sidney Poitier (1927–). Born in Miami, Florida, Poitier grew up in the Bahamas, moving to New York City at the age of sixteen. Known for his dignified portrayals of black males, he was initially rejected for an acting role and took a job as a janitor at the American Negro Theater. He eventually understudied for actor-singer Harry Belafonte in the company's production of *Days of Our Youth,* gaining the attention of critics and attracting more work. He made his film debut in the 1950 feature *No Way Out.* This was followed by *Cry the Beloved Country, Blackboard Jungle,* and *The Defiant Ones.* Stage and film appearances in Lorraine Hansberry's *A Raisin in the Sun* brought new critical acclaim, but it was his role in *Lillies of the Field* that earned him an Academy Award as best actor. He was the first black actor to win this honor. He made his directorial debut in 1972 in *Buck and the Preacher.*

Adam Clayton Powell Jr. (1908–1972). Born in New Haven, Connecticut, only days before his father became pastor of Abyssinian Baptist Church, Powell Jr. succeeded him in 1937. A graduate of Colgate University and Columbia University Teachers College, Powell established himself quickly as a church, social, and civic leader. He successfully organized Harlem consumers with his "Don't Buy Where You Can't Work" campaigns in the 1930s. Elected to the U.S. House of Representatives in 1944, he became the first black chairman of the House Education and Labor Committee in 1960. He championed Head Start, federal aid for school programs, and an increased minimum wage. President Lyndon Johnson's domestic agenda maximized Powell's influence, and he was instrumental in the passage of almost every element of the War on Poverty campaign. Expelled from Congress in 1967, he won a special election to fill his own vacant seat. In 1969, the Supreme Court vindicated Powell, ruling that he had been removed from Congress unconstitutionally.

Colin L. Powell (1937–). The son of Jamaican immigrants, Powell was born in Harlem and grew up in the South Bronx. He graduated from the City College of New York, excelling in the Reserve Officer Training Program. He was commissioned a second lieutenant in the U.S. Army. After two tours of duty in Vietnam during the 1960s, during which he received two Purple Hearts, a Bronze Star, a Soldier's Medal, and the Legion of Merit, Powell earned an M.B.A. at George Washington University and graduated from the National War College. Alternating between civilian and military assignments in the Defense Department and the Army, he served as assistant to the President for national security affairs from 1987 to 1989, rising to the rank of general. In 1989, President Bush named him to the nation's top military post, Chairman of the Joint Chiefs of Staff. At age 52, he was the youngest man and the first black to hold that position. In 1990 he successfully directed the largest military movement in history, Operation Desert Storm.

Leontyne Price (Mary Violet Leontine Price, 1927–). Moving to New York City to attend the Juilliard School of Music, Price, born in Laurel, Mississippi, made her first professional appearance during a European tour of *Porgy and Bess*. Emerging in the 1950s as a major artist, she was the first African American lyric soprano to achieve international diva status. In 1955 she became the first black to appear in opera on television in *Tosca* shown on NBC-TV's nationally televised *Opera Workshop*. Her Metropolitan Opera debut in 1961 received a forty-two-minute ovation, leading to her selection as the first African American to open a season at the Met the following year. When the company moved to its new home at Lincoln Center in 1966, she opened the season in an opera written especially for her, Samuel Barber's *Anthony and Cleopatra*. Price retired from opera in 1985.

A. Philip Randolph (1889–1979). Born to a poor family in Crescent City, Florida, Randolph, attracted by the ideas of W. E. B. DuBois, moved to New York City after graduat-

ing from high school. Co-founder with Chandler Owen of *The Messenger,* a radical socialist newspaper that championed black rights, he was reportedly labeled "the most dangerous Negro in America" by a U.S. District Attorney. In 1925, he organized the Brotherhood of Sleeping Car Porters, the first successful black union in the country. Founder of the Negro American Labor Council, Randolph became the first black vice-president of the powerful AFL-CIO, the largest federation of unions in the United States. In 1941, he organized the first March on Washington movement, the threat of which forced President Franklin Delano Roosevelt to issue Executive Order 8802 banning discrimination in the defense industry. Dean of the African American civil rights movement leadership during the 1960s, Randolph was also the organizer and director of the 1963 March on Washington, scene of Martin Luther King Jr.'s "I Have a Dream" speech.

Charles B. Rangel (1930–). Born and raised in Harlem, Rangel attended DeWitt Clinton High School in the Bronx and, after service in the Army, earned a law degree at St. John's University. He was appointed U.S. Attorney in the Southern District of New York in 1961 and elected New York State Assemblyman for the 72nd District in Central Harlem in 1966 and U.S. Representative from New York's 16th Congressional District in 1970. Rangel was named chairman of the Congressional Black Caucus in 1974. A member of the House Judiciary Committee during the Nixon impeachment proceedings, in 1975 he became the first African American appointed to the powerful House Ways and Means Committee, which makes key revenue decisions. He is currently the ranking minority member of the committee.

Max Roach (1924–). Born in Elizabeth City, North Carolina, Roach grew up in Brooklyn, where he graduated from Brooklyn Boys' High School. He studied composition and tympani at the Manhattan School of Music. He started performing in the 1940s with Charlie Parker at Minton's and Charles Monroe's Uptown House in Harlem. He made his recording debut in 1943 with the Coleman Hawkins group, and worked with Dizzy Gillespie, Duke Ellington, and Charlie Parker's bands throughout the 1940s. By 1945, Roach and Kenny Clarke had become cornerstones of the bebop movement, creating a new solo role for modern jazz drum performance, shifting the rhythmic foundations from the bass drum to the cymbals and the drum sound from the background to front-line status. Roach has composed for film, theater, and television. He was awarded a MacArthur Foundation "genius award" in 1988, the first awarded to a jazz musician.

Paul Robeson (1898–1976). Born in Princeton, New Jersey, Robeson gained renown as a student and athlete during his years at Rutgers, where he was elected to Phi Beta Kappa in his junior year, graduated as valedictorian, and was selected twice as an All-American football player. Graduating in 1920, he moved to Harlem, where he enrolled at Columbia University Law School, and supported himself by playing professional football on weekends. After earning a law degree and passing the bar, however, he opted for the stage. With his longtime accompanist Lawrence Brown, he presented the first public recital composed entirely of Negro spirituals in 1925. A distinguished acting career on stage and screen was highlighted by his show-stopping performance of "Old Man River" in *Showboat,* and his critically acclaimed portrayal of Othello in the record-breaking 1943–1944 run at the Shubert Theatre. A perennial scholar, he was fluent in more than twenty languages and produced writings on cultures of the East, the West, and Africa. An eloquent spokesman on behalf of oppressed peoples everywhere, Robeson was revered throughout the United States and abroad.

Bill "Bojangles" Robinson (Luther B. Robinson, 1878–1949). Born in Richmond, Virginia, and nicknamed "Bojangles" by a childhood friend, he is said to have coined the phrase "everything's copasetic," meaning "fine, better than all right" by the time he was twelve years old and dancing for nickels and dimes in Washington, D.C. Robinson joined a traveling show called *The South Before the War* and first performed in New York City in 1891. Limited by vaudeville's "two-colored" rule, which restricted blacks to performing in pairs, he teamed with comic dancer George W. Cooper in 1902. Though both refused to wear the customary blackface makeup, Cooper and Robinson were a popular act on the touring circuit. Stardom came at age fifty for Robinson, when his popular stair-dance routine was featured in *Blackbirds of 1928.* Gaining his greatest fame in movies, his films, including *The Little Colonel, The Littlest Rebel,* and *Rebecca of Sunnybrook Farm,* were among Hollywood's biggest financial successes.

Jackie Robinson (John Roosevelt Robinson, 1919–1972). Born in Cairo, Georgia, Robinson grew up in Pasadena, California. He graduated from UCLA, where he was an outstanding athlete in football, basketball, base-ball, and track. After a stint in the army, he signed to play professional baseball with the Kansas City Monarchs of the Negro American League in 1944. In 1948, he accepted an offer from the Brooklyn Dodgers, becoming the first African American in major league baseball in the modern era. Excelling in all aspects of the game, Robinson was voted to the National League All-Star team six times during his ten-year career; compiled a lifetime batting average of .311, becoming the first black batting champion in 1949; and stole 197 bases during his career, leading the National League in 1947 and 1949. He helped the Dodgers win six National League pennants and one world championship. He was named the League's Rookie of the Year in 1947 and Most Valuable Player in 1949. In 1962, he became the first African American inducted into the Baseball Hall of Fame.

Augusta Savage (1892–1962). Born in Green Cove Springs, Florida, Savage arrived in New York City with $4.60. She enrolled at Cooper Union, studying there until 1923. Denied a scholarship she had won to study at Fontainebleau by an American committee of seven white men, she found solace in her work, completing three major sculptures, W. E. B. DuBois, Marcus Garvey, and *Gamin.* A plaster model of her nephew, Ellis Ford, *Gamin* won her a Rosenwald Fellowship, which allowed her to study in Europe. Following her return to New York in 1931, her position as a supervisor for the Works Progress Administration (WPA) Art Projects enabled her to influence the careers of many artists, including Jacob Lawrence, Gwendolyn Knight, Norman Lewis, Georgette Seabrooke, and the photographers Morgan and Marvin Smith. Commissioned in 1937 to create a sculpture for the 1939 New York World's Fair, Savage created her most publicized work, *The Harp,* inspired by the black national anthem, "Lift Every Voice."

Arturo Alfonso Schomburg (1874–1938). Born in Santurce, Puerto Rico, Schomburg moved to New York in 1891, apparently to work in the Cuban and Puerto Rican struggle for independence. In 1892, he helped organize and was elected secretary of Las Dos Antillas, a political group affiliated with Cuban liberation leader Jose Marti. He worked as a law clerk and a Spanish teacher, and in 1906 became a messenger at the Bankers Trust Company, eventually becoming head of its foreign mail division until he retired in 1926. Best known as a bibliophile, he was also a patron of the arts, an exhibit curator, an Odd Fellow, a Mason, a Kappa (Alpha Psi), a scholar, and a leading authority on black history worldwide. In 1925, his collection of over 10,000 items on black history and culture was acquired by The New York Public Library and deposited in its 135th Street Branch in the center of Harlem. Schomburg's visionary work in developing this collection created the nucleus of the Schomburg Center for Research in Black Culture, the national research library on black history and culture. He served as the curator of the collection from 1932 until his death in 1938.

Percy E. Sutton (1920–). Born in San Antonio, Texas, Sutton served as an intelligence officer with the Tuskegee Airmen (the Ninety-Ninth Fighter Squadron) during World War II. A 1950 graduate of Brooklyn Law School, he re-entered military service for the Korean War as an intelligence officer before returning and starting his Harlem law practice. A civil rights activist and Freedom Rider in the 1960s, Sutton was elected Manhattan Borough President from 1966 to 1977. He was the founder and is currently Chairman Emeritus of Inner City Broadcasting Corporation, a New York–based company that owns and operates radio and cable television companies, and radio and television production companies around the United States. He is also Chairman of African Telecommunications, Ltd. (ACTEL), a satellite-based telecommunications company.

Billy Taylor (1921–). A native of Greenville, North Carolina, Taylor obtained his musical education from the Washington, D.C., public schools, Virginia State College, and the University of Massachusetts at Amherst. He moved to New York in the early 1940s, where he played with Ben Webster, Charlie Parker, Miles Davis, and Ella Fitzgerald, among others. He was the house pianist at Birdland from 1949 to 1951, and musical director of the Emmy Award–winning *David Frost Show.* During the 1960s, he co-founded Jazzmobile, a grassroots summer concert series in New York City. An arts educator and recording artist, he is the recipient of two Peabodys, an Emmy, the National Medal of Arts, and *Downbeat*'s Lifetime Achievement Award.

Gardner Taylor (1918–). Born in Baton Rouge, Louisiana, Taylor aspired to be a lawyer, but after surviving a near-fatal traffic accident, he devoted his life to religion. A graduate of Oberlin Theological Seminary, he was ordained a Baptist minister in 1939. After serving congregations in New Orleans and Baton Rouge, he became pastor of the Concord Baptist Church of Christ in Brooklyn's Bedford-Stuyvesant neighborhood. When fire destroyed the church in 1952, Taylor led the successful campaign to build a new edifice. An advocate for better educational opportunities for black children, he was appointed to the New York City Board of Education in 1958. Often at odds with the Board's majority, in 1959 he supported a city-wide boycott by the parents of African American and Puerto Rican students, who were protesting against inferior schools for children. A national civil rights and Baptist church leader renowned for his dynamic preaching, Taylor is known as the "Dean of Black Preachers."

Franklin A. Thomas (1934–). Thomas was born into a West Indian family in the Bedford-Stuyvesant section of Brooklyn. At Columbia University he became the first African American to captain an Ivy League basketball team and was twice voted the league's Most Valuable Player. Following a short stint in the Air Force, he earned a law degree at Columbia and worked in a variety of government positions in New York City. He was appointed President of the Bedford-Stuyvesant Restoration Corporation at the age of thirty-three. During his tenure there, he raised $63 million in public and private funds, built three apartment complexes, a 200,000 square foot shopping center, and 400 brownstone units, and helped start or expand 120 businesses. In 1980 Thomas was appointed head of the Ford Foundation, the world's largest foundation.

Walter Turnbull (1944–). A native of Greenville, Mississippi, Turnbull graduated *cum laude* from Tougaloo College, earned degrees from the Manhattan School of Music, and began pursuing a career in opera. Working as a singer at the Trinity Episcopalian Church in Connecticut, however, he became interested in their boys choir and proposed a choir for Harlem's Ephesus Church in 1968. From a nucleus of twenty boys, Turnbull's dream expanded as the choir became the Boys Choir of Harlem, a nonprofit organization. A former public school teacher, Turnbull worked to establish discipline and maintain enthusiasm among his young choir members, and the choir made its first national tour in 1983. The Choir Academy of Harlem was established in 1986, and graduated its first twelfth-grade class in 1996. The choir has contributed to film soundtracks, recorded, toured nationally and internationally, and performed on Broadway. The girls choir made a highly acclaimed debut at Lincoln Center in 1997.

Madame C. J. Walker (1867–1919). Walker was born on a plantation near Delta, Louisiana. She worked as a washerwoman in St. Louis to support herself and her daughter A'Lelia. In 1905 she began to perfect a formula and the process of using a hot iron for straightening hair. After moving to Denver, she first demonstrated and sold her methods door-to-door, but eventually began hiring agents and expanding her business to other cities. She moved to New York in 1913, and in 1914 built a townhouse in Harlem at 108-110 West 136th Street, including a fully equipped beauty parlor at 110. Her mansion at Irvington-on-Hudson, Villa Lewaro, was built in 1918, just a few years before her death at fifty-two. Employing more than 3,000 people, mainly women, Madame Walker built a fortune that allowed her to live in high style and invest in real estate, while also contributing to the NAACP, homes for the aged, scholarships, and other charitable causes.

Barbara M. Watson (1918–1983). Born in New York City, Watson earned degrees from Barnard College and New York Law School. In 1946, she founded (with Edward Branford) one of the first black modeling agencies in the United States to serve mainstream advertisers. Joining the U.S. State Department in 1966, she was head of the Bureau of Security and Consular Affairs from 1968 to 1974, responsible for implementing all laws and policies relating to U.S. citizens abroad. In 1977, she was appointed Assistant Secretary of State for Consular Affairs, the first woman and the first African American to hold the position of Assistant Secretary of State. She was named the United States Ambassador to Malaysia in 1980 by President Carter.

Robert C. Weaver (1907–1997). Well established as a leading expert on race relations and a leader of "The Black Cabinet" during the New Deal administration, Weaver, a native of Washington, D.C., served in several academic positions in New York before his appointment as State Rent Administrator in 1955, the first black to hold cabinet rank in the state. He was appointed Vice Chairman of the New York City Housing and Redevelopment Board in 1960, and named administrator of the U.S. Housing and Finance Agency in 1961. President Lyndon B. Johnson appointed Weaver as Secretary of the Department of Housing and Urban Development (HUD) in 1966, the first African American to hold a cabinet-level position. After leaving HUD, he returned to academic life in New York City.

Lenny Wilkens (Leonard Randolph Wilkens, 1937–). Born in the Bedford-Stuyvesant section of Brooklyn to a black father and a white mother, Wilkens won an athletic

scholarship to Providence College, where he majored in economics and earned a B.A. in 1960. Drafted by the St. Louis Hawks of the National Basketball Association (NBA) in 1960, Wilkens became a starting point guard as a rookie and in the ten years between 1963 and 1973 was voted to nine All-Star teams. He was named to the NBA Hall of Fame at the end of his fifteen-year playing career. In 1969, he started his coaching career as player-coach of the struggling Seattle SuperSonics. Over the course of the next twenty-nine years, he held head coaching positions with the Seattle SuperSonics, the Portland Trail Blazers, the Cleveland Cavaliers and the Atlanta Hawks. Wilken's Seattle SuperSonics won the NBA championship in 1978, and his teams have regularly qualified for the NBA playoffs ever since. In January 1995, Wilkens became the all-time leader in coaching victories when his Atlanta Hawks team registered his 939th win. He coached the U.S. Olympic team that won the championship in Atlanta in 1996.

Roy Wilkins (1901–1981). Born in St. Louis, Missouri, Wilkins began his journalistic career as editor of his high school newspaper in St. Paul, Minnesota. While a student at the University of Minnesota, he served as night editor of the university's *Minnesota Daily* and the *St. Paul Appeal*, a black weekly. After graduating, he moved to Kansas City, Missouri, to work as a reporter for the prestigious black weekly the *Kansas City Call*, eventually rising to managing editor. A crusading journalist, his successful work on a campaign to unseat racist U.S. Senator Henry J. Allen brought him to the attention of Walter White, executive secretary of the national NAACP. Accepting White's offer to become his assistant in the organization's New York City office in 1931, he succeeded W. E. B. DuBois as editor of the NAACP's *The Crisis* in 1934. He was unanimously elected executive secretary on White's death in 1955, and led the organization through the height of the civil rights movement of the 1950s and 1960s, until his retirement in 1977.

Bert Williams (Egbert Austin Williams, 1874–1922). Born in Nassau, Bahamas, and raised in Riverside, California, Williams was a talented young singer whose plans to study civil engineering at Stanford University never materialized. Instead, Williams joined a minstrel troupe and later teamed with George Walker, creating one of America's most successful entertainment acts. Originated by whites as a caricature of black life, minstrelsy, with its burnt-cork blackface makeup, was adapted by Williams and other black performers to suit their own purposes. The team appeared in *The Gold Bug* in 1896, and helped set off the cakewalk craze. They gained critical acclaim in *In Dahomey* in 1902, the first black musical comedy to open on Broadway, and later in *Abyssinia* and *Bandanna Land*. Williams's fame continued after Walker's retirement because of illness in 1909. The next year, Williams became the first African American to star in the Ziegfeld *Follies*.

Louis Tompkins Wright, M.D. (1891–1952). Born in La Grange, Georgia, Wright graduated from Harvard Medical School. Denied internships at predominantly white hospitals, he accepted a post at Freedman's Hospital in Washington, D.C., in 1916. He moved to New York City's Harlem Hospital in 1919, where he was reluctantly named a clinical assistant visiting surgeon on the all-white Harlem Hospital staff. He led the struggle to hire black doctors there and served with distinction on its staff for more than thirty years, rising to become director of the Department of Surgery. Wright was the first black physician to be appointed to the staff of a New York municipal hospital, the first black surgeon in the police department of New York City, the first to experiment on humans with the antibiotic aureomycin, the first black surgeon to be admitted to the American College of Surgeons, and the first black physician in America to head a public interracial hospital. A leading research scholar in the field of surgery, he published over eight-nine articles in medical journals. He was also active in the NAACP and served as chairman of its national board of directors for seventeen years.

Albion, Robert Greenhalgh. *The Rise of New York Port, 1815–1860*. Boston: Northeastern University Press, 1984.

Anderson, Jervis. *A. Philip Randolph: A Biographical Portrait*. Berkeley: University of California Press, 1986.

Andrews, Charles C. *The History of the African Free Schools*. New York: Mahlon Day, 1930.

Aptheker, Herbert. *American Negro Slave Revolts*. New York: Columbia University Press, 1983.

———, ed. *A Documentary History of the Negro People in the United States*. 7 volumes. New York: Citadel Press, 1951–1991.

Ashe, Arthur. *A Hard Road to Glory: A History of the African-American Athlete*. New York: Warner Books, 1988.

Bayor, Ronald H., and Timothy J. Meagher, ed. *The New York Irish*. Baltimore: Johns Hopkins University Press, 1996.

Bernstein, Iver. *The New York City Draft Riots*. New York: Oxford University Press, 1990.

Bontemps, Arna Wendell, ed. *The Harlem Renaissance Remembered*. New York: Dodd, Mead, 1972.

Burrows, Edwin G., and Mike Wallace. *Gotham: A History of New York City to 1898*. New York: Oxford University Press, 1999.

Caro, Robert A. *The Power Broker: Robert Moses and the Fall of New York*. New York: Alfred A. Knopf, 1974.

Charters, Samuel B., and Leonard Kunstadt. *Jazz: A History of the New York Scene*. New York: Doubleday, 1962.

Clark, Kenneth. *Dark Ghetto*. Middleton, Conn.: Wesleyan University Press, 1955.

Clarke, John Henrik, ed. *Marcus Garvey and the Vision of Africa*. New York: Vintage Books, 1974.

———. *Harlem: A Community in Transition*. New York: Citadel, 1964.

Contemporary Black Biography. Detroit: Gale Research Inc., 1992.

Cooper, Wayne F. *Claude McKay: Rebel Sojourner in the Harlem Renaissance: A Bibliography.* Baton Rouge: Louisiana State University Press, 1987.

Cronon, E. *Black Moses: The Story of Marcus Garvey and the Universal Negro Improvement Association.* Madison: University of Wisconsin Press, 1955.

Curtin, Philip D. *The Atlantic Slave Trade, A Census.* Madison: University of Wisconsin Press, 1969.

Danckaerts, Jasper. *Journal of Jasper Danckaerts 1679–1680.* New York: Charles Scribner's Sons, 1913.

Donnan, Elizabeth. *Documents Illustrative of the History of the Slave Trade.* Washington, D.C.: Carnegie Institution, 1932.

Duberman, Martin. *Paul Robeson.* New York: Alfred Knopf, 1988.

Essien-Udom, E. U. *Black Nationalism: The Rise of the Black Muslims in the USA.* Harmondsworth: Penguin Books, 1966.

Foner, Jack. *Blacks and the Military in American History.* New York: Praeger Publishers, 1974.

Foner, Nancy, ed. *New Immigrants in New York.* New York: Columbia University Press, 1987.

Foner, Philip S. *Organized Labor and the Black Worker, 1619–1918.* New York: International Publishers, 1982.

Garfinkel, Herbert. *When Negroes March.* New York: Atheneum, 1969.

Garwood, Alfred N., ed. *Black Americans: A Statistical Sourcebook.* Boulder, Colo.: Numbers and Concepts, 1990.

Genovese, Eugene. *From Rebellion to Revolution: Afro-American Slave Revolts in the Making of the Modern World.* Baton Rouge: Louisiana State University Press, 1979.

Glennon, Lorraine, ed. *Our Times: The Illustrated History of the 20th Century.* Atlanta: Turner Publishing, 1995.

Goodfriend, Joyce B. *Before the Melting Pot: Society and Culture in Colonial New York City, 1664–1730.* Princeton: Princeton University Press, 1992.

Greenberg, Cheryl. *"Or Does It Explode?" Black Harlem in the Great Depression.* New York: Oxford University Press, 1991.

Handlin, Oscar. *The Newcomers: Negroes and Puerto Ricans in a Changing Metropolis.* Cambridge, Mass.: Harvard University Press, 1959.

Harris, Joseph E. *African-American Reactions to War in Ethiopia, 1936–1941.* Baton Rouge: Louisiana State University Press, 1994.

Harris, William H. *Keeping the Faith: A. Philip Randolph, Milton P. Webster, and the Brotherhood of Sleeping Car Porters, 1925–1937.* Urbana: University of Illinois Press, 1977.

Haynes, George E. *The Negro at Work in New York City.* New York: Columbia University Press, 1912.

Hemenway, Robert. *Zora Neale Hurston: A Literary Biography.* Urbana: University of Illinois Press, 1977.

Higgenbotham, A. Leon. *In the Matter of Color.* New York: Oxford University Press, 1978.

Hill, Robert A., ed. *The Marcus Garvey and Universal Negro Improvement Association Papers.* Berkeley: University of California Press, 1983.

Hine, Darlene Clark, ed. *Black Women in America: An Historical Encyclopedia.* Brooklyn, N.Y.: Carlson Publishing, 1993.

Holder, Calvin. *West Indian Immigration in New York City, 1900–1952: A Study in Acculturation.* Ph.D. diss., Harvard University, 1976.

———. "The Rise of the West Indian Politician in New York City, 1900–1952," *Afro-Americans in New York Life and History*. Vol. 4, no. 1, January 1980.

———. "The Causes and Composition of West Indian Immigration to New York City, 1900–1952," *Afro-Americans in New York Life and History*. Vol. 11, no. 1, January 1987.

Huggins, Nathan Irvin. *The Harlem Renaissance*. New York: Oxford University Press, 1971.

Hughes, Langston. *Black Magic: A Pictorial History of the African-American in the Performing Arts*. New York: Da Capo Press, 1990.

Jackson, Kenneth T., ed. *The Encyclopedia of New York City*. New Haven: Yale University Press, 1995.

Jaffe, Julian E. *Crusade Against Radicalism: New York During the Red Scare, 1914–1924*. New York: Praeger, 1972.

Johnson, James Weldon. *Black Manhattan*. New York: Da Capo Press, 1990.

Kammen, Michael. *Colonial New York: A History*. New York: Charles Scribner's Sons, 1975.

Kaplan, Sidney, and Emma N. Kaplan. *The Black Presence in the Era of the American Revolution*. Revised edition. Amherst: University of Massachusetts Press, 1989.

Kasinitz, Philip. *Caribbean New York, Black Immigrants and the Politics of Race*. Ithaca, N.Y.: Cornell University Press, 1992.

Katz, William Loren. *Black Indians: A Hidden Heritage*. New York: Atheneum, 1986.

———. *Black Legacy: A History of New York's African Americans*. New York: Antheneum, 1997.

———. *Eyewitness: A Living Documentary of the African American Contribution to American History*. New York: Simon & Schuster, 1995.

Kellner, Bruce, ed. *The Harlem Renaissance: A Historical Dictionary of the Era*. Westport, Conn.: Greenwood Press, 1984.

Kiser, Clyde V. *Sea Island to City*. New York: Atheneum, 1932.

Kornweibel, Theodore. *No Crystal Stair: Black Life and the Messenger, 1917–1928*. Westport: Greenwood Press, 1975.

Lankevich, George J. *American Metropolis: A History of New York City*. New York: New York University Press, 1998.

Lewis, David Levering, ed. *The Portable Harlem Renaissance Reader*. New York: Viking, 1994.

———. *W. E. B. DuBois: Biography of a Race*. New York: Henry Holt, 1993.

———. *When Harlem Was in Vogue*. New York: Alfred A. Knopf, 1981.

Litwack, Leon. *North of Slavery*. Chicago: University of Chicago Press, 1961.

Locke, Alain, ed. *The New Negro*. New York: A. and C. Boni Publishers, 1925.

Logan, Rayford. *The Negro in American Life and Thought: The Nadir 1877–1901*. New York: The Dial Press, 1954.

Logan, Rayford, and Michael R. Winston, eds. *Dictionary of American Negro Biography*. New York: W. W. Norton, 1982.

McKay, Claude. *Home to Harlem*. Boston: Northeastern University Press, 1987.

McManus, Edgar J. *A History of Negro Slavery in New York*. Syracuse, N.Y.: Syracuse University Press, 1996.

Mollenkopf, John, ed. *Power, Culture and Place: Essays on New York City*. New York: Russell Sage Foundation, 1988.

Mullen, Robert. *Blacks in America's Wars*. New York: Pathfinder Press, 1973.

Naison, Mark. *Communists in Harlem During the Depression*. Urbana: University of Illinois Press, 1983.

New York City Department of City Planning. *The Newest New Yorkers: An Analysis of Immigration into New York City During the 1980s*. New York: Department of City Planning, 1992.

———. *The Newest New Yorkers 1990–1994: An Analysis of Immigration to NYC in the Early 1990s*. New York: Development of City Planning, 1996.

Ortiz, Victoria, "Arthur A. Schomburg: A Biographical Essay," in The Schomburg Center for Research in Black Culture, *The Legacy of Arthur Alfonso Schomburg: A Celebration of the Past, a Vision for the Future*. New York: Schomburg Center for Research in Black Culture, 1986.

Osofsky, Gilbert. *Harlem: The Making of a Ghetto, 1890–1930*. New York: Harper & Row, 1966.

Ottley, Roi. *New World A-Coming: Inside Black America*. 1943. Reprint. New York: Ann Press, 1969.

Ottley, Roi, and William J. Weatherby, eds. *The Negro in New York: An Informal Social History, 1626–1940*. New York: Praeger, 1969.

Phelps Stokes, N. *The Iconography of Manhattan Island, 1498–1909*. New York: Robert H. Dodd, 1918.

Ploski, Harry A., and James Williams, eds. *Reference Library of Black America*. New York: Gale Research Inc., 1990.

Quarles, Benjamin. *The Negro in the American Revolution*. Chapel Hill: University of North Carolina Press, 1961.

———. *Black Abolitionists*. New York: Oxford University Press, 1969.

Rampersad, Arnold. *The Life of Langston Hughes. Vol. 1: 1902–1941: I, Too, Sing America*. New York: Oxford University Press, 1986.

———. *The Life of Langston Hughes: Vol. II: 1941–1967: I Dream A World*. New York: Oxford University Press, 1988.

Ripley, C. Peter, et al., eds. *Witness for Freedom*. Chapel Hill: University of North Carolina Press, 1993.

Rosenwaike, Ira. *Population History of New York City*. Syracuse, N.Y.: Syracuse University Press, 1972.

Runcie, John. "Marcus Garvey and the Harlem Renaissance," *Afro-Americans in New York Life and History*. Vol. 10, no. 2, July 1986.

Samuels, Wilfred E. "Five Afro-Caribbean Voices in American Culture, 1917–1929: Hubert Harrison, Wilfred A. Domingo, Richard B. Moore, Cyril V. Briggs, and Claude McKay". Ph.D. diss., University of Iowa, 1977.

Sanchez Korrol, Virginia E., *From Colonia to Community: The History of Puerto Ricans in New York City*. Westport, Conn.: Greenwood Press, 1983.

Scheiner, Seth M. *Negro Mecca, A History of the Negro in New York City, 1865–1920*. New York: New York University Press, 1965.

Schoener, Allon. *Harlem on My Mind: Cultural Capital of Black America*. New York: The New Press, 1995.

———. *New York: An Illustrated History of the People*. New York: W. W. Norton, 1998.

Scott, William. *Sons of Sheba's Race: African Americans and the Italo-Ethiopian War, 1935–1941*. Bloomington: Indiana University Press, 1993.

Sinnette, Elinor Des Verney. *Arthur Alfonso Schomburg: Black Bibliophile and Collector: A Biography*. New York: New York Public Library and Wayne State University Press, 1989.

Smith, Jessie Carney, with Casper L. Jordan and Robert L. Johns, eds. *Black Firsts: 2,000 years of Extraordinary Achievement*. Detroit: Visible Ink, 1994.

Snyder-Grenier, Ellen M. *Brooklyn!: An Illustrated History*. Philadelphia: Temple University Press, 1996.

Thernstrom, Stephan, ed. *Harvard Encyclopedia of American Ethnic Groups*. Cambridge, Mass.: Harvard University Press, 1980.

Valade, Roger M. III, with Denise Kasinec, eds. *The Schomburg Center Guide to Black Literature from the Eighteenth Century to the Present*. Detroit: Gale Research, 1995.

Vincent, Theodore. *Black Power and the Garvey Movement*. Berkeley: Ramparts Press, 1971.

Waters, Mary. "Ethnic and Racial Identities of Second-Generation Black Immigrants in New York City," *International Migration Review*. Vol. xxviii, no. 4, Winter 1994.

Watkins-Owens, Irma. *Blood Relations: Caribbean Immigrants and the Harlem Community, 1900–1930*. Bloomington: Indiana University Press, 1996.

Watson, Steven. *The Harlem Renaissance: Hub of African-American Culture, 1920–1930*. New York: Pantheon Books, 1995.

West, Cornel. *Encyclopedia of African-American Culture and History*. New York: Simon & Schuster Macmillan, 1996.

White, Shane. *Somewhat More Independent: The End of Slavery in New York City, 1770–1810*. Athens: The University of Georgia Press, 1991.

ACKNOWLEDGMENTS

We are indebted to Regina Andrews, who conceived of the idea of writing a chronological history of black New York more than thirty years ago. Her draft manuscript, written in 1968 but never published, has served as an inspiration for and an important resource in the development of this book.

We are also indebted to Malaika Adero for working to revise and update the Andrews manuscript and for bringing it to the attention of Carole Hall, Editor-in-Chief of African American books at John Wiley & Sons.

During the early stages of this project, an advisory committee comprised of authorities on all facets of black New York life and history reviewed Ms. Andrews's original draft manuscript and recommended corrections and changes to bring it into conformity with the new scholarship that had developed since the late 1960s. The advisory committee included William Loren Katz, Allon Schoener, John Graziano, Irma Watkins Owens, Sherrill Wilson, William Miles, Byron Saunders, Carlton Mabee, Walter Stafford, Richard Dickenson, and Jervis Anderson. We wish to thank them for their critical insights and for leading us to new sources that have made this volume possible. *The Black New Yorkers* has benefited from the explosion of research and scholarship on the black New York experience that has occurred over the last three decades. The works included in the bibliography have been used extensively in developing this chronology. We wish to thank all of the authors listed.

Craig Wilder prepared the first draft of chapter six with the assistance of his research assistant, Cordell Reaves. Mr. Wilder also provided entries on the black experience in Brooklyn, which have been incorporated throughout the manuscript. We thank him and Mr. Reaves for their invaluable assistance.

The staff of the Schomburg Center also made significant contributions. Mary Yearwood, James Huffman, and Anthony Toussaint assisted with the illustration research and reproduction. Manu Sassonian provided photographs and Alice Adamczyk and Betty Odabashian assisted with fact verification. Victor Smythe and Gennette McLaurin provided research support, and Maribel Pimentel and Theresa Martin provided clerical support.

Carole Hall and Marcia Samuels, Senior Managing Editor, shepherded the project through the editorial and production processes at Wiley and served as liaisons between the Center and the press throughout. We thank them and their co-workers in the Wiley organization for their investments of time, energy, and commitment.

CREDITS

PERMISSIONS ACKNOWLEDGMENTS

Grateful acknowledgment is made for permission to reprint selections from the following:

"A Litany for Survival," from *The Black Unicorn* by Audre Lorde. Copyright © 1978 by Audre Lorde. Reprinted by permission of W. W. Norton & Company, Inc.

From the book *Homegirls and Handgrenades* by Sonia Sanchez. Copyright © 1984 by Sonia Sanchez. Appears by permission of the publisher, Thunder's Mouth Press.

ILLUSTRATION CREDITS

All illustrations are from the collections of the Schomburg Center for Research in Black Culture except where otherwise indicated.

Pages 11, 19, 34: Charles Lilly.

Page 53: John Joseph Holland. "A View of Broad Street, Wall Street, and the City Hall." Watercolor, 1797. The Phelps Stokes Collection, Miriam and Ira D. Wallach Division of Art, Prints and Photographs, The New York Public Library.

Page 74: Edwin Whitefield. "View of Brooklyn, L.I. / From the U.S. Hotel, New York." Color lithograph, printed by F. Michelin, 1846. Eno Collection, Miriam and Ira D. Wallach Division of Art, Prints and Photographs, The New York Public Library.

Page 82: Milton Meltzer Collection.

Page 113 (top and bottom): Augustus Sherman. William B. Williams Papers, Manuscripts Division, The New York Public Library.

Page 137: Bennett Rosner Collection.

Page 164: James Latimore Allen.

Page 165: James VanDerZee.

Page 166: Morgan & Marvin Smith.

Page 172: James VanDerZee.

Page 174 (bottom): Apeda, NY.

Page 178: James C. Campbell.

Page 185: White Studio.

Page 187: James VanDerZee.

Page 192: Morgan & Marvin Smith.

Page 193: Acme Art Studio.

Page 195: James VanDerZee.

Page 198: White Studio.

Page 202: Mills-Rockwell, Inc.

Page 205: A. de Lawrence.

Page 209: New York City W.P.A. Art Project.

Page 214: Morgan & Marvin Smith.

Page 218: Austin Hansen.

Page 219: Wide World Photos.

Pages 233, 241: Morgan & Marvin Smith.

Page 244: James Latimore Allen.

Page 248: Johnson Publishing Company (Ebony).

Page 251: Andrew Herman/W.P.A. Art Project.

Page 256: Cecil Layne.

Page 261: Vandamm Studio.

Page 267: Austin Hansen.

Page 277: Cecil Layne.

Page 279: Morgan & Marvin Smith.

Page 282: Austin Hansen.

Page 286: Robert L. Haggins.

Page 287: Brown Brothers.

Page 288: Alvin Ailey American Dance Theater photograph by Bill Hilton.

Page 289 (top): Courtesy of Hansberry/Nemiroff Estate.

Page 291: *New York Times.*

Page 295: Kwame Braithwaite.

Page 298: Klytus Smith.

Page 302: Kwame Braithwaite.

Page 303: Chester Higgins, Jr.

Page 317: Matt Heron.

Page 320: Robert A. Sengstacke.

Page 323: Kwame Braithwaite.

Page 328: Courtesy of Bob Beamon.

Page 331: The Studio Museum of Harlem.

Page 332: Bert Andrews.

Page 340 (top and bottom): Weeksville Society.

Page 343: Karen Pell.

Page 346: Adam Scull/Globe Photos.

Page 348: Bert Andrews.

Page 349: *Black Enterprise.*

Page 350: Scott Cunningham/Globe Photos.

Page 353: Globe Photos.

Page 354: Duane Winfield.

Page 367: Sulaiman Ellison.

Page 371: Christian Steiner.

Page 373: Austin Hansen.

Page 375 (top): NBC-TV.

Page 376: David Lee.

Page 378: David Seidner.

Page 381: James W. Gilbert.

Page 383: Kwame Braithwaite.

Page 389: Sulaiman Ellison.

Pages 392, 395: Chester Higgins, Jr.

Page 399: E. Lee White.

Page 400: Chester Higgins, Jr.

Page 404: Steve J. Martin.

Page 405: Suzanne Dechillo/*New York Times.*

Page 407: Budd Williams/*New York Times.*

Page 408: Jim Estrin/*New York Times.*

Page 410: Eli Reed.

Page 414: James W. Gilbert.

Page 416: Gerald E. Hayes.

Page 417 (top): Steve J. Martin.

Page 422: Dwight Carter.

Page 424: Ron Campbell.

Numbers indicate the year under which the subject or name appears. Names in **bold**
indicate people who are included in the Selected Biographies section.